*f*P

FOR YOUR OWN GOOD

The Anti-Smoking Crusade and the Tyranny of Public Health

JACOB SULLUM

THE FREE PRESS
New York   London   Toronto   Sydney   Singapore

_f_P

THE FREE PRESS
A Division of Simon & Schuster Inc.
1230 Avenue of the Americas
New York, NY 10020

Manufactured in the United States of America

10 9 8 7 6 5 4 3 2 1

Library of Congress Cataloging–in–Publication Data

Sullum, Jacob.
    For your own good : the anti-smoking crusade and the tyranny of
public health / Jacob Sullum.
        p.   cm.
    Includes bibliographical references and index.
    ISBN 0–684–82736–0
    1. Antismoking movement—United States.   2. Smoking—Public
opinion—United States.   3. Public opinion—United States.
4. Smoking—Government policy—United States.   5. Passive smoking
—Government policy—United States.   I. Title.
HV5751.S85   1998
363.4—dc21   98-10798
                                                                  CIP

TO MICHELE

Who reads everything first

I believe the ultimate goal should be a smoke-free society by the year 2000.

—Surgeon General C. Everett Koop, 1984

From my point of view, anything that stops smoking is good.

—C. Everett Koop, 1996

CONTENTS

Author's note   xi

Introduction: Without a Doubt   1

1. From Devil's Weed to Soldier's Friend   15

2. Appropriate Remedial Action   40

3. Coughing Cowboys   82

4. Vice Charge   119

5. Smoke Alarm   138

6. Try, Try Again   181

7. Little White Slavers   220

8. Doctor's Orders   256

Appendix: Ten Myths of the Anti-Smoking Movement   277

Notes   281
Bibliography   321
Acknowledgments   328
Index   329

AUTHOR'S NOTE

If you are looking for a reason to dismiss this book without going to the trouble of reading it, you should start here. In 1994 I wrote an op-ed piece for the *Wall Street Journal* about a report on secondhand smoke by the Environmental Protection Agency (EPA). R. J. Reynolds subsequently used the article in an ad campaign and paid me for the reprint rights. This is the only time I've had any financial dealings with a tobacco company. I also wrote an article about press coverage of the secondhand smoke issue, which appeared in the summer 1994 issue of *Forbes Media-Critic*. Philip Morris reprinted that article in a series of ads. I did not give the company permission to do so (*MediaCritic* had all rights to the article), and I was not paid. Finally, *Reason* magazine, where I work, is published by the Reason Foundation, a think tank that has received contributions from Philip Morris Companies to support its research (none of it tobacco related). Philip Morris has also bought space in the magazine for corporate image ads. The combination of the donations and the ad revenue has always been less than 1 percent of the foundation's budget.[1]

From this information, people who disagree with me about secondhand smoke and other tobacco-related issues have concluded that I am part of an industry-financed conspiracy to undermine the anti-smoking movement. Stanton Glantz, a University of California researcher and cofounder of Californians (now Americans) for Nonsmokers' Rights, calls me "a conservative commentator who has been paid by the tobacco industry for his views on the EPA" and refers to "Mr. Sullum and his tobacco patrons."[2] In his book *Smokescreen,* journalist Philip J. Hilts claims the tobacco companies "paid writers to get stories out attacking the science and the scientists." He continues, "In one series of ads, a piece by Jacob Sullum, who works for a foundation supported by tobacco, was run whole. In other ads, it was excerpted with the headline, 'If we said it, you might not believe it.' But of course, they did say it. Sullum not only works for a tobacco-supported foundation, but was paid directly by the company when they used his story."[3] John Banzhaf, executive director of Action on Smoking and Health, once appeared with me on a TV talk show and said, "We also want to tell the folks out there that you're in the pay of the tobacco industry."[4]

Each of these descriptions is inaccurate in its own special way: Glantz invented a political identity for me, Hilts confused two different articles, and Banzhaf simply asserted a nonexistent financial relationship. But more important than the direct misstatements of fact is the implication that I am not to be trusted because I have been tainted by tobacco money. Readers can judge for themselves, based on the content of this book and my other work, whether the possibility of future reprint fees has made me eager to please the tobacco companies. As for Philip Morris's donations to the Reason Foundation: Since they have no impact at all on my job security or compensation, it's hard to imagine what financial interest my critics have in mind. And if refusing to write for publications that accept ads from cigarette manufacturers is a requirement for credibility, all I can say is that most journalists in America would probably fail that test. In seven years at *Reason,* no one has ever suggested that I write about a particular topic, or approach it from a certain angle, in order to please a donor or advertiser. Indeed, one of the main advantages of working at a think magazine is that you can write what you like, as long as the editor considers it worthwhile.

More to the point, my critics are guilty of a logical fallacy, namely, that you can weaken someone's arguments by impugning his motives. If I really believed what I say, they imply, I might be worthy of attention, but since I am only interested in financial gain (anti-smokers rarely consider the possibility that their opponents might be acting on principle), I can be easily dismissed. It turns out that I'm in distinguished company. In 1994 Scott Ballin, then chairman of the Coalition on Smoking or Health, took issue with a *Wall Street Journal* op-ed piece about tobacco taxes by two economists, the University of Chicago's Gary Becker and the City University of New York's Michael Grossman. Ballin considered it "worth noting that Mr. Becker is a fellow at the Hoover Institution, and that Mr. Grossman is an associate at the National Bureau of Economic Research, both of which have received substantial funding from Philip Morris, America's largest cigarette manufacturer." The "substantial funding," it turns out, amounted to about 0.1 percent of each organization's budget. But in Ballin's universe, it seems, the Hoover Institution and the National Bureau of Economic Research are fronts for the tobacco industry, and two highly respected scholars—Becker is a Nobel laureate, Grossman a Distinguished Professor at CUNY—are a couple of Philip Morris flacks.[5]

Similarly, anti-smoking activists and their allies have portrayed criticism of the case against secondhand smoke as a tobacco industry plot. Defending the "broad consensus among the legitimate scientific community that secondhand smoke kills," Glantz describes the skeptics as "apologists" who are "repeating the standard industry arguments."[6] He and other promoters of the idea that secondhand smoke is deadly note that some skeptics, including Yale University epidemiologist Alvan Feinstein and Texas lung specialist Gary Huber, have received research grants from or done consulting work for cigarette companies, as if this permanently disqualifies them from commenting on tobacco issues. In a 1994 press release headlined "The Tobacco Industry's Misinformation Campaign," the majority staff of the House Subcommittee on Health and the Environment claimed, "Virtually the only scientists who support the industry's contentions are scientists with financial ties to the tobacco industry."[7] Not only is this untrue (see chapter 5), it's irrelevant. If the dissenters' arguments are plausible, they are worth listening to; if not, their opponents should explain why. Either way, the money makes no difference. Truth is truth, no matter who speaks it.

Tobacco's opponents usually fail to recognize that questions about funding cut both ways. It's probably safe to say, on the subject of environmental tobacco smoke, that virtually the only scientists who support the EPA's contentions are scientists with financial ties to the anti-smoking movement. If researchers modify their opinions or slant their findings to improve their chances of getting more grants, the conclusions of scientists who are funded by anti-smoking sources such as the National

Cancer Institute or the American Cancer Society are no less suspect than the conclusions of scientists who are funded by the industry. Some researchers have received money from both sides. Whom do they try to please? The reality is that researchers whose results are useful to the tobacco companies will tend to receive industry grants and consulting fees, while researchers whose results are useful to the anti-smoking movement will tend to receive money from government agencies and voluntary health organizations. In this sense, the funding reflects the findings, rather than the other way around. It should be noted, too, that research funding from the tobacco industry generally comes without strings attached, and the studies are published in peer-reviewed journals. While such grants are increasingly controversial, the critics do not claim that the research itself is compromised. Rather, they worry that the industry is buying "innocence by association" or trying to distract attention from smoking as a cause of cancer by paying for studies of other factors.[8]

Nevertheless, I realize that some readers will want to know about funding sources, especially if a study's results seem congenial to the cigarette companies. I have taken an evenhanded approach to research funding in this book: When a paper notes a grant, whether it's from the industry or from an anti-smoking source, I include that information in the reference. But when I quote people, whatever their views on a given issue, I simply note their position, specialty, or affiliation; I do not provide a history of the grants they've received.

Following the money will always be easier than following a line of reasoning or examining a body of data, but this approach is completely antithetical to rational discourse. If (real or imagined) personal motives invalidate evidence and argument, then none of us has anything worthwhile to say, because we all have personal motives. I state mine plainly in the introduction: I oppose paternalistic policies on philosophical grounds. Activists, scientists, and bureaucrats may be driven by ideology; by a reluctance to admit error; by a hunger for power, publicity, or funding; or simply by a desire to reduce smoking and thereby improve "the public health." If we have independent reasons to believe that someone is shading the truth, these agendas can help explain why. But the motives themselves do not discredit the conclusions.

WITHOUT A DOUBT

*If President Roosevelt knew what we know now about the dangers of
tobacco, he would have quit smoking.*

—Joseph W. Cherner, SmokeFree Educational Services, 1995

HOW DARE YOU?

When I was about ten years old, my father brought an old sign machine
home from his furniture store. It was a big, heavy contraption with mov-
able wooden and metal type. After setting the type and applying some
gooey ink out of a tube, you would put a piece of cardboard on top of
the letters and run a roller over it. One of the first signs I made with the
machine was THANK YOU FOR NOT SMOKING. I produced several copies
and distributed them around the house. I also hid all the ashtrays, which
were there mainly for company. My father, who smoked cigars, rarely
did so at home. Neither of my parents smoked cigarettes, but sometimes
their visitors did. Not anymore, I had decided. About the same time, I
began waging a passive-aggressive campaign against my father's cigars.
When he dared light up in my presence, I would glare at him and
cough. If we were in the car, I would ostentatiously roll down a window.

I was born in 1965, the year after the Surgeon General's Advisory
Committee on Smoking and Health issued its landmark report conclud-
ing that "cigarette smoking is a health hazard of sufficient importance in
the United States to warrant appropriate remedial action."[1] I had never
read the report, of course, but I grew up with its consequences. From

1

TV and school I learned that smoking was bad. So here I was, engaging in a little remedial action of my own. I'd like to say that I did it because I was genuinely concerned about my father's health or because I was especially sensitive to tobacco smoke. But the truth is, I was on a power kick. By condemning tobacco, I could demonstrate my moral superiority to adults, and they had no effective way to respond. What were they going to say? That my teachers and the government were lying? That smoking was OK?

Since adults are constantly setting limits for them, children jump at the chance to turn the tables. Try throwing out a bottle in front of a kid who's been taught that recycling is the key to saving the planet, and see what happens. During the same period when I was irritating my parents with my anti-smoking signs, I was also collecting signatures to save baby harp seals. Self-righteousness comes naturally to children (or so I like to think, when I reflect upon my obnoxious behavior).

The punishment for my early intolerance came twenty years later, when I was castigated by an anti-smoking activist during a tobacco policy debate on a Ft. Lauderdale radio talk show. Alan Landers, a former model for Winston cigarettes, was suing several tobacco companies for manufacturing the product he used to promote. Then in his fifties, Landers had tried his first cigarette when he was nine and had begun smoking heavily as an adult. He was diagnosed with lung cancer in 1988. "At what point did you realize that smoking was bad for you?" the talk show's host asked him. "I got lung cancer," Landers replied, "and heard the truth about how the tobacco industry, the cigarette companies, lie to you." He said the first surgeon general's warning, which began appearing on cigarette packages in 1966, did not impress him: "That label said, 'Cigarette smoking may be hazardous to your health.' Well, I lived in New York at the time. So is walking across the street. That meant nothing. From 1970 to 1984, the next label was, 'Warning: The surgeon general has determined that cigarette smoking is hazardous to your health.' Well, that doesn't say the truth, either. Now, 1984 to present, they finally came out and said, 'Surgeon General's Warning: Smoking causes lung cancer, heart disease, and emphysema.' . . . By the time I found out that it causes lung cancer, it was in 1984. I got my cancer in '88. It was too late."[2]

The host asked Landers about the many statements by scientists and government officials regarding the hazards of smoking. "That means nothing," he said. "That's announced like one time, or put in a newspaper. I didn't happen to see that. What means something is what they're putting on their labeling. . . . If I saw a pack of cigarettes and it said 'Addictive Poison,' I never would have smoked."[3] Landers's claim that he did not know about the link between smoking and lung cancer until 1984 is hard to believe; the hazards of smoking, especially the risk of lung cancer, had been widely publicized since the early 1950s. Thousands of scientific studies on smoking had been published, the most important of which were covered in the general press; the surgeon general had issued seventeen reports on the health consequences of smoking, beginning in 1964; and voluntary health organizations had been urging smokers to quit for decades through posters, pamphlets, and ads. In the late 1960s and early '70s, when Landers was hawking Winstons in magazine ads and billboards, anti-smoking public service announcements were aired frequently on radio and TV. Little kids like me got the message. It's hard to see how anyone could have missed it.

Since the hazards of cigarettes have long been common knowledge, I argued, smokers cannot reasonably blame the tobacco companies if they get sick as a result of their habit. Not surprisingly, Landers did not like this argument. "You know," he said, "you ought to be ashamed of yourself. Do you smoke? . . . Do you have any children? . . . What I'm trying to tell you is, we're not talking about the common cold. We're talking about lung cancer. Smoking-related illness kills half a million a year. . . . In the world, three million a year are dying. So how you could defend the cigarette companies is beyond me. It's killing people. We're murdering our children." A little later, after the host asked me who was publishing this book, Landers interjected, "Make money off the pain and suffering of others. That's really something. I don't know how you can live with yourself." I asked him what he meant. "You're defending the tobacco companies," he said. "They're merchants of death. Do you know what it's like to have lung cancer? . . . How dare you defend them!"[4]

How, indeed. Between the time of my precocious anti-smoking activism and my encounter with Landers, a couple of things happened that help explain why I no longer identify with the crusade for a smoke-free society. As I grew up, I realized that something can be bad for you, raising your chance of disease or injury, yet also good for you, providing pleasure or relieving stress. I also realized that people have different tastes and preferences. For me, the rewards of smoking cigarettes have never justified the risks involved, but I'm sure a lot of smokers would have a hard time understanding why I like bungee jumping, a considerably safer activity. When I started giving serious thought to this sort of thing, it seemed to me that people should be allowed to decide for themselves which risks to take, as long as they don't pose a danger to others. This basic notion, I discovered, was part of a venerable tradition in political philosophy, one with which I felt an immediate rapport.

As John Stuart Mill famously put it, "The sole end for which mankind are warranted, individually or collectively, in interfering with the liberty of action of any of their number is self-protection. . . . The only purpose for which power can rightfully be exercised over any member of a civilized community, against his will, is to prevent harm to others. His own good, either physical or moral, is not a sufficient warrant."[5] This principle rules out the use of coercion, which includes taxes and regulations as well as the criminal law, to discourage people from engaging in risky habits. With the freedom to make such choices, however, comes the obligation to accept responsibility for the consequences. And that Alan Landers seemed unwilling to do.

Under the circumstances, Landers's emotional response was understandable. He had recently suffered a grave illness, he did not know how long his cancer would be in remission, and he was intent on atoning for his work as a cigarette model. But if Landers got carried away, that does not explain why so many anti-smokers approach debates in a similar way. Indeed, the rhetorical techniques he used—the decontextualized death tolls; the gross exaggeration ("We're murdering our children"); the red herring questions ("Do you smoke? Do you have children? Do you know what it's like to have lung cancer?"); and, above all, the substitution of personal attacks for logical argument—are typical of the anti-smoking movement. This is not to say that every opponent of smoking is a raving fanatic. During the course of my research, I have encountered reasonable, fair-minded critics of the tobacco industry who understand that people who disagree with them are not necessarily in league with the "merchants of death." Unfortunately, these are not the people who set the tone for the movement.

TO BE SURE

Among tobacco's opponents, citing "financial ties" to the industry is by far the most popular form of *ad hominem* attack, as I have learned from personal experience (see Author's Note). Such attacks reflect the unshakable certainty that many anti-smokers feel about the rightness of their cause. For some, the moral imperative to eliminate smoking is so clear that they assume anyone who opposes them must be collaborating with the tobacco companies. Others may not really believe this but are willing to pretend they do if it will help overcome obstacles to a smoke-free society. Either way, anti-smoking activists and public health officials rarely concede that there is any legitimate opposition to their agenda.

Alan Blum, a physician who has been an anti-smoking activist for twenty years, worries that the movement might be perceived as "a bunch of jerks . . . morally outraged, Carry Nation types. I think it's more sophisticated than that." At the same time, having indulged in some extreme rhetoric of his own over the years, he recognizes that the perception has some basis in fact: "Folks see evil, and you know how evil is—you want to go after it and slay it. But they don't see the people who are looking at evil and not objecting as much as they are. It's a very elite, liberal argument. . . . They're so absolutely certain of how right they are, and everybody else is wrong. Eventually, they wind up turning you off."[6]

Joseph W. Cherner, a successful bond trader who left Wall Street in 1989 to found SmokeFree Educational Services, nicely illustrated that attitude in an interview with the *New York Times*. "It's the only issue I know of where there aren't two sides—two intelligent sides," he said. "I have a comic-book mentality—I grew up with comic books—and I see this as good versus evil."[7] Cherner, who said he identifies with Spider Man in particular, has lobbied for smoking restrictions in New York City businesses, campaigned against a Marlboro billboard in Shea Stadium, and sponsored anti-smoking poster contests for children. He has dark, earnest eyes and a friendly but intense manner. Soon after meeting me at a radio studio where we debated tobacco policy, he asked me the three big questions: Do you smoke? Do you have children? Have you ever seen someone die of emphysema? He seemed to be looking for an explanation of my puzzling failure to agree with him.

A similar sort of dismay was apparent in a 1994 editorial in the *Journal of the American Medical Association* (*JAMA*), coauthored by David Satcher, director of the U.S. Centers for Disease Control and Prevention, and Michael Eriksen, head of the CDC's Office on Smoking and Health. Despite all the evidence that smoking is dangerous, Satcher and Eriksen wrote, "we are still plagued by an entirely preventable problem, and this is the paradox of tobacco control."[8] Yet there is nothing paradoxical about the fact that people continue to smoke, unless you assume that there are no benefits to balance against the hazards. This does seem to be a governing assumption of the anti-smoking movement. As chairman of the Coalition on Smoking or Health, a joint project of the American Cancer Society, the American Heart Association, and the American Lung Association, Scott Ballin claimed, "There is no positive aspect to [smoking]. The product has no potential benefits."[9]

Many smokers, of course, would disagree. Journalist Christopher Hitchens says, "Cigarettes improve my short-term concentration, aid my digestion, make me a finer writer and a better dinner companion, and, in several other ways, prolong my life. So when you tread, tread softly—for you tread on my dreams."[10] *National Review* columnist Florence King writes, "I believe life should be savored rather than lengthened, and I am ready to fight the misanthropes among us who are trying to make me switch."[11] Similarly, Nader Mousavizadeh writes in the *New Republic*, "The issue, to put it perhaps a bit grandly, is the freedom of adult men and women to live and die as they choose. And who are these health-zealots anyway with their clinical sensibilities who presume such omniscience about the means and ends of the good life? What ever made them think that they are models for anything, except perhaps for the choice of a life bought at the cost of living?"[12]

Julie DeFalco, a policy analyst at a Washington think tank, notes that tobacco's opponents "are making a personal judgment—that a long life without cigarettes is better than a shorter life with cigarettes—and attempting to turn it into a law applicable to everybody. I and many other people like to smoke. We get unquantifiable, but real, benefits from smoking. I like the entire ritual of lighting a cigarette, and I enjoy the first drag. Cigarettes are really nice when you feel stressed out. So this is to be a crime?"[13]

Tobacco's opponents typically dismiss such statements out of hand. "The argument is, 'They don't enjoy it; they just do it because they have to,' " says David Brenton, founder of the Smokers' Rights Alliance. "This assumes that people don't derive any pleasure at all from smoking."[14] As Ballin put it, "It's addictive, so people don't have the choice to smoke or not to smoke."[15] Hence, smokers who acknowledge the risks of their habit but cite countervailing rewards are dishonest or deluded, displaying the classic defense mechanisms of rationalization and denial. Sociologist Anne Wortham, herself a smoker, says tobacco's opponents believe that if you smoke, "you are in a state of false consciousness, because you are not aware of what is in your interests. It's the refusal to acknowledge people's capacity to make choices. You just define them out of the discourse. 'Addiction' says they can't even talk about their own likes and dislikes. We can decide for them."[16]

Participating in a discussion on CNN a few years ago, Christopher Buckley, author of the satirical novel *Thank You for Smoking*, suggested that "hectoring smokers to death" might backfire. NPR correspondent and fellow guest Susan Stamberg replied: "I say hector them to death is better than their dying of lung cancer. . . . And what's a government for if it doesn't step in and say, 'You can't commit suicide'?"[17] The late Oklahoma representative Mike Synar, who was one of the tobacco industry's leading critics in Congress, once lamented that "millions of smokers haven't accepted the fact that they should give it up."[18] If the need to stop smoking is a *fact,* there is no room for disagreement. A faith that can leap the is/ought gap so readily is a powerful force to contend with.

The U.S. Postal Service chose to avoid a confrontation with the faithful in 1994 when it released a twenty-nine-cent stamp featuring the early blues guitarist Robert Johnson. In the photograph on which the engraving is based (one of the few extant images of the enigmatic bluesman), Johnson has a cigarette dangling from his lips; in the stamp, the cigarette is gone. According to a postal service spokeswoman, an advisory committee recommended the modification "because they didn't want the stamps to be perceived as promoting cigarettes."[19] The incident might have been dismissed as an example of excessive caution by silly bureaucrats, but the postal service had good reason to worry that a stamp accurately depicting Johnson, cigarette and all, might prompt complaints from tobacco's opponents. The year before, Joe Cherner's SmokeFree Educational Services had taken out ads in *Daily Variety* criticizing Ron Howard, director of *Backdraft,* and Robert Redford, director of *A River Runs Through It,* for daring to depict important characters in their films as smokers. Never mind that some firefighters really do smoke or that Redford's movie was a period piece. Giving smokers such a prominent place in a major motion picture was just *irresponsible.* "We're not trying to restrict artistic freedom," Cherner said. "We're just saying, if it's not important to the role of the character, why help the tobacco industry kill people?"[20]

In 1995 similar protests greeted a proposal to adopt a silhouette of Franklin D. Roosevelt, with a cigarette in a holder protruding from his mouth, as the official symbol of Hyde Park, New York. "I wouldn't want Hyde Park to be seen as promoting a deadly habit," said Dutchess County health commissioner Michael C. Caldwell. "If President Roosevelt knew what we know now about the dangers of tobacco," Cherner asserted, "he would have quit smoking." Kevin Bergin, the town councilman who proposed the symbol, was bemused by the complaints. "Roosevelt with a cigarette was Roosevelt to a generation of people," he noted. "Do we try to be so politically correct that we end up rewriting history?"[21]

A good question. This business of falsifying historical images so they jibe with contemporary sensibilities has a totalitarian flavor to it. Writing in the *Washington Post* about the smoke-free Robert Johnson stamp, Charles Paul Freund noted that the governments of Albania and China retouched old pictures of Enver Hoxha and Mao Tse-tung, respectively, to eliminate cigarettes that were deemed undignified, while Adolf Hitler, a rabid anti-smoker, ordered Joseph Stalin's cigarette obliterated from an official photograph taken after the signing of the nonaggression pact between Germany and the Soviet Union.[22] Cherner's notion that art should conform to a political agenda—that filmmakers should be doing their part to help achieve a smoke-free society—also has disturbing precedents.

TERMS OF ENGAGEMENT

The vigilance against deviation from the correct portrayal of smoking is accompanied by absurd rhetorical excesses, even in supposedly sober scientific journals. *JAMA*'s vociferousness on the issue of smoking, like Alan Landers's, may be an attempt to make up for past sins: The journal carried cigarette ads until 1953, and the AMA accepted research money from the tobacco industry in the '60s and '70s, during which decades activists accused the organization of inexcusable timidity on an important public health issue. Since the 1980s, however, *JAMA* has been second to none in its denunciations of tobacco. A 1986 editorial compared smoking-related deaths to Nazi genocide, calling for "a declaration of all-out war" to save "the victims of the tobaccoism holocaust."[23] A 1990 editorial, this one by a former CDC director, said tobacco executives and the advertising firms that work for them "daily make the decision to kill for money, to become 'hit men' on a colossal scale."[24] Picking up on the same theme in yet another *JAMA* editorial, then-secretary of health and human services Louis Sullivan called revenue from tobacco advertising accounts "blood money."[25]

Longtime anti-smoking activist Stanton Glantz, a professor at the University of California at San Francisco, has compared the tobacco companies to Timothy McVeigh, convicted of murdering 168 people in Oklahoma City. "The tobacco industry has killed 10 million Americans since 1964," he wrote in a 1997 *Los Angeles Times* op-ed piece. "No attorney general or politician even considered letting McVeigh cop a plea; the same should be true for the tobacco industry."[26] *New York Times* reporter Philip J. Hilts, who portrays himself as a moderate on smoking issues, nevertheless likens tobacco industry employees to "the guards and doctors in the Nazi death camps."[27] According to Texas Attorney General Daniel Morales, "History will record the modern-day tobacco industry alongside the worst of civilization's evil empires."[28]

Facing such an enemy, tobacco's opponents feel justified in using any weapon that comes to hand. "From my point of view," former surgeon general C. Everett Koop told the *Philadelphia Inquirer* in 1996, "anything that stops smoking is good."[29] Former AMA president Lonnie Bristow, who serves on the board of the National Center for Tobacco-

Free Kids, has called the fight against smoking a "black flag" battle, explaining, "During the Civil War, when some Union troops with black soldiers went into combat against Confederate troops, both sides would wave a black flag. This meant the opposite of a white flag—a fight to the death, with no surrenders, no prisoners. Mercy was neither expected nor given. That's what it's like fighting against tobacco interests."[30]

In reality, however, the anti-smoking movement is not fighting "tobacco interests" so much as smokers themselves, without whom the cigarette companies would not exist. The fraction of American adults who smoke has dropped from more than two-fifths in the 1960s to about one-quarter today, but the trend has been gradual and seems to have leveled off in recent years.[31] Meanwhile, tobacco's opponents, who initially emphasized education and persuasion, have turned to increasingly coercive measures, including punitive taxes, censorship, and government-imposed smoking bans on private property. The Food and Drug Administration is poised to take charge of tobacco regulation, and the authority it claims would allow a wide range of restrictions, including a partial or complete ban on cigarettes. Prohibition would be disastrous for the tobacco companies, of course, but the results would not be very pleasant for smokers, either (or for the rest of us, given the nasty side effects of creating a black market). Even private and state-sponsored lawsuits against cigarette companies have been aimed, in part, at their customers, who would have to pay higher prices—which tobacco's opponents hope will deter smoking—to cover the cost of damage awards or settlements.

The point, in short, is to make life harder for smokers so they will stop misbehaving. The pressure works at a practical level, making smoking more expensive and less convenient, and at a symbolic level, transforming what was once a mainstream habit into a shameful addiction. Bans on smoking in public places (meaning any building other than a private residence) operate at both levels, literally and figuratively pushing smokers out into the cold—a phenomenon satirized in those Benson & Hedges ads that show smokers congregating on airplane wings and the tops of trains.

One of my colleagues, Charles Paul Freund, works at home in Washington rather than put up with the inconvenience of a smoke-free office.

Back when smoking was still permitted in local restaurants, he would nevertheless refrain when he sensed that fellow diners might be disturbed. As complaints about secondhand smoke became more common, he also stopped smoking in other people's homes; recognizing that a guest might object even if the host did not, Freund would just step outside for a cigarette. "I don't have any problem not smoking around people who don't like it," he says. "I never have. What I object to are the idiotic things like smoking bans in open-air places such as stadiums. People who never used to care when I smoked now think that I'm shortening their lives, that it's a form of assault. It's simply not rational."[32]

Freund, who smokes between one and two packs a day, finds that certain kinds of smoking bans are easier to tolerate than others. The first time he took a long smoke-free flight, he expected an ordeal. Instead, the flight was just more boring than usual, without cigarettes to mark the passage of time. When he visits an office or someone's home, he will usually go without a cigarette for an hour or two. But in bars or other contexts involving drinking and conversation, he tends to smoke more frequently. During a dinner with the rest of *Reason*'s editorial staff in Los Angeles, where smoking in restaurants is forbidden, he left the table repeatedly to consume a quick cigarette on the sidewalk. He would make a joke each time he went out: "I think I'll go check the weather again." The ban did not change the reality of what he was doing—ingesting a psychoactive substance—but it changed its social significance. We could alter our consciousness with alcohol and remain inside, but Freund had to go outside to alter his consciousness with nicotine. Had he been allowed to light up at the table, he would have been just a guy smoking while talking to his friends over drinks. The ban made him seem more like an addict in need of a fix.

The cigar boom of the 1990s can be seen as a rebellion against this attempt to redefine smoking. Sales of premium cigars (costing more than a dollar each) rose 42 percent from 1989 to 1994, and overall cigar sales, which had been declining since 1970, rose 45 percent from 1993 to 1996.[33] The demand for some premium cigars outstripped supplies, with customers waiting months for delivery. Launched in 1992, the glossy magazine *Cigar Aficionado*, fat with ads and featuring celebrity smokers on the cover, has been a big success, inspiring imitators. In increasingly smoke-free cities such as Los Angeles and New York, cigar banquets and cigar bars offer havens for smokers who can afford them. Rejecting the attempt to stigmatize smoking as low-class and anti-social, the new cigar smokers see it as sophisticated and convivial. Their mood is summed up by an ad campaign for Johnnie Walker Red Label scotch that shows a man sitting in a chair with a glass in one hand and a cigar in the other. The copy reads: "Big fat cigar. Glass of Red Label. Back whether they like it or not."

The Johnnie Walker slogan calls attention to the true nature of the crusade for a smoke-free society. It is an attempt by one group of people to impose their tastes and preferences on another—a point that is often obscured by focusing on the misdeeds of the tobacco industry. As I write, Congress is considering a nationwide settlement proposal under which the tobacco companies would cough up a ton of money and swallow a mass of humiliating requirements in exchange for protection against the vicissitudes of regulation and litigation. Among other things, the companies have agreed to pay what amounts to a huge fine ($368.5 billion) for the crime of selling cigarettes; have conceded the authority of the Food and Drug Administration (FDA) over tobacco products; have accepted sweeping restrictions on advertising and promotion; have endorsed a federal ban on smoking in most nonresidential buildings; have promised to finance a $500-million-a-year national media campaign aimed at discouraging consumption of their products; and have committed themselves, under the threat of further fines, to utterly unrealistic goals for reducing smoking by teenagers. Tobacco's opponents are complaining that the agreement does not go far enough.

Whatever Congress decides, the crusade for a smoke-free society will continue, because it is aimed at the behavior of individuals, not the behavior of corporations. Long before Philip Morris and R. J. Reynolds existed, the tobacco habit had plenty of detractors (see chapter 1). Initially condemned as an unsavory practice of savages, smoking quickly caught on in Europe and throughout the world, but attempts to suppress tobacco use, including cigarette bans in nineteen U.S. states early in this century, have been a recurring theme. The emergence of definitive scientific evidence that smoking is hazardous, discussed in chapter 2, has given a new impetus to anti-tobacco forces. According to contemporary public health doctrine, the government has a right and a duty to discourage behavior that might lead to disease or injury, a principle that gives the anti-smoking movement a rationale for enlisting the state's assistance.

Given this country's tradition of limited government, however, most Americans are not prepared to accept "public health" as an adequate reason for joining the march toward a smoke-free society. Hence, tobacco's opponents have offered additional rationales, all designed to overcome suspicions of paternalism. They have argued that tobacco advertising is an insidious force that seduces people into acting against their interests (see chapter 3). They have said that smoking imposes costs on society that need to be recouped through special taxes (chapter 4). They have claimed that secondhand smoke poses a grave threat to bystanders and that smoking should therefore be confined to private residences (chapter 5). They have accused the tobacco companies of hiding the truth about smoking, thereby preventing their customers from making informed decisions (chapter 6). They have described nicotine addiction as a compulsive and possibly contagious illness, a portrayal that fits nicely with the public health mission to control disease (chapter 7). Often these arguments are combined with appeals to protect children, who are said to be especially vulnerable to advertising, secondhand smoke, and addiction. The best-funded anti-smoking group in Washington these days is the National Center for Tobacco-Free Kids, which played a key role in the negotiations that led to the nationwide settlement proposal. Former FDA commissioner David A. Kessler calls smoking a "pediatric disease," and who could be in favor of that?[34]

Since, as this book tries to show, none of these claims is very convincing, we are left with the argument that I understood and fervently adopted as a ten-year-old: You shouldn't smoke because it's bad for you. In the realm of public policy, the impulse behind this injunction takes the form of two complementary beliefs: that the government should suppress the use of hazardous drugs and that it should deter activities that impair "the public health." As I argue in the final chapter, the dangerous implications of these ideas extend far beyond tobacco.

Chapter 1

FROM DEVIL'S WEED TO SOLDIER'S FRIEND

They who smoke tobacco can be compared only to men possessed, who are in need of exorcizing. While their throats belch forth the stinking, poisonous fumes, they remain nonetheless thralls to the tobacco fiend to whom they cling with an idolatrous devotion, exalting him as their god above all others, and striving to entice all they meet to imitate their folly. One thing at least it teaches them, the better to endure the reek of hell.

—Johann Michael Moscherosch, 1650

DRINKING SMOKE

Rodrigo de Jerez, who accompanied Christopher Columbus on his first voyage to the New World, stumbled upon a strange practice while exploring Cuba. He saw villagers light dried leaves and hold them to their mouths, alternately blowing on them and inhaling the smoke. These were the same sort of leaves that Arawak Indians had presented to Columbus when he landed in the Bahamas. Europeans would eventually find that the plant was cultivated throughout North and South America. It could be chewed, snorted as a powder, or mixed with a liquid and drunk, but it was generally smoked, either in a pipe or rolled up inside a leaf. The inhabitants of the Antilles often burned the leaves and inhaled the smoke through a Y-shaped tube, which they called *tobacco,* a term the Spaniards applied to the plant.

Jerez experimented with smoking and found that he liked it. When he returned to his hometown of Ayamonte, he brought some tobacco with him. But fifteenth-century Spaniards were not accustomed to seeing smoke billow from a man's mouth and nose. Suspecting that the Devil was at work, the townspeople consulted a priest, who reported the incident to the Inquisition. As a result, the explorer spent several years in prison.[1]

Jerez's experience was a sign of things to come. Enthusiasm for tobacco has been greeted with hostility, in varying degrees, for five hundred years. Sometimes the reaction has been fierce and repressive, sometimes perfunctory. Attempts to discourage tobacco use have ranged from exhortation to the death penalty. None of these measures prevented the spread of tobacco around the world or steadily rising consumption wherever it was introduced. But no matter how popular tobacco became, a vocal minority continued to condemn smoking as disgusting, immoral, addictive, and unhealthy.

Although most Americans probably think of the anti-smoking movement as something that began in the 1960s, tobacco's contemporary opponents echo complaints first expressed centuries ago. The weed's detractors have long warned that smoking ravages the body, leaving it vulnerable to a variety of ills, including deadly diseases. They have said that it impairs the ability to work and pay taxes, thereby draining the state's coffers and hurting society as a whole. They have strenuously objected to secondhand smoke as a nuisance and a health hazard. They have argued that tobacco use is evidence of madness or possession, since no sane, rational person could possibly choose to continue this vile, self-destructive, inconsiderate, and irresponsible habit. Since the late nineteenth century, they have complained that tobacco companies are luring children into the habit, and they have used that concern to justify restrictions on adults.

Especially striking is the failure of tobacco's opponents to understand its appeal, a blindness that did not begin with Scott Ballin and the Coalition on Smoking or Health. In his 1526 history of the West Indies, Fernandez de Oviedo y Valdes wrote, "Among other evil practices, the Indians have one that is especially harmful, the inhaling of a certain kind of smoke which they call tobacco, in order to produce a state of stupor. . . . I cannot imagine what pleasure they derive from this practice."[2] About the same time, Bishop Bartholomé de las Casas noted that Spanish settlers in the West Indies had begun to smoke cigars. "I have seen many Spaniards in the Island of Hispaniola who used them and who, when reproached for such a disgusting habit, replied that they found it impossible to give up," he wrote. "I cannot understand what enjoyment or advantage they derive from it."[3]

Others did understand, finding that tobacco was pleasantly stimulating in small doses and calming in larger doses; it also helped relieve fatigue and hunger. Spanish and Portuguese sailors spread the habit by their example and by bringing tobacco plants and seeds back to Europe for cultivation. Since European physicians were eager for new botanical remedies and since the inhabitants of the Americas had long used tobacco to treat a wide range of maladies (including headaches and respiratory problems), the plant came to be viewed as a medicine. Jean Nicot, the French ambassador to Lisbon from 1559 to 1561, enthusiastically promoted tobacco as a topical treatment for sores, lesions, tumors, and headaches, sending samples of the plant to Paris. (In recognition of his efforts, his name would be applied to both the tobacco plant's genus, *Nicotiana,* and its main psychoactive ingredient, nicotine.) In a 1571 book on the medicinal plants of the New World, the renowned University of Seville physician Nicolò Monardes discussed tobacco at length, recommending it as a cure for more than twenty ailments, including coughs, asthma, toothache, headache, stomach cramps, gout, intestinal worms, and cancer. The book was translated into several languages and widely distributed in Europe, boosting tobacco's reputation as a panacea.

James VI, king of Scotland, was not impressed. He detested smoking and watched in disgust as it gained a following in England, where it was tolerated by Elizabeth I, who even let Sir Walter Raleigh smoke in the palace. Shortly after succeeding Elizabeth as James I in 1603, the new king published *A Counterblaste to Tobacco,* one of the first anti-smoking polemics. James doubted that tobacco was much use as a medicine; in any case, he said, healthy men should not be taking it. He emphasized the plant's uncivilized origins: "Shall we . . . abase ourselves so farre, as to imitate these beastly *Indians?* . . . Why doe we not as well imitate them in walking naked as they doe? . . . yea why doe we not denie God and adore the Devill as they doe?"[4]

The king worried that dependence on tobacco would make his people unsuited for war—since they would yearn for the weed during battle—and deplete their property. (Tobacco was still a luxury; during the Elizabethan period, the historian Egon C. Corti reports, it sold for its weight in silver.) "Is it not the greatest sinne of all," James asked, "that you the people of all sortes of this Kingdome, who are created and or-deined by God to bestowe both your persons and goods for the mainte-nance both of the honour and safetie of your King and Commonwealth, should disable your selves in both?" Thus he forthrightly asserted a premise that today's anti-smoking activists, who also complain about to-bacco's impact on the public treasury, prefer to leave unspoken: that the function of the individual is to serve the state.[5]

James also complained about secondhand smoke, noting the appalling practice of lighting pipes at the dinner table. He averred that many people started smoking as a way of making the smoke of others more tolerable. The wife of a smoker, he said, can either take up a pipe herself and "corrupt her sweete breath therewith, or else resolve to live in perpetuall stinking torment." In short, he concluded, smoking is "a cus-tome lothsome to the eye, hatefull to the Nose, harmefull to the braine, dangerous to the Lungs, and in the blacke stinking fume thereof, neerest resembling the horrible Stigian smoke of the pit that is bottomlesse."[6]

The king's pamphlet was widely read and prompted a spate of books on tobacco. Most of them, not surprisingly, agreed with him about smoking, though many praised tobacco's medicinal properties. In *The Anatomy of Melancholy* (1621), Robert Burton wrote, "A good vomit, I confess, a virtuous herbe, if it be well qualified, opportunely taken, and medicinally used, but, as it is commonly abused by most men, which take it as Tinkers do Ale, 'tis a plague, a mischief, a vicious purger of goods, lands, health, hellish, devilish and damned *Tobacco,* the ruin and overthrow of body and soul."[7]

Despite the complaints, English tobacco consumption soared, en-couraged partly by the belief that tobacco smoke helped ward off the plague. James I ordered an increase in the duty on tobacco to discourage smoking, but because of opposition from Parliament the measure was never enforced. The second Virginia colony thrived by growing tobacco. In 1619, to protect the colonial revenue, the king forbade domestic cultivation and made the tobacco trade a royal monopoly. Thus, one of history's most vociferous opponents of smoking recognized the profit in tobacco even as he railed against it. James I was hardly the last ruler to reject smoking but welcome the money it generated.

THE REEK OF HELL

During the seventeenth century, a combination of religious objections, annoyance at tobacco smoke, concern about the fire hazard posed by smoking, and disappointment with tobacco's performance as a medicine generated a backlash against the weed. Among the clergy the controversy centered on tobacco's pagan origins, its addictiveness, its reputed aphrodisiac properties, and its use in church.

The Puritans of New England, who presaged our modern-day ambivalence about drugs, granted tobacco's medicinal value but frowned upon using it as an intoxicant. In the 1630s Massachusetts banned tobacco sales and smoking in public. In 1647 Connecticut passed a law forbidding the use of tobacco in public and restricting even private use to adults above the age of twenty-one who had already acquired the habit or who had obtained a physician's certificate and a court license. These Puritan laws were not seriously enforced, and they were soon repealed or forgotten. But the spirit behind them was apparent in a 1726 book by Cotton Mather offering guidance to ministerial candidates. In the section on "Rules of Health," he warned: "If once you get into the way of *Smoking*, there will be extreme hazard, of your becoming a *Slave* to the *Pipe*; and ever *Insatiably* craving for it. People may think what they will; But such a *Slavery*, is much below the Dignity of a *Rational Creature*; and much more of a *Gracious Christian*."[8]

Tobacco's more fervent detractors identified it as the Devil's weed. In 1650 Johann Michael Moscherosch addressed those who had acquired the smoking habit "through the cunning wiles of the Devil": "Consider well, beloved mortals, brothers and sisters in your madness, how the Devil hath deceived you! For even as they who grow fat and fleshy through much gluttony do clearly show that their god is their belly, so you, who use the filthy weed, do fill yourselves with the spirit of fire, and belch forth from your mouths the smoke of perdition."[9]

Others, in an argument with a more contemporary ring (it would be familiar to NPR's Susan Stamberg), condemned smoking as a kind of suicide. "What difference is there between a smoker and a suicide," asked the Jesuit priest Jakob Balde in 1658, "except that the one takes longer to kill himself than the other? Because of this perpetual smoking, the pure oil of the lamp of life dries up and disappears, and the fair flame of life itself flickers out and goes out, all because of this barbarous habit."[10]

Tobacco's opponents were especially offended by smoking and snuff taking in church. The spitting and smoke associated with tobacco use dirtied church property and created an unpleasant odor. Furthermore, priests who inhaled snuff prior to Mass ran the risk of expelling the host by sneezing or spitting during communion. In 1642 Pope Urban VIII issued a bull that threatened excommunication of priests who "take tobacco in leaf, in powder, in smoke by mouth or nostrils in any of the churches of Seville, [or] throughout the archbishopric."[11] Eight years later, his successor, Innocent X, applied the same rule to St. Peter's Church in Rome.

In the seventeenth century, Holy Roman Emperor Ferdinand III, the Swiss National Assembly, and other authorities banned "tobacco drinking" under threat of fines, but smoking continued unabated. Indeed, the habit proved resistant to far more heavy-handed attempts at suppression. In 1633, after hearing dissidents in tobacco houses denounce his government, the Turkish sultan Murad IV forbade smoking under pain of death and ordered the demolition of all places where people met to smoke. The sultan liked to visit the coffeehouses of Constantinople incognito; anyone he saw smoking would turn up dead the next morning. Blood lust and paranoia were not the only reasons for Murad the Cruel's enthusiastic pursuit of smokers: the assets of executed smokers, like the assets of drug offenders in twentieth-century America, became the property of the state. During military campaigns Murad would catch soldiers in the act of smoking and order their immediate execution by hanging, beheading, or quartering. Sometimes he would have their hands and feet crushed and leave them on the battlefield to die. In *The Balance of Truth* (1656), the Turkish writer Katib Chelebi reports that during Murad's campaign against Baghdad fifteen to twenty officers were tortured to death for smoking at one resting place. But as the sultan's repression intensified, Chelebi notes, "so did people's desire to smoke. . . . 'Men desire what is forbidden,' and many thousands of men were sent to the abode of nothingness."[12] The Turkish ban on smoking was repealed by Mohammed IV, himself a smoker, who became sultan in 1648. Smokers had the last laugh in 1900 when Murads, a brand of Turkish cigarettes, appeared on the market.

Brutal methods also failed to eradicate smoking in Russia. Czar Michael, whose rule began in 1613, declared smoking a deadly sin and made possession of tobacco a crime. Arrested smokers could expect to be flogged or have their lips slit. Repeat offenders might be exiled to Siberia, in which case their property would go to the czar. A 1643 visitor to Moscow later described enforcement of the tobacco ban: "Offenders are usually sentenced to slitting of the nostrils, the bastinado, or the knout; those convicted of taking snuff have their noses torn away. We ourselves have met with many victims of these forms of torture, which were inflicted alike on men and women."[13] Still, smoking persisted, and the ban was eventually lifted by Peter the Great, who ascended the throne in 1689. Like Mohammed IV, he was a smoker.

European governments increasingly recognized that so hardy a habit could be a valuable source of revenue. In 1629 Louis XIII, at the recommendation of his first minister, Cardinal Richelieu, imposed a duty of thirty sols on every pound of tobacco imported into France. Richelieu disapproved of smoking and hoped to discourage the habit through taxation, but his policies established a link between the French treasury and tobacco consumption that continues to this day. Two centuries later Napoleon III would observe: "This vice brings in one hundred million francs in taxes every year. I will certainly forbid it at once—as soon as you can name a virtue that brings in as much revenue."[14] In the mid-seventeenth century several Italian republics established tobacco monopolies that became a model for the rest of Europe. Monopolies in the importation and sale of tobacco could be operated by the government or farmed out for large fees. The government monopolies proved so lucrative that they persisted in several European countries late into the twentieth century.

Although Louis XIV hated tobacco, he dared not ban it, since this would have meant giving up the money from the state monopoly. Nevertheless, he encouraged his court physician, Fagon, who shared his views, to speak out against the increasingly popular weed. During a debate at the Paris School of Medicine in 1699, Fagon offered an eloquent version of contemporary warnings about nicotine addiction, describing the tobacco habit as fatal yet somehow irresistible: "Who is the rash man that first tasted a poison that is more dangerous than hemlock, deadlier than opium? When he opened his snuff-box, did he not know that he was opening Pandora's box, from which would spring a thousand ills, one worse than another? Assuredly, when we try it for the first time, we feel an uneasiness that tells us that we have taken poison. . . . When, unfortunately, against all advice, he falls under this dangerous habit, all reasoning, all warning, is in vain. He cannot shake off his enemy. . . . All other pleasures bring satiety, which weakens their ill effects; tobacco alone becomes a fatal, insatiable necessity. It has been said that love is a brief epileptic fit, but smoking is a permanent epilepsy."[15]

Both Fagon and his master were dismayed by the increasingly common sight of dignified aristocrats removing scented, ground tobacco from little boxes and snorting the powder into their noses. Snuff, which the Spanish royal monopoly was manufacturing by the second half of the seventeenth century, was soon being produced throughout Europe. European sophisticates eagerly adopted dainty snuff rituals and collected elaborately decorated snuff boxes. During the eighteenth century snuff's popularity in trend-setting France and its association with clergy and royalty helped make it the most fashionable way to consume tobacco.

From a contemporary perspective the popularity of snuff is hard to understand (though it is not so different from the more recent fashion of inhaling cocaine powder). Snuff stained fingers and clothes, brought on sneezing fits and runny noses, and impaired the sense of smell. Nevertheless, it had several advantages over smoking as then practiced. In those days smoking was associated with a great deal of spitting, and lighting a pipe required an existing flame or the skillful application of flint and steel. Those who were concerned about the ill effects of smoking viewed snuff as safer, and its tendency to induce sneezing was considered beneficial, helping to rid the body of "corrupt humours." Finally, as the German historian Wolfgang Schivelbusch observes, in an era when olfactory assaults were constant, an impaired sense of smell was probably a welcome side effect.

In 1725, bowing to fashion, Pope Benedict XIII decided to permit the use of snuff in St. Peter's Church, lifting the ban imposed seventy-five years before by Innocent X. In 1779 the Vatican opened its own to-bacco factory. Snuff's triumph was so dramatic that in 1773 Samuel Johnson declared: "Smoking has gone out. To be sure, it is a shocking thing, blowing smoke out of our mouths into other people's mouths, eyes, and noses, and having the same thing done to us. Yet I cannot ac-count, why a thing which requires so little exertion, and yet preserves the mind from total vacuity, should have gone out."[16] His ambivalent announcement of smoking's demise turned out to be premature—its greatest popularity still lay ahead—but he was right that many people would continue to find it shocking.

SMOKE RETURNS

A form of cigar—tobacco wrapped in vegetable matter—had long been consumed by the Indians of South America, and Spanish settlers imi-tated the practice. But the ready-made cigar in a tobacco-leaf wrapper did not gain a large following until the beginning of the nineteenth cen-tury. French and British soldiers fighting in Spain during the Napoleonic Wars learned to smoke cigars and helped popularize them upon returning home. Cigars were more compact, portable, and conve-nient than the pipe; they became even easier to smoke after the inven-tion of the friction-activated phosphorous match in 1827. In England and France cigars became so fashionable that they rehabilitated smoking for the upper classes, much as they would in the United States during the 1990s. A "smoking room" was established in the House of Com-mons in the 1820s, and smoking compartments were introduced on English railways in 1868.

Smokers were still hemmed in by taboos and restrictions. Queen Vic-toria hated tobacco, especially when it was smoked. Royal guests who smoked had to exhale into fireplaces. And though men of high rank could smoke without raising eyebrows, smoking by women was still seen as low-class behavior.

Smoking was considered improper on the street and in other public places that were not set aside for the purpose. In the German states, police imposed heavy fines for smoking in the street, which was deemed hazardous as well as indecent. But the rule was unpopular and frequently broken. In Prussia, Corti writes, "smoking in public was often regarded as a demonstration against the system of government. Just as anyone who wore a soft felt hat instead of the fashionable top-hat was suspected of holding revolutionary views, everyone smoking in the streets was regarded as a dangerous democrat."[17] The idea of smoking as a political statement would have seemed bizarre a few decades ago, but it is not so implausible in the current atmosphere of intolerance, which has transformed smoking into an act of protest against the meddling of bureaucrats and busybodies.

In the United States, opposition to tobacco was closely tied to the temperance movement—a link that continues today, with groups such as the Center for Science in the Public Interest railing alternately against drinking and smoking. The eighteenth-century physician Benjamin Rush, who declared alcoholism a disease, conceded tobacco's medical utility but cautioned against casual use, which he said could lead to impaired appetite, indigestion and other stomach disorders, tremors, palsy, apoplexy, tooth loss, and cancer of the lip. Rush, who had earlier described the inexorable slide into habitual drunkenness among those who developed a taste for liquor, said "the progress of habit in the use of Tobacco is exactly the same." Furthermore, he claimed, chewing or smoking tobacco contributes to drunkenness by creating a peculiar kind of thirst: "This thirst cannot be allayed by water, for no sedative or even insipid liquor will be relished after the mouth and throat have been exposed to the stimulus of the smoke, or juice of Tobacco. A desire of course is excited for strong drinks, and these when taken between meals soon lead to intemperance and drunkenness."[18]

Rush's arguments had a strong influence on nineteenth-century anti-alcohol crusaders, who echoed his charge that tobacco use encourages drinking. In 1829 the respectable *Journal of Health* endorsed the notion: "The almost constant thirst occasioned by smoking and chewing has, in

numerous instances, it is to be feared, led to the intemperate use of ar-
dent spirits." The journal's explanation of this phenomenon repeated
Rush's claim almost verbatim.[19] J. Smyth Rogers, a physician and professor of chemistry and pharmacy, expressed the same concern in a lecture
before the New York Anti-Tobacco Society, published as an essay in
1836. "INTEMPERANCE," he said, *owes thousands of its victims to indulgence in tobacco. . . .* The direct effects of tobacco are to produce a
love,—a *craving* I may say, for strong drinks."[20] Rogers drew an analogy
between tobacco and opium, saying that both produce tolerance (larger
doses are required to achieve the same effect), both act as stimulants in
small amounts and depressants in large amounts, and both produce initially pleasant effects but take their toll in the long run. "There is
scarcely to be found a practical writer on medical subjects, who does not
bear witness to the frequent occurrence of the most grave and alarming
consequences from [tobacco's] employment," he wrote, "and they all
unite in declaring, that the general tendency of tobacco in any form, is
to prostrate the powers of life, and to bring on ultimate disease."[21] In addition to drunkenness, Rogers said, tobacco use can lead to "vertigo, loss
of appetite, tremors, and prostration of strength" as well as "dyspepsia,
with its dire train; atrophy, consumption, palsy, [and] prostration of the
mental with the bodily powers."[22]

One of the most fervid opponents of tobacco was the Reverend
George Trask of Fitchburg, Massachusetts, a former smoker who called
himself the Anti-Tobacco Apostle. In the first issue of his *Anti-Tobacco
Journal,* he described his conversion: "Ten years ago I was a victim of tobacco,—a tremulous, haggard clergyman, on the verge of the grave. I re-
linquished the poison; God smiled upon me, and I have been a robust
and active man ever since; all who know me can testify. Believing then,
as I now do, that Tobacco is as great a curse as can be named, I gave myself to battling it without compromise."[23] In 1850 Trask founded the
American Anti-Tobacco Society, which he served as president, vice president, secretary, treasurer, and auditor. The purpose of the society, he explained, was to "break up a death-like prevalent stupidity in relation to
the evils of tobacco" and "create a public conscience, which, we trust in
God, will lead to the removal of so great a curse."[24] Like contemporary
anti-smokers, Trask had little patience with people who did not share his

sense of urgency: "A smoking clergyman observes, 'I see no harm in smoking.'—'No harm in smoking!' Smoking only leads to drinking—drinking to intoxication—intoxication to bile—bile to indigestion—indigestion to consumption—consumption to death—nothing more!"[25] The *Anti-Tobacco Journal,* which appeared sporadically between 1859 and 1873, presented a daunting array of warnings about tobacco's effects, ranging from the dubious (delirium tremens) to the plausible (cancer of the lip and tongue). The list of problems attributed to tobacco began to resemble the list of ailments it once had been said to cure.

In addition to publishing the journal, Trask distributed anti-tobacco tracts, addressed schools and colleges around the country, and urged young people to take the Band of Hope pledge: "I hereby solemnly promise to abstain from the use of all Intoxicating Liquors as a beverage; I also promise to abstain from the use of Tobacco in all forms, and all Profane Language."[26] Like activists in the temperance movement, which despite its name was soon dominated by an absolutist philosophy, Trask rejected the idea of moderation and insisted on total abstinence. In 1852 he published *Thoughts and Stories on Tobacco for American Lads; or Uncle Toby's Anti-Tobacco Advice to his Nephew Billy Bruce,* a series of fictitious letters chronicling the evils of tobacco. Uncle Toby warned that tobacco leads to drunkenness ("I call Tobacco and Rum Siamese Twins"), uncleanliness, acute poisoning, addiction, poverty, crime, and spiritual corruption.[27]

Despite his extreme rhetoric and hyperbolic claims, Trask was by no means an isolated oddball. The appendix to *Thoughts and Stories on Tobacco for American Lads* includes messages from such prominent figures as Horace Mann, P. T. Barnum, and John Quincy Adams. The *Anti-Tobacco Journal* printed letters from grateful clergymen, educators, and physicians throughout the country. But during a period when Americans were occupied by the momentous issues of slavery and the Union's future, it became increasingly hard for people like Trask to get a hearing. "*This cause encounters scorn and derision,*" he complained in 1860. "It has been laughed at by superficial men, in the church and out of it, from Maine to Georgia, from Plymouth Rock to California. We have needed temples of brass—we have needed faith in God like Abraham's, to brave this tide of sarcasm and nonsense."[28] The next issue of the journal did not appear for more than a decade, and by December 1873 Trask had discontinued publication again due to lack of support.

CIGARETTE FIENDS

Had Trask waited another decade, he would have had a new target, a menace from abroad that was corrupting the youth of America. Although cigarettes, like cigars, originated in South America, it was not until after they became fashionable in London that Americans started smoking them. When cigarettes were introduced in the United States, chewing tobacco was more popular than cigars, pipes, or snuff. It remained the leading form of tobacco until the turn of the century, but cigarettes began making inroads in the 1870s. The first U.S. cigarettes were produced in 1869 by F. S. Kinney and Company of New York, which used flue-cured American tobacco, an innovation that made the smoke much milder. During the next decade three other companies opened cigarette factories in New York, Rochester, and Richmond.

In 1881 James B. Duke decided that his family's tobacco company, based in Durham, North Carolina, should get into the cigarette business. That same year, a Virginian named James Bonsack invented a machine that could produce 100,000 to 120,000 cigarettes a day, replacing the labor of thirty to forty workers. Duke immediately ordered two Bonsack machines and eventually obtained the exclusive right to use the invention. Introduction of the machine cut production costs by more than 50 percent. By 1889 W. Duke, Sons & Co. was the largest cigarette producer in the world. It eventually became the huge American Tobacco Company, which in 1911 was broken up by a federal antitrust lawsuit into several components, including a smaller company of the same name, R. J. Reynolds, British-American Tobacco, Lorillard, and Liggett & Myers. Another familiar name, Philip Morris, has been an independent company since it was established in 1902.

Mechanized production made it possible for cigarettes to become a mass-market product. The U.S. Department of Agriculture has been tracking domestic cigarette consumption since the late nineteenth century, and dividing this number by the adult population (eighteen and older) gives a good measure of the product's popularity. Per capita consumption of cigarettes, about 0.4 in 1870, rose to 8.2 in 1880 and 35.5 in 1890—roughly a hundredfold increase over twenty years. By 1910 cigarettes had become the most widely used form of tobacco. Per capita consumption skyrocketed from 85.5 that year to nearly 1,000 in 1930.[29]

The mildness and low cost of cigarettes expanded the appeal of smoking, to the consternation of those who had always condemned the habit. But alarm about the new "cigarette fiends" was not limited to die-hard anti-tobacco crusaders. Many cigar and pipe smokers (correctly) perceived cigarettes as more addictive and hazardous than the products they used. "The cigarette is designed for boys and women," the *New York Times* declared in 1884. "The decadence of Spain began when the Spaniards adopted cigarettes, and if this pernicious practice obtains among adult Americans the ruin of the Republic is close at hand."[30]

At first the anti-cigarette movement focused on restricting children's access to cigarettes. "There is no question that demands more public attention than the prevailing methods of cigarette manufacturers to foster and stimulate smoking among children," an angry New Yorker said in 1888, expressing a complaint that has become familiar in the century since. "At the office of a leading factory in this city you can see any Saturday afternoon a crowd of children with vouchers clamoring for the reward of self-inflicted injury."[31] He was referring to the coupons that smokers could collect and exchange for prizes such as pocket knives and lithograph albums. Pioneered by James Duke, these coupons were the precursors to contemporary promotional devices such as "Camel cash" and "Merit awards," which also have been criticized as enticements to children.

By 1890, twenty-six states had passed laws banning cigarette sales to minors, but many children continued to smoke.[32] Charles B. Hubbell was one of many educators who spoke out against smoking by minors. "The cigaret habit," he wrote in 1904, "is more devastating to the health and morals of boys and young men than any habit or vice that can be named. . . . Once the cigaret habit becomes established its servitude is almost certain and unending." Hubbell rejected widespread rumors that cigarette papers were impregnated with poison and that cigarettes contained opium, noting that it would hardly make sense to substitute a costlier drug for tobacco. He explained that the cigarette habit is dangerous not because of additives but because, unlike other modes of to-bacco consumption, it involves taking smoke into the lungs. (He has-tened to add that he did not object to the "rational, reasonable, and nor-mal use of tobacco"—in cigars, pipes, or chaw—by adults, which he said appeared to be "comparatively harmless.") Hubbell said the cigarette not only hurt boys physically, leaving their health "more or less shattered," but also corrupted them morally. He recalled that during his service as president of New York City's Board of Education, "it was found that nearly all of the incorrigible truants were cigaret fiends." He added that "the Police Magistrates of this and other cities have stated again and again that the majority of juvenile delinquents appearing before them are cigaret fiends whose moral nature has been warped or destroyed through the instrumentality of this vice."[33]

Saving children from such a fate became the mission of Lucy Page Gaston, an Illinois teacher and journalist who has been described as the Carry Nation of the anti-cigarette movement. She appears in a photo-graph accompanying a story entitled "Killing the Cigaret Habit" in the December 6, 1913, issue of the *Literary Digest.* In the foreground D. H. Kress, a physician who served as general secretary of the Chicago Anti-Cigarette League, is swabbing the tongue of a boy named Tommy Don-nahue with a silver-nitrate solution intended to discourage smoking. Tommy, who wears a crew cut and a messenger's uniform, sits with his hands on his legs and his shoulders hunched, gazing off into the distance and opening his mouth compliantly. The dark-suited, gray-haired doc-tor looks at him benignly, one hand on the boy's chin, the other holding the swab. In the background, holding a glass of the silver-nitrate solu-tion, sits a middle-aged woman wearing a long-sleeved dress, granny glasses, and a tight bun of dark hair. Her mouth is a straight line be-tween sunken cheeks as she stares at the boy. Her expression makes you glad you are not Tommy Donnahue.

Gaston, who was born in Ohio in 1860 and grew up in Illinois, began her social-reform work as a member of the Women's Christian Temperance Union, which opposed smoking as well as drinking. While studying at the Illinois State Normal School, she led raids on local tav-erns and tobacco shops. She launched her anti-cigarette campaign in the 1890s, urging boys and girls in schools and churches to abstain from smoking and leading them in the "Clean Life Pledge": "I hereby pledge myself with the help of God to abstain from all intoxicating liquors as a beverage and from the use of tobacco in any form."[34] (This pledge was less demanding than the one George Trask had urged, since it left the kids free to continue swearing.) In 1899 Gaston founded the Chicago Anti-Cigarette League, which became the model for similar groups throughout the country. In 1901 several hundred anti-cigarette groups joined together under Gaston's leadership to form the National Anti-Cigarette League, which claimed a membership of nearly three hundred thousand. The organization, which later became the Anti-Cigarette League of America and then the International Anti-Cigarette League, aimed not just to prevent children from smoking but to completely eliminate cigarettes.

In response to intense lobbying by Gaston and her fellow activists, almost every state considered some form of anti-cigarette legislation. Between 1893 and 1909, fourteen states and one territory (Oklahoma) enacted laws banning the sale—and, in some cases, possession—of cigarettes. Two other states, Tennessee and West Virginia, imposed prohibitive taxes. Such laws were supported not only by Gastonites but also by the cigar industry, which saw its business slipping away to a new competitor. Washington passed the first anti-cigarette law in 1893, followed by North Dakota in 1895, Iowa in 1896, and Tennessee in 1897.[35]

In *Austin v. Tennessee,* a distributor who was fined for buying cigarettes from a North Carolina factory and shipping them to his business in Tennessee challenged that state's law on constitutional grounds, arguing that it infringed on Congress's authority to regulate interstate commerce. In 1898 the Supreme Court of Tennessee rejected that claim and upheld the law as a public health measure. "Are cigarettes legitimate articles of commerce?" the court asked. It then supplied the answer: "We think they are not because they are wholly noxious and deleterious to health. Their use is always harmful; never beneficial. They possess no virtue, but are inherently bad, bad only. They find no true commendation for merit or usefulness in any sphere. On the contrary, they are widely condemned as pernicious altogether. Beyond any question, their every tendency is toward the impairment of physical health and mental vigor."[36] Since tobacco's contemporary opponents likewise argue that cigarettes are "inherently bad, bad only," it is instructive that Tennessee's highest court—in an era when judges took constitutional limits more seriously than they do nowadays—thought cigarettes could be banned because they had no redeeming value.

On appeal in 1900, the U.S. Supreme Court ruled that Tennessee could not constitutionally prevent cigarettes bound for other states from crossing its borders, but it could control them once they left their original shipping containers. The Court did not offer its own assessment of cigarettes, yielding instead to the judgment of the state legislature that they threatened public health.[37] The decision gave a boost to the anti-cigarette movement, encouraging passage of more bans and stricter enforcement of the existing laws.

During this period cigarettes attracted a host of epithets: coffin nails, little white slavers, dope sticks, paper pills, brain capsules, coffin pills, Devil's kindling wood. Among other things, they were said to cause stunted growth, weakened immunity, insomnia, shattered nerves, shaky hands, poor motor coordination, heart palpitations, cardiovascular disease, high blood pressure, lowered vitality, restlessness, drunkenness, and impaired mental ability. Although research and experience have provided evidence for some of these claims, many of them seem quaint today. This is particularly true of the allegation that smoking cigarettes causes brain damage. "I have had a large experience in brain diseases, and I am satisfied that smoking is a most noxious habit," a British physician said in a pamphlet published by the Chicago Anti-Cigarette League in 1900. "I know of no other cause or agent that so much tends to bring on functional disease, and through this in the end to lead to organic disease of the brain." An American physician warned, "The use of tobacco in any form previous to sixteen years of age has an undoubted tendency to lower very materially the mental force and acumen, and to render the user a person without ambition, and may even cause insanity or death."[38]

Our Bodies and How We Live, an elementary school textbook published in 1910, warned: "The cells of the brain may become poisoned from tobacco. The ideas may lack clearness of outline. The will power may be weakened, and it may be an effort to do the routine duties of life. . . . The memory may also be impaired. . . . The honors of the great schools, academies, and colleges are very largely taken by the abstainers from tobacco. . . . The reason for this is plain. The mind of the habitual user of tobacco is apt to lose its capacity for study or successful effort. This is especially true of boys and young men. The growth and development of the brain having been once retarded, the youthful user of tobacco has established a permanent drawback which may hamper him all his life. The keenness of his mental perception may be dulled and his ability to seize and hold an abstract thought may be impaired."[39]

Although cigarettes would later be seen as an aid to concentration perfectly compatible with work, turn-of-the-century critics tied them to distraction and idleness. The cigarette smokers depicted by these writers resemble the dull and lazy marijuana smokers in contemporary anti-drug commercials. "The time is already at hand when smokers will be barred out of positions which demand quick thought and action," wrote Charles B. Towns, operator of a New York drug and alcohol hospital, in March 1912.[40] The biologist David Starr Jordan similarly advised: "The boy who smokes cigarettes need not be anxious about his future. He has none."[41] The notion that smokers do not make fit employees was promoted by prominent businessmen. In 1914 Henry Ford published a booklet called *The Case Against the Little White Slaver,* which included condemnations of cigarettes from entrepreneurs, educators, community leaders, and athletes. "If you will study the history of almost any criminal you will find that he is an inveterate cigarette smoker," Ford averred. "Boys, through cigarettes, train with bad company. They go with other smokers to the pool rooms and saloons. The cigarette drags them down."[42] Thomas Edison (himself a cigar smoker and tobacco chewer) noted the well-known brain degeneration associated with cigarettes: "Unlike most narcotics, this degeneration is permanent and uncontrollable. I employ no person who smokes cigarettes."[43]

Like Edison, Towns labeled tobacco a narcotic. As J. Smyth Rogers had in 1836, he compared tobacco to opium, widely condemned as a drug of foreigners and criminals. And following in the footsteps of Benjamin Rush, he charged that tobacco leads to alcohol and alcohol leads to morphine—an early version of what today is called the "gateway" or "stepping-stone" theory. Towns also anticipated later anti-drug propaganda by confusing correlation with causation: "The action of any narcotic is to break down the sense of moral responsibility. If a father finds that his boy is fibbing to him, is difficult to manage, or does not wish to work, he will generally find that the boy is smoking cigarettes. . . . The action of a narcotic produces a peculiar cunning and resource in concealment." Noting the rudeness of smokers who light up despite the complaints of bystanders, Towns concluded that "callous indifference to the rights of others" was another effect of the drug.[44]

Annoyance about exposure to tobacco smoke was a significant element in the anti-cigarette movement, though not as important as it would later become. Like the activists of the 1980s and '90s, the people who were most irked by secondhand smoke argued that it violated their rights. In 1911 Charles G. Pease, a New York physician, founded the Non-Smokers Protective League of America to lobby for stricter enforcement of the city's bans on smoking in public waiting rooms and on streetcars and trains. He explained his group's position in a November 10, 1911, letter to the *New York Times*: "The right of each person to breathe and enjoy fresh and pure air—air uncontaminated by unhealthful or disagreeable odors and fumes—is a constitutional right, and cannot be taken away by legislatures and courts, much less by individuals pursuing their own thoughtless or selfish indulgence."[45] Towns had the same complaint: "On all sides, the attitude seems to be, 'What right has anyone to object to my smoking!' The matter is really on just the *opposite* basis: 'What right has anyone to smoke, when other people object to it?'"[46]

This sentiment was shared by many who did not otherwise oppose smoking. In 1904 *Harper's Weekly* observed that "the standard of manners among smokers seems to be low. The men who bring lighted cigars into street-cars and smoke in the face of every passenger who crowds past them to get on or off, clearly and scandalously disregard the rights of others. . . . These street-car smokers ought not to be tolerated."[47] In 1924 the *Literary Digest* noted that "smoking is now the rule, and the inhalation of smoke from the surrounding atmosphere is compulsory if refuges are not provided."[48]

I LIKE IT

As the complaints about secondhand smoke indicate, despite all the agitation, legislation, and condemnation, smoking continued to rise. Although there was considerable sympathy for preventing children from smoking and confining the practice to appropriate places, the extravagant claims of the anti-cigarette movement met with disbelief. *Harper's Weekly* was expressing skepticism as early as 1900. "All hostility to tobacco seems nowadays to be concentrated on cigarettes," the magazine noted in 1905. "Time was when it was thought expedient to discourage tobacco-chewing. It was denounced as a filthy habit—and it is pretty filthy—but it was never charged, as cigarettes are now charged, with withering the mental faculties and destroying the moral fibre of men. . . . How deadly cigarettes are to the average consumer we don't know, but the London *Lancet* has declared that they are not nearly so bad as their reputation is, and we suspect that they are more maligned than they deserve."[49]

So did many others. The general lack of enthusiasm for the anti-cigarette cause is illustrated by a poem that appeared in the *Penn State Froth* in 1915:

> Tobacco is a dirty weed. I like it.
> It satisfies no normal need. I like it.
> It makes you thin, it makes you lean,
> It takes the hair right off your bean,
> It's the worst darn stuff I've ever seen.
> I like it.[50]

In the states that had banned possession of cigarettes, the courts often proved unwilling to apply the law to consumers, who were then free to obtain cigarettes by mail. Even dealers found that they were unlikely to be prosecuted, and cigarette consumption climbed despite the bans. Indiana repealed its cigarette ban in 1909, followed by Washington in 1911, Minnesota in 1913, Wisconsin and Oklahoma in 1915, and South Dakota in 1917.

American soldiers in Europe found that cigarettes helped pass the time and calm their nerves. Tobacco's value in wartime was not a new discovery. In 1798 Benjamin Rush had remarked that "fear creates a desire for tobacco. Hence it is used in a greater quantity by soldiers and sailors than by other classes of people."[51] James I might have worried that dependence on tobacco would be a liability in battle, but fighting men through the centuries have disagreed, which is why wars have so often been followed by surges in tobacco use. "In time of war," writes Richard Klein in *Cigarettes Are Sublime,* "it is with gratitude and love that one holds, between fingers and lips, the small, compact cylinder of paper and tobacco—cinder, fire, ash—like worry beads, rosary, or some other divine consoler: a little daemon, mediator of the gods, and a most intimate friend, a companion who never fails to speak to the loneliness of the self in moments of greatest heroism or of empty or splenetic boredom."[52] During World War I, General John J. Pershing, commander-in-chief of the American forces in France, cabled Washington, "Tobacco is as indispensable as the daily ration; we must have thousands of tons of it without delay."[53] Tobacco companies sent cigarettes overseas with much hoopla and featured soldiers in their ads. Thus, cigarettes came to be identified with patriotism, and U.S. troops brought the habit home with them after the war.

Another sign of the cigarette's new respectability was its growing popularity among women. At first the Victorian taboo against smoking by women prevailed in the United States as well as England. In 1900 *Harper's Weekly* observed that "reputable and well-mannered American women rarely smoke nowadays. . . . The general sentiment among our women is that for women to smoke is vulgar. Whether it is all merely a matter of habit and custom, or whether women's occupations and environments are such that they have less need of tobacco than men, let the learned discuss. All we know is that as a rule men smoke and women don't, and we wonder why women are so docile about it."[54]

They did not remain docile for long. In 1908 the New York City Board of Aldermen approved a ban on public smoking by women. Although the ordinance was vetoed by the mayor two weeks later, at least one woman, Katie Mulcahey, was arrested by an overzealous policeman for violating the rule. "No man shall dictate to me," she declared.[55] In 1910 *Harper's Weekly* reported, "Dealers say that women cigarette-smokers are increasing in number tremendously every year."[56] In a development that would inspire a memorable ad campaign for Virginia Slims ("You've come a long way, baby"), the cigarette became identified with the movement for sexual equality. "For a woman," said an *Atlantic Monthly* writer in 1916, "it is the symbol of emancipation, the temporary substitute for the ballot."[57]

According to one estimate, women accounted for 5 percent of U.S. tobacco consumption in 1924, 12 percent in 1929, and 14 percent in 1931. A 1935 survey by *Fortune* found that more than 26 percent of women over the age of 40 smoked.[58] Taking advantage of this trend, the tobacco companies began gearing their ads toward women. A 1919 ad for the Lorillard brand Helmar's depicted a woman with a cigarette between her lips. A 1926 ad for Chesterfields showed a man smoking while his lady friend said, "Blow some my way." Philip Morris was more direct in a 1927 Marlboro ad that showed a woman smoking and announced, "Women, when they smoke at all, quickly develop discriminating taste." Beginning in 1928, Lucky Strike ads urged women to "Reach for a Lucky instead of a Sweet." In 1929 R. J. Reynolds ran an ad playing off its familiar Camel slogan: it showed a woman offering a cigarette to a man who responds, "I'd Walk a Mile for a Camel—but a 'Miss' Is as Good as a Mile."[59]

Even people who were willing to tolerate smoking by men drew the line when the cigarette became a menace to womanhood. "Women smokers, young and old, are increasing in legions," a 1922 article in the *Ladies' Home Journal* entitled "Women Cigarette Fiends" reported with alarm. "In New York City, women smoke everywhere, even on the streets. It is not an uncommon sight to see women atop Fifth Avenue busses puffing away at their cigarettes. The theaters are opening smoking rooms for women, and during intermission it is no longer unusual to find women smoking in the lobbies or on the sidewalks with men." The author explained that women smoked only because it was fashionable to defy convention, not because they enjoyed it. Furthermore, he said, women's weaker constitutions left them more vulnerable to the hazards of smoking. The article quoted Samuel Lambert, former physician to Theodore Roosevelt: "Intemperate smoking causes nervousness and may lead to something worse. Women who use cigarettes cannot be temperate. At best it is a horrible weed and should be let alone. It fouls the breath and makes women unwomanly."[60] We may smile at the patronizing tone of such warnings, but much of today's anti-smoking propaganda is remarkably similar in spirit, portraying women as vulnerable and smoking as unfeminine.

The focus on women—suggesting that tobacco's enemies had basically given up on men—was a sign that the broader battle against the cigarette had already been lost. After ratification of National Alcohol Prohibition in 1919, there was speculation that the temperance movement would press for a Nineteenth Amendment outlawing smoking. "Prohibition is won," announced the evangelist Billy Sunday. "Now for tobacco."[61] But the Women's Christian Temperance Union rejected that course, choosing instead to continue its anti-smoking propaganda campaign. Although Nebraska, Iowa, Arkansas, and Tennessee repealed their cigarette bans after the war, the anti-smoking movement managed to achieve passage of two new state laws. One, a ban on cigarette sales passed by Idaho in 1921, was repealed almost immediately. The other, a ban on cigarette sales and public smoking backed by the Mormon Church, was approved by the Utah legislature in 1921 but was not initially enforced. When Salt Lake County Sheriff Benjamin R. Harries, who won election on a promise to take Utah's ban on public smoking seriously, staged a crackdown in 1923, arresting three prominent citizens who had lit up in a restaurant, he prompted a storm of criticism. In the face of nationwide ridicule and open rebellion by the state's citizens, the Utah legislature quickly legalized cigarette sales to adults and sharply cut back the restrictions on smoking.

Lucy Page Gaston continued to campaign against cigarettes after the war, but it soon became clear that her time had passed. On December 31, 1919, she was ousted from the International Anti-Cigarette League. The next day, Gaston announced that she was running for president on a platform of "clean morals, clean food and fearless law enforcement." She withdrew from the race six months later and formed a new group with a recycled name—the National Anti-Cigarette League. In 1920 she went to Kansas to lobby for stricter enforcement of that state's anti-cigarette law, but despite some modest success her tactics were too overbearing for the Kansas Anti-Cigarette League, which fired her in January 1921. In August she also parted ways with the National Anti-Cigarette

League, which noted that "Miss Gaston's methods were more aggressive than the methods approved by the League Board of Managers."[62] She returned to Chicago, where she died of throat cancer in 1924. Three years later, Kansas repealed its anti-cigarette law, and by 1930 cigarettes were again legal in every state.[63]

In 1925 Carl Avery Werner, writing in the *American Mercury,* declared "The Triumph of the Cigarette." He noted that despite "persistent, organized opposition on the grounds of health and morals," cigarette consumption had shot far past cigar consumption. "The more violently [the cigarette] has been attacked," he observed, "the more popular it has become." Werner argued that the anti-cigarette movement's "melodramatic" propaganda had backfired. He noted that scientists had "failed to find evidence for the appalling charges made against smoking" and added, "A dispassionate review of the findings compels the conclusion that the cigarette is tobacco in its mildest form, and that tobacco, used moderately by people in normal health, does not appreciably impair either the mental efficiency or the physical condition."[64]

Although a minority would continue to proclaim the unhealthy effects of smoking, Werner's conclusion remained the conventional view for decades. Having rejected the anti-cigarette movement's warnings about the disastrous short-term consequences of smoking, most Americans gave little credence to the possibility of serious long-term damage. Certainly no one thought he was doing his body any good by smoking; even after overcoming the initial dizziness, nausea, and palpitations, a smoker could anticipate throat irritation, coughing, shortness of breath, and other symptoms that tended to confirm the suspicion that sucking smoke into one's lungs was not a healthy practice. But physicians generally advised the public that the main danger from smoking lay in excess, and smokers tended to assume that their bodies would tell them when they were overdoing it.

In 1933 *Scientific American* reported that a Chicago researcher had tentatively linked the "tar" in cigarette smoke to the increase in lung cancer that had been observed in recent years. But the same article quoted other researchers who were skeptical of this hypothesis: "Any substance so widely and commonly used as the cigarette cannot be as dangerous and deleterious as the propaganda of the more fanatical 'no-tobacco' advocates might lead one to infer." The researchers reaffirmed that a "moderate amount of smoking may not produce visible injury in a sound individual." The article ended with a caveat: "However, the possibility of damage not perceptible by casual observation cannot yet be ruled out."[65] To the next generation of smokers, that obligatory note of caution would take on a new significance.

Chapter 2

APPROPRIATE REMEDIAL ACTION

*Cigarette smoking is a health hazard of sufficient importance in the
United States to warrant appropriate remedial action.*

—The Surgeon General's Advisory Committee on Smoking and Health, 1964

THE SURGEON GENERAL'S WARNING

As if working on a Saturday morning were not bad enough, the two
hundred or so reporters who showed up at a State Department auditorium on January 11, 1964, for a press conference called by Surgeon
General Luther L. Terry were held under guard and handed a 387-page
government report. They had ninety minutes to digest *Smoking and
Health: Report of the Advisory Committee to the Surgeon General of the
Public Health Service* before asking a bunch of scientists questions about
it. If the pressure of the situation brought on the urge for a cigarette, the
reporters had to seek refuge in the hallway or lobby; as newly posted
signs made clear, smoking was forbidden in the auditorium.

The timing and tight security were intended to prevent a Wall Street
panic and the spread of misinformation. Both concerns had been expressed by President John F. Kennedy during a press conference two
years before in the same room. Asked about the hazards of smoking in
May 1962, he had replied, "That matter is sensitive enough and the
stock market is in sufficient difficulty without my giving you an answer
which is not based on complete information, which I don't have."[1] A
few weeks later, after examining material gathered by the Public Health

Service, Kennedy instructed Terry to go ahead with a plan he had proposed in April to appoint an Advisory Committee on Smoking and Health. After consulting with the tobacco industry, private health organizations, and several federal agencies, Terry picked ten distinguished scientists, none of whom had taken a public position on the health effects of smoking. The group held nine meetings between November 1962 and December 1963, reviewed more than seven thousand articles, and reported its findings two months after Kennedy's assassination.

"In view of the continuing and mounting evidence from many sources," the report said, "it is the judgment of the Committee that cigarette smoking contributes substantially to mortality from certain specific diseases and to the overall death rate." The committee found that "cigarette smoking is causally related to lung cancer in men" and that "the magnitude of the effect of cigarette smoking far outweighs all other factors." It noted that "the data for women, though less extensive, point in the same direction." Furthermore, "the risk of developing lung cancer increases with duration of smoking and the number of cigarettes smoked per day, and is diminished by discontinuing smoking." The panel also reported that cigarette smoking was the most important cause of chronic bronchitis and could lead to laryngeal cancer. It noted statistically significant, possibly causal, associations between smoking and esophageal cancer, bladder cancer, coronary artery disease, emphysema, peptic ulcers, and low birth weight. It said that men who smoked were, on average, about ten times as likely to die of lung cancer as men who didn't and that their overall death rate in a given year was 70 percent higher. Studies had also found higher mortality for female smokers, though the magnitude of the difference was unclear. The Surgeon General's Advisory Committee on Smoking and Health concluded, "Cigarette smoking is a health hazard of sufficient importance in the United States to warrant appropriate remedial action."[2]

Three decades later, almost everyone concedes that cigarette smoking is a serious health hazard. Indeed, even before the 1964 surgeon general's report, surveys found that most Americans associated cigarettes with cancer. Beginning in the 1930s and intensifying in the '50s, a stream of scientific reports had implicated smoking in lung cancer. The function of the surgeon general's advisory committee was not to discover any-

thing new but to ratify a growing scientific consensus. "They met in secret," Terry later wrote, "but there was no doubt about the conclusion
they would reach because the scientific evidence against cigarettes was
by that time overwhelming."[3] The accumulation of evidence through
systematic research—especially large-scale epidemiological studies that
examined the relationship between smoking and diseases that take
decades to develop—elevated warnings about tobacco above anecdote,
folklore, and superstition. It gave tobacco's opponents new credibility
and added to their ranks. But it did not, by itself, indicate what the *government* should do about smoking, if anything. That is why Americans
are still arguing about what, exactly, "appropriate remedial action" is.

Physicians had been suggesting a link between tobacco and cancer for
centuries. Likewise, tobacco's opponents had been warning about the
impact of smoking on the lungs at least since the time of James I. Yet it
appears that no one put these two concerns together, suggesting a connection between smoking and lung cancer, prior to the twentieth century. That is mainly because lung cancer was hardly seen during the first
four hundred years of tobacco use in the Western world. In 1912 the
American pathologist Isaac Adler said, "Primary malignant neoplasms of
the lung are among the rarest forms of disease." His search of the world
medical literature turned up just 374 confirmed cases.[4] One reason lung
cancer was so unusual is that it generally appears late in life. In 1900 life
expectancy at birth in the United States was about forty-seven, compared to about seventy-six today.[5] Until relatively recently, people who
might have developed lung cancer tended to die of something else first,
often a viral or bacterial infection. When it did occur, lung cancer was
probably often confused with tuberculosis. Thus, the control of infectious diseases increased both the likelihood that people would live to get
lung cancer and the likelihood that it would be detected.

The most important development affecting lung cancer rates, however, was the increasing popularity of the cigarette. Other forms of tobacco involved either no inhalation of smoke (snuff, chewing tobacco)
or relatively little (pipes, cigars). Cigarette smokers, on the other hand,
typically inhale, regularly exposing their lungs to the products of tobacco combustion. Turn-of-the-century critics such as Charles Hubbell
argued that inhalation made cigarettes more dangerous, and as early as

1912 Adler speculated that cigarettes might cause lung cancer. But the evidence for this hypothesis did not appear for several decades. The rise in U.S. cigarette consumption was paralleled by a dramatic increase in the lung cancer death rate, from about 1 per 100,000 in 1920 to 13 in 1950 (by 1990 it was more than 50).[6] Although longer life spans and better diagnosis accounted for some of this increase, it seemed clear that another factor was at work.

During the 1930s several researchers suggested that the factor was cigarette smoking. In a 1932 *American Journal of Cancer* article, William D. McNally, assistant professor of medicine at Rush Medical College in Chicago, said the tar (dark gunk) in cigarette smoke might account for the recent increase in the incidence of lung cancer. Mc-Nally failed, however, to induce cancer by applying tar to the backs of mice. Alton Ochsner, a lung cancer expert at the Tulane University School of Medicine, published papers in 1939 and 1941 that noted what he would later call "a distinct parallelism between the sale of cigarettes and the incidence of bronchogenic carcinoma."[7] In 1939 the German researcher F. H. Müller, who had also noted a rise in lung cancer, reported that of eighty-six patients with the disease, all but three smoked. Raymond Pearl, professor of biology at Johns Hopkins Medical School, took a broader approach in a 1938 *Science* article. In a sample of 6,813 subjects, Pearl found that 67 percent of the nonsmokers lived past sixty, compared to 61 percent of the moderate smokers and 46 percent of the heavy smokers.[8] A report in *Time* said Pearl's findings "should make tobacco users' flesh creep."[9]

SMOKING MORE, IN MODERATION

The research reports of the 1930s and '40s were not conclusive. It was still unclear whether smoking caused lung cancer and, if it did, what level of consumption posed a substantial risk. Raymond Pearl's results suggested that smokers had little to worry about if they didn't smoke *too much,* which corresponded neatly with the conventional wisdom of the time. As one physician put it in the *American Mercury* in 1943, "If you are in good health, and use tobacco moderately, you needn't worry much about your smoking."[10] Since people tend to define moderation by their own behavior, the scattered warnings of the 1930s and '40s did not have a noticeable impact on smoking. After a three-year dip at the beginning of the Great Depression, per capita cigarette consumption rose from 1,245 in 1932 to 3,886 in 1952.[11]

As in the past, the war years were a period of dramatic growth in tobacco use, with double-digit percentage increases in 1941, 1942, 1943, and 1945. Like John J. Pershing before him, General Douglas McArthur emphasized the need to keep U.S. troops supplied with tobacco. Cigarette ads during World War II, like those during World War I, linked the product with patriotism and the boys in uniform.

In the hands and mouths of movie stars like Humphrey Bogart and Bette Davis, the cigarette became a pop culture icon, an all-purpose prop that could signify glamor, fun, seductiveness, power, courage, confidence, toughness, determination, thoughtfulness. This multiplicity of meanings reflects the versatility of tobacco, a drug that, depending upon dosage and context, can relieve boredom or lull anxiety, keep you alert or help you relax. Unlike many other psychoactive substances, nicotine does not cloud judgment or impair coordination; indeed, contrary to the claims of early cigarette opponents, it enhances performance at tasks that require concentration. Like coffee, cigarettes were affordable, combined mild psychoactive effects with taste and other sensations, and could be enjoyed in many different settings. It is hardly surprising that they became so pervasive. By the mid-1950s more than a quarter of American women and more than half of American men smoked cigarettes.[12]

Until 1950, Evarts A. Graham, a pioneering chest surgeon at Barnes Hospital in St. Louis, was one of them. That was the year that Graham and Ernst L. Wynder, a student at Washington University School of Medicine, published "Tobacco Smoking as a Possible Etiologic Factor in Bronchiogenic Carcinoma" in the *Journal of the American Medical Association*. Breaking their subjects into five groups, ranging from nonsmokers to chain smokers, Graham and Wynder found that 97 percent of 605 patients with lung cancer were at least moderately heavy smokers, compared to 74 percent of 780 patients without lung cancer. "The temptation is strong to incriminate excessive smoking, and in particular cigaret smoking, over a long period as at least one important factor in the striking increase of bronchiogenic carcinoma," they wrote. "In general it appears that the less a person smokes the less are the chances of cancer of the lung developing and, conversely, the more heavily a person smokes the greater are his chances of becoming affected with this disease."[13] Graham, who quit smoking after completing the study, died of lung cancer in 1957.

Other studies lent support to Graham and Wynder's hypothesis. The same issue of *JAMA* included a study of 1,650 patients admitted to Roswell Park Memorial Institute in Buffalo. A team of researchers led by Morton L. Levin of the New York State Department of Health found that lung cancer was more than twice as common among those who had smoked for twenty-five years or more than among other smokers or nonsmokers. At the Fifth International Cancer Congress in Paris later that year, both research teams, along with a third led by Alton Ochsner, emphasized the link between smoking and lung cancer.

Ochsner, an early proponent of the hypothesis, was by now convinced that cigarette smoking caused lung cancer. But he did not have an easy time persuading his colleagues. "Physicians are not of one mind on the reported link between smoking and lung cancer," the *New York Times* noted in an October 1951 story about an address that Ochsner gave to a group of cancer specialists in Detroit. "This was demonstrated here today in a smoke-filled auditorium." The *Times* reported that "cancer specialists in the audience continued to puff at their cigars and cigarettes" even as Ochsner blamed cigarettes for the recent sharp increase in lung cancer. As he recommended periodic chest X rays for smokers, "the doctors smoked relentlessly."[14]

A series of reports during the next few years made the link between smoking and chronic disease harder to ignore. In December 1952 two British researchers, Richard Doll and A. Bradford Hill, reported the results of a large-scale, four-year study in which they compared 1,465 lung cancer patients to an equal number of patients with other diseases, matched for age, sex, and region. Doll and Hill—who had reported preliminary results in 1950, several months after Graham and Wynder's article appeared in *JAMA*—found that the lung cancer patients were considerably more likely to be smokers and much more likely to be heavy smokers. They suggested that "the mortality from carcinoma of the lung may increase in approximately simple proportion with the amount smoked."[15] In November 1953 Graham and Wynder reported that they had succeeded where William McNally had failed in 1932, producing skin cancer in laboratory mice by painting tar on their backs. Said Graham, "This shows conclusively that there is something in cigarette smoke which can produce cancer."[16]

At the Greater New York Dental Meeting in December 1953, researchers presented four reports implicating smoking as a cause of lung cancer and cardiovascular disease. Ochsner said he was "extremely concerned about the possibility that the male population of the United States will be decimated by cancer of the lung in another fifty years if cigarette smoking increases as it has in the past, unless some steps are taken to remove the cancer-producing factor in tobacco." Summarizing the findings of thirteen studies in various countries, Ernst Wynder concluded that "the prolonged and heavy use of cigarettes increases up to twenty times the risk of developing cancer of the lung." Two other researchers, one from the Mayo Clinic and one from Cornell, warned people with heart disease to abstain from smoking.[17]

In June 1954 the American Cancer Society announced preliminary results from a study that had tracked 187,766 men between the ages of fifty and seventy for two and a half years. The ACS had originally planned to present its findings in 1955, but according to the lead researcher, E. Cuyler Hammond, "We found cigarette smokers had so much higher death rates that we didn't think we could withhold the information another year." Hammond and his associate, Daniel Horn, reported that lung cancer deaths were three to nine times as common among smokers as among nonsmokers, while heart disease deaths were one and a half times as common. Death rates for other forms of cancer were higher as well, and mortality increased with the amount of smoking (a result confirmed in a study of forty thousand British doctors that Doll and Hill published about the same time in the *British Medical Journal*). Hammond and Horn concluded that "the associations found between regular cigarette smoking and diseases of the coronary arteries and between smoking and cancer reflect cause-and-effect relationships."[18] In a follow-up report the next year, they said the lung cancer death rate was much lower for ex-smokers than for current smokers.

This stream of well-publicized reports—the work of Ochsner, Wynder, and Graham was reported in a *Reader's Digest* article entitled "Cancer by the Carton," and the ACS study made the front page of the *New York Times*—had the sort of impact you might expect. The day after the December 1953 Greater New York Dental Meeting, at which Ochsner and Wynder had confidently asserted that smoking causes lung cancer, tobacco stocks, which had been declining for several weeks, took a sharp dip. Total cigarette consumption dropped for two consecutive years, 1953 and 1954. The only other time that had happened since the turn of the century was during the Great Depression.

SOOTHING SMOKERS' NERVES

The tobacco companies tried to reassure smokers in several ways. First, they questioned the evidence on the health effects of smoking. Early on, this was not so hard to do, nor was it unreasonable. The researchers themselves often used cautious language, described their findings as inconclusive, or noted the possibility of alternative explanations for the statistical association between smoking and lung cancer. In April 1953 John R. Heller, director of the National Cancer Institute, told a House of Representatives subcommittee that a causal link between smoking and lung cancer had not been established "to our satisfaction." Although "there is a very high correlation between heavy cigarette smoking and the occurrence of lung cancer," he said, "our . . . scientists seem to feel that there are some additional factors which we have not yet discovered or studied sufficiently which may have a bearing on this particular problem."[19] The American Cancer Society, which commissioned the Hammond and Horn study precisely because it considered the evidence inadequate, did not take a position on the issue until 1954. Even after the ACS report, some physicians and statisticians remained skeptical. A May 1955 edition of Edward R. Murrow's *See It Now* that focused on the topic was described as "almost mathematically divided between scientists who believe cigarette smoking is responsible for lung cancer and those who believe no cause and effect relationship has been established."[20]

In November 1953 Paul M. Hahn, president of the American Tobacco Company, condemned what he called "loose talk" in the press

about the health effects of cigarettes. He noted that "authorities themselves differ widely"; that correlation is not causation; that some scientists had suggested the rise in lung cancer might be due to other causes,
such as air pollution; that researchers had not been able to induce lung
cancer in laboratory animals by exposing them to normal concentrations
of tobacco smoke; and that "no one has yet proved that lung cancer in
any human being is directly traceable to tobacco."[21] He recalled that tobacco had been blamed, with little or no evidence, for almost every mal-
ady under the sun at one time or another. Thus, scientists who were
concerned about the health effects of smoking had to contend with the
suspicion engendered by the reckless claims of tobacco's previous opponents, from James I to Henry Ford. In April 1954 the industry released
"A Scientific Perspective on the Cigarette Controversy," a collection of
statements by thirty-six cancer experts who agreed that the case against
cigarettes was not yet conclusive.

This defensive posture was a striking change from the blithe reassurances that tobacco companies had been offering their customers for
decades. In 1926 Lorillard introduced its Old Gold brand with the slogan "Not a cough in a carload." In 1935 R. J. Reynolds ads for Camels
claimed, "They don't get your wind," and called them "so mild . . . you
can smoke all you want." A 1949 ad announced, "Not one single case of
throat irritation due to smoking Camels!" The claim was based on a
"test" in which smokers were examined once a week while smoking
"Camels—and *only* Camels—for 30 consecutive days." The impression
of healthfulness was reinforced by the familiar slogan "More doctors
smoke Camels than any other cigarette."[22] A 1952 Liggett & Myers ad
offered a broader guarantee: NOSE, THROAT, AND ACCESSORY ORGANS
NOT ADVERSELY AFFECTED BY SMOKING CHESTERFIELDS.[23] The claim was
based on a similarly rigorous six-month study. But from the mid-1950s
on, the tobacco companies generally avoided such sweeping claims—
which, in light of the emerging evidence, would have invited breach-of-
warranty lawsuits. Instead of asserting that their product was innocent,
they insisted that it had not been proven guilty—a position that became
increasingly untenable over the years.

In addition to criticizing the existing evidence, the tobacco companies said they were sponsoring independent research to help settle the

issue. "We are confident that long-range, impartial investigation and other objective research will confirm the view that neither tobacco nor its products contribute to the incidence of lung cancer," American Tobacco president Paul M. Hahn said in November 1953.[24] In January 1954 nine tobacco companies, together with groups representing growers and distributors, announced the formation of the Tobacco Industry Research Committee—later renamed the Council for Tobacco Research (CTR)—in newspaper ads throughout the country. Under the headline A FRANK STATEMENT TO CIGARETTE SMOKERS, they said, "We believe the products we make are not injurious to health." Still, "We accept an interest in people's health as a basic responsibility, paramount to every other consideration of our business." Guided by a panel of independent scientists, TIRC would allocate industry funding to researchers looking into "all phases of tobacco use and health."[25]

From the beginning, TIRC was viewed with suspicion. As *Christian Century* commented shortly after the announcement, "It is impossible for any research which they set up and ultimately control, whatever the eminence of its staff and advisory committee, to convince the public that it is telling the truth, the whole truth and nothing but the truth."[26] Litigation would later reveal that some of the CTR's funding, reportedly less than 10 percent, went to "special projects" chosen by industry executives and lawyers.[27] These projects, which included literature reviews and research on other causes of the diseases associated with smoking, were intended to bolster the industry's position in product liability suits and regulatory controversies. But most of the CTR grantees were selected by a panel of prominent scientists, and they were free to publish their research regardless of the results.

Contrary to the popular notion that industry-sponsored research is inevitably self-serving, the results were not always congenial to the cigarette companies. A 1958 study found that "cigarette smoke condensate is a weak mouse skin carcinogen." A 1961 autopsy study concluded that "a history of cigarette smoking is significantly related to the incidence of carcinoma." A 1963 study found that smokers suffered coronary artery disease earlier and coronary occlusion more often than nonsmokers. A 1965 study said women who smoked during pregnancy had lighter babies and were more likely to give birth prematurely.[28] The most dramatic example of industry-funded research that did not turn out the way the tobacco companies might have liked was a fourteen-year project managed by a committee of the American Medical Association. Completed in 1978, it cost the industry $15 million, and it confirmed the role of cigarette smoking in lung cancer and heart disease.[29] The findings of such studies should give pause to anyone who believes that tobacco money automatically taints research.

Still, the tobacco companies hoped that their ongoing funding of research would help create the impression that the connection between smoking and disease remained controversial. As Ernest Pepples, vice president and general counsel at Brown & Williamson, privately put it in 1976, "The significant expenditures on the question of smoking and health have allowed the industry to take a respectable stand along the following lines—'After millions of dollars and over twenty years of research, the question about smoking and health is still open.'"[30]

The third prong of the industry's response to the cancer scare was to push filter-tipped and king-size brands as safer alternatives to standard cigarettes. (The longer brands were supposed to be healthier because the extra tobacco served as a filter.) This was a tricky matter, since the tobacco companies were not conceding that there was anything unsafe about regular cigarettes. A 1951 Brown & Williamson ad simply reported that Viceroy king-size filtered cigarettes yielded less tar and nicotine than other brands. "When a filter tip cigarette is desired," it said, "Viceroy's double-filtering action can be counted upon for a significant reduction in nicotine and tars. At the same time, however, the comforts of full smoking satisfaction can still be enjoyed." Except for a reference to "a report to doctors—published in leading medical journals," there was no indication of *why* a filter tip might be desired.[31] But sales of Viceroys, then the only major brand with a filter, jumped by more than 50 percent between 1950 and 1951.[32]

Lorillard introduced a filter-tipped brand (Kent) in 1952 and was followed by R. J. Reynolds (Winston) and Liggett & Myers (L&M) in 1953 and Philip Morris (Marlboro) in 1954. Filtered brands accounted for 1 percent or less of the market in 1950, but their share rose to 42 percent by the end of the decade. By the early '60s most of the cigarettes sold in the United States were filtered, and by the '80s their share was more than 90 percent.[33] Ads for Kent, the fifth largest cigarette brand in the country by 1958, were relatively candid about the intended function of its amazing "Micronite" filter. Among the twenty-seven leading brands, a 1957 ad claimed, "One gives sensitive smokers far greater health protection than any other. This cigarette is Kent with the Micronite Filter—and the only question is whether *you* need Kent's extra health protection."[34] (Ironically, the original Micronite filter contained asbestos.) Although this pitch was ostensibly aimed only at "sensitive" consumers ("at least one third of this country's smokers"), it implicitly acknowledged that cigarettes can be harmful, something the cigarette companies were loath to admit explicitly.

Despite the internal inconsistencies, the industry's three-prong strategy apparently worked. Total and per capita cigarette consumption rebounded after 1954 and continued to rise for another decade. But the strategy locked the cigarette companies into a defensive, wait-and-see position that ultimately destroyed their credibility and, along with it, the public's good will. Probably more than anything else, this refusal to concede the well-established hazards of smoking has made the cigarette business the most reviled and distrusted industry in America.

In 1954 Philip Morris vice president George Weissman declared, "If we had any thought or knowledge that in any way we were selling a product harmful to consumers, we would stop business tomorrow."[35] In 1986—after more than three decades and thousands of studies, including animal and autopsy research that confirmed the findings of epidemiologists—R. J. Reynolds President Gerald H. Long said: "If I saw or thought that there were any evidence whatsoever that conclusively proved that, in some way, tobacco was harmful to people, and I believed it in my heart and my soul, then I would get out of the business and I wouldn't be involved in it. Honestly, I have not seen one piece of medical evidence that has been presented by anybody, anywhere that absolutely, totally said that smoking caused the disease or created it."[36] What began as an understandable reluctance to accept the early evidence hardened into a demand for 100 percent proof, a demand that can never be satisfied in a world of uncertainty.

MAKING IT OFFICIAL

Between 1950 and 1963 researchers published more than three thousand articles on the health effects of smoking. In 1957 Surgeon General Leroy Burney said, "The Public Health Service feels the weight of the evidence is increasingly pointing in one direction: that excessive smoking is one of the causative factors in lung cancer." Two years later, he said, "The weight of evidence at present implicates smoking as the principal factor in the increased incidence of lung cancer." In 1962 Britain's Royal College of Physicians issued a report that said, "Cigarette smoking is the most likely cause of the recent world-wide increase in deaths from lung cancer." The report also concluded that smoking contributes to bronchitis; aggravates ulcers; probably raises the risk of dying from heart disease; and may be a factor in cancer of the mouth, pharynx, esophagus, and bladder. Luther L. Terry, Burney's successor, cited the British report later that year when, at the urging of several private health organizations, he proposed the appointment of an advisory committee to study the issue.[37]

The committee's report, released on January 11, 1964, made front-page headlines throughout the country and was featured prominently on news broadcasts. Although its conclusions came as no surprise to Terry or to others familiar with the research, they had a noticeable impact on the country's smokers. Cigarette sales fell immediately. In New York State, cigarette tax revenue for January was about 5 percent less than in January 1963, and February's total was down 18 percent from the year before.[38] Nationwide, per capita cigarette consumption fell 3.5 percent between 1963 and 1964. (By comparison, consumption dropped 2.8 percent and 6.1 percent, respectively, in the cancer scare years of 1953 and 1954.) Per capita consumption rose a bit in 1965 and 1966, dropped for four consecutive years, and rebounded slightly in the early 1970s. But it never returned to the 1963 peak of 4,345, and in 1974 it began a steady decline that continued for two decades. In 1966, about 43 percent of American adults regularly smoked cigarettes; today about 25 percent do.[39]

The report alone did not accomplish all of this. But it marked the beginning of the most concerted, sustained, and successful effort in history to discourage the use of tobacco. The first step was to publicize the findings of the surgeon general's advisory committee. One week after Terry's press conference, the Federal Trade Commission announced that it planned to require health warnings on every cigarette package and advertisement. Congress superseded FTC action with the Cigarette Labeling and Advertising Act of 1965, which required the warning "Caution: Cigarette Smoking May Be Hazardous to Your Health" on all cigarettes packages (but not ads) as of January 1, 1966. The wording, milder than what the FTC had proposed, resulted from industry lobbying and the influence of legislators from tobacco states. To protect manufacturers from a multiplicity of state and federal regulations, the law prohibited any other health warning. The Public Health Cigarette Smoking Act of 1969 (actually passed in 1970) required a new, more confident, message: "Warning: The Surgeon General Has Determined that Cigarette Smoking Is Dangerous to Your Health." After the expiration in June 1971 of the moratorium imposed by the law on FTC action, the agency threatened to file complaints against cigarette companies for failing to include health warnings in their ads. In March 1972 the industry agreed to use the standard surgeon general's warning in advertisements as well as on packages.

By 1981 the FTC had decided that the familiar warning was no longer having any impact, and it recommended a series of specific, rotating labels. Congress adopted this basic idea in the Comprehensive Smoking Education Act of 1984, which took effect in October 1985 and established the four messages now in use, each preceded by the phrase "SURGEON GENERAL'S WARNING": (1) "Smoking Causes Lung Cancer, Heart Disease, Emphysema, and May Complicate Pregnancy"; (2) "Quitting Smoking Now Greatly Reduces Serious Risks to Your Health"; (3) "Smoking by Pregnant Women May Result in Fetal Injury, Premature Birth, and Low Birth Weight"; (4) "Cigarette Smoke Contains Carbon Monoxide."

Paradoxically, these ubiquitous messages about the hazards of smoking encouraged the tobacco companies to continue questioning those hazards. No one buying cigarettes after January 1, 1966, could reasonably claim to be unaware that smoking is a risky practice, regardless of what tobacco company executives might say. Furthermore, the courts have generally held that awarding damages for smoking-related diseases to plaintiffs who claim cigarette warnings are inadequate would, in effect, impose additional labeling requirements, which are forbidden by federal law. Hence, the cigarette companies decided there was little risk of liability in continuing to dispute the health hazards of smoking. On the other hand, a sudden reversal of their position would make it easier for plaintiffs to prevail and would invite charges that the industry had been lying to the public for years. As it turned out, however, sticking to Plan A did not stop plaintiffs from accusing the tobacco companies of a conspiracy to deceive consumers. Quite the contrary. (See chapter 6.)

In August 1964 the Council for Tobacco Research released a seventy-one-page booklet summarizing the findings of 350 reports on research it had funded during the previous decade. Clarence Cook Little, the former managing director of the American Cancer Society who served as the council's scientific director, said the studies had found little evidence to support a causal link between smoking and lung cancer, heart disease, or peptic ulcers. But he expressed the hope that continued research funded by the CTR, private health organizations, and the federal government would eventually resolve such issues. Testifying before the House Subcommittee on Health and the Environment thirty years later, the chief executives of the major tobacco companies were still reserving judgment. Asked whether smoking causes lung cancer, heart disease, emphysema, bladder cancer, stroke, or low birth weight, R. J. Reynolds CEO James W. Johnston answered "It may" to each question. Philip Morris CEO William Campbell agreed that a causal connection between smoking and lung cancer remained unproven. Lorillard CEO Andrew H. Tisch went further, saying he did not believe smoking causes lung cancer.[40]

Lately cracks have developed in this stonewall. In March 1997, as part of a settlement with the attorneys general and plaintiffs' lawyers suing the industry, the Liggett Group became the first tobacco company to concede publicly that cigarettes can cause cancer, heart disease, emphysema, and other illnesses. The other companies, in a deal announced three months later, did not offer a Liggett-style confession. But they did acknowledge "a consensus within the scientific and medical communities that tobacco products are inherently dangerous and cause cancer, heart disease and other serious adverse health effects." They also agreed to stronger warning labels, including "Smoking can kill you."[41] In pretrial testimony later that summer, Philip Morris Companies chairman Geoffrey Bible speculated that over several decades perhaps one hundred thousand Americans "might have" died from smoking. The next day, RJR-Nabisco chairman Steven F. Goldstone said, "I have always believed that smoking plays a part in causing lung cancer. What the role is, I don't know, but I do believe it."[42] Even before the settlement agreement, Philip Morris and R. J. Reynolds were tacitly acknowledging what Liggett said explicitly. In a 1995 interview, Philip Morris attorney Michael York told me it's "totally false" to say that "cigarette companies deny that smoking [poses] a risk of disease." He later told *Time,* "You'd have to be living under a rock not to know there are risks associated with smoking."[43] In May 1997, RJR senior vice president Daniel Donahue, commenting on an industry victory in court, referred to the "well-known risks of the use of this product."[44]

THE BODY COUNT

Based on data from a large prospective study conducted by the American Cancer Society from 1982 to 1988, the 1989 surgeon general's report offered estimates of the risks facing cigarette smokers. Over all, smokers in the ACS study were roughly twice as likely to die during the study as nonsmokers. Among men over the age of thirty-five, smokers were about 22 times as likely to die of lung cancer as nonsmokers; 27 times as likely to die of lip, oral, or pharyngeal cancer; 10 times as likely to die of chronic obstructive lung disease and cancer of the larynx; 8 times as likely to die of esophageal cancer; and twice as likely to die of coronary heart disease and stroke. The risk ratios for women were in the same ballpark, except for most of the cancers, where their rates lagged behind the men's. These disparities probably reflect historical differences in smoking behavior.[45]

By combining the risk ratios from the ACS study with information about smoking prevalence and mortality from specific causes in the general population, the surgeon general's 1989 report estimated smoking-attributable deaths for 1985. According to those figures, smoking accounted for 87 percent of lung cancer deaths (106,000), 82 percent of deaths from chronic obstructive lung disease (57,000), 21 percent of deaths from coronary heart disease (114,000), and 18 percent of stroke deaths (27,500). After adding in several other smoking-related causes of death, the total was 390,000.[46] In 1993, using similar methods, the Centers for Disease Control and Prevention estimated that smoking-attributable deaths in 1990 totaled 419,000, about 20 percent of all deaths.[47]

Tobacco's opponents, some of whom use higher numbers than the federal government, like to quantify the impact of smoking because it helps dramatize the issue. In her 1984 book *Smoking Gun: How the Tobacco Industry Gets Away with Murder,* Elizabeth Whelan, president of the American Council on Science and Health, writes, "If every single day two filled-to-capacity jumbo jets crashed—killing all on board—the death toll (about 212,000) would not approach that accounted for each year by cigarette smoking."[48] Journalist Larry C. White, in his 1988 book *Merchants of Death,* says, "Smoking has killed more Americans than have died in all the wars against our enemies from the British to the Japanese."[49] In a 1990 editorial in the *Journal of the American Medical Association,* Louis Sullivan, then secretary of Health and Human Services, offered a different war comparison: "The number of Americans who die each year of diseases caused by smoking exceeds the number of Americans who died in World War II."[50] In the same issue of *JAMA,* former CDC Director William H. Foege said, "It is quite predictable that in the coming years the annual global death toll of tobacco will equal the total death toll of the Holocaust in Nazi Germany."[51] The epidemiologist R. T. Ravenholt, in a 1985 paper offering his own estimate of the deaths caused by tobacco use, declared that "only the unquantifiable threat of nuclear annihilation poses a greater threat to health and life."[52]

Despite their rhetorical usefulness, smoking mortality estimates should be approached with caution. They are based on epidemiological research with samples that are not representative of the general population, and they do not take account of confounding variables—differences between smokers and nonsmokers (aside from tobacco use) that might affect disease rates. For example, smokers tend to drink more, eat poorer diets, exercise less, earn lower incomes, and engage in more haz-

ardous occupations than nonsmokers. A 1992 Royal Society study estimated that "possibly between 10% and 20%" of the deaths attributed to
smoking are in fact due to confounding variables.[53] Other researchers
have put the percentage higher.[54]

However accurate the numbers, the emphasis on total deaths is misleading. The rhetoric of tobacco's opponents implies a rough equivalence between a sixty-five-year-old smoker who dies of lung cancer and a
forty-year-old businessman killed in a plane crash, a nineteen-year-old
soldier shot in the trenches of World War I, or a child murdered by the
Nazis at Auschwitz. But there is a big difference between someone who
dies suddenly at the hands of another person or in an accident and
someone who dies as a result of a long-term, voluntarily assumed risk.
Aside from the clear moral distinctions—which tobacco's opponents too
often ignore—there is the issue of timing. On average, the people who
die from smoking-related diseases lose far fewer years than people who
die in plane crashes, wars, or acts of genocide. These points tend to be
lost in discussions of smoking, where the body count is all that matters.

Joe Califano, Jimmy Carter's secretary of health, education, and welfare, had the body count in mind on January 11, 1978, when he declared smoking "Public Health Enemy Number One." Harking back to
Jesuit priest Jakob Balde's admonition in 1658, Califano said, "People
who smoke are committing slow-motion suicide."[55] Or as he later put it
in his memoirs, "The cigarette industry sells a product that has killed
more Americans more painfully—through heart disease, lung cancer
and choking to death from emphysema—than have all our wars and all
our traffic accidents combined."[56] A former three-pack-a-day smoker
who liked to tell the story of how he kicked the habit as a birthday present to his eleven-year-old son, Califano recommended an increase in
the federal cigarette tax, a ban on smoking aboard airplanes, more funding for anti-smoking research and education, restrictions on smoking in
federal buildings, and stronger warning labels.

Most of the points in Califano's list were not under his control, but
he did testify before Congress about the hazards of smoking; restrict
smoking in his department's buildings; and obtain more money for the
National Clearinghouse for Smoking and Health, which he moved from
Atlanta (home of the Centers for Disease Control) to Washington and

renamed the Office on Smoking and Health. He held press conferences to highlight the dangers of smoking, wrote letters to every school superintendent in the country to emphasize the importance of teaching children about smoking and health, and arranged prominent press coverage for the release in January 1979 of the fifteenth-anniversary surgeon general's report.

Anti-smoking activists thought Califano's campaign was mostly flash. One critic called it "a very weak program, since most of its elements are merely suggestions."[57] Another, writing in the *Washington Monthly,* accused Califano of "presenting nearly nothing as if it were a bombshell." He speculated that the HEW secretary was hungry for attention: "Califano is one of the press-happiest fellows in a town where the philosophy is, 'I'm in the papers, therefore, I exist.'"[58]

Still, Califano's preaching aroused considerable hostility. In a letter to the *New York Times,* a Boston physician recommended that the portly bureaucrat set an example for the country by going on a diet. "Let us not forget that heart disease is a major killer of Americans," he wrote, "and obesity is a risk factor in the genesis of heart disease."[59] After North Carolina Governor Jim Hunt invited Califano for a visit so he could see how important tobacco was to the state, Representative Charlie Rose, a North Carolina Democrat, said, "We're going to have to educate Mr. Califano with a two-by-four, not a trip." When Califano criticized cigarette advertising, saying it was aimed at convincing young people that "smoking is glamorous, adult, and sexually attractive," a tobacco company executive called him "a silly ass." Anti-Califano bumper stickers ("Califano Is Dangerous to My Health") and billboards ("Califano Blows Smoke") started appearing, courtesy of the tobacco companies.[60]

In July 1979, when President Carter fired Califano along with two other Cabinet members, the HEW secretary cited "friction" with the White House staff and Carter's need "to get the Cabinet ready for the 1980 election."[61] Some observers took this to mean that the president was concerned about political problems in the South caused by Califano's anti-smoking efforts and his push to desegregate state universities. During an August 1978 visit to North Carolina, Carter had joked: "I had planned today to bring Joe Califano with me. But he decided not to come. He discovered that not only is North Carolina the No. 1 tobacco-producing state, but that you produce more bricks than anyone in the nation as well."[62] The South was not the only place where Califano made enemies. *Newsweek* said he had "perhaps the biggest ego in Jimmy Carter's Cabinet," while *Science* noted, "He made enemies because he carried out his duties in an aggressive way that nearly always cast his adversaries as moral inferiors."[63] It's not clear how important a role Califano's vocal opposition to smoking played in his dismissal, but it certainly didn't help.

Five years later, when Surgeon General C. Everett Koop called for "a smoke-free society by the year 2000," the reaction was much more subdued, perhaps because he had considerably less power than Califano and offered no specific policy proposals. Koop announced the goal at a meeting of the American Lung Association (ALA) in May 1984, and he did not say exactly what he meant by "a smoke-free society."[64] In December 1985 he told the *New York Times* that "what I mean is not the complete absence of smoking, but a society in which you will not find people smoking in the presence of people who don't want it."[65] He repeated this explanation in *Reader's Digest* two years later and in his memoirs, published in 1991.[66]

Yet "a smoke-free society" was almost universally understood, naturally enough, to mean a society without smoking. In his speech to the ALA, Koop did discuss private and government bans on smoking in certain locations, and he urged nonsmokers to demand more such restrictions. His main focus, however, was reducing cigarette consumption, primarily through educational efforts by physicians, the media, civic groups, and professional organizations. It was implausible, of course, to suggest that more than fifty million Americans could be persuaded to stop smoking in a decade and a half. (The *New York Times*, in a favorable editorial, called it "Surgeon General C. Everett Koop's impossible dream."[67]) But that is what most people took Koop to be saying.

This interpretation of the surgeon general's speech was adopted not only by newspapers and general interest magazines but by specialized publications such as *Alcoholism and Drug Abuse Week* and the CDC's *Morbidity and Mortality Weekly Report*.[68] Koop himself frequently used *smoke-free society* in the broader sense, as in his foreword to a 1988 book on the tobacco industry. Noting that "approximately fifty-three million

Americans still smoke," he wrote, "There's still a very big job left to do. I assure you that the U.S. Public Health Service and its surgeon general—I and whoever comes after me—will do whatever we can to make the dream of a smoke-free society come true."[69]

Koop's inconsistent use of the slogan reflects an ambiguity in the drive for bans on smoking in stores, offices, restaurants, bars, theaters, stadiums, parks, taxis, and other "public places." Promoted in the name of "nonsmokers' rights," such restrictions also serve to reduce cigarette consumption by making it less convenient and less socially acceptable. As chapter 5 shows, tobacco's opponents seek bans on smoking to discourage the habit, not just to shield bystanders from secondhand smoke. Hence, achieving a smoke-free society in the narrow sense (no smoking in public) is part of the strategy to achieve a smoke-free society in the broad sense (no smoking at all).

Koop's millenarian vision was consistent with his style as surgeon general. A distinguished pediatric surgeon who attracted Ronald Reagan's attention through his conspicuous anti-abortion efforts, Koop was frequently compared to an Old Testament prophet. Noting that friends described him as "a man with missionary zeal and a hefty ego to match," a glowing 1986 *People* profile said, "Koop has always lived as if he were on a mission from God."[70] A tall, hefty fellow with an authoritative voice, metal-framed glasses, and a silver Mennonite-style beard, Koop attracted attention (and a fair amount of ridicule) by wearing the gold-braided uniform that goes with the surgeon general's honorary rank of vice admiral. "I put it on immediately," he explains in his memoirs, "because I felt it would help to reestablish the languishing authority of the Surgeon General and revive the morale of the Commissioned Corps of the United States Public Health Service. There is something about a uniform."[71]

An evangelical Christian who emphasized the importance of faith in his career, Koop brought a quasi-religious certainty to what he called "the anti-smoking crusade."[72] So far as he was concerned, smoking was an unmitigated evil. In a dispute with Defense Secretary Caspar Weinberger over the sale of discounted cigarettes at military bases, Koop asked, "How could the removal of cigarettes be viewed as a reduction of benefits, when the only benefit would be a lifetime of illness or early death?"[73] During his eight years as surgeon general, Koop oversaw an impressive series of reports on tobacco-related topics: cancer, cardiovascular disease, chronic obstructive lung disease, smoking in the workplace, secondhand smoke, smokeless tobacco, nicotine addiction, and the impact of anti-smoking efforts. Like Califano, he condemned tobacco advertising for seducing children, and he testified before Congress in favor of a ban. He also supported the switch from the old surgeon general's warning for cigarettes to the current system of four rotating messages. At Koop's urging, the Coalition on Smoking or Health developed a twelve-year anti-smoking curriculum designed to ensure that the high school class of 2000 would be "smoke-free." Like George Trask and Lucy Page Gaston, Koop toured the country, giving anti-smoking speeches and leading schoolchildren in a no-smoking pledge. To adults he gave buttons that announced, THE SURGEON GENERAL *PERSONALLY* ASKED ME TO QUIT SMOKING. A companion button declared, AND I DID.

SMOKING AS A DISEASE

Califano and Koop, like most contemporary opponents of tobacco use, considered smoking a public health issue, a matter of life and death requiring government attention. From a public health perspective, smoking is not an activity or even a habit. It is "Public Health Enemy Number One," "the greatest community health hazard,"[74] "the single most important preventable cause of death,"[75] "the manmade plague,"[76] "the global tobacco epidemic."[77] It is something to be stamped out, like smallpox or yellow fever. This view of smoking is part of a public health vision that encompasses all sorts of risky behavior, including not just smoking but drinking, using illegal drugs, overeating, failing to exercise, owning a gun, speeding, riding a motorcycle without a helmet—in short, anything that can be said to increase the incidence of disease or injury.

Although this sweeping approach is a relatively recent development, we can find intimations of it in the public health rhetoric of the nineteenth century. In the introduction to the first major American book on public health, U.S. Army surgeon John S. Billings explained the field's concerns: "Whatever can cause, or help to cause, discomfort, pain, sickness, death, vice, or crime—and whatever has a tendency to avert, destroy, or diminish such causes—are matters of interest to the sanitarian."[78] Despite this ambitious mandate, and despite the book's impressive length (nearly 1,500 pages in two volumes), *A Treatise on Hygiene and Public Health* had little to say about the issues that occupy today's public health professionals. There were no sections on smoking, alcoholism, drug abuse, obesity, vehicular accidents, mental illness, suicide, homicide, domestic violence, or unwanted pregnancy. Published in 1879, the book was instead concerned with things like compiling vital statistics; preventing the spread of disease; abating public nuisances; and assuring wholesome food, clean drinking water, and sanitary living conditions.

A century later, public health textbooks discuss the control of communicable diseases mainly as history. The field's present and future lie elsewhere. "The entire spectrum of 'social ailments,' such as drug abuse, venereal disease, mental illness, suicide, and accidents, includes problems appropriate to public health activity," explains *Principles of Community Health*. "The greatest potential for improving the health of the American people is to be found in what they do and don't do to and for themselves. Individual decisions about diet, exercise, stress, and smoking are of critical importance."[79] Similarly, *Introduction to Public Health* notes that the field, which once "had much narrower interests," now "includes the *social and behavioral aspects of life*—endangered by contemporary stresses, addictive diseases, and emotional instability."[80]

The extent of the shift can be sensed by perusing a few issues of the American Public Health Association's journal. In 1911, when the journal was first published, typical articles included "Modern Methods of Controlling the Spread of Asiatic Cholera," "Sanitation of Bakeries and Restaurant Kitchens," "Water Purification Plant Notes," and "The Need of Exact Accounting for Still-Births."[81] Issues published in 1995 offered articles like "Menthol vs. Nonmenthol Cigarettes: Effects on Smoking Behavior," "Compliance with the 1992 California Motorcycle Helmet Use Law," "Correlates of College Student Binge Drinking," and "The Association Between Leisure-Time Physical Activity and Dietary Fat in American Adults."[82]

In a sense, the change in focus is understandable. After all, Americans are not dying the way they once did. The chapter on infant mortality in *A Treatise on Hygiene and Public Health* reports that during the late 1860s and early 1870s two-fifths to one-half of children in major American cities died before reaching the age of five.[83] The major killers included measles, scarlet fever, smallpox, diphtheria, whooping cough, bronchitis, pneumonia, tuberculosis, and "diarrheal diseases." Beginning in the 1870s, the discovery that infectious diseases were caused by specific microorganisms made it possible to control them through vaccination, antibiotics, better sanitation, water purification, and elimination of carriers such as rats and mosquitoes. At the same time, improvements in nutrition and living conditions increased resistance to infection.

Americans no longer live in terror of smallpox or cholera. Despite occasional outbreaks of infectious diseases such as rabies and tuberculosis, the fear of epidemics that was once an accepted part of life is virtually unknown. The one exception is AIDS, which is not readily transmitted and remains largely confined to a few high-risk groups. For the most part, Americans are dying of things you can't catch: cancer, heart disease, trauma. Accordingly, the public health establishment is focusing on those causes and the factors underlying them. Having vanquished most true epidemics, it has turned its attention to metaphorical epidemics of unhealthy behavior.

In 1979 Surgeon General Julius Richmond released *Healthy People: The Surgeon General's Report on Health Promotion and Disease Prevention,* which broke new ground by setting specific goals for reductions in mortality. "We are killing ourselves by our own careless habits," Joe Califano wrote in the introduction, calling for "a second public health revolution" (the first being the triumph over infectious diseases).[84] *Healthy People,* which estimated that "perhaps as much as half of U.S. mortality in 1976 was due to unhealthy behavior or lifestyle," advised Americans to quit smoking, drink less, exercise more, fasten their seat belts, stop driving so fast, and cut down on fat, salt, and sugar. It also recommended motorcycle helmet laws and gun control to improve public health.[85]

Healthy People drew on a "national prevention strategy" developed by what is now the U.S. Centers for Disease Control and Prevention. Established during World War II as a unit of the U.S. Public Health Service charged with fighting malaria in the South, the CDC today includes seven different centers, only one of which deals with its original mission, the control of infectious disease. The Office on Smoking and Health, now back in Atlanta, is part of the National Center for Chronic Disease Prevention and Health Promotion.

The CDC's growth can be seen as a classic example of bureaucratic empire building. More generally, it is easy to dismiss public health's ever-expanding agenda as a bid for funding, power, and status. Yet the field's practitioners argue, with evident sincerity, that they are simply adapting to changing patterns of morbidity and mortality. In doing so, however, they are treating behavior as if it were a communicable disease, which obscures some important distinctions. Behavior cannot be transmitted to other people against their will. People do not choose to be sick, but they do choose to engage in risky behavior. The choice implies that the behavior, unlike a viral or bacterial infection, has value. It also implies that attempts to control the behavior will be resisted.

FORMIDABLE OBSTACLES

Healthy People noted that "formidable obstacles" stand in the way of improved public health. "Prominent among them are individual attitudes toward the changes necessary for better health," it said. "Though opinion polls note greater interest in healthier lifestyles, many people remain apathetic and unmotivated. . . . Some consider activities to promote health moralistic rather than scientific; still others are wary of measures which they feel may infringe on personal liberties. However, the scientific basis for suggested measures has grown so compelling, it is likely that such biases will begin to shift."[86] In other words, people engage in risky behavior because they don't know any better. Once they realize the risks they are taking, they will change their ways.

Accordingly, the anti-smoking movement that emerged in the 1960s initially emphasized information and exhortation. "We believe in the freedom of the individual in the matter of cigarette smoking," the president of the American Cancer Society told a congressional committee in 1964. "We are opposed to legislation that would prohibit the smoking of cigarettes. . . . To achieve our goal we rely on persuasion and public and professional education."[87] After the first surgeon general's report, writes public health historian Allan M. Brandt, "the presumption was widely held that smokers—now apprised of the risks—would quickly quit."[88] Observing the immediate drop in cigarette sales, Luther Terry recalled, "We were jubilant! As sensible physicians, public health officers, educators and scientists, we imagined for a moment that we had 'conquered' cigarette smoking."[89]

But while the prevalence of smoking started to drop, the decline was more gradual than expected. In 1971 Daniel Horn, coauthor of the 1954 American Cancer Society study and director of the National Clearinghouse for Smoking and Health, predicted that in four years only a quarter of the adult population would be smoking, a goal that was not reached until the 1990s.[90] Many Americans continued to smoke, despite a pervasive public education campaign that included not only warning labels and surgeon general's reports but also press coverage, radio and TV spots, print ads, posters, buttons, bumper stickers, pamphlets, books, and curricula for primary and secondary schools.

Survey data reviewed in the 1989 surgeon general's report show that the message came through loud and clear. As early as 1964, 81 percent of adults agreed that smoking is harmful to one's health. That figure rose to 90 percent by 1975. The share of adults who believed smoking causes lung cancer rose from 66 percent in 1964 to 95 percent in 1985. For heart disease (where the evidence was not as strong), acceptance rose from 40 percent in 1964 to 90 percent in 1985. The share agreeing that smoking is a cause of emphysema or chronic bronchitis increased from 50 percent in 1964 to 86 percent in 1985. The percentages were somewhat lower for current smokers than for nonsmokers, but in all cases a large majority of smokers had accepted these health claims by the 1980s. Even those who did not agree that smoking causes these diseases must surely have been aware of the warnings. As the 1989 report concluded, "A vast majority of adults agree that smoking is hazardous to health and correctly recognize the conditions that are associated with smoking."[91]

Nevertheless, critics of the tobacco industry often argue that the average American is not adequately informed about the health consequences of smoking. Says Kenneth E. Warner, a health economist at the University of Michigan, "Once you get beyond the simple basics—it causes lung cancer, heart disease, and emphysema—knowledge is strikingly superficial, often wrong."[92] Elizabeth Whelan, president of the American Council on Science and Health, writes, "If cigarette manufacturers were to supply, up front, a complete and detailed list of the risks assumed by smokers and describe how those risks relate to the numbers of cigarettes smoked (information that would fill a volume the size of the Manhattan phone book), we might argue more legitimately that smokers were 'informed'—or at least had the opportunity to become so."[93] This standard hardly seems realistic. It's true that most Americans do not know all the details about the hazards associated with smoking. But the same could be said of many potentially hazardous activities, including drinking, driving, skiing, and swimming. The voluntary assumption of risk does not require expert knowledge.

Furthermore, Harvard University economist W. Kip Viscusi has found that, if anything, Americans tend to *overestimate* the risks associated with smoking. Viscusi used data from a survey that asked people to estimate how many smokers in a group of one hundred could be expected to die (1) as a result of smoking and (2) from lung cancer specifically. He compared their responses to risk estimates based on epidemiological data available at the time of the survey. On average, the respondents put the risk of dying from smoking at 54 percent, compared to a "true" risk between 18 and 36 percent. They estimated that a smoker has a 38 percent chance of dying from lung cancer, while the "true" risk was between 6 and 13 percent. Smokers' estimates were lower than nonsmokers' but still higher than the risks indicated by the epidemiological data.[94]

In a second survey, Viscusi told respondents the average life expectancy for a twenty-one-year-old nonsmoker and asked them to estimate the life expectancy for a smoker of the same age and sex. For a benchmark he used an estimate from the 1989 surgeon general's report, which said that each death postponed by anti-smoking efforts represented an average gain in life expectancy of about 20 years.[95] Multiplying 20 years by an overall mortality risk of 18 to 36 percent, Viscusi came up with an average life expectancy loss per smoker of 3.6 to 7.2 years. By contrast, the average response to his survey indicated a life expectancy loss of 11.5 years. Again, the smokers' average estimate (9 years), though lower than the nonsmokers' (12.3 years), was beyond the benchmark range.[96]

Given the widespread knowledge of the hazards posed by smoking, the notion that people smoke out of ignorance is no longer tenable. An alternative explanation is that people smoke because they are addicted. As I will argue in chapter 7, addiction is, at best, a description, not an explanation. There is nothing about nicotine (or any drug, for that matter) that compels the user to continue taking it. As Koop noted in his "smoke-free society" speech, smoking is "a voluntary act: one does not have to smoke if one does not want to."[97] In practical terms, all of the talk about nicotine addiction boils down to a point that has been widely recognized for hundreds of years: It's hard to quit smoking. Hard, but not impossible, as forty-four million former American smokers could tell you.[98] The 1988 surgeon general's report estimates that 90 percent of quitters give up the habit on their own, without formal treatment or smoking cessation devices.[99] As Richard Klein observes in *Cigarettes Are Sublime*, "The fact of addiction in itself explains nothing; after all, millions choose to stop, or never start. Becoming addicted and continuing to smoke implies a persistent disposition to find some benefit or pleasure in the drug."[100]

But anti-smoking activists do not seem to understand this "benefit or pleasure," to which enthusiasts over the centuries have devoted treatises, novels, and poetry. Like Fernandez de Oveido y Valdes in the sixteenth century, tobacco's current opponents look at smokers and "cannot imagine what pleasure they derive from this practice."[101] Elizabeth Whelan maintains that the decision to smoke is fundamentally irrational. "To engage in a behavior that is going to put your life and health in jeopardy, and have you assume all kinds of risks of disease and premature death—you can't rationally decide that," she says. "That would be an aberrant decision."[102]

It may be especially hard for a nonsmoker to imagine what benefits the habit could offer to outweigh the substantial risks associated with it. According to the 1989 surgeon general's report, "research has shown that one-fourth or more of all regular cigarette smokers die of smoking-related diseases."[103] Some researchers believe the fraction is closer to one-half.[104] Everyone dies of something, of course, so the timing of these deaths is important. According to CDC data, the 419,000 deaths attributed to smoking in 1990 represented about 5 million years of potential life lost, or about 12 years per death.[105] It is worth emphasizing that this figure is both an estimate (some of the life-expectancy loss attributed to smoking may in fact be due to other causes) and an average (heavier smokers tend to die earlier, lighter smokers later). Furthermore, given the dramatic reduction in cigarette tar levels that has occurred during the last few decades, calculations based on mortality figures for people who started smoking in the '50s or '60s probably exaggerate the risks facing people who started smoking more recently. But the official estimate is useful for the sake of illustration. If one-fourth to one-half of all smokers die from the habit and die twelve years early on average, cigarettes reduce the life expectancy of the average smoker by three to six years.[106]

For millions of Americans, smoking is a source of daily comfort and gratification. Could it be worth three to six years of life? To answer that question, it may be helpful to reflect on your own pleasures. Would you give up three to six years for red meat? (I would.) How about chocolate? (My wife says she would.) Sex? TV? Music? Most people could probably think of *something* that would be worth three to six years.

But the public health perspective, which seeks collective prescriptions to reduce morbidity and mortality, does not take individual tastes and preferences into account. Having noted that smoking can lead to illness, public health specialists now identify smoking itself as a disease, something inherently undesirable that happens to unwilling victims. The foreword to the 1988 surgeon general's report informs us, "Tobacco use is a disorder which can be remedied through medical attention."[107]

FIRST, DO LESS HARM

Since public health specialists seek to reduce morbidity and mortality, they should welcome less hazardous forms of tobacco (less virulent strains of the "disease"). And, in fact, the search for a safer cigarette initially drew support both from the federal government and from private health organizations such as the American Cancer Society. Over the years, however, the anti-smoking movement became increasingly hostile not only toward new cigarette designs but also toward cigars, pipes, and smokeless tobacco. Many anti-smoking activists see these products not as safer alternatives to standard cigarettes but as dangerous distractions from the goal of eliminating tobacco use. In this respect (as in others), the contemporary anti-smoking movement resembles the temperance movement of the nineteenth century, which at first emphasized the hazards of distilled spirits and excessive drinking but eventually opposed all forms of alcohol and called for complete abstinence.

The tobacco companies responded to the cancer scare of the 1950s and the 1964 surgeon general's report by introducing brands with lower tar and nicotine yields. (Tar seems to play a much more important role in smoking-related disease than nicotine, which is not carcinogenic and has not been linked to lung damage, though it may contribute to cardiovascular disease.) Cigarette makers brought the tar and nicotine levels down through a variety of methods, including filtration, ventilation, increases in the burn rate, and the use of fillers such as reconstituted and puffed tobacco. Brands with tar yields of less than fifteen milligrams, representing 2 to 3 percent of the domestic market in the late '60s, accounted for 56 percent in 1981 and 69 percent in 1992.[108] Today that category includes such ultra-low brands as Now and Carlton, which advertise tar yields of 1 milligram or less. By contrast, tar yields of forty milligrams or more were common in the 1950s.

Responding to the trend toward lower-yield cigarettes and the ensuing "tar derby" among cigarette makers, the Federal Trade Commission banned claims of medical approval or health benefits in 1955. It continued to allow statements of tar and nicotine yields but only if substantiated. In 1959 the FTC, frustrated by the lack of uniform standards for measuring tar and nicotine, announced that "all representations of low or reduced tar or nicotine, whether by filtration or otherwise, will be construed as health claims."[109] In 1966, after warning labels started appearing on cigarette packages, the FTC reversed itself again, allowing statements of tar and nicotine yields as determined by a testing method it had approved. Three years later, the FTC asked Congress to *require* such statements in cigarette ads and on packages. In 1970, the commission proposed a regulation mandating tar and nicotine numbers in advertising. The regulation was never formally implemented; instead, the tobacco companies agreed to comply with the FTC's wishes, and since 1971 all cigarette ads have included average tar and nicotine yields as measured by the "FTC method." Though it is not required, packages (generally those of the lower-yield brands) sometimes include this information as well.

The change in the FTC's position reflected the belief that information about tar and nicotine content would encourage smokers to switch to lower-yield, presumably less hazardous, brands. That goal was part of a pragmatic public health approach recognizing that, as AMA president Edward R. Annis remarked after the release of the surgeon general's 1964 report, "it is unrealistic to assume that the American people are suddenly going to quit smoking."[110] Given that reality, it made sense to encourage innovations that would reduce the risks of smoking. Accordingly, Surgeon General Terry called for a safer cigarette as well as education about the hazards of smoking, and the National Cancer Institute sponsored research toward that end in the 1960s and '70s.

By the late 1970s, however, tobacco's opponents had become less keen on the idea of a safer cigarette, as Gio Batta Gori discovered. In 1976 Gori, a microbiologist who oversaw the government's safer-cigarette research as director of the NCI's Smoking and Health Program, argued in *Science* that "low-toxicity cigarettes hold significant promise in the prevention of diseases related to smoking." Gori looked at various epidemiological studies to see at what level of smoking they were able to detect an increased risk of disease. For lung cancer, the average was 5.7 cigarettes a day. For coronary heart disease, it was 3.5. For all smoking-related diseases, it was 2. Based on these data and information about the composition of smoke from pre-1960 cigarettes (the kind smoked by subjects in the studies), he estimated "critical values" for tar, nicotine, carbon monoxide, nitrogen oxides, hydrogen cyanide, and acrolein. Gori emphasized that "it would be erroneous to interpret these critical values as indicators of safe smoking levels." But he concluded that "a rapid shift in cigarette consumption habits toward the proposed range of critical values would make it reasonable to expect that the current epidemic proportions of smoking-related diseases could be reduced to minimal levels in slightly over a decade."[111]

Two years later, Gori went a step further. Writing in *JAMA,* he and Cornelius J. Lynch, a scientist involved in the NCI-funded research, noted that the levels of toxic components in cigarette smoke had changed dramatically since 1960. On the basis of laboratory analyses of the smoke from twenty-seven low-yield brands, they estimated how many of each would be equivalent to two pre-1960 cigarettes in terms of the six components they measured. Nine Benson & Hedges Lights, twenty-eight Lucky 100s, and seventy-two Carlton Menthols, for example, yielded as much tar as two pre-1960 cigarettes. You could smoke four Benson & Hedges Lights, eight Lucky 100s, or twenty-three Carlton Menthols without exceeding the "critical value" for any of the six measured components. Gori and Lynch again emphasized that "these are by no means safe levels but merely imply that, for a smoker whose daily consumption does not exceed these levels, any attendant tobacco-related mortality risk may be epidemiologically indiscernible from that of a nonsmoker."[112]

Gori's suggestions for harm reduction did not fit well with the mood of the public health establishment. As he later put it, "The new policy was: Smokers shouldn't be helped; smokers should be eliminated."[113] Press coverage of Gori and Lynch's findings set off a storm of criticism. It started with an August 1978 story in the *Washington Post* under the inaccurate headline SOME CIGARETTES NOW 'TOLERABLE,' DOCTOR SAYS. What Gori actually said was, "We can now begin to talk about 'tolerable' levels of smoking *from an overall, public health standpoint.*" He stressed: "I am not calling any cigarette 'safe.' The only cigarette that is safe is the cigarette that is not lit. I am not talking about what might happen to any individual. I am talking about averages. There may be a risk that may still be there even though we might not see it in overall, large population studies." The story quoted a National Cancer Institute spokesman who said, "[Gori] probably represents the best expertise we have on smoking and health." It also quoted Gori's boss, NCI director Arthur Upton, who reiterated that "no cigarette now on the market can be considered wholly without risk to health."[114]

The next day, presumably after he saw the headline in the *Post,*

Upton had a stronger reaction. He called Gori's use of the word *tolerable* "unfortunate," because smokers might misinterpret it as meaning that low-yield cigarettes were safe. He said, "[Gori's comments] set back our cause, and even if we can correct the misinterpretation, we will have lost valuable momentum." HEW Secretary Califano, who had recently announced his anti-smoking campaign, said public health officials were "all very disturbed" by Gori's comments. "There is no such thing as a safe cigarette," he said. Surgeon General Julius Richmond likewise insisted, "There is no known safe level of smoking any cigarette of any type." Sidney Wolfe, head of the Ralph Nader Health Research Group, called Gori "reckless" and said he should be fired for "the most damaging statement that has been made about smoking in the last 10 years."[115]

Thus Gori was accused of saying something he had explicitly and repeatedly denied: that people could smoke without danger. While he may have been excessively optimistic about the benefits of low-yield cigarettes, his aim was to reduce risk, not eliminate it. Two prominent authorities interviewed by the *Post*—Ernst Wynder, the pioneering lung cancer researcher, and Arthur Holleb, the American Cancer Society's medical director—agreed that low-yield cigarettes were less hazardous. That belief has been supported by several studies. In one, E. Cuyler Hammond analyzed data gathered by the ACS between 1960 and 1972. He found that lung cancer, heart disease, and total death rates were lower among smokers who switched to low-yield brands, even after initial differences in smoking behavior (light smokers were more likely to switch) were taken into account.[116] A 1979 autopsy study by Oscar Auerbach designed to assess the impact of reduced cigarette yields found that precancerous changes in lung tissue were much less common in smokers who died in the '70s than in smokers who died in the '50s.[117] The 1989 surgeon general's report summarized the evidence this way: "Studies have shown that smoking filtered lower tar cigarettes reduces the risk of lung cancer compared with smoking unfiltered higher tar cigarettes. However, there is no conclusive evidence that the lower yield cigarettes are associated with reduced risk of overall mortality, cancers other than lung, [chronic obstructive lung disease], or heart disease."[118]

DEADLY DELUSION?

Many anti-smokers insist that, as a 1985 article in the *New York State Journal of Medicine* put it, "the 'less hazardous' cigarette is a deadly delusion."[119] This claim is based mainly on evidence that the official tar and nicotine ratings are a poor measure of what smokers actually absorb. The FTC-approved method for measuring tar and nicotine yields uses a smoking machine that puffs on a cigarette once a minute, down to a specified length. The tar and nicotine drawn from the cigarette are then weighed. Critics of this method, including the surgeon general and the FTC itself, have noted that people and machines do not smoke cigarettes the same way. In particular, smokers, unlike machines, may adjust their behavior to achieve the nicotine dose to which they are accustomed. When they switch to low-yield brands, they may take more puffs, inhale more deeply, retain the smoke longer, or subconsciously cover the ventilation holes.[120]

But the existence of such compensatory behavior does not mean there is *no* benefit from switching to low-yield brands. A 1989 summary of seventeen studies estimated that "smokers who reduce the tar yields of their cigarettes by half will, on average, reduce their intake of tar by 24 percent."[121] That conclusion, together with the epidemiological evidence, supports the belief that low-yield brands are significantly less hazardous. Nevertheless, the desire to maintain a certain level of nicotine intake is an important consideration, one that Gori, pilloried for overselling the benefits of low-yield cigarettes, took into account. In his *Science* article, he argued that nicotine levels should remain high enough to keep smokers satisfied, and in the *JAMA* article, he and Lynch calculated yields of various smoke components per milligram of nicotine for each of the brands they examined.

Hostility to cigarette innovation extends beyond today's low-yield brands. One critic went so far as to deny even the possibility of developing a safer cigarette. Insisting that "there will never be a 'less hazardous' cigarette," he said, "All funding for the development of a 'less hazardous' cigarette should be discontinued."[122] Similarly, some anti-smoking activists and public health specialists have opposed recent innovations in cigarette design that promise substantial risk reduction.

In 1988 R. J. Reynolds introduced Premier, a cigarette with a piece of carbon at the tip that, when lit, heated the air drawn into the cylinder, which contained a roll of tobacco and beads coated with tobacco extract, flavorings, and glycerol. Because Premier did not burn like an ordinary cigarette, it produced very little ash or smoke and no tar. R. J. Reynolds said it also produced less carbon monoxide than 70 percent of the cigarettes sold in the United States and less nicotine than 97 percent of them. The Coalition on Smoking or Health filed a petition with the Food and Drug Administration, asking it to review Premier for "safety and efficacy" as if it were a new drug, which would have kept the brand off the market. The AMA asked state regulators to prevent distribution of the product in test markets. In the end, Premier was withdrawn mainly because of disappointing sales. Customers did not like the taste and found it difficult to keep lit.

In 1994 the *New York Times* reported that R. J. Reynolds planned to try again. The new brand, Eclipse, also used a charcoal tip to heat air, but the flavored beads were gone; instead, the hot air passed through processed tobacco treated with glycerine, which vaporized, picking up nicotine and flavor from blended tobacco near the filter. R. J. Reynolds claimed the design reduced the amount of tar delivered to the smoker by 90 percent as compared to a standard cigarette. Company tests also showed sharp reductions in benzo(a)pyrene, nitrosamines, and acrolein. Like Premier, Eclipse produced little ash or smoke, but it delivered a full dose of nicotine and about as much carbon monoxide as a regular cigarette. Two days after the *New York Times* story about Eclipse appeared, the Coalition on Smoking or Health said it would again ask the FDA to keep the brand off the market, on the ground that it was not a cigarette but a "drug delivery device." The FDA's subsequent decision to regulate *all* cigarettes as drug delivery devices (see chapter 7) did not bode well for Eclipse—or any other innovative cigarette design. The proposed nationwide tobacco settlement announced in June 1997 said the FDA would have to approve any "less hazardous tobacco products" and could then force the manufacturer to license the technology to competitors.[123]

The response to Premier and Eclipse revealed a split within the anti-smoking movement. Representative Henry Waxman, a California Democrat who is one of the tobacco industry's most vociferous critics in Congress, said Eclipse was a positive development. "It may have the advantage of being safer, relatively speaking," he said. "That is impressive and could be a big advantage." John Pauly, a smoking expert at Roswell Park Cancer Center, said: "We have come to realize that despite numerous warnings since 1964, there exists a very large segment of the smoking population who are either unwilling or unable to give up smoking. It's worthwhile to come in with a safer cigarette. I interpret Eclipse as an effort by the industry to have a safer cigarette."[124]

Other opponents of smoking viewed the new brands with alarm. "We think it's just a desperate attempt on their part to reverse the growing social taboo against smoking," an American Lung Association spokeswoman said of Premier, adding that the organization was "alarmed at the possibility that young people in particular may be encouraged by this marketing ploy by R. J. Reynolds to take up smoking."[125] Conceding that "it sounds like the level of tar is far reduced," Jan Hitchcock, associate director of Harvard's Institute for the Study of Smoking Behavior and Policy, said, "It would be too bad to see the current momentum—which has encouraged a lot of people to quit smoking—defused or confused."[126] As Matthew Myers, then staff director of the Coalition on Smoking or Health, explained, "The fact that a product is safer doesn't mean that there is a net health gain if it ends up leading more people to smoke."[127]

Similarly, the physician and addiction specialist John Slade has argued that innovation in cigarette design threatens public health because it encourages people to keep smoking. "If the new products were not available, more people would be able to respond directly to concerns about illness and death from smoking and become completely abstinent from nicotine," he wrote in *Priorities,* a publication of the American Council on Science and Health. Slade argued that the government should "prohibit any new products" whose safety had not been demonstrated. "Had such a policy been in effect in 1950," he wrote, "the only cigarettes on the market today would be unfiltered 70 mm smokes, and far fewer people would be smoking."[128]

This argument against innovation hinges, in part, on an empirical question: Do safer cigarettes encourage so many people to keep smoking or start smoking that the ultimate result is an increase in tobacco-related deaths? But that question is decisive only from the collectivist perspective of public health, which says that what matters is the total number of smokers—the fewer, the better. From the perspective of an individual consumer, what matters is the risk–benefit ratio offered by cigarettes—the lower, the better. As cigarettes become safer, some people who enjoy smoking but abstain for health reasons might take up the habit or return to it because they have decided that the benefits now outweigh the risks. For them, safety improvements are a good thing. For public health specialists, they are fraught with peril.

ALL OR NOTHING

Attitudes toward forms of tobacco other than cigarettes have also hardened. Pipe and cigar smoking declined more rapidly than cigarette consumption after 1964; the share of men smoking cigars or pipes but not cigarettes dropped by two-thirds, from 9 to 3 percent, between 1965 and 1985.[129] Yet it has long been known that cigar and pipe smokers are much less prone to smoking-related diseases (especially lung cancer) than are cigarette smokers, mainly because they inhale less. In a 1958 American Cancer Society study, for example, the overall death rate was 57 percent higher for cigarette smokers than for nonsmokers, but only 12 and 22 percent higher, respectively, for pipe and cigar smokers.[130] A subsequent ACS study found that "death rates were far higher in cigarette smokers than in nonsmokers," while "cigar smokers had somewhat higher death rates than nonsmokers" and "there was little difference between the death rates of pipe smokers and the death rates of men who never smoked regularly."[131]

Recognizing that cigars and pipes are much less hazardous than cigarettes, the 1972 Consumers Union report *Licit and Illicit Drugs* suggested that people concerned about the health effects of smoking should try to "convert smokers from cigarettes to cigars or pipes."[132] By contrast, the chapter on tobacco in the 1991 Consumers Union report *The Facts About Drug Use* says only that "pipe and cigar smoking are far from risk free."[133] Anxious to discourage teenagers from experimenting with cigars, public health officials go to great lengths to obscure the truth. "Tobacco is tobacco is tobacco," Michael Eriksen, director of the CDC's Office on Smoking and Health, told the *New York Times* in 1997. The *Times* itself went further, incorrectly asserting that cigars pose "higher risks than . . . cigarettes."[134]

The anti-smoking movement is especially hostile, oddly, toward smokeless tobacco. Again, it's instructive to compare the two Consumers Union books. The 1972 report said, "Efforts should be made to popularize ways of delivering frequent doses of nicotine to addicts without filling their lungs with smoke." Accordingly, one of its suggestions was to "popularize chewing tobacco and snuff."[135] That recommendation was conspicuously absent from the 1991 book. Instead, the authors expressed concern about the rising popularity of smokeless tobacco, especially among adolescents. "The evidence is compelling that smokeless tobacco produces nicotine levels in the body comparable to those produced by smoking and carries additional risk of cancer of the mouth," they said, giving no indication that snuff and chewing tobacco might pose less of a health hazard than cigarettes.[136]

This one-sided treatment of the topic reflects the attitude of the public health establishment. In 1986 Surgeon General C. Everett Koop issued a report that condemned smokeless tobacco as carcinogenic and addictive. He warned against "the tragic mistake of replacing the ashtray with the spittoon." That same year, Congress banned broadcast ads for smokeless tobacco and required warning labels. One of those labels sums up the prevailing view, echoed by public health officials, anti-smoking activists, self-help books, and newspaper columnists: Smokeless tobacco "is not a safe alternative to cigarettes."[137]

Like Califano's observation that "there is no such thing as a safe cigarette," this is true enough, but it's hardly helpful to someone trying to assess the relative risks of different forms of tobacco. In particular, as Brad Rodu has observed, it is no help to a smoker who is looking for a less hazardous alternative to cigarettes. Rodu, an oral pathologist at the University of Alabama at Birmingham (UAB), thinks smokers ought to give up tobacco completely. But if they choose not to, he says, they are much better off with smokeless tobacco than with cigarettes. In his 1995 book *For Smokers Only: How Smokeless Tobacco Can Save Your Life,* Rodu notes that oral cancer is the only well-established life-threatening risk associated with the use of smokeless tobacco, and even that disease is twice as common among smokers. A 1981 study published in the *New England Journal of Medicine* found an oral cancer rate of 26 per 100,000 among long-term users of smokeless tobacco, compared to 6 per 100,000 among nonusers. Noting that the survival rate for oral cancer is 50 percent, Rodu estimates that "if all 46 million smokers used smokeless tobacco instead, the United States would see, at worst, 6,000 deaths from oral cancer [a year], versus the current 419,000 deaths from smoking-related cancers, heart problems, and lung disease."[138]

By this measure, Rodu argues, smokeless tobacco is 98 percent safer than smoking. He and his colleagues have estimated that life expectancy for a thirty-five-year-old smokeless tobacco user is 80.9, virtually the same as for nonusers. The average thirty-five-year-old cigarette smoker, by contrast, lives to be 73.1. (The eight-year gap is not due entirely to smoking, since cigarette smokers also die more frequently from other causes, including accidents, suicide, and cirrhosis of the liver.) Rodu's message to smokers is straightforward: You can enjoy tobacco flavor and nicotine at a fraction of the risk, without the pesky smoke. Still, Rodu emphasizes, "Smokeless tobacco should only provide a viable and comparatively safe *damage control measure* for the current and last generation of nicotine addicts. Forty years or so from now I hope there are no tobacco users left on the planet."[139]

Like Gio Gori, Rodu has been condemned by other opponents of tobacco because they consider his message detrimental to the cause. "To say that one form of tobacco is safer than the other at this point in the debate is just irresponsible," Gregory Connolly, director of the Massachusetts Tobacco Control Program, told the Associated Press after Rodu discussed his ideas in scientific journals and on television in 1994. "Tobacco is tobacco. . . . It's like telling someone to jump from the fifth floor instead of the 10th floor."[140] The American Association of Oral and Maxillofacial Surgeons preferred a different analogy: "Suggesting this switch is like telling someone to use a rifle instead of an Uzi."[141] Robert Mecklenburg, dental coordinator for the

National Cancer Institute's tobacco control program, offered yet another comparison: "We know that more children are killed by cars than trains, but you wouldn't tell children to play on railroad tracks instead of in the street."[142] The president of the American Dental Association (ADA) called Rodu's proposal "naive at best and irresponsible at worst."[143]

Beginning in 1993, Rodu and his colleagues conducted a pilot study in which they showed volunteer smokers how to use smokeless tobacco and then followed them for a year to see if the switch had been successful. The initial results were encouraging, but the researchers had a hard time publishing them. "The disappointing thing is that the ideas are not being rejected on the basis of sound science or logic," Rodu said. "They're being rejected on the basis of philosophy. . . . We are getting very emotionally wrought rejections. They're attacking me personally, my ethics, [saying] this shouldn't be tried at all. . . . You simply would not see this kind of vicious attack in the normal scientific process."[144]

The ADA unsuccessfully urged Rodu's professional organization, the American Academy of Oral and Maxillofacial Pathology, to repudiate his work.[145] In July 1994, after Rodu and University of Alabama epidemiologist Philip Cole published a letter in *Nature* suggesting the benefits of switching from cigarettes to smokeless tobacco,[146] the National Cancer Institute prepared a statement rejecting "the substitution of one known carcinogen for another," which it called "medically and ethically unwarranted." The statement, which the NCI sent to University of Alabama officials for comment, said recommending a switch to smokeless tobacco "sends the wrong message" and "raises questions of both legal liability and medical malpractice."[147] After requesting records related to Rodu's study, NCI deputy director Edward J. Sondik contacted the Office for Protection from Research Risks at the National Institutes of Health, suggesting that the project violated NIH guidelines for human research. (Rodu's study did not receive any federal money, but the NIH is a major funding source for research at the university.) In an angry letter to NIH director Harold Varmus, a UAB vice president said, "NCI officials have overstepped both their authority and responsibility and have, in so doing, come perilously close to harassment and censorship."[148]

The Office for Protection from Research Risks launched a yearlong investigation of Rodu's study and, eventually, of other research projects at the university. "They were on a fishing expedition," Rodu says. "It became clear after the first two or three months that they weren't going to get anywhere with this." The university's Institutional Review Board, which had unanimously approved Rodu's study, did so again after the investigation started. "The implication that there might be ethical problems or legal problems in this research I find a little insulting," the board's chairman said in a letter to the OPRR.[149] "They never found any significant problem with my study, but it did get kind of nasty," Rodu says. "You get this kind of pressure from some tiny effort to get smokers to quit. It's just ridiculous."[150]

The vehemence of the opposition to smokeless tobacco, together with the objections to the very concept of a safer cigarette, suggest that public health is not the only thing at stake here. After all, trying to keep tobacco use as dangerous as possible for the sake of deterrence is a very risky strategy if your aim is a net reduction in morbidity and mortality. It makes more sense if your goal is to eliminate all forms of tobacco use, regardless of their relative hazards. Which suggests that the contemporary anti-smoking movement has more in common with prior efforts to suppress tobacco use than is generally recognized. Tobacco's opponents have always been concerned about its impact on the body, but they also worried about its impact on the soul—and they still do. The revulsion of sixteenth-century clergymen at heathen tobacco rituals and the alarm of early anti-cigarette crusaders about the corrupting effects of "little white slavers" may seem quaint to us now. But the moral objections to tobacco remain. As Gregory Connolly explained in a TV report about the control of nicotine in cigarettes, "It's a drug, it's a drug, it's a drug."[151]

Americans have long had an ambivalent attitude toward psychoactive substances. To help resolve our mixed feelings, we like to put drugs into neat categories: medicinal or recreational, good or evil, legal or illegal. Once hailed as a miracle remedy, tobacco was later praised as a comfort in times of distress, a stimulant to relieve boredom, an aid to concentration and conviviality. Today it is widely seen as a plague and a poison, an enslaver of children, a deadly seductress. Its users, once perfectly respectable, are now portrayed as sick, sinful, and anti-social—more like heroin addicts than coffee drinkers. This dramatic reversal goes beyond concerns about physical health. It reflects a feeling of betrayal. We may finally be heeding Johann Michael Moscherosch, the seventeenth-century anti-tobacco polemicist. "Consider well," he said, "how the Devil hath deceived you!"[152]

Chapter 3

COUGHING COWBOYS

Cigarettes—they're killers.

—American Cancer Society commercial, 1969

INTO THE SUNSET

On January 1, 1971, the Marlboro Man rode across the television screen one last time. At midnight a congressional ban on broadcast advertising of cigarettes went into effect, and the smoking cowboy was banished to the frozen land of billboards and print ads. With the deadline looming, bleary-eyed, hung-over viewers across the country woke to a final burst of cigarette celebration. "Philip Morris went on a $1.25-million ad binge New Year's Day on the Dick Cavett, Johnny Carson and Merv Griffin shows," the *New York Times* reported. "There was a surfeit of cigarette ads during the screening of the bowl games."[1] And then they were gone. American TV viewers would no longer be confronted by happy smokers frolicking on the beach or by hapless smokers losing the tips of their extra-long cigarettes between cymbals and elevator doors. They would no longer have to choose between good grammar and good taste.

This was widely considered an important victory for consumers. The *Times* wondered whether the ad ban was "a signal that the voice of the consumer, battling back, can now really make itself heard in Washington." A *New Yorker* article tracing the chain of events that led to the ban concluded, "To an increasing degree, citizens of the consumer state seem to be perceiving their ability to turn upon their manipulators, to place widespread abuses of commercial privilege under the prohibition of laws that genuinely do protect the public, and, in effect, to give back to the people a sense of controlling their own lives."[2]

As these comments suggest, many supporters of the ban viewed advertising not as a form of communication but as an insidious force that seduces people into acting against their own interests. This was a common view then (and now), popularized by social critics such as John Kenneth Galbraith and Vance Packard. In *The Affluent Society* (1958), Galbraith argued that manufacturers produce goods and then apply "ruthless psychological pressures" through advertising to create demand for them.[3] In *The Hidden Persuaders* (1957), Packard described advertising as an increasingly precise method of manipulation that can circumvent the conscious mind, influencing consumers without their awareness. He reinforced his portrait of Madison Avenue guile with the pseudoscientific concept of subliminal messages: seen but not seen, invisibly shaping attitudes and actions.[4] The impact of such ideas can be seen in the controversy over tobacco advertising. The federal court that upheld the ban on TV and radio ads for cigarettes quoted approvingly from another ruling that referred to "the subliminal impact of this pervasive propaganda."[5]

The anti-smoking movement responded to this propaganda in two main ways: with censorship and with more propaganda. From the ban on broadcast ads to the Clinton administration's attempted prohibition of Marlboro caps and Joe Camel T-shirts, tobacco's opponents sought to suppress the speech of cigarette manufacturers, always emphasizing its corrupting effect on young minds. At the same time, they tried to counter tobacco advertising with information, arguments, and satire. The second strategy gave consumers more credit, treating them like independent moral agents instead of mindless automatons. In the 1990s, however, these two approaches began to blend together. Instead of attempting to influence individual behavior, anti-smoking advertising increasingly sought to affect public policy by undermining the legitimacy of the tobacco industry. Ads sponsored by the California Department of Health Services emphasized the industry's dishonesty and greed, while the National Center for Tobacco-Free Kids ran advertorials in the *New*

York Times that urged further restrictions on tobacco advertising. In the battle between force and persuasion, force seemed to be winning.

Criticism of tobacco advertising has been remarkably consistent during the last three decades. A few days after the release of the 1964 surgeon general's report, the *New York Times* revealed that the Federal Trade Commission, which had tangled with tobacco companies over misleading ads during the '40s and '50s, hoped "to be able to force the cigarette industry to change the whole tone of its advertising." Reported the *Times*: "Specifically, it will attempt to force the elimination from cigarette advertising of statements or indications that people 'feel good' when smoking, that smoking is a social grace, a sign of maturity or a part of sophisticated living. Advertisements aimed at making smoking attractive to young people and those that mention athletes may be banned entirely." The new regulations "would virtually oblige the industry to stop trying to make cigarettes seem attractive or desirable."[6] Less than a week later, probably anticipating resistance from Congress, the FTC started backpedaling. Instead of the sweeping controls outlined in the *Times,* it suggested banning ads that implied smoking promoted good health, along with unsubstantiated statements that one brand was less harmful than another.

But the tobacco companies knew which way the wind was blowing. In April 1964 they announced an industry advertising code, to be enforced by an independent administrator who would review every ad before it ran. The code, which incorporated suggestions made by the Tobacco Institute in 1963, barred "virility" themes, unsubstantiated health claims, endorsements by athletes or entertainers, and ads aimed mainly at people under twenty-one (meaning that programs and publications intended primarily for that group would be off-limits). It said ads should not depict smoking as "essential to social prominence, distinction, success or sexual attraction." It also required that models in cigarette ads be and appear at least twenty-five years old. Strictly interpreted, the code went nearly as far as the FTC's initial proposal, but in practice the requirements were pretty loose. The main function of the advertising code was rhetorical. The cigarette companies said it showed they cared, while their opponents said it showed they couldn't even live up to their own standards.[7]

Although the industry's code probably helped delay legislation and regulation dealing with advertising, concerns about children's exposure to cigarette ads persisted. In May 1967 the National Congress of Parents and Teachers passed a resolution that said television stations should stop airing cigarette commercials before 9 P.M. It also called upon cigarette companies to refrain from depicting smoking in their ads. A supporter of the resolution explained, "The constant seduction of cigarette advertising on TV gives children the idea that cigarettes are associated with all they hold dear—beauty, popularity, sex, athletic success."[8]

FORCING FAIRNESS

A brash young New York lawyer named John F. Banzhaf III decided to do something about the commercials that the PTA found so troubling. As described in a 1971 *Reader's Digest* profile, his epiphany came at 2:34 P.M. on Thanksgiving Day, 1966. Banzhaf was watching a football game on TV when a commercial (presumably for Marlboros) came on, showing "handsome, rugged men confidently smoking cigarettes in an outdoor western setting. It implied that any man who wanted to be truly masculine should smoke cigarettes. To the tobacco industry, it was a routine advertisement; to [Banzhaf], it was the final outrage. 'Suddenly,' he recalls, 'I determined to do whatever I could to wipe out those evil commercials.' "[9]

Nowadays, Banzhaf tells a less dramatic story. He says he did not have especially strong feelings about smoking. "It probably was not the most important issue from my point of view, or, obviously, from the country's point of view," he says. "If I had seen a way to use some legal rule or principle I had learned to do something as an individual about another significant social problem—saving the whales, auto safety, or whatever else—I probably would have done that also." But Banzhaf came up with a legal tactic that was appropriate for the anti-smoking movement, and it was the tactic that determined the mission. "Something clicked in my mind," he says. "It was that something I had learned in law school, the fairness doctrine, might have application to this issue."[10]

The fairness doctrine, formulated by the Federal Communications Commission in 1949 and abolished in 1987, required broadcasters to provide time for opposing views when they covered controversial topics. Banzhaf figured that cigarette commercials amounted to a one-sided treatment of a controversial topic—namely, smoking—and that TV and radio stations should give the other side time to respond. It was an audacious argument, since the FCC had never applied the fairness doctrine to product commercials. First Banzhaf wrote to WCBS-TV in New York, requesting air time to rebut the cigarette ads carried by the station. "I had some queasy times," he says, "wondering what would happen if CBS wrote me back and said, 'Sure, come on down and tape something.' I'm not sure I would have known, at 26, what to do or how to do it."[11] But the station turned down the novel request, and Banzhaf filed a complaint with the FCC.

In June 1967 the commission shook up the broadcasting industry by ruling that stations airing cigarette commercials had to provide "a significant amount of time" for "the other side of this controversial issue of public importance—that however enjoyable, such smoking may be a hazard to the smoker's health."[12] The ruling did not specify how much time was "significant," but FCC general counsel Henry Geller, responding to a question, said a ratio of one anti-smoking message to every three cigarette commercials would be reasonable. "I recall talking with him many years later," says Banzhaf, "and he said, 'You know, if they had said 10 to 1, I might have said yes also.'"[13] In response to protests from broadcasters, the FCC reaffirmed the ruling in September. The tobacco industry challenged the requirement on First Amendment and statutory grounds, but it was ultimately upheld by the federal courts.

To monitor compliance with the new policy, Banzhaf established Action on Smoking and Health in February 1968. During the next two years ASH, with the assistance of Seventh Day Adventist volunteers, filed dozens of complaints with the FCC against stations that it claimed were violating the fairness doctrine by airing too few anti-smoking messages or running them when audiences were small. "I felt that what I had to do was create a fear among the broadcasters that I could do something to them if they didn't comply fully," Banzhaf later explained.[14] The FCC never actually revoked any licenses, but in some cases it instructed stations to expand the time allotted to anti-smoking spots. The publicity surrounding the complaints encouraged other stations to be more generous.

After his success with the fairness doctrine, Banzhaf pursued other anti-smoking projects, lobbying Congress, producing litigation kits, and campaigning for "nonsmokers' rights." In the late 1960s he began teaching at George Washington University and moved ASH's headquarters to his law school office. In 1969 he told the *New York Times*, "I know I sound presumptuous, taking on an establishment that must spend $1 million a year lobbying for the industry, but I've been up against impossible odds before and I've won."[15] Banzhaf began issuing press releases in which he called himself "the [Ralph] Nader of the cigarette industry"— to which journalist Elizabeth Drew replied, "Nader he is not, for among other things Ralph Nader would never issue such a release." Drew also noted that Banzhaf had "an entire wall covered with articles about and photographs of himself."[16]

Banzhaf's exploits as a tobacco industry gadfly attracted admiration from people sympathetic to the anti-smoking cause. Still, wrote Thomas Whiteside in a 1970 *New Yorker* article, "Their admiration for his resourcefulness is tempered by reservations concerning what they think is his occasional propensity for personal publicity, in contrast to the manner of other and more self-effacing people whose contributions over the years to the cause of informing the public of the relationship between smoking and health were at least as fundamental. And, indeed, to talk with Banzhaf at any length about public awareness of the relationship between cigarette smoking and health, one would hardly think that such prime movers in the field as Drs. Hammond and Horn, whose study in 1954 first brought the issue to wide public attention, and Dr. Luther Terry, the Surgeon General of the United States between 1961 and 1965, had ever existed."[17]

More than twenty-five years later, Banzhaf is still head of ASH and still teaching law at George Washington University, where he encourages (and gives course credit for) legal activism. (He says ASH "in a sense pioneered the whole idea of what today we call legal activism."[18]) His motto, displayed in his office and in abbreviated form on his license plate, is, "Sue the bastards." In recent years the "bastards" have included barbers and dry cleaners who charge men and women different prices.

Banzhaf's litigious efforts prompted ABC correspondent John Stossel to call him a "bully" on national television. It didn't seem to faze Banzhaf. Nor does the charge that he's a publicity hound. "Do I actively seek and court publicity?" he asked in 1995. "Sure. My primary reason is because it gives you tremendous power and clout. . . . Is there psychic satisfaction or gratification in it? Of course."[19] Banzhaf still sends out press releases (now by fax), selling himself as a quotable expert on a wide range of topics, and his list of "Major Professional Accomplishments," which he gives to reporters, is four pages long.

DON'T BE A LOSER

John Banzhaf's most important accomplishment remains the feat he performed fresh out of law school. When the FCC agreed to apply the fairness doctrine to cigarette commercials, it cleared the way for a flood of anti-smoking "public service announcements" (PSAs) that helped achieve unprecedented reductions in smoking. Although some anti-smoking ads had been aired prior to 1967, their volume and prominence increased dramatically after the FCC said the fairness doctrine required something like one rebuttal for every three cigarette commercials. The American Cancer Society reported that it provided 4,723 spots to stations in the ten months following the FCC ruling, compared to fewer than a thousand in the previous three and a half years.[20] By 1970, broadcasters had been compelled to donate roughly $75 million in air time (more than $300 million in 1997 dollars) for the messages.[21]

The PSAs, produced mainly by the American Cancer Society, ranged from subtle to explicit, humorous to deadly serious. In one ten-second TV spot, a man held up a cigarette and asked, "Have you ever thought what happens when you smoke a cigarette? . . . *We* have." Then the words *American Cancer Society* appeared on the screen. Other PSAs used dramatic images to get people's attention. In one, a cigarette came to life, coiling and rattling like a snake, then striking at the camera. The announcer asked, "What does a cigarette have to *do* to you before you get the message?" Another PSA opened with the sound of a siren and images of a FLAMMABLE sign, a bottle labeled POISON, and a blinking red traffic light. Then it showed the warning label on a package of cigarettes. "We receive many warnings in our life," the narrator said. "And sometimes they can save our life." With the sound of a cough in the background, he concluded, "This message is brought to you by the American Cancer Society."

Some PSAs took a satirical approach. The most memorable one, which played off the Marlboro campaign, began with a cowboy hero standing at a bar under the watchful gaze of two bad guys, both of them smoking. The main villain entered the saloon, a cigarette dangling from his mouth. The good guy turned toward the villain, who said, "We figured *(cough)* you'd *(cough)* be here." Before they could get off a shot, the bad guys were overwhelmed by coughing fits. The good guy brushed past his would-be assailants and left the saloon. Then the words *American Cancer Society* appeared on the screen while the announcer intoned, "Cigarettes—they're killers."

An ACS ad featuring the TV actor William Talman, a three-pack-a-day smoker who died of lung cancer in 1968, was more straightforward. Talman, who played the prosecutor on *Perry Mason,* made the spot at his home six weeks before his death. At the beginning of the ad, he introduced his wife and children. Then, sitting next to a picture of Raymond Burr, who played Perry Mason, Talman noted that Burr's character "used to beat my brains out on TV every week for about 10 years. . . . I didn't really mind losing those courtroom battles. But I'm in a battle right now I don't want to lose at all because if I lose it, it means losing my wife and those kids you just met. I've got lung cancer. . . . So take some advice about smoking and losing from someone who's been doing both for years. If you haven't smoked, don't start. If you do smoke, quit. Don't be a loser."

Many people took this advice to heart. Beginning in 1967, per capita cigarette consumption dropped four years in a row, which had not happened at any time since the turn of the century.[22] Between 1966 and 1970, the prevalence of smoking among adults declined from 43 percent to 37 percent. By 1970 it was no longer true that most men smoked.[23] In 1979 Kenneth E. Warner, a leading tobacco control scholar, concluded that of all the techniques that had been used to reduce smoking none had been "demonstrably more effective than the antismoking messages broadcast on TV and radio from 1968 through 1970."[24]

Despite the apparent success of the PSAs, tobacco's opponents continued to complain about the "constant seduction" of cigarette ads, especially on TV and radio. Broadcast ads were conspicuous, and banning them seemed to present few First Amendment problems. Under the theory that use of "the public airwaves" was a privilege to which the government could legitimately attach conditions, the U.S. Supreme Court had already approved limits on broadcast speech.[25] The FTC endorsed a ban on TV and radio ads for cigarettes in 1968, and the FCC followed suit in 1969. The FTC also proposed that cigarette ads, like packages, carry a warning, and it recommended stronger language. Under the Cigarette Labeling and Advertising Act of 1965, both agencies were barred from imposing new advertising regulations until June 30, 1969. So the focus of the debate shifted to Congress, which could extend the regulatory moratorium, let it expire, or impose its own requirements. The tobacco industry wanted the moratorium renewed, while anti-smoking groups wanted the regulatory agencies free to act—or, alternatively, legislation imposing new restrictions on the industry.

During the debate, John Banzhaf and his students roamed the halls of Congress, giving out ashtrays. Mounted on each ashtray was a pair of clear plastic lungs, one of which would gradually turn black as cigarette smoke flowed into it. ASH had enough of these novelty items to "inundate Congress," Banzhaf recalls. "We called them 'silent lobbyists.' In virtually every office, there were people who smoked. . . . For many years, those ashtrays were still up there and very clearly showed exactly what smoking did." But he concedes that the silent lobbyists were not welcomed everywhere: "There were one or two, particularly tobacco state congressmen, who got very angry, and I think literally threw some of our people out of their offices and hurled the ashtrays after them."[26]

Tobacco company executives may have felt like throwing something, too, after the National Association of Broadcasters unilaterally gave in to demands for an end to cigarette commercials. In July 1969, while the Senate was considering an industry-backed bill that had been passed by the House of Representatives, the NAB's Television Code Review

Board proposed the elimination of cigarette commercials by September 1973. Although Banzhaf dismissed this concession ("In effect they are asking Congress to allow them to continue killing for another four years," he said in a letter to the *New York Times*),[27] it had a dramatic impact. Two weeks later, the tobacco companies, stung by what they saw as a betrayal, provisionally agreed to stop advertising on TV and radio by September 1970. The proposed timing was a slap at the broadcasters, who preferred a more gradual phaseout so they could adjust to the loss of revenue. The law that Congress ultimately approved, the Public Health Cigarette Smoking Act of 1969 (actually passed in 1970), set January 2, 1971, as the deadline. It also strengthened the warning on cigarette packages and allowed the FTC to require warnings in ads after July 1, 1971.

Several factors explain the capitulation of the broadcasters and tobacco companies. Senate passage of the bill renewing the regulatory moratorium was in doubt, and both industries were facing intense criticism for exposing children to pitches for a hazardous product. Some stations had already decided not to carry cigarette commercials, and a ban would prevent other broadcasters from gaining a competitive advantage by continuing to accept revenue from tobacco companies. Furthermore, the FCC's PSA requirement had made cigarette ads less attractive to broadcasters, since they had to give away roughly a minute of air time for every three minutes they sold. The anti-smoking messages also made the medium less attractive to the tobacco companies. By giving it up they would dramatically reduce the subsidy for ads attacking their product.

In the summer of 1969, a former tobacco company executive told Thomas Whiteside, "The opinion of many top-level tobacco people is that as things stand they'd just as soon have cigarette commercials banned if by that they could in effect get the anti-smoking commercials banned, too." That view of the ad ban has led a number of public health researchers to question the wisdom of forcing cigarette commercials off TV. They note that per capita cigarette consumption, which dropped four years in a row from 1967 to 1970, rose for three years following the ban before resuming a downward trend. According to Kenneth Warner, "The ad ban was myopic public policy."[28]

THE PITCH IS BACK

The ban on TV and radio ads for cigarettes saved the tobacco companies over $200 million a year in 1970 dollars (more than $800 million in 1997 dollars), and much of it flowed into billboards, magazine and newspaper ads, and various promotion efforts, including sponsorship of sporting and cultural events. Cigarettes had been the most heavily advertised product on TV, and they became the second most heavily advertised product (after cars) in the outdoor and print media. In 1993 the industry spent about $6 billion on advertising and promotion. Most of this money was absorbed by promotion, with coupons, customer premiums (lighters, key chains, clothing, etc.), and allowances to distributors accounting for 81 percent of the spending. Cigarette companies spent a bit less than $1 billion on newspaper, magazine, outdoor, transit, direct-mail, and point-of-sale advertising.[29]

Eliminating TV and radio commercials for cigarettes did not eliminate criticism of tobacco advertising. In 1985 the American Cancer Society, which three decades earlier had called for an end to cigarette ads through "voluntary self-regulation,"[30] endorsed a government ban on all forms of tobacco advertising and promotion. The American Medical Association, the American Public Health Association, the American Heart Association, and the American Lung Association also began advocating a ban. At various times since the mid-'80s, members of Congress have introduced bills that would have banned tobacco advertising, limited it to "tombstone" messages (black text on a white background), or reduced its tax deductibility.

In August 1996 the Food and Drug Administration issued regulations imposing sweeping restrictions on the advertising and promotion of cigarettes and smokeless tobacco. Among other things, the regulations prohibited promotional items such as hats, T-shirts, and lighters; forbade brand-name sponsorship of sporting events; banned outdoor advertising within one thousand feet of a playground, elementary school, or high school; and imposed a tombstone format on all other outdoor signs, all indoor signs in locations accessible to minors, and all print ads except those in adult-oriented publications. (To use color or pictures, the advertiser was required to show, based on survey data, that minors represented

15 percent or less and fewer than two million of a publication's readers.)[31] The tobacco companies challenged the regulations in federal court, and in April 1997 U.S. District Judge William L. Osteen ruled that the FDA had no statutory authority to regulate the advertising and promotion of "restricted devices," the category in which the agency had placed cigarettes and smokeless tobacco.[32] In the proposed nationwide liability settlement, however, the tobacco companies agreed not only to the FDA rules but to additional restrictions, including bans on outdoor ads, the use of human or cartoon figures, Internet advertising, and product placement in movies, TV shows, or video games.

The fundamental objection to cigarette advertising remains the same: that it depicts the product in a positive light, which is said to be "misleading by its very nature."[33] As Elizabeth Whelan, president of the American Council on Science and Health, puts it, cigarette ads "have nothing to do with the reality of what cigarettes do. They're associated with glamor and sex and outdoor activity."[34] Writes syndicated columnist Ellen Goodman, "I have never seen a cigarette ad that wasn't fundamentally misleading. Any promotion of a healthy, energetic, glamorous lifestyle is at odds with a smoking, gasping reality."[35] Of course, almost all advertising could be said to communicate implicit messages that plainly are not true. The right car, beer, soft drink, breath mint, or perfume will not make you cool, fun, popular, attractive, and happy. Most people take such images with a grain of salt.

What makes tobacco advertising different is the sense that, as the Tennessee Supreme Court declared in 1898, cigarettes are not "legitimate articles of commerce." In the words of contemporary critics, they are "the only legal product that when used as intended causes death,"[36] manufactured by "an industry that is literally getting away with murder."[37] The cigarette companies are "a cancer that has metastasized," "a killer industry" that "depends on a technique perfected by the Nazis: the Big Lie."[38] Since its very existence is considered morally objectionable, the tobacco industry has generated controversy simply by using standard advertising and promotion tools, including attractive models, "image" advertising, cartoon characters, target marketing, store displays, free samples, brand-logo clothing, and customer premiums. "I think a lot of people imagine that when you study marketing, there's a separate track for tobacco," says R. J. Reynolds spokeswoman Peggy Carter. "We don't do anything different from anybody else. It's just that we have a whole industry of critics to contend with."[39]

If you want to get a rise out of those critics, remark favorably on how much Philip Morris has done for women's tennis. For a quarter of a century, tobacco's opponents have charged that tobacco companies circumvent the ban on broadcast ads by sponsoring televised sporting events such as the Virginia Slims tennis tournament. Similarly, they have complained about cigarette billboards at televised baseball, football, basketball, and hockey games, prompting several stadiums and arenas to restrict or remove such signs. In 1995, under the threat of a Justice Department lawsuit, Philip Morris promised to confine its billboards to areas that are not likely to be seen on TV. Tobacco opponents have also argued that sponsorship of sporting events falsely implies a connection between smoking and athleticism. "When the tobacco industry sponsors an event in order to push their deadly product," said Secretary of Health and Human Services Louis Sullivan in 1990, "they are trading on the health, the prestige and the image of the athlete. . . . The sponsorship itself uses the vigor and energy of athletes as a subtle but incorrect and dishonest message that smoking is compatible with good health."[40]

This charge was plausible with respect to tennis, ice skating, or soccer but was less so for bowling, golf, sailing, darts, and motorcycle, speedboat, or auto racing. Most of the sports that tobacco companies have sponsored can be performed just fine by smokers. Again, the real objection seemed to be that tobacco companies (like every other business) were trying to associate their product with something positive. Thus, tobacco's opponents complained about the industry's sponsorship of cultural events and charitable causes. "Donning the mask of philanthropy," wrote Jason DeParle in the *Washington Monthly,* "the tobacco companies have courted not only athletes but ballerinas, modern dancers, jazz musicians, museum curators, unions, civil rights groups, feminists, religious leaders—almost anyone with a glimmer of uprightness and a use for cash. The Guggenheim Museum. The Joffrey Ballet. The Whitney. The purpose of this fevered gift-giving has been to divert the public's attention from what tobacco companies really do: lure people, particularly young ones, into buying a highly addictive drug, which, if used as intended, courts death."[41] In almost any other industry, "this fevered gift-giving" might be praised as high-minded generosity or admired as savvy public relations. But to critics like DeParle, the tobacco companies are inherently evil, so everything they do is tainted.

This attitude helps explain the controversy over "target marketing" of cigarettes. Companies often create brands or run ads aimed at particular demographic groups. Secret deodorant, we are told, "is strong enough for a man but made for a woman." People who drink Mountain Dew and watch MTV tend to be younger than people who drink Diet Pepsi and watch VH-1. Ads for consumer products in black-oriented maga-zines tend to feature black models. Tobacco companies likewise gear their marketing toward specific audiences. The most conspicuous exam-ple is Virginia Slims, introduced in 1968 with the slogan "You've come a long way, baby" (since replaced by the vapid "It's a *woman* thing") and later joined by women's brands such as Eve, Misty, and Capri. Mentho-lated cigarettes such as Brown & Williamson's Kool, sponsor of the Kool Jazz Festival, are especially popular with black smokers.

So in 1990, when R. J. Reynolds began to test-market a new menthol brand, Uptown, in Philadelphia, the move was not completely unprece-dented. But the attempt to introduce a cigarette brand explicitly aimed at blacks aroused intense opposition from anti-smoking groups and public health officials. Louis Sullivan, who is black, condemned Uptown during a speech at the University of Pennsylvania, urging "an all-out ef-fort to resist the attempts of tobacco merchants to earn profits at the ex-pense of our poor and minority citizens."[42] RJR quickly shelved the brand. A few months later, a similar fate befell Dakota, an RJR brand that was reportedly aimed at young, white working-class women.

The Uptown controversy helped trigger a wave of vandalism against cigarette billboards in black neighborhoods during the spring of 1990. In New York, the Reverend Calvin O. Butts III, pastor of Harlem's Abyssinian Baptist Church, led volunteers on search-and-deface missions against billboards advertising cigarettes and alcoholic beverages. In Dal-las, county commissioner John Wiley Price and a group of whitewashers hit about twenty-five billboards. In Chicago, the Reverend Michael Pfleger, a Catholic priest, was arrested for splashing red paint on South Side billboards advertising cigarettes, beer, and vodka. A jury acquitted him after he presented a necessity defense, arguing that his crimes were aimed at preventing a greater evil. "When you target a particular race of people with [ads for] two of the nation's top killers," he said, "that's genocide."[43]

Father Pfleger's argument carried weight only for those who accepted the equation between selling cigarettes and committing murder. Others were left to wonder why cigarette advertising aimed at specific demographic groups was particularly objectionable. "I don't think there's an objection to niche marketing as such," John Banzhaf said. "The objection is to picking the most vulnerable segments of society and trying to take advantage of their vulnerabilities. I don't think anybody would object if Philip Morris came out tomorrow with a cigarette they wanted to market to doctors or university professors or magazine writers."[44] The implication is that blacks and young women, especially poor or working-class blacks and young women, are not adequately equipped to make decisions about smoking. As NAACP executive director Benjamin Hooks observed in March 1990, the billboard defacers seemed to be saying "that white people have enough sense to read the signs and disregard them and black people don't."[45]

SAVE THE CHILDREN

While a protective attitude toward adult smokers is patronizing at best, it seems more reasonable for children, who are not supposed to smoke and may be less sophisticated in the way they respond to advertising (though the vulnerability of kids raised on *Mad* magazine, *Saturday Night Live,* and other lampooners of Madison Avenue has surely been exaggerated). Indeed, for three decades the debate over tobacco advertising has been driven largely by concerns about its influence on children. The industry's advertising code, the fairness-doctrine PSAs, the ban on TV and radio ads, and subsequent efforts to restrict or prohibit tobacco advertising can all be viewed as responses to anxiety about the "constant seduction" of children, decried by the PTA in 1964. In the 1990s tobacco's opponents found an emblem for that concern: a cartoon character named Joe Camel.

Introduced in 1988 with the slogan "smooth character," Joe Camel was a cartoon version of the dromedary (known as Old Joe) that has appeared on packages of Camel cigarettes since 1913. Print ads and billboards depicted Joe Camel shooting pool in a tuxedo, hanging out at a nightclub, playing in a blues band, and sitting on a motorcycle in a leather jacket and shades. He was cool, hip, and popular—in short, he was like a lot of other models in a lot of other cigarette ads, except that he was a cartoon animal instead of a flesh-and-blood human being. Even in that respect he was hardly revolutionary. In the 1870s and '80s, more than a century before the debut of Joe Camel, W. T. Blackwell & Co., manufacturer of Bull Durham smoking tobacco, ran newspaper ads throughout the country depicting the Durham Bull "in anthropomorphic situations, alternating between scenes in which the bull was jovial and boisterous and those where he was serious and determined."[46]

But Joe Camel, it is safe to say, generated more outrage than any other cartoon character in history. Critics of the ad campaign said the use of a cartoon was clearly designed to appeal to children. *Washington Post* columnist Courtland Milloy said that "packaging a cartoon camel as a 'smooth character' is as dangerous as putting rat poison in a candy wrapper."[47] In response to such criticism, R. J. Reynolds noted that Snoopy sells life insurance and the Pink Panther pitches fiberglass insulation, yet no one assumes those ads are aimed at kids.

The controversy intensified in 1991, when the *Journal of the American Medical Association* published three articles purporting to show that Joe Camel was indeed a menace to the youth of America. The heavily promoted studies generated an enormous amount of press coverage, under headlines such as CAMELS FOR KIDS (*Time*); I'D TODDLE A MILE FOR A CAMEL (*Newsweek*); JOE CAMEL IS ALSO PIED PIPER, RESEARCH FINDS (the *Wall Street Journal*); and STUDY: CAMEL CARTOON SENDS KIDS SMOKE SIGNALS (*Boston Herald*). Dozens of editorialists and columnists condemned Joe Camel, and many said he should be banned from advertising.

In March 1992 the Coalition on Smoking or Health asked the FTC to prohibit further use of the smooth character. Surgeon General Antonia Novello and the American Medical Association also called for an end to the campaign. In August 1993 the FTC's staff backed the coalition's petition, and a month later twenty-seven state attorneys general added their support. In June 1994, by a three-to-two vote, the FTC decided not to proceed against Joe, finding that the record did not show he had increased smoking among minors. (During the first five years of the campaign, in fact, teenage smoking actually declined, starting to rise only in 1993.[48]) In March 1997, after several members of Congress asked the FTC to reexamine the issue, the commission's staff again urged a ban, citing new evidence that R. J. Reynolds had targeted underage smokers. This time the commission, with two new members appointed by the Clinton administration, decided to seek an order instructing RJR not only to keep Joe out of children's sight but to conduct a "public education campaign" aimed at deterring underage smoking.

The two dissenting commissioners were not impressed by the new evidence, which failed to show that Joe Camel had actually encouraged kids to smoke. One wrote, "As was true three years ago, intuition and concern for children's health are not the equivalent of—and should not be substituted for—evidence sufficient to find reason to believe that there is a likely causal connection between the Joe Camel advertising campaign and smoking by children."[49] In any event, the FTC's action turned out to be doubly irrelevant. R. J. Reynolds, along with its competitors, agreed to stop using cartoon characters as part of the proposed nationwide tobacco settlement, and in July 1997 it announced that it was discontinuing the "smooth character" campaign, replacing it with one that made more subtle use of camels.

Although the *JAMA* articles were widely cited by Joe's enemies, including the FTC and President Clinton, they demonstrated much less than the uproar would lead one to believe. In the first study, researchers led by Paul M. Fischer, a professor of family medicine at the Medical College of Georgia, asked preschoolers to match brand logos to pictures of products. Over all, about half the kids correctly matched Joe Camel with a cigarette. Among the six-year-olds, the share was 91 percent, about the same as the percentage who correctly matched the Disney Channel logo to a picture of Mickey Mouse.[50] But recognizing Joe Camel is not tantamount to smoking, any more than recognizing the logos for Ford and Chevrolet (which most of the kids did) is tantamount to driving. The researchers seemed to assume that familiarity breeds affection, but this is not necessarily the case. A subsequent study published in the *Journal of Marketing* confirmed that recognition of Joe Camel rises with age and that most six-year-olds correctly associate him with cigarettes. Yet 85 percent of the kids in this study expressed a negative attitude toward cigarettes, and the dislike rose with both age and recognition ability. Among the six-year-olds, less than 4 percent expressed a positive attitude toward cigarettes.[51]

In the second *JAMA* study, Joseph R. DiFranza, a researcher at the University of Massachusetts Medical School, led a team that showed Joe Camel ads to samples of high school students and adults. They found that the teenagers were more likely than the adults, whose average age was about forty, to recognize Joe Camel, to recall the ads, and to evaluate them positively. Since R. J. Reynolds contended that the Joe Camel campaign was aimed at young adults, these results were hardly surprising. On the basis of such comparisons, it is impossible to distinguish between an ad aimed at sixteen-year-olds and an ad aimed at eighteen-year-olds (or twenty-one-year-olds). DiFranza et al.'s most striking claim was that the Joe Camel campaign had caused a huge shift in brand preferences. Using data from seven surveys conducted in three states between 1976 and 1988, they estimated that 0.5 percent of underage smokers preferred Camels before the campaign began. By comparison, 33 percent of the teenage smokers in their study, conducted during 1990 and 1991, said they smoked Camels—a *66-fold* increase. "Our data demonstrate that in just 3 years Camel's Old Joe cartoon character had an astounding influence on children's smoking behavior," the researchers wrote.[52] But neither the pre-1989 surveys nor the *JAMA* study used random samples of the national population, so it's doubtful that the results are representative of American teenagers in general.[53] Data from the CDC's Teenage Attitudes and Practices Survey, which does use a nationwide sample, suggest a much less dramatic shift toward Camels. In 1993, 13.3 percent of the TAPS respondents said they usually bought Camels, compared to 8.1 percent in 1989.[54]

The third *JAMA* article presented data from a 1990 California telephone survey. The researchers, led by John P. Pierce, head of the University of California at San Diego's Cancer Prevention and Control Program, reported that teenagers were more likely than adults to identify Marlboro or Camel as the most advertised brand. The survey also found that Marlboro's market share increased with age until twenty-four, when it started to decline gradually. Camel, on the other hand, was considerably more popular among teenagers than among young adults.[55] Comparing the California data to the results of a national survey conducted in 1986, Pierce et al. concluded that the market shares for both Marlboro and Camel had increased among adults (the 1986 survey did not include minors). Camel's increase was bigger, particularly among adults under the age of thirty (i.e., the segment R. J. Reynolds claimed to be targeting).[56]

Taken together, these studies suggest that (1) most children know Joe Camel has something to do with cigarettes and (2) the Joe Camel campaign helped increase the brand's market share, especially among young smokers. Since most smokers pick up the habit before they turn eighteen, it's plausible that the tobacco companies would take an interest in the brand choices of teenagers, as some internal documents suggest. In 1974, for example, Philip Morris hired the Roper Organization to interview young smokers about their brand choices, and more than a third of the 1,879 respondents were described as eighteen or younger.[57] In 1997, as part of an agreement settling twenty-two state lawsuits, the Liggett Group said tobacco companies have deliberately targeted underage smokers.

The other companies continued to deny that charge. R. J. Reynolds maintained that Joe Camel was aimed at eighteen-to-twenty-four-year-olds, although the company had no way of assuring that he would not also appeal to people younger than eighteen. In response, FDA commissioner David A. Kessler said, "Tell me how you design an advertising campaign that affects only eighteen-year-olds."[58] Which is sort of the point. If cigarette companies have to avoid any ad that might catch the eye or tickle the fancy of a sixteen-year-old, they might as well not advertise at all (which would suit Kessler fine). In any case, the important question is whether advertising encourages kids to smoke, not whether it steers them toward Camels instead of Marlboros.

In each of the Joe Camel studies, the researchers' conclusions (and the subsequent press coverage) went beyond what the data indicated. Fischer et al., whose comparison between Joe Camel and Mickey Mouse got the most attention, were relatively cautious: "Given the serious health consequences of smoking, the exposure of children to environ-mental tobacco advertising may represent an important health risk and should be studied further."[59] DiFranza et al. said, "A total ban of tobacco advertising and promotions, as part of an effort to protect children from the dangers of tobacco, can be based on sound scientific reasoning."[60] Pierce et al. flatly concluded that "cigarette advertising encourages youth to smoke and should be banned."[61] These are all statements of opinion that have little to do with what the studies actually showed.

Information that came to light in a California lawsuit suggests that at least some of the researchers may have prejudged the issue. In a letter he wrote to a coauthor before the research began, DiFranza complained that he had not been able to give reporters "proof that the tobacco com-panies [were] advertising to children." He wrote, "I can't point to any one piece of evidence as a smoking gun and say 'here, this proves it.' Well I have an idea for a project that will give us a couple of smoking guns to bring to the national media." He explained, "I am proposing a quick and easy project that should produce . . . evidence that RJR is going after kids with their Camel ads." Toward the end of the letter, he wrote, "There, the paper is all ready, now all we need is some data."[62]

BAN AID

Neither DiFranza's "smoking gun" nor the other studies provided any evidence about the impact of advertising on a teenager's propensity to smoke, which is the crux of the issue. When critics complain that adver-tising encourages people to smoke, the tobacco companies reply that it encourages smokers to buy particular brands. Strictly speaking, these claims are not mutually exclusive. In principle, advertising can promote an industry's overall sales as well as drum up business for a specific com-pany. An ad for a Compaq portable computer might encourage people to buy a Compaq (the company certainly hopes so), or it might get them thinking about laptops generally. But the tobacco companies argue that the U.S. market for cigarettes is mature, meaning that the product is universally familiar, like toothpaste or deodorant, and attempts to boost overall consumption are no longer cost-effective. Indeed, with smoking rates declining, the tobacco companies are fighting for pieces of

a shrinking pie. Tobacco's opponents say this trend makes cigarette manufacturers all the more desperate to maintain their profits; they need advertising like the Joe Camel campaign to attract replacements for smokers who quit or die.

Advocates of an advertising ban contend that brand competition does
not adequately explain the behavior of the tobacco companies. According to a widely cited article by Joe B. Tye, Kenneth Warner, and Stanton
A. Glantz, "A simple calculation shows that brand-switching, alone,
could never justify the enormous advertising and promotional expenditures of the tobacco companies." Tye et al. started with an estimate,
based on marketing research, that about 10 percent of smokers switch
brands each year. Then they calculated that the industry's spending on
advertising and promotion in 1983 amounted to nearly as much per
switcher as a typical smoker would have spent on cigarettes that year.
Furthermore, since each cigarette maker produces various brands, smokers who switch are not necessarily taking their business to another company. "Thus," the authors concluded, "advertising and promotion can
be considered economically rational only if they perform a defensive
function—retaining company brand loyalty that would otherwise be
lost to competitors who promote their products—of if they attract new
entrants to the smoking marketplace, or discourage smokers from quitting." If defending market share were the only aim, Tye et al. added, the
tobacco companies should support a ban on advertising and promotion,
which would eliminate the threat from competitors. If, on the other
hand, "advertising and promotion increase cigarette consumption, then
less than two million new or retained smokers—5.5 percent of smokers
who start each year or try to quit (most failing)—alone would justify the
annual promotional expenditure."[63]

There are several flaws in this argument. To begin with, the estimate
for the number of brand switchers does not include people who usually
smoke, say, Benson & Hedges but occasionally smoke Camels. Based on
its own marketing surveys, R. J. Reynolds reports that about 70 percent
of smokers have a second-choice brand that they smoke now and then.
About 25 percent regularly buy more than one brand each month.[64]
Even smokers who don't have a second favorite sometimes try other
brands because of coupons, premiums, and promotional offers. Further-

more, when estimating the value of brand switchers, Tye et al. did not take into account the continuing revenue from a new customer; they considered only the money he spends on cigarettes in one year. By contrast, when they estimated the gain from getting someone to start smoking or keeping a smoker who otherwise would have quit, they used the net present value of the additional profit over a twenty-year period, which they calculated as $1,085, more than three times a year's revenue. Most important, Tye et al. did not acknowledge that tobacco companies could be competing for new smokers, trying to build brand loyalty at an early age, without actually creating them.

Tye et al. considered the industry's opposition to an advertising ban prima facie evidence that tobacco advertising increases total consumption. But the tobacco companies might also have opposed a ban because it would help delegitimize the industry, opening the way to other kinds of regulation and defeats in product liability suits. Furthermore, a company's attitude toward restrictions on advertising (and brand competition in general) depends on its market position. Philip Morris and R. J. Reynolds, the market leaders, might well be less worried about an advertising ban than their competitors. Tellingly, these were the companies that spearheaded the settlement talks and included dramatic restrictions on advertising and promotion in their opening offer.

In any case, it is not clearly foolish for the tobacco companies to spend so much money on advertising and promotion, even without the hope of market expansion. More evidence is necessary to support the claim that tobacco advertising increases consumption. Broadly speaking, there are three ways of investigating this issue. You can look at the historical relationship between changes in advertising and changes in smoking. You can compare smoking trends in places with different levels of advertising. And you can ask people questions in the hope that their answers will suggest how advertising influences attitudes and behavior. None of these approaches has yielded consistent or definitive results. Each has limitations that leave plenty of room for interpretation. The state of the research was aptly, if unintentionally, summed up by the title of an article making the case for a causal link: "The Evidence Is There for Those Who Wish to See It."[65]

Some analyses of historical data have found a small, statistically significant association between increases in advertising and increases in smoking; others have not. In an overview of the evidence, Michael Schudson, professor of communication and sociology at the University of California at San Diego, writes, "In terms of a general relationship between cigarette advertising and cigarette smoking, the available econometric evidence is equivocal and the kind of materials available to produce the evidence leave much to be desired."[66] This sort of research is open to challenge on technical grounds, such as the time period chosen and the methods for measuring advertising and consumption. There is also the possibility that advertising goes up in response to a rise in consumption, rather than the reverse. Industry critics often cite the increases in smoking by women that occurred in the 1920s and the late '60s to early '70s as evidence of advertising's power. "Yet in both cases," Schudson notes, "the advertising campaign followed rather than preceded the behavior it supposedly engendered."[67] In other words, the tobacco companies changed their marketing in response to a trend that was already under way.

International comparisons have also produced mixed results. There is no consistent relationship between restrictions on advertising and smoking rates among adults or children. In some countries where advertising is severely restricted, such as Sweden, smoking rates are relatively low. In others, such as Norway, they are relatively high. Sometimes smoking drops after advertising is banned; sometimes it doesn't. It is hard to say what such findings mean. Countries where smoking is already declining may be more intolerant of the habit and therefore more likely to ban advertising. Alternatively, a rise in smoking might help build support for a ban. Furthermore, advertising bans are typically accompanied by other measures, such as tobacco tax increases and restrictions on smoking in public, that could be expected to reduce cigarette purchases. The one conclusion it seems safe to draw is that many factors other than advertising affect tobacco consumption.

The best way to resolve the issue of advertising's impact on smoking would be to conduct a controlled experiment: Take two groups of randomly selected babies; expose one to cigarette advertising but otherwise treat them identically. After eighteen years or so, compare smoking rates. Since such a study would be impractical, social scientists have had to make do with less tidy methods, generally involving interviews, questionnaires, or survey data. This kind of research indicates that the most important factors influencing whether teenagers will smoke are the behavior of their peers, their perceptions of the risks and benefits of smoking, and the presence of smokers in their home. Exposure to advertising does not independently predict the decision to smoke, and smokers themselves rarely cite advertising as an important influence on their behavior.

Critics of the industry have been quick to seize upon studies indicating that teenage smokers disproportionately prefer the most advertised cigarette brands. But such research suggests only that advertising has an impact on brand preferences, which the tobacco companies have conceded all along. Several studies have found that teenagers who smoke (or who say they might) are more apt to recall cigarette advertising and to view it favorably. Such findings do not necessarily mean that advertising makes adolescents more likely to smoke. It is just as plausible to suppose that teenagers pay more attention to cigarette ads after they start smoking or that teenagers who are inclined to smoke for other reasons are also more likely to have a positive view of cigarette ads.

In reporting on research in this area, the mainstream press tends to ignore such alternative interpretations. Consider the coverage received by a 1995 study published in the *Journal of the National Cancer Institute*. The study, coauthored by John Pierce, found that teenagers who scored high on a "receptivity" index—which included "recognition of advertising messages, having a favorite advertisement, naming a brand [they] might buy, owning a tobacco-related promotional item, and willingness to use a tobacco-related promotional item"—were more likely to say they could not rule out smoking in the near future. Such "receptivity" was more strongly associated with an inclination to smoke than was smoking among parents and peers.[68] According to the *New York Times,* this meant that "tobacco advertising is a stronger factor than peer pressure in encouraging children under 18 to smoke."[69] Similarly, the *Boston Globe* reported that the study showed "cigarette advertising has more influence on whether adolescents later start smoking than does having friends or family members who smoke."[70] The Associated Press went even further: "Of all the influences that can draw children into a lifelong habit of smoking, cigarette advertising is the most persuasive."[71] In reality, the study showed only that kids who like smoking-related messages and merchandise are more receptive to the idea of smoking—not exactly a startling finding.

Overall, the evidence that advertising plays an important role in getting people to smoke is not very convincing. In 1991 the economist Thomas Schelling, former director of Harvard's Institute for the Study of Smoking Behavior and Policy, said: "I've never seen a genuine study of the subject. . . . Most of the discussion that I hear—even the serious discussion—is about as profound as saying, 'If I were a teenage black girl, that ad would make me smoke.' I just find it altogether unpersuasive. . . . I've been very skeptical that advertising is important in either getting people to smoke or keeping people smoking. It's primarily brand competition."[72] The 1989 surgeon general's report conceded that "there is no scientifically rigorous study available to the public that provides a definitive answer to the basic question of whether advertising and promotion increase the level of tobacco consumption. Given the complexity of the issue, none is likely to be forthcoming in the forseeable future."[73] The 1994 surgeon general's report, which focused on underage smoking, also acknowledged the "lack of definitive literature."[74]

This does not mean that tobacco advertising has no impact at all on the level of consumption. The 1989 surgeon general's report concluded that while "the extent of the influence of advertising and promotion on the level of consumption is unknown and possibly unknowable," the weight of the evidence "makes it more likely than not that advertising and promotional activities do stimulate cigarette consumption."[75] The 1994 report concluded, on the basis of suggestive evidence, that "cigarette advertising appears to increase young people's risk of smoking."[76] Similarly, Michael Schudson—who says "advertising typically attempts little and achieves still less"—argues that cigarette advertising "normally has only slight effect in persuading people to change their attitudes or behaviors." But he adds, "It is reasonable to believe that some teens become smokers or become smokers earlier or become smokers with less guilt or become heavier smokers because of advertising."[77]

Serious critics of tobacco advertising, including Schudson, Warner, and Whelan, do not subscribe to a simple stimulus-and-response theory in which kids exposed to Joe Camel automatically become smokers. They believe the effects of advertising are subtle and indirect. They argue, for example, that the very existence of cigarette ads suggests that "it really couldn't be all that bad, or they wouldn't be allowed to advertise, that it's really OK, that it's not like cocaine."[78] They say advertising imagery reinforces the notion, communicated by peers and other role models, that smoking is cool. They say dependence on advertising revenue from tobacco companies discourages magazines from running articles about the health consequences of smoking.[79] They do not claim such effects are sufficient, by themselves, to make people smoke. Rather, they argue that at the margin—say, for an ambivalent teenager whose friends smoke—the influence of advertising may be decisive.

Stated this way, the hypothesis that tobacco advertising increases consumption is impossible to falsify. "Fundamentally," observes Jean J. Boddewyn, a professor of marketing at Baruch College, "one cannot prove that advertising does *not* cause or influence smoking, because one cannot scientifically prove a negative."[80] So despite the lack of evidence that advertising has a substantial impact on smoking rates, tobacco's opponents can argue that we should play it safe and ban the ads—just in case. The problem with this line of reasoning is that banning tobacco advertising can be considered erring on the side of caution only if we attach little or no value to freedom of speech. Especially given the state of the evidence, it is hard to square an advertising ban with a presumption against censorship.

SPEECH DEFECTS

Many of tobacco's opponents say cigarette manufacturers do not deserve a presumption against censorship. In his book *Merchants of Death,* journalist Larry C. White accuses the tobacco companies of "hiding behind the First Amendment," undermining its "prestige" by using it as "a license to lie."[81] In a *Washington Monthly* article entitled "Has the ACLU Lost Its Mind?" sociologist Amitai Etzioni criticizes the civil liberties group for defending the free speech rights of tobacco companies. By handling such "truly bizarre cases," he says, the ACLU "is undermining its reputation and cheapening free speech."[82] One could just as easily

argue that opposition to censorship of white supremacists or commu-
nists or animal rights activists cheapens free speech and undermines the
prestige of the First Amendment. Consistent application is the essence
of civil liberties. Free speech does not mean much if it applies only to
popular speakers saying noncontroversial things.

In general, the Constitution protects speech, no matter how hateful,
destructive, or wrongheaded. But proponents of a ban on tobacco advertising see a loophole: The Supreme Court has repeatedly ruled that
"commercial" speech merits less protection under the First Amendment
than other kinds of speech. The ban on broadcast advertising of cigarettes passed muster with the courts largely because of this distinction.
In the 1942 case *Valentine v. Chrestensen,* the Supreme Court unanimously declared that "the Constitution imposes no . . . restraint on government as respects purely commercial advertising."[83] The four-page
opinion cited no authority and offered no explanation for this assertion,
and the Court has since backed away from it. In the 1976 case *Virginia
State Board of Pharmacy v. Virginia Citizens Consumer Council,* the
Court decided that commercial speech is protected by the First Amendment after all, though to a lesser degree than other speech.[84] The Court
explained what this meant in the 1980 case *Central Hudson Gas & Electric Corp. v. Public Service Commission:* When commercial speech deals
with legal activity and is not misleading, regulation will be upheld only
if (1) it serves a substantial government interest, (2) it directly advances
that interest, and (3) it is no more extensive than necessary.[85]

As we've seen, some critics argue that image-oriented tobacco advertising is inherently misleading. But the courts are not likely to adopt this
position, since it could be applied to many other industries. Nor are
they likely to buy the argument, advanced by President Clinton and
White House counsel Abner Mikva in defense of the FDA's regulations,
that cigarette ads are proposing an unlawful activity because they are targeting children. Without a confession from the tobacco companies, that
contention will be difficult to prove. And given the weak evidence for a
causal link between advertising and underage smoking, it is hard to see
how a ban can be said to directly advance a legitimate government interest. Finally, less extensive alternatives, such as stricter enforcement of the
laws against cigarette sales to minors, are clearly available.

Supporters of a ban on tobacco advertising and promotion drew hope from the 1986 case *Posadas de Puerto Rico Associates v. Tourism Company of Puerto Rico*. In *Posadas* the Supreme Court held that since Puerto Rico's legislature had the authority to ban gambling outright, it also had the authority to ban casino advertising within the common-wealth.[86] On its face, this five-to-four decision seemed to give legislatures permission to ban the advertising of any activity that is not itself constitutionally protected. But Court watchers cautioned against such an interpretation. Philip B. Kurland, professor of law at the University of Chicago, noted that it was "inconsistent with everything that has gone before."[87]

In subsequent cases the Court has not pursued the implications of *Posadas*. To the contrary, it has closely scrutinized restrictions on com-mercial speech. In 1993, by a six-to-three vote, the Court overturned Cincinnati's ban on vending machines dispensing free publications con-sisting entirely of advertisements.[88] In 1995 the Court unanimously ruled that a federal regulation barring brewers from listing alcohol con-tent on their labels violated the First Amendment.[89] In 1996 the Court unanimously overturned a Rhode Island ban on the advertising of liquor prices, and eight justices disavowed the reasoning in *Posadas*.[90] The trend toward greater protection of commercial speech does not bode well for a complete ban on tobacco advertising and promotion, or even for restrictions similar to those proposed by the FDA, which is one rea-son industry concessions in this area played such an important role in the settlement talks.

Aside from the issue of how a ban would fare under current prece-dents, there is reason to question the distinction at the heart of the com-mercial speech doctrine. As Alex Kozinski, a judge on the U.S. Court of Appeals for the Ninth Circuit, and attorney Stuart Banner noted in a 1990 *Virginia Law Review* article, "the Supreme Court plucked the commercial speech doctrine out of thin air." The distinction between commercial speech and fully protected speech has never been clearly ex-plained, let alone justified. What makes nude dancing or a Jackie Collins novel more worthy of protection than a Coca-Cola commercial? All three are intended to make money, and all three (arguably) have artistic content. Kozinski and Banner argue persuasively that the second-class status of so-called commercial speech threatens to undermine protection of artistic, political, and scientific expression. The commercial speech doctrine "gives government a powerful weapon to suppress or control speech by classifying it as merely commercial. If you think carefully enough, you can find a commercial aspect to almost any first amendment case."[91]

Consider advertorials: For more than forty years the tobacco companies have been running ads that fall into the gray zone between commercial and noncommercial speech. In 1954 they argued that the evidence concerning the health consequences of smoking was inconclusive and announced the formation of the Tobacco Industry Research Committee. In 1967 the Tobacco Institute reprinted an editorial from *Barron's* condemning the FCC's extension of the fairness doctrine to cigarette commercials. In 1984 and 1985 R. J. Reynolds ran a series of ads on various topics, including the health consequences of smoking and relations between smokers and nonsmokers. In 1986 Philip Morris announced a $150,000 prize for the best essay defending the right to advertise. In recent years RJR and Philip Morris have run ads questioning the case against secondhand smoke, emphasizing that cigarettes should not be sold to minors, and attacking the Clinton administration's proposed regulations.[92] Such advertisements take positions on scientific and political issues, but they also serve a commercial interest. Do they merit full First Amendment protection?

The issue is not simply speculative. A 1984 RJR ad claiming it was "far from the truth" that "the case against smoking is closed" prompted a yearlong FTC investigation before the commission's attorneys decided not to pursue the case. The FTC launched another investigation in 1985, after RJR ran an ad suggesting that a large epidemiological study had failed to provide evidence of a link between smoking and heart disease. The study, known as the Multiple Risk Factor Intervention Trial (MR FIT), was designed to assess the impact of several measures aimed at reducing risk factors for disease, including smoking. After ten years, the researchers did not find a statistically significant difference in death rates between subjects in the experimental group, who had been urged to quit smoking, and subjects in the control group. Nevertheless, the rate of heart disease was significantly lower among the subjects who had quit smoking than it was among those who continued to smoke, a fact the RJR ad omitted.

In June 1986 the FTC issued a formal complaint against RJR, charging that the ad was misleading. The lone dissenter, chairman Daniel Oliver, said, "It is valuable for the public to hear all sides of an issue, and I am concerned about taking any action that may inhibit free expression of views that might not be popular [with] government regulators."[93] RJR, represented by First Amendment attorney Floyd Abrams, appealed to an administrative law judge, who agreed with Oliver, finding that the ad was noncommercial speech and dismissing the complaint. In April 1988 the commission reversed that ruling and revived the complaint. The matter was ultimately settled in October 1989, when RJR promised "not to misrepresent in future advertisements" the results of research on the health effects of smoking.[94]

These skirmishes illustrate how the commercial speech doctrine can be used to stifle debate. There was no issue of consumer fraud here; RJR was not selling a product under false pretenses. It was making a case for a particular view of the evidence on smoking and health. To be sure, the case was not very convincing. But in a free society, the government is not supposed to decide such matters. The proper response to misleading statements and weak arguments is correction and counterargument, not censorship.

That point was recognized by Circuit Judge J. Skelly Wright when he dissented from the 1971 ruling that upheld the ban on broadcast advertising of cigarettes. Wright said, "The Government is emphatically not entitled to monopolize the debate or to suppress the expression of opposing points of view on the electronic media by making such expression a criminal offense." Noting the "clear and present danger" exception to the First Amendment, he added, "The state can stop speech in order to protect the innocent bystander, but it cannot impose silence merely because it fears that people will be convinced by what they hear and thereby harm themselves. . . . At the very core of the First Amendment is the notion that people are capable of making up their own minds about what is good for them and that they can think their own thoughts so long as they do not in some manner interfere with the rights of others."[95]

Two decades later, Quebec Superior Court Justice Jean-Jude Chabot
expressed a similar concern when he overturned Canada's ban on cigarette advertising, a decision upheld by the Canadian Supreme Court in
1995. "The question," Chabot wrote, "is whether the State has the
right, through the elimination of all competing messages, to impose on
its citizens its view and only its view of what is right in an attempt to
mould their thoughts and behavior."[96] He concluded that "this form of
paternalism or totalitarianism is unacceptable in a free and democratic
society."[97]

TALKING BACK

In contrast with an advertising ban, the anti-smoking public service announcements of the late '60s and early '70s seem at first glance to be a
classic example of countering speech with more speech. But these ads
achieved high visibility because of a government edict that would have
been clearly unconstitutional had it been applied to newspapers or magazines. When it upheld the fairness doctrine in 1969, the Supreme
Court justified this disparity by citing the "scarcity of broadcast frequen-
cies."[98] This argument never made much sense—all resources, including
newsprint, ink, and printing presses, are "scarce" in economic terms—
and it became increasingly unconvincing over the years. With the multi-
plication of broadcast outlets, most towns had more local radio and TV
stations than newspapers. The rise of cable TV further increased the
number of options available and raised the ticklish question of why a
signal transmitted over a wire should receive more constitutional protection than the same signal broadcast over the airwaves.

In 1987 these contradictions, coupled with the realization that the
burdens imposed by the fairness doctrine were actually discouraging discussion of controversial issues, led the FCC to formally abandon the
policy. That decision has been upheld by the federal courts, and attempts to enact a statutory version of the fairness doctrine have repeatedly failed. The idea of mandating balance nevertheless remained popular among anti-smoking activists. In 1994 opponents of a California
ballot initiative backed by the tobacco industry asked the FCC to rein-
state the doctrine and require stations that aired commercials supporting

the proposition to offer free rebuttal time. Some anti-smokers would go further than the fairness doctrine ever did. In an article published about six months before the FCC scrapped the doctrine, Brian R. Flay, a public health researcher at the University of Southern California, suggested "extending the scope of the Fairness Doctrine, or something like it, to cover all forms and forums of the advertising and promotion of cigarettes."[99] In 1994 Ahron Leichtman, executive director of Citizens for a Tobacco-Free Society, said the government should "require newspapers and magazines which accept tobacco ads to provide equal space for anti-smoking groups to run pro-health messages about smoking."[100] The Supreme Court has explicitly rejected the idea of applying a "right of reply" to the print media, finding that the First Amendment forbids government orders to publish as well as orders not to publish.[101]

Government mandates are not the only way to communicate anti-smoking messages. In addition to TV and radio spots, private organizations have long produced print ads, posters, and educational materials aimed at discouraging smoking. The early messages were pretty mild by today's standards. A 1964 American Heart Association poster simply warned, WHERE THERE'S SMOKE . . . THERE'S DANGER FROM HEART DISEASE. In a 1969 AHA poster, a drawing of a doctor was accompanied by the observation/admonition THEY QUIT SMOKING/WHY DON'T YOU?/MOST DOCTORS WHO USED TO SMOKE HAVE STOPPED. Another poster from the same year superimposed the words *emphysema, bronchitis, cancer,* and *heart disease* over a cloud of cigarette smoke. A third featured a drawing of a man and a boy smoking, next to the headline LIKE FATHER, LIKE SON. During the '70s and '80s the AHA produced a series of THANKS FOR NOT SMOKING signs featuring cute cartoons. It also distributed some fairly tough posters, illustrated with photographs, that warned about setting a bad example for children, about the effects of smoking during pregnancy, and about the impact of a smoker's early death on his family.

In the tradition of the "coughing cowboys" commercial, anti-smoking groups continue to produce satires of cigarette advertising. The official goal of Doctors Ought to Care, founded in 1977 by Miami (now Houston) physician Alan Blum, is to "laugh the pushers out of town." Accordingly, DOC has sponsored a Barfboro Barfing Team van that follows the Marlboro Adventure Team van around the country, providing mobile counteradvertising. DOC's line of Barfboro products includes posters, bumper stickers, lapel pins, T-shirts, and (of course) barf bags imprinted with the message DOES CIGARETTE ADVERTISING MAKE YOU SICK? US TOO! DOC also mocks Newport (Newcorpse), Red Man chewing tobacco (Dead Man Chew), and Virginia Slims (Emphysema Slims: "You've coughed up long enough, baby"). Says Blum, "When you can get people to lighten up and laugh at Marlboro, and ridicule the whole nature of the industry—don't take it so damned seriously—I think you've got a much better way to go about it than the moral outrage approach. The Devil can't stand to be mocked."[102]

Blum, who called the fuss about cartoon characters in cigarette ads "flogging a dead camel," believes in fighting advertising with advertising. "As long as I have the right to counteradvertise," he says, "it seems to me that's pretty good. I used to believe we should ban [tobacco advertising], but as much as I might find some aspects of that appealing, I found very early on that when you have the opportunity to counter something that's visible, it works a lot better." DOC pays to have its ads displayed on park benches, on billboards, and in publications. In 1990, when R. J. Reynolds was planning to test-market Dakota cigarettes in Houston, where DOC is based, Blum created an ad that showed the new brand accompanied by the slogan "Dakota . . . Da Cough . . . Da Cancer . . . Da Coffin."[103]

Joseph Cherner, the New York bond trader who left his job at Kidder, Peabody to found SmokeFree Educational Services, is also fond of hard-hitting anti-smoking ads. Some of the winning entries in his anti-smoking poster contests have appeared on subways and taxis. One of the ads, created by a fifth-grader, shows a skeleton in a cowboy hat riding a horse through a graveyard, under the headline COME TO WHERE THE CANCER IS. A simplified and more polished version of the same concept, showing a smoking skeleton in a red shirt and white cowboy hat on a blue background between the words CANCER COUNTRY, appears on cabs all over Manhattan. Another ad, designed by a high school senior, features a drawing of a wrinkled, skeletal woman with red eyes, thinning hair, and yellow teeth and fingernails, clutching a burning cigarette. Above the picture are the words VIRGINIA SLIME. Blood drips from the edges of the drawing onto the slogan below: YOU'VE COME THE WRONG WAY, BABY!

In contrast to such private efforts, which are funded by voluntary contributions, the tobacco settlement proposal said the cigarette companies (and, ultimately, their customers) would pick up the tab for a $500-million-a-year anti-smoking campaign. Several states already compel smokers to pay for their own vilification. California, where a 1988 ballot initiative known as Proposition 99 raised the tax on each pack of cigarettes by twenty-five cents and set aside a portion of the new revenue for anti-smoking programs, is the most conspicuous example. Although Proposition 99 said nothing about an advertising campaign, the money it raised has paid for one of the largest anti-smoking media efforts in history. Public health researchers credit the campaign, which had spent about $100 million by 1997, with encouraging a substantial decline in smoking among Californians. Per capita cigarette consumption in California dropped about 35 percent between 1988 and 1994, compared to about 19 percent nationwide.[104]

Cigarette consumption was falling faster in California even before passage of Proposition 99, but the trend accelerated after 1988. Factors other than the mass-media campaign, such as the tax hike and increasing restrictions on smoking outside the home, must have contributed to the change, which began before the first ads appeared. The tax hike went into effect in January 1989, and total cigarette consumption fell sharply that year, by about 14 percent. The ad campaign began in April 1990, and consumption that year actually rose by about 1 percent. It dropped about 7 percent in 1991 but less than 2 percent in 1992, when the ads were interrupted because of a funding dispute. Consumption fell 2.4 percent in 1993 and 14.5 percent in 1994, when the cigarette tax was raised by another two cents a pack to fund breast cancer research.[105] Meanwhile, smoking among California teenagers was flat until 1993, when it began rising, following a national trend.[106] Despite uncertainty about the impact of the ad campaign, anti-smoking activists consider it a major success, and it has been imitated by Massachusetts and Arizona.

In the Proposition 99 ads, smokers come across as unattractive and insensitive, if not criminally negligent. One TV spot shows a man smoking in the presence of his pregnant wife. As she begins coughing, expelling plumes of smoke, the man puffs on, oblivious, while the camera zooms in on his wife's bulging abdomen. The ad closes with the line "Smokers aren't the only ones who smoke." Another ad follows a smoker on a typical day, counting the people he exposes to secondhand smoke: thirty-seven bystanders, including his wife and daughter, who "will die a little, because they were forced to breathe the smoke from his cigarette." An ad aimed at a younger audience shows a teenager in a gas mask standing in a smoky rest room. He asks another kid whether a bulldog or a smoker has worse breath. The dog's breath, it turns out, is "slightly less putrid."

The ads are even harder on the cigarette companies. One TV spot shows a group of executives in a smoke-filled room. The man running the meeting says, "We need more cigarette smokers, pure and simple. Every day, two thousand Americans stop smoking, and another eleven hundred also quit. Actually, technically, they die. That means that this business needs three thousand fresh, new volunteers every day. So forget about all that heart disease, cancer, emphysema, stroke stuff. We're not in this business for our health." The scene fades out to the sound of sinister laughter.

Another ad prompted R. J. Reynolds to threaten a defamation suit, leading several California stations to stop running it. The spot shows tobacco company executives, including RJR CEO James W. Johnston, testifying before Congress in April 1994. First we see them being sworn in. Then we see two of them denying that nicotine is addictive, while in the background the words "under oath" are repeated again and again. "Now the tobacco industry is trying to tell us that secondhand smoke isn't dangerous," says the announcer. A question appears on the screen: "Do they think we're stupid?" In a letter to S. Kimberly Belshe, director of the California Department of Health Services, RJR's lawyers argued that playing the phrase "under oath" in the background implied that Johnston was lying. In response, Belshe maintained that "the issue of the ads is not the veracity of any individual. The issue of the ads is the credibility of the tobacco industry."[107]

Ads unveiled in 1997 use similar themes. One TV spot shows cowboys herding children into a cattle pen "as a metaphor for manipulative tobacco industry marketing practices." Another shows cigarettes raining down on children in a playground while an adult male voice explains, "We have to sell cigarettes to your kids." It's designed to make the point that "even while playing, children are bombarded by tobacco and pro-tobacco imagery."[108]

These anti-industry ads go well beyond informing people about the hazards of smoking. They seek to shape public attitudes toward the to-bacco companies and tobacco control. Writing in *Public Health Reports,* Lori Dorfman and Lawrence Wallack, public health researchers at the University of California at Berkeley, note that the TV spot depicting a behind-the-scenes strategy session "struck directly at the tobacco indus-try. The message was that the industry itself is evil, out to kill for profit. It tried to shift the level of discussion from the actions of smokers to the actions of corporate executives. Rather than questioning why people do not quit smoking, it questioned why such a deadly product is so widely marketed." Dorfman and Wallack also cite a California billboard bear-ing the message WARNING: THE TOBACCO INDUSTRY IS NOT YOUR FRIEND, printed to resemble the health warning on cigarette packages. "The target audience here," they note, "was the wider society and public opinion about the questionable acceptability of the tobacco industry doing business at all."[109] This is also the approach taken by the National Center for Tobacco-Free Kids, which has run ads intended to "delegit-imize the tobacco industry" and "sway public opinion toward the to-bacco control effort."[110]

Dorfman and Wallack praise this strategy, arguing that true counter-ads "challenge the dominant view that public health problems reflect personal habits" and that "it is political action and attitudes rather than personal behavior on which counter-ads are focused." They consider such ads a natural outgrowth of the public health mission. "A public health perspective on alcohol, tobacco, and other drug problems de-mands a shift in emphasis from personal habits to social conditions," they explain. "The task for public health advocates who focus on social conditions is to reassign part of the responsibility for health problems to industry and other institutions that shape the social and physical envi-ronment. . . . This is a formidable challenge in a society in which the ethic of individualism has elevated business and industry to a privileged position."[111]

We've come a long way from "If you haven't smoked, don't start. If you do smoke, quit." In the 1960s, opponents of smoking criticized the use of cowboys, the classic symbol of American individualism, to sell cigarettes. Today they criticize individualism itself, because it implies that people are responsible for their own behavior. The coughing cowboy has been replaced by the laughing merchant of death.

Chapter 4

VICE CHARGE

*I hope they price them out of my range, because I'm really wanting
to stop.*

—Kentucky smoker on the 1990 cigarette tax increase

I SAID, 'NO *NEW* TAXES'

The single most effective anti-smoking measure ever enacted by Congress was not intended to reduce smoking. It was intended to reduce the federal deficit. The Tax Equity and Fiscal Responsibility Act of 1982 was a compromise in which the Reagan administration agreed to tax hikes in exchange for substantial cuts in domestic spending. The spending cuts never quite materialized, but the tax hikes were felt immediately. Among other things, TEFRA doubled the federal excise tax on cigarettes, from eight to sixteen cents a pack, as of January 1, 1983. Around the same time, the cigarette companies, recognizing that smokers were already expecting to pay more, repeatedly raised wholesale prices, compounding the impact of the tax increase. Per capita cigarette consumption fell 6.7 percent that year, the biggest drop since 1932.[1]

The tax hike, which brought in an additional $1.5 billion or so a year, was originally scheduled to expire in October 1985.[2] But the deficit continued to grow, despite many expressions of concern and resolutions to do something about it. "By the end of 1982," writes David Stockman, Reagan's first budget director, "the fiscal situation was an utter, mind-numbing catastrophe."[3] Determined to be fiscally responsible, Congress repeatedly extended the temporary tax increase, making it permanent in 1986.

The fact that Congress originally set an expiration date, observed health economist Kenneth Warner, demonstrated that the motivation for the eight-cent increase was "fiscal exigency and not public health." But tobacco's opponents recognized the opportunity to combine increased revenue with reductions in smoking—"Doing Good by Doing Well," as Warner put it.[4] In a February 1982 op-ed piece, Michael F. Jacobson, executive director of the Center for Science in the Public Interest, said tobacco and alcohol "are blamed for tens of thousands of deaths each year, and higher taxes would reduce this toll." Noting that the real value of the federal tax on cigarettes had declined by about 70 percent in the thirty-one years since it had last been raised, he argued that a higher tax would "both promote health and be politically acceptable."[5] After the tax hike went into effect, tobacco's opponents urged Congress not to let it lapse. "It's one tax that's certifiably good for our health," enthused syndicated columnist Ellen Goodman.[6] The *New York Times* recommended another eight-cent increase, calling it "poetic justice" and "a small payback . . . for what the cigarette habit costs government each year."[7]

The *Times* got its wish in 1990 when George Bush abandoned his "no new taxes" pledge. David Stockman had argued that raising excise taxes was "not inconsistent with the supply-side idea of restoring *income* tax incentives for production, savings, investment, and entrepreneurial activity."[8] Thus, Stockman reasoned, Reagan could accept an increase in the cigarette levy without violating the spirit of his promise to cut taxes. But Bush's pledge did not seem to leave any wiggle room. During the campaign he had written a letter to North Carolina Governor James Martin that said, "I will not raise taxes, period," specifically adding that he was "opposed to any increase in excise taxes, including those on tobacco or cigarettes."[9] At his January 1989 confirmation hearings, Bush budget director Richard Darman had explicitly ruled out excise tax increases, since they would fail the "duck test": "If it looks like a duck and walks like a duck and quacks like a duck, it is a duck."[10]

But that fall the Bush administration went duck hunting. After the *Wall Street Journal* reported that a Treasury Department task force was considering higher taxes on cigarettes, Tobacco Institute vice president

Walker Merryman expressed confidence that Bush would keep his promise.[11] Seven months later, the president announced that "the size of the deficit problem and the need for a package that can be enacted" required, among other things, "tax revenue increases."[12] Congress and the White House ultimately agreed on $134 billion in new revenue over five years, including about $6 billion from two four-cent hikes in the cigarette tax, taking effect in 1991 and 1993.[13]

It probably wouldn't have helped him win reelection, but Bush could have tried to explain away the increase in the cigarette levy by noting that he had promised "no *new* taxes." In the United States, tobacco taxes are nearly as old as the republic. Since the days of James I and Cardinal Richelieu, governments have recognized tobacco as a reliable source of income, and the record suggests that war is just as good for tobacco taxes as it is for tobacco consumption. Congress imposed a tax on snuff in the 1790s, eliminated it in 1804, and brought it back briefly in 1814 to help finance the War of 1812. The Civil War revived federal tobacco taxes, including a cigarette tax, and they've been with us ever since. In 1865, facing a huge war debt, Congress tripled the tobacco tax from eleven to thirty-three cents a pound, unintentionally prompting a sharp drop in per capita tobacco consumption, which fell from 1.3 pounds to 1 pound during the next three years.[14] The cigarette tax went up temporarily during the Spanish-American War and permanently during World War I, World War II, and the Korean War, reaching eight cents a pack in 1951. In 1964 Wisconsin Senator Gaylord Nelson, taking a cue from history, suggested a five-cent increase to help finance Lyndon Johnson's War on Poverty.[15] But apparently a metaphorical war just didn't rate another hike, and the tax remained at 8 cents until the Reagan-Bush double whammy.

Spread over three years, the second eight-cent increase did not have a noticeable impact on cigarette consumption. That fact did not discourage anti-smokers who had come to view the excise tax as a public health tool; they simply believed that bigger increases were necessary. In 1982 Michael Jacobson had recommended a tripling of the cigarette tax, from eight to twenty-four cents, a level it did not reach for more than a decade.[16] In 1989, the *New York Times* urged an increase in the neighborhood of twenty cents, which it said would mean half a million fewer smokers.[17] By 1993, when the Clinton administration was floating the idea of raising the cigarette tax to help pay for its health care plan, the proposals had become even more ambitious. Anti-smoking groups such as the American Medical Association and the Coalition on Smoking or Health endorsed a *ninefold* hike, from twenty-four cents to $2.24. Such an increase would have more than doubled the price of a pack of cigarettes, something guaranteed to get the attention of smokers.

In a March 1993 poll by Lou Harris and Associates, 74 percent of the respondents (roughly the nonsmoking proportion of the population) supported a one-dollar cigarette tax hike to pay for health care reform. The idea was politically astute, tying an increase in the tax on a product used by a minority of voters to the highly popular goal of universal health coverage. And it seemed to make a rough kind of sense, since cigarettes contribute to disease. The combination was so potent, *National Journal* reported in April 1993, that "even Rep. Charlie Rose, D.-N.C., sometimes known as 'Mr. Tobacco,' realizes that some tax increase is inevitable." Anti-smoking activists at the Advocacy Institute were cocky enough to write a ditty about their impending victory, sung to the tune of "The Monster Mash":[18]

> We were working on the bill late one night
> Had an idea that would cause a fright
> Blaring through the halls came the sound of a sax
> Bill playing the tune of the monster tax
> The monster tax
> (We did the tax)
> It was a monster tax
> (The monster tax)
> The idea spread by fax
> (We did the tax)
> Opposed by industry hacks
> (The monster tax)
> We'll give ol' Joe the ax!

After months of speculation, in October 1993 President Clinton called for a seventy-five-cent increase—huge by historical standards but modest compared to some of the numbers that had been tossed around (which may have been the whole idea). The tobacco companies campaigned aggressively against the tax hike, arguing that it would hit the poor hardest, that it would contribute to black-market activity, and that it would eliminate hundreds of thousands of jobs. In March 1994 some eighteen thousand tobacco farmers and industry employees attended a protest rally outside the White House organized by several cigarette makers, which closed down their factories and bused in their workers for the occasion.[19]

Less than two weeks later, the Health Subcommittee of the House Ways and Means Committee approved a $1.25 increase in the cigarette tax, fifty cents more than Clinton had suggested. In June the full committee voted for a forty-five-cent hike, thirty cents less than the administration's proposal. That month the *Atlanta Journal and Constitution* reported that "the industry [hoped] to hold the tax to 48 cents"; in other words, the tobacco companies now viewed a doubling of the tax as a victory.[20] But compromise proved unnecessary. The reason had less to do with the tobacco industry's clout than with the program that was supposed to justify a higher cigarette tax. "One of the last best hopes for the industry," the *New York Times* reported prophetically in March 1993, "is that the details of the Administration's health-care plan will prove so unpopular, or so unwieldy, that it will be unable to get through Congress, allowing cigarettes to escape unscathed."[21] By fall 1994 Clinton's health care plan was dead, and so was his cigarette tax hike.

With the election of a Republican Congress that November, the chance of raising the tax seemed even more remote. In May 1997, attempting to save a budget agreement between the White House and Congress, Clinton himself helped kill a proposal to raise money for children's health insurance through a forty-three-cent hike in the cigarette tax. But Congress approved a more modest version of the plan that summer, after the proposed national tobacco settlement highlighted the industry's vulnerability. The budget bill that Clinton signed in early August will raise the federal cigarette tax by ten cents a pack in 2000 and another five cents in 2002. This fifteen-cent hike—aimed mainly at revenue, rather than deterrence—is the biggest federal increase ever, but it's tiny compared to what anti-smoking activists want.

Tobacco's opponents complained that the settlement proposal announced in June 1997 did not include any tax hikes. But the plan did require the cigarette companies to pass the $368.5 billion cost of the deal on to their customers through higher prices, which would have the same impact as a tax increase. In September the president said if underage smoking did not decline according to the government's schedule, the tobacco companies should have to pay penalties high enough to raise cigarette prices by up to $1.50 a pack—an amount calculated to deter teenagers from smoking and help meet the official targets.

LABORATORIES OF TAXATION

State legislatures have been more willing than Congress to increase cigarette taxes. While the federal tax has been raised just three times since 1951, state taxes have gone up more than three hundred times.[22] In fact, the National Governors' Association opposed the 1983 federal tax hike on the ground that it preempted a traditional source of state revenue. By 1969 every state and the District of Columbia taxed cigarettes, with rates ranging from two cents a pack in North Carolina to sixteen cents in Connecticut.[23] In 1996, when the rates ranged from two and a half cents in Virginia to eighty-two and a half cents in Washington state, the weighted average was about thirty-two cents, one-third more than the federal tax.[24] State legislators have often found it easier to extract money from an increasingly unpopular minority than from broad-based taxes on sales, income, or property. Since 1993 the Washington legislature, seeking money for the cleanup of Puget Sound, for anti-violence programs, and for health insurance subsidies, has raised the state's cigarette tax from thirty-four to eighty-two and a half cents a pack. In 1994 Michigan voters approved a referendum that tripled the cigarette tax to seventy-five cents a pack as part of a plan to reduce property taxes.

During the last decade several states have increased their cigarette taxes with the explicit aim of reducing smoking. In 1985 the Minnesota legislature raised the state's tax from eighteen to twenty-three cents a pack, earmarking some of the additional revenue for health education, including anti-smoking ads.[25] California's Proposition 99, approved by voters in 1988, increased the state's cigarette tax from ten to thirty-five cents a pack, setting aside about a quarter of the money for anti-tobacco efforts, which have included research, promotion of local smoking ordinances, and a media campaign (discussed in chapter 3).[26] Taking a cue from California, anti-smoking activists in Massachusetts proposed a similar ballot measure, Question 1, in 1992. It raised the state's cigarette tax from twenty-six to fifty-one cents a pack, with some of the money paying for an anti-smoking ad campaign that began in 1993. In 1994 voters in Arizona also passed an initiative resembling Proposition 99, raising the state's cigarette tax from eighteen to fifty-eight cents a pack. All three initiatives prevailed despite well-funded opposition by the tobacco industry, which spent about $10 million in California, $5 million in Massachusetts, and $4 million in Arizona.[27] The industry had more success in Colorado, where voters defeated a Proposition 99–style ballot measure by a large margin in 1994.

That year the Robert Wood Johnson Foundation announced $10 million in grants for campaigns to raise cigarette taxes in nineteen states.[28] In 1996 Oregon voters approved an initiative raising the state's cigarette tax from thirty-eight to sixty-eight cents a pack, allocating the extra money to health insurance for the poor. In 1997 eight states—Alaska, Arkansas, Hawaii, Maine, New Hampshire, Rhode Island, Utah, and Wisconsin—raised their cigarette taxes. The increases ranged from a modest two and a half cents in Alaska (from thirty-one and a half cents to thirty-four cents) to a whopping forty cents in Hawaii (from sixty cents to a dollar, as of July 1998).[29] "We're getting clobbered," an industry official said. "Raising tobacco taxes is our No. 1 strategy to damage the tobacco industry," an American Cancer Society official told the *New York Times,* which reported that anti-smoking activists "hope to have campaigns going in all 50 [states] by next year."[30]

Like the 1983 federal tax hike, sizable increases in state cigarette taxes are generally followed by significant drops in sales. Cigarette purchases in California fell 14 percent in 1989, the year after the state tax rose by twenty-five cents a pack, compared to 4 percent nationwide.[31] In his statistical analysis of several state tax hikes, University of Scranton business scholar Richard McGowan found that increases of more than fifteen cents a pack in Massachusetts and Washington led to "a sharp and permanent decline in cigarette sales." He concluded that "the cigarette excise tax has proven to be the most effective public policy measure in decreasing cigarette sales if public policy makers have the will to raise the rate substantially."[32]

Most studies of the issue have found that the price elasticity of demand for cigarettes is somewhere between –0.4 and –1.0—that is, for every 10 percent increase in the price of cigarettes, consumption drops 4 to 10 percent.[33] Research suggests that price increases cut consumption mainly by reducing the number of smokers (as opposed to reducing the amount consumed per smoker). One study indicated that a 10 percent price increase reduces smoking prevalence by roughly 3 percent.[34] Tobacco's opponents combine such figures with epidemiological data to estimate the impact of changing the cigarette tax. In 1985, when Congress was considering whether to extend the 1983 tax increase, Kenneth Warner cautioned, "If that tax is allowed to fall in half, upwards of half a million Americans will die earlier than if the tax had been left at 16 cents."[35] In 1993, urging Congress to raise the cigarette tax "by a minimum of $2 a pack," a physician representing the Coalition on Smoking or Health said, "By your action you can save 2 million lives, and you can do it without spending a dime of taxpayers' money."[36]

That's a pretty appealing proposition. But a legislator who votes for a cigarette tax hike should not expect the sort of gratitude that a surgeon or a firefighter might receive. To be sure, some smokers who are inclined to quit may welcome the added incentive of higher prices. In 1990, with rumors of a cigarette tax hike in the air, a Kentucky smoker told a reporter, "I hope they price them out of my range, because I'm really wanting to stop."[37] Such smokers, like overweight people who enroll in fat farms, are looking for external assistance to reinforce their own will power. But many others will react like the California smoker who said of Proposition 99, "It's a form of extortion. The initiative is punitive and it's scary. It singles out a part of the population that is seen as offensive by another group."[38] Or like the spokesman for the Kentucky Smokers Rights Organization, who said of Bill Clinton's proposed seventy-five-cent tax increase, "This isn't about health-care reform. . . . What the administration wants is to reduce the use of tobacco by citizens of this country. This is about behavior modification. Where will it end?"[39]

Smokers of modest means are apt to resent tax hikes the most. Tobacco taxes are highly regressive, both because the poor are more likely
to smoke and because poor smokers spend a larger share of their income
on cigarettes than affluent smokers do. In 1990 smokers represented 19
percent of Americans earning $50,000 or more a year and about 32 per-
cent of those earning less than $10,000. Tobacco taxes consumed 0.4
percent of the median income for smokers in the first group, versus 5.1
percent for smokers in the second group—nearly thirteen times as
much. Compared to cigarette taxes, a head tax is a model of fairness.[40]

Yet tobacco's opponents seem to overlook the possibility that smokers
might object to a cigarette tax hike. Defending a policy of reducing
smoking through taxation against the charge that it amounts to "blaming the victim," Kenneth Warner wrote, "Given the effective deterrence
function of a cigarette tax, one might consider a tax increase as a help-
the-victim measure."[41] Responding to the argument that Proposition 99
hit the poor especially hard, the author of a letter to the *Western Journal
of Medicine* said, "The benefits of the tax in terms of discouraging smoking are likely . . . to be progressive. A disproportionate number of lives of
the poor are likely to be saved by a cigarette tax."[42] What about the "victims" who don't want to be "helped," the "lives" who don't want to be
"saved"? The public health model ignores that question. It deals with
populations, not people.

Advocates of higher tobacco taxes assume that legislators are doing
smokers a favor by making cigarettes more expensive. That counterintu-
itive notion rests on the belief that people continue to smoke because
they don't know any better or because they can't help it. "People do not
understand the results of the market behavior called smoking," Warner
insisted in 1985. "By raising the dollar price, we're providing information. We're saying, 'This is costly.' That's not just in dollars; that's in
terms of health implications too."[43] In other words, tobacco taxes are
supposed to communicate the same message as all those warning labels,
surgeon general's reports, and anti-smoking ads: Cigarettes are bad for
you. But as the Congressional Research Service concluded in 1994,
"available data indicate the average smoker is aware of, or overestimates,
the health risks of smoking."[44] Warner also argued that "we're dealing
with a highly addictive process. Ninety percent of adults say they'd like

to quit if it were easy to do so; 60 percent claim they have tried within the past year."[45] Chapter 7 will explore the meaning of addiction, including the significance of those survey results. For now it should suffice to observe that giving up cigarettes when the price of a pack goes up twenty-five cents is not the behavior of someone who is powerless over nicotine.

As with the advertising ban, anti-smoking activists reinforce their argument for increasing cigarette taxes by urging us to save the children. They note that most smokers start before the age of eighteen and that teenagers are especially sensitive to price increases. "To reduce new recruits," writes Jack Nicholl, campaign manager for Proposition 99, "the price of tobacco must be elevated beyond the reach of teens. Boosting the tobacco tax is the best method yet tried for discouraging teen smokers."[46] Similarly, the Coalition on Smoking or Health argues that "raising tobacco taxes is the most effective way to rapidly and significantly reduce tobacco use by young people."[47] Even if that's true, this approach imposes a burden on all smokers, regardless of age, to deter a small minority who are not legally permitted to buy cigarettes in the first place. It's akin to taxing pornographic magazines so children can't afford them. Since every state already prohibits the sale of cigarettes to minors, a serious effort to enforce those laws seems a more appropriate response to underage smoking.

NONSMOKER'S BURDEN

For those who are not persuaded that we need higher cigarette taxes to protect smokers from themselves or to discourage minors from taking up the habit, tobacco's opponents have another argument: Cigarette taxes are a way of bringing home to smokers the costs they impose on society. "I believe that people should pay their own way and not pass their costs on to society," says Elizabeth Whelan, president of the American Council on Science and Health. "I wouldn't call it a tax. I would call it a user's fee."[48] John Banzhaf, executive director of Action on Smoking and Health, says "the fairest thing to do . . . would be to figure out the cost to society from smoking and then impose that in the form of a tax."[49] The "social cost" argument is more appealing than the other rationales for raising cigarette taxes because it emphasizes fairness and individual responsibility. But it suffers from severe empirical and conceptual weaknesses. "I can't really defend the various economic numbers," Whelan concedes, "because I didn't get involved in how they were done. I also know that the dollar estimates put on the cost of smoking in society are almost impossible to come up with. . . . You can come up with any numbers you want. We've tried, and we just find it an impossible situation."[50]

Part of the problem is that basic issues about smoking-related costs remain unresolved. Tobacco's opponents often assert, for example, that smokers take more sick leave and generate higher medical expenses than nonsmokers. But the extent, significance, and even the existence of such differences have been questioned. A 1991 study published in *Applied Economics* found that when factors such as occupation, age, and drinking habits were considered, smokers were no more likely than nonsmokers to be absent from work. "Our results suggest that smokers miss no more work than non-smokers because they smoke," wrote Auburn University economist Richard W. Ault and his coauthors. "Rather smokers tend to be younger, heavier drinkers, blue collar workers, etc., and these groups will miss more work regardless of whether or not they smoke."[51] Similarly, a 1995 study by San Jose State University economist J. Paul Leigh, reported in the *Quarterly Review of Economics and Finance*, found that factors other than smoking accounted for much (though not all) of the difference in absenteeism between smokers and nonsmokers. After adjustment, the absence rate was about one percentage point higher for male smokers than for male nonsmokers; among women, the difference was less than one-third of a percentage point.[52]

The evidence concerning health care costs is also mixed. A decade ago the economist Thomas C. Schelling, who headed Harvard's Center for the Study of Smoking Behavior and Policy, observed, "It is not at all evident that over their lifetimes smokers incur greater medical-care costs than nonsmokers. . . . It seems a reasonable guess that the health-care costs that are obviated by premature deaths attributable to smoking are at least the order of magnitude of the health-care costs attributable to fatal smoking-induced illness."[53] A 1990 study reported in *Preventive Medicine* seemed to confirm Schelling's hunch, finding that lifetime medical expenses are actually *lower* for smokers than for nonsmokers.[54] A 1992 article in the *Milbank Quarterly* criticized this conclusion, arguing that the study used too narrow a definition of smoking-related disease and overestimated the medical expenses of nonsmokers.[55] The most recent study of this issue, published by the *New England Journal of Medicine* in 1997, estimated that "health care costs for smokers at a given age are as much as 40 percent higher than those for nonsmokers, but in a population where no one smoked the costs would be 7 percent higher among men and 4 percent higher among women" because of longer life spans. Therefore, the authors concluded, "If people stopped smoking, there would be a savings in health care costs, but only in the short term. Eventually, smoking cessation would lead to increased health care costs."[56]

In addition to measurement problems, discussion of smoking-related costs is clouded by analytical confusion. Anti-smoking activists routinely fail to distinguish between costs that smokers pay and costs that other people pay. In a 1995 briefing paper, the Coalition on Smoking or Health asserted that "the total economic cost of tobacco exceeds $100 billion per year." It cited a CDC estimate that treatment of smoking-related diseases cost $50 billion in 1993 and an estimate by the U.S. Office of Technology Assessment that "lost economic productivity caused by smoking cost the U.S. economy $47 billion in 1990."[57] The CDC figure includes all health care expenses related to smoking, regardless of who paid them. Less than half of the total ($22 billion) represents taxpayer money. The OTA figure includes $7 billion for "lost time at work" and "lost housekeeping services by homemakers," along with $40 billion for the "forgone earnings of those dying prematurely."[58] Both estimates combine costs paid by the smoker (e.g., out-of-pocket health care, lost wages) with costs paid by others. Yet the Coalition on Smoking or Health simply divided $100 billion by the number of cigarette packs sold in 1993 and declared, "On average, every pack of cigarettes is directly responsible for more than $3.90 in health care costs and lost productivity."[59] In the context of an argument for raising cigarette taxes, this calculation is irrelevant and misleading.

Tobacco's opponents not only include inappropriate costs but also ignore important sources of savings. As noted above, smokers consume less health care in old age than nonsmokers because they tend to die earlier. They also spend less time in nursing homes and take less money out of Social Security and pension funds. From an economic perspective, these savings have to be considered along with the costs, even though it may seem distasteful. As the OTA noted, "Reduction or elimination of smoking would improve health and extend longevity, but may not lead to savings in health care costs. In fact, significant reductions in smoking prevalence and the attendant increase in life expectancy could lead to future increases in total medical spending, in Medicare program outlays, and in the budgets of the Social Security and other government programs."[60]

The first study to include long-term savings and distinguish costs paid by smokers from costs paid by third parties was published in the *Journal of the American Medical Association* in 1989. A group of researchers associated with the RAND Corporation, led by Willard G. Manning, considered the impact of smoking on fires, sick leave, nursing home care, pension programs, and payments under health, life, and disability insurance. They estimated that the external costs of smoking (those borne by people other than smokers and their families) totaled about fifteen cents a pack, based on a 5 percent discount rate. (The discount rate translates future dollars into present dollars.[61]) "On balance," Manning et al. concluded, "smokers probably pay their way at the current level of excise taxes."[62] The average state and federal excise tax burden was thirty-eight cents at the time.[63]

In 1994 the Congressional Research Service updated the findings of the RAND study. Adjusted for inflation, Manning et al.'s estimate of fifteen cents per pack became thirty-three cents in 1995 dollars, compared to a combined state and federal tax that averaged about fifty-seven cents.[64] The CRS noted that raising the discount rate to 10 percent would increase the per-pack cost to forty-two cents. At a discount rate a bit under 4 percent, the cost would drop to zero, and below that rate smoking would result in net savings. The CRS also considered the impact of including deaths attributed to secondhand smoke (a topic discussed in the next chapter) as a component of smoking's cost. While "the link between passive smoking and disease is uncertain," the report said, "the best available estimate of this link implies external costs of no more than a few cents per pack."[65]

In a 1994 paper published by the National Bureau of Economic Research, W. Kip Viscusi updated the RAND data and adjusted them to take into account reductions in tar consumption since the 1950s. Viscusi used a 3 percent discount rate, "corresponding to the long-run real rate of return in the U.S. economy." He found that smoking generates net external savings between twenty-three and fifty-three cents a pack, depending upon whether lost income tax revenue is counted as a cost. "At reasonable rates of discount," he concluded, "the cost savings that results because of the premature deaths of smokers through their lower Social Security and pension costs will more than compensate for the added costs imposed by smokers. . . . On balance there is a net cost savings to society even excluding consideration of the current cigarette taxes paid by smokers." Based on these calculations, he noted, one could argue that "cigarette smoking should be subsidized rather than taxed." Like the CRS, Viscusi considered the evidence concerning the health effects of secondhand smoke shaky. But he found that even when deaths from secondhand smoke were included in the cost calculation, there was no basis for raising cigarette taxes.[66]

Although they were careful not to count costs paid by smokers, the authors of these studies did not distinguish between costs paid by others voluntarily and costs imposed on others. Private insurers and HMOs, for example, agree to cover smokers in exchange for their premiums. If smokers generate bigger medical bills, that may be a reason to charge them higher premiums, but it is not an argument for government intervention. Similarly, if smokers take more sick leave than nonsmokers, are less productive on the job, or draw on group health insurance more, employers are in the best position to know and respond. Some companies already charge employees who smoke or who have smoking dependents more for health coverage. In principle, employers can also pay smokers less or refuse to hire them, though employment laws, including misguided "anti-discrimination" statutes backed by the tobacco industry, interfere with this freedom.

The government also forces people (a.k.a. taxpayers) to pick up the

tab for smoking-related illness through Medicaid and Medicare. As long
as the government subsidizes health care, it will subsidize risky behavior,
including not just smoking but heavy drinking, overeating, and hazardous recreation. Politicians and bureaucrats will then use those subsidies as an excuse for further meddling. The implications are troubling.
In a 1976 essay commissioned by *Time,* John H. Knowles, president of
the Rockefeller Foundation, reviewed the rise of taxpayer-funded health
insurance and declared that "the cost of sloth, gluttony, alcoholic
overuse, reckless driving, sexual intemperance, and smoking is now a national, not an individual responsibility."[67] Writing in *Daedalus* the following year, he said, "I believe that the idea of a 'right' to health should
be replaced by the idea of an individual moral obligation to preserve
one's own health—a public duty if you will."[68]

Even if we ignore that chilling prospect, the cost of treating smoking-related illness under taxpayer-funded programs still has to be
weighed against the claims that smokers would make on Medicare and
Social Security if they lived longer. Taking the long view, the CRS concluded that "reduced smoking probably would cause an increase in net
budgetary costs."[69]

Many anti-smokers are offended by all this talk about the savings associated with smoking. In congressional testimony during the 1993 debate over Clinton's proposed tax hike, Jeffrey Harris, a physician and
MIT economist, estimated that the "direct health care costs of smoking"
were $88 billion a year, or $3.71 per pack. He cited the OTA's estimate
for "lost productivity" and used it to calculate "forgone income taxes."
But when it came to the costs avoided because smokers die earlier, he
was suddenly squeamish. "This is not the kind of calculation in which a
civilized society engages," he declared. "Premature deaths are not
counted as a 'benefit' in decisions to fund research to cure diseases such
as breast cancer or prostate cancer, or in decisions to stop the spread of
AIDS or violence. . . . This is not a matter of cold economic calculation,
but a matter of health."[70]

Harris's analogies make sense only if smoking is an unequivocal evil,
like cancer, AIDS, or murder. But while public health specialists may
consider smoking inherently undesirable, many smokers clearly have a
different view. (Otherwise there would be no need for higher cigarette

taxes.) In any case, tobacco's opponents are the ones who introduced "cold economic calculation" to justify tobacco tax hikes. They switched the focus from the individual to the group, asking about the impact of smoking on "society as a whole." The question is reminiscent of the complaint made by James I that tobacco impaired the health and drained the property of his subjects, who were "created and ordeined by God to bestowe both [their] persons and goods for the maintenance both of the honour and safetie of [their] King and Commonwealth."[71] Today's anti-smoking activists similarly blame smokers for reduced tax revenue and "lost productivity," as if every individual owes the state a full lifetime of income (at the highest possible wage?). Criticizing economists who do not treat cigarette tax hikes like funding for cancer research, Harris complained, "There is a double standard at work here."[72] Indeed.

SMOKE SMUGGLING

Even if the case for higher cigarette taxes were convincing, practical problems would remain. Just as surely as they discourage consumption, taxes encourage evasion and smuggling. In 1996 the average price for a pack of cigarettes sold in the United States (including discount brands) was about $1.85. The average state and federal tax burden represented more than 30 percent of that price.[73] Smokers are happy to avoid some or all of that burden, and sellers who can oblige them and supply cigarettes at a substantial discount stand to make a nice profit.

Many smokers can cut out the middleman by simply crossing the border to a state where the tax is lower. Business scholar Richard McGowan found that cigarette sales increased in New Hampshire after Massachusetts raised its cigarette tax in 1993. He reported that "New Hampshire appears to have directed its own state police to protect Massachusetts residents who buy cigarettes and alcohol in New Hampshire. New Hampshire state police harass undercover Massachusetts state police who sit in parking lots relaying license plate numbers of the cars of Massachusetts residents who are seen buying large quantities of cigarettes and alcohol in New Hampshire." McGowan also found that cigarette sales in Oregon rose after Washington increased its tax in 1994.

Two years later, when Washington raised its tax again, Oregon cut its tax. "States do indeed covet potential cigarette excise tax revenue from neighboring states," McGowan concluded. "Rather than raising their own cigarette excise taxes to raise additional revenue, many states are maintaining or even lowering their cigarette excise tax rate to attract smokers from neighboring states that have substantially increased their cigarette excise tax rate."[74] The Tax Foundation estimated that, because of growing disparities in cigarette taxes, cross-border shopping nearly quintupled between 1980 and 1994.[75]

In addition to interstate purchases by smokers, organized crime has long been involved in trucking cigarettes from low-tax states such as Virginia and North Carolina to high-tax states such as New York and Massachusetts. According to the Tax Foundation, the number of smuggled cigarettes rose more than 250 percent from 1980 to 1994.[76] When Michigan tripled its cigarette tax in May 1994, it created a tempting business opportunity for interstate smugglers. During the year after the tax hike, tax-paid sales in Michigan dropped 19 percent. By comparison, sales in North Carolina, where the cigarette tax was seventy cents lower, rose 14 percent. Sales also rose significantly in three other tobacco states—Kentucky, Virginia, and Tennessee—and in three states bordering Michigan that have lower cigarette taxes—Wisconsin, Indiana, and Ohio.[77] Since overall cigarette consumption in the United States did not change significantly between 1993 and 1994, these figures indicate that many Michigan smokers started buying cigarettes from other states, on their own or through bootleggers.

A 1995 report by the investigative accounting firm Lindquist Avey MacDonald Baskerville described several routes by which low-tax cigarettes reach Michigan. Some smugglers drive rented vehicles to North Carolina, where they purchase cigarettes from wholesalers and retailers in quantities of 299 or fewer cartons at a time, since records of larger sales are kept for inspection by the Bureau of Alcohol, Tobacco, and Firearms. Others buy cigarettes from Indian reservations in New York State. A typical smuggler might pay $11 for a carton of premium-brand cigarettes and get $15 from a retailer, who would then sell it for $18 or $19, compared to more than $22 for fully taxed cigarettes.[78]

Smugglers who can avoid federal as well as state taxes stand to make even more money. A 1994 report by Lindquist Avey MacDonald Baskerville estimated that untaxed cigarettes—which are smuggled from Mexico or diverted from duty-free shops, export shipments, or other un-taxed sources—accounted for about 6 percent of U.S. consumption. One sign that smuggling is on the rise: Department of Agriculture fig-ures indicate that exports of U.S. cigarettes to Mexico increased by a sus-picious 2,424 percent between 1990 and 1994. Most of these tax-free cigarettes were presumably smuggled back into the United States. In California, just across the border, the state Board of Equalization esti-mated that 7 percent of the cigarettes sold in 1994 were contraband. A spokesman said smuggling "keeps getting worse every month."[79]

If Mexico offers one reason to be cautious about raising cigarette taxes, our neighbor to the north offers another. In Canada, where the national government sharply increased cigarette taxes in 1989 and 1991, the consequences precipitated a crisis and a dramatic policy reversal. Be-fore taxes were cut, a legal carton of cigarettes in Canada sold for about $45, compared to between $15 and $20 in the United States.[80] Because of this big gap, smuggling by individuals and groups, including Mo-hawks operating out of reservations along the U.S.–Canadian border, rose dramatically. Smugglers brought in cigarettes and tobacco on boats and kayaks, in trucks carrying produce, on snowmobiles, even inside the bodies of cars and vans.[81] The number of contraband tobacco seizures by the Royal Canadian Mounted Police jumped from 303 in 1990 to 5,033 in 1993.[82]

A January 1994 story in the *New York Times* described Cornwall, On-tario, a small town near the Akwesasne Reserve along the border with New York State, as "Dodge City East" because of the violence associated with cigarette smuggling. "Shootings erupt almost nightly," the *Times* reported. "In recent weeks cars have been torched with firebombs, shots have been fired into a civic complex on the waterfront and at a building housing the radio station, and the hallway outside a pool hall has been bombed."[83]

By 1994 one-third of the cigarettes sold in Ontario and two-thirds of the cigarettes sold in Quebec were said to be contraband (either smug-gled from the United States or diverted from Canadian exports).[84] Canadians bought the black-market cigarettes on the street, at flea markets, and in bars, restaurants, and convenience stores. Many merchants started keeping double inventories, with legal cigarettes on display and tax-free smokes below the counter. In January 1994, seventy-five retailers in St. Eustache, Quebec, defied police by openly selling contraband cigarettes. Hundreds of customers lined up for cigarettes at half the legal price. No arrests were made.[85]

In response to the smuggling, the violence, and the citizen rebellion, Prime Minister Jean Chretien announced big tax cuts in February 1994. "Smuggling is threatening the safety of our communities and the livelihood of law-abiding merchants," he said. "It is a threat to the very fabric of Canadian society." Solicitor General Herb Gray added: "Organized crime has become a major player in the contraband market. What we are seeing is a frightening growth in criminal activity. We are seeing a breakdown in respect for Canadian law. Canadian society is the victim."[86]

You might think that Canada's experience would give pause to people who want the price of cigarettes to be doubled or tripled. But John Banzhaf, who'd like to see a tax of about four dollars a pack, is not very concerned. "Are we going to have somewhat of a problem?" he says. "Sure. But we already have a problem with smuggling with all of the other drugs. Cigarettes, by and large, are harder to smuggle. They're a lot bulkier. The amount of space that it takes to bring in a kilo of coke is less than [you'd need] for a carton of cigarettes. So that's not going to be very profitable." Since the number of Americans who smoke cigarettes every day is more than a hundred times the number who use cocaine every day, smugglers might disagree.[87]

Chapter 5

SMOKE ALARM

If you can smell it, it may be killing you.

—New York City subway ad, 1995

THE NO-SMOKING SIGN GOES ON

In 1986 U.S. Representative Richard J. Durbin had to sit in the smok-ing section of an airplane. The flight was overcrowded, and when he checked in at the gate he was seated between two smokers. "Can't you do anything about it?" he asked the gate agent. "No, I can't," she said. "But you can, Congressman."[1]

This is the story that the Illinois Democrat, now a senator, would tell to explain how he came to sponsor legislation that eventually led to the elimination of smoking from almost all domestic airline flights. "It was an inconvenience, of course," he said at an anti-smoking conference in 1989. "What came to mind were the passengers who might suffer from some respiratory disease, or small children who might be thrust into the same situation."[2]

Ahron Leichtman, founder of Citizens Against Tobacco Smoke, was one of those passengers who suffered more than inconvenience. Leicht-man, who once sued a radio talk show host for breathing cigar smoke in his face, says just a whiff of tobacco smoke can give him a headache and prolonged exposure causes sinus problems. He first noticed that he was unusually sensitive to secondhand smoke in the late 1960s, when he was working as a press secretary for the National Education Association. "I really felt there was something wrong . . . about forcing someone like myself to sit in a meeting where there might have been twelve people, and seven were smoking," he says. "Back then, you just did not say, 'Excuse me, could we not have smoking in this small conference room?' I mean, it just wasn't socially acceptable to even raise the issue. So I used to leave the damned meetings. I used to have my secretary come in and say, 'Mr. Leichtman, you have a phone call,' and I'd just never come back." That wasn't an option on airplane flights. "I was made ill virtually every time I got on an airplane from all the tobacco smoke," he recalls. "I would get sinus infections from the damned tobacco smoke."[3]

An early member of Action on Smoking and Health (ASH), Leichtman worked on two unsuccessful anti-smoking initiatives in California before moving to Cincinnati in 1980. Four years later he led a fight for a city smoking ordinance, a campaign that he says made him "the most controversial character in town." It all started with a smoker at the fish counter in a Kroger's supermarket who refused to put out his cigarette. After complaining to the manager, an indignant Leichtman called the local newspaper, which ran a story saying that he was about to lead a "nonsmokers' rights strike." That Sunday, Leichtman received more than a hundred telephone calls, almost all favorable. Within a year the Cincinnati chapter of the Group Against Smokers' Pollution (GASP) had attracted five hundred members and the city had adopted new restrictions on smoking.

Fresh from his victory in Cincinnati, Leichtman started Citizens Against Tobacco Smoke during the First World Conference on Nonsmokers' Rights, sponsored by Action on Smoking and Health, in October 1985. A coalition of state and local nonsmokers' rights groups, CATS initially had just one goal: getting tobacco smoke off airplanes. "If you use pinpoint concentration," Leichtman explains, "you can accomplish a lot more than if you do some scatter-fire thing." He says CATS lobbied the news media rather than the public, holding press conferences, sending out mailings to newspapers, and encouraging reporters to do investigative pieces about conditions on airplanes. The organization spotlighted airline employees who complained about the effects of tobacco smoke; one flight attendant had lost her job because she insisted on wearing a surgical mask while on duty. An airline mechanic would demonstrate how tar from cigarette smoke gummed up the ventilation system. "We had a dog and pony show all over South Florida," says Leichtman, "and the media ate it up."[4]

The public was receptive, too. Polls found that a large majority of Americans favored an airline smoking ban. Although the federal government had required airlines to set aside nonsmoking sections since 1973, segregation did not eliminate unwanted exposure to secondhand smoke. Members of Congress, who flew frequently, were especially familiar with the nuisance of tobacco smoke on airplanes. So were flight attendants, who made sympathetic lobbyists for a ban. One wrote to a senator, "I will be so grateful when burning eyes, sinuses, and lungs, as well as headaches, nausea, lightheadedness, and blocked ears . . . will be a part of the past."[5] Two reports released in 1986 raised the prospect of more serious health consequences. Both the surgeon general and the National Research Council concluded that secondhand smoke can cause lung cancer in nonsmokers. As Surgeon General C. Everett Koop put it, "Now, instead of people saying, 'You know, smoking annoys me, it irritates me, my sinuses ache at night, and my eyes burn and my clothes smell,' they can also say, 'We now have solid evidence that this is dangerous to my health.' "[6] In addition to health concerns, advocates of a ban cited the danger of fires.

In 1987 Representative Durbin introduced an amendment to a transportation spending bill aimed at banning smoking on flights of two hours or less. "The rights of smokers to smoke end where their smoking affects the health and safety of others," he argued.[7] The House of Representatives narrowly approved the amendment, by a vote of 198 to 193, in July. That fall the Senate, responding to the demands of tobacco state legislators, such as North Carolina Republican Jesse Helms, approved a transportation bill that imposed a less stringent ban, covering flights of ninety minutes or less. But the bill that emerged from the House–Senate conference included the stricter version. Signed into law by President Reagan in December, it took effect in April 1988 for a two-year trial period.

Leichtman faults the voluntary health organizations, represented by the Coalition on Smoking or Health, for seeking less than a complete ban. "If you're going after an objective to get tobacco smoke off airplanes, that two-hour ban was the most ridiculous thing in the world," he says. "If tobacco smoke is truly that harmful, it is going to be much more harmful if you sit on a four-hour plane flight."[8] But the two-hour, trial approach turned out to be a clever tactical move. On the one hand, it sounded modest. As Durbin put it, "Why can smokers willingly abstain for the two hours it takes to watch a movie, yet step on an airplane and claim some constitutional right to light up?"[9] On the other hand, the ban covered about 80 percent of domestic flights, so when it came up for renewal in 1989, extending it to the remaining flights did not seem like such a big deal. In fact, supporters could argue that it was simply a matter of logical consistency.

In the face of this argument, the tobacco industry considered it a victory when the House of Representatives voted in August 1989 merely to make the existing ban permanent. The Senate went further in September, heeding New Jersey Democrat Frank Lautenberg's call to "get on with protecting the public health and safety."[10] The Senate approved Lautenberg's amendment extending the ban to all domestic flights after a 77-to-21 vote to cut off debate on the topic. At the House–Senate conference in October, the momentum for a total ban was so strong that the only compromise tobacco lobbyists could win was an exception for about two dozen flights a day—to and from Hawaii, Alaska, and Guam—lasting longer than six hours. "We'll take whatever we can get," said a Tobacco Institute lobbyist, "anything short of a total ban."[11] The final legislation was approved by both houses in November, and the ban went into effect in February 1990.

Durbin reported that airline executives had been privately rooting for a ban, eager to be rid of the extra maintenance costs associated with smoking and the hassle involved in segregating smokers from nonsmokers. Yet even after smoking was banned on short flights, Northwest was the only U.S. airline that chose to go completely smoke-free. It later said the policy, which was announced with much fanfare, had helped attract customers. Nevertheless, the other airlines were clearly afraid that they would lose business if they followed suit, since smokers could switch to carriers that still allowed them to light up. An industry-wide rule would eliminate that threat, so it's not surprising that the airlines, though officially opposed, did not fight the smoking ban as aggressively as the cigarette companies did.

The tobacco industry's strong opposition shows that more was at stake than the rules governing passenger behavior on airplanes. The cigarette companies recognized that the airline smoking ban was part of the campaign to discourage consumption of their product. It would make smoking less convenient and less socially acceptable, and it would set a precedent for more restrictions. Advocates of the ban also recognized its broader significance. "There are early signs that the limitations on smoking that have lately been imposed in many offices and public buildings have prompted some smokers to smoke less, and others to quit entirely," the *Los Angeles Times* editorialized. "The ban on smoking in airliners might encourage similar behavioral changes."[12] After the House approved the extended ban, Durbin—who was fourteen when his father, a two-pack-a-day smoker, died of lung cancer—declared, "Today, millions of Americans who have lost loved ones from tobacco-related diseases are the real winners."[13] A triumphant Leichtman (who, tellingly, changed the name of his organization to Citizens for a Tobacco-Free Society in 1991) announced, "Smokers have an additional reason for quitting now. . . . This clear and obvious victory for non-smokers, in time, will be recognized by smokers as in their best interest as well."[14]

Most supporters of the airline smoking ban probably did not see it as an effort to protect smokers from themselves; they just wanted to get tobacco smoke off airplanes. Tobacco's opponents declared that desire a right and used it to expand public support for their agenda. As Senator Lautenberg put it, "Airline passengers have the right not to have their health jeopardized by the smoke of others."[15] The combination of these two ideas—that secondhand smoke (1) violates people's rights and (2) endangers their health—gave a powerful boost to a movement that otherwise would have appealed mainly to public health specialists. It validated the distaste and discomfort that many people feel in the presence of tobacco smoke and justified enlisting the coercive power of the state to address their complaints. At the same time, it put smokers on the defensive, depicting them as not only inconsiderate but dangerous and anti-social. "Nonsmokers' rights" became the rallying cry for a campaign to ostracize smokers, gradually eliminating the locations outside their homes where they could light up. Since smoking is something that people tend to do throughout the day in various places, the campaign to

protect nonsmokers' rights dovetailed nicely with the crusade to eliminate tobacco use, helping to achieve "a smoke-free society" in both
senses of the phrase.

YEARNING TO BREATHE FREE

Complaints about tobacco smoke are hardly a recent development.
James I, in his *Counterblaste to Tobacco*, showed much concern for the
bystanders who had to endure "the black stinking fume" from pipes. He
reported that many men had reluctantly taken up the habit "to be as one
that was content to eat Garlicke (which hee did not love) that he might
not be troubled by the smell of it, in the breath of his fellowes." And he
called it "a great iniquitie . . . against all humanitie" that a smoker "shall
not bee ashamed, to reduce thereby his delicate, wholesome, and cleane
complexioned wife, to that extremitie, that either shee must also corrupt
her sweete breath therewith, or else resolve to live in perpetuall stinking
torment."[16] Tobacco's detractors were not the only ones to recognize
that secondhand smoke could be irksome. Samuel Johnson conceded
that "it is a shocking thing, blowing smoke out of our mouths into other
people's mouths, eyes, and noses, and having the same thing done to
us."[17] And *Harper's Weekly*, which was highly skeptical of anti-tobacco
propaganda early in the twentieth century, nevertheless criticized smokers who brought their cigars into streetcars and blew smoke in passengers' faces.[18]

During the period when Lucy Page Gaston and Henry Ford were
campaigning against the newly popular cigarette, it was common for
nonsmokers to express their complaints about secondhand smoke in
terms of rights. Charles G. Pease, founder of the Nonsmokers Protective
League of America, asserted in 1911 that "the right of each person to
breathe and enjoy fresh and pure air" was guaranteed by the Constitution.[19] In 1912 Charles B. Towns asked, "What right has anyone to
smoke, when other people object to it?"[20] In his 1910 health textbook
Our Bodies and How We Live, Alfred F. Blaisdell wrote: "The effect of tobacco on the moral nature often shows itself in a selfish disregard for the
rights of others. The smoker has no right to make with his tobacco
smoke the air about him unfit for others to breathe. He has no right to

puff his smoke into the faces of people on the streets, or thus to pollute the air of public places which others are obliged to share with him."[21]

Such critics probably did not share the sweeping view of "nonsmokers' rights" that prevails today. Despite his claim of constitutional support, Pease was mainly interested in getting New York City to enforce existing bans on smoking in public waiting rooms and on trains and streetcars. Towns cited smoking in the subways (which was against the law) and smoking in other people's homes without their permission to illustrate smokers' "callous indifference to the rights of others."[22] Blaisdell's examples—blowing smoke into people's faces on the street, polluting the air of public places that "others are obliged to share"—likewise suggest a narrow understanding of nonsmokers' rights, limited to situations where smoke is truly unavoidable. Nowadays, by contrast, tobacco's opponents claim that nonsmokers have a right to demand that smoking be eliminated from just about any place they might want to go, whether on public or private property.

Though it eventually came back with a vengeance, the idea of nonsmokers' rights did not get much attention once cigarettes became widely accepted. During an era when most men and more than a quarter of women smoked, exposure to secondhand smoke was taken for granted. True, the polite thing to say before lighting up was "Mind if I smoke?" But the polite response was "No." (In the 1970s, comedian Steve Martin offered an alternative answer: "No. Mind if I fart?") Even after the 1964 surgeon general's report, the people who minded when others smoked were considered a bit odd. That perception began to change as smoking became less common, especially after public health officials started to suggest that secondhand smoke might be a health hazard as well as a nuisance.

In January 1971 Surgeon General Jesse L. Steinfeld said smoking should be banned in restaurants, theaters, airplanes, buses, and trains. In a speech to the Interagency Council on Smoking and Health, he revived Charles Pease's notion of a constitutional right to a smoke-free environment. "Nonsmokers have as much right to clean air as smokers have to their so-called right to smoke," he said. "It's time we interpreted the Bill of Rights for the nonsmoker as well as the smoker."[23] (Like Pease, he was rather vague on this point, failing to specify which of the first ten amendments he had in mind.) A year later, in the 1972 surgeon general's report, Steinfeld warned that high levels of carbon monoxide could accumulate in a closed room or car as a result of smoking, which would be especially hazardous to people with heart or lung disease.[24] The *New York Times* commented that "the smoking of cigarettes in the presence of a nonsmoker might be considered an act of aggression."[25]

Tobacco's opponents were quick to pick up on that implication. John Banzhaf, executive director of Action on Smoking and Health, cited Steinfeld's findings in an April 1972 article entitled, none too subtly, "Please Put Your Cigarette Out; the Smoke Is Killing Me!" Banzhaf began by comparing smokers to drunken drivers, who "go to jail because their actions put innocent people's lives in mortal danger." He continued, "I have little understanding for those men and women whose nasty nervous habit forces me to breathe carbon monoxide. Quite frankly—as well as literally—they make me sick." Banzhaf claimed that "a nonsmoker may actually be forced against his will to breathe almost as much carbon monoxide, tar and nicotine as the active smoker sitting next to him." He said nonsmokers should "demand that smokers [not] inflict their foolishness on the rest of us."[26] Steinfeld's report was also mentioned in the November 1972 issue of *Reader's Digest.* In "Non-Smokers, Arise!" Max Wiener said that "at least 34 million Americans are sensitive to cigarette smoke" and that "those who suffer from respiratory allergies may be seriously threatened." Suggesting that "smoking should be confined to consenting adults in private," Wiener declared, "It is time for you, the innocent bystander, to assert your rights."[27]

Despite the militant rhetoric, the recommendations offered by Banzhaf and Wiener were mild by current standards. After noting approvingly that federal regulators intended to require no-smoking sections on airplanes and buses, Banzhaf added, "There's no reason there can't be smoking cars on trains, and smoking rooms in public places."[28] Wiener suggested that nonsmokers could "help curb smoking in restaurants, planes, sporting arenas and the like by demanding a non-smoking area, preferably a separate room, as a prior condition for patronage."[29] Nowadays, of course, advocates of nonsmokers' rights want to *eliminate* smoking areas, and they would automatically reject the idea of using economic pressure, rather than the force of law, to achieve smoking restrictions.

The initial victories of the nascent nonsmokers' rights movement involved separation of smokers from nonsmokers. In 1971 the Interstate Commerce Commission required that smokers be confined to designated sections on interstate buses (the last few rows) and trains. In 1973 the Civil Aeronautics Board, responding to petitions from Banzhaf and Ralph Nader, ordered all U.S. airlines to establish no-smoking sections with enough seats to accommodate any passenger who requested one. These measures, which in retrospect may seem quite moderate, packed a symbolic wallop. The government was, after all, segregating smokers and making them sit in the back of the bus. The social significance of such policies became clear over time. By the 1980s, when references to "militant smokers" started appearing in the press, a backlash had developed.

But in the '70s it was nonsmokers who were rebelling. They formed organizations such as GASP, which eventually had dozens of affiliates throughout the country (including Leichtman's group in Cincinnati), and Californians for Nonsmokers' Rights, which later became Americans for Nonsmokers' Rights. They urged people irked by tobacco smoke to assert themselves, and they lobbied for state and local smoking restrictions. In 1973 Arizona became the first state to limit smoking as a way of protecting nonsmokers (some states already restricted smoking as a fire prevention measure). Proponents of the law—which confined smoking to designated areas in theaters, museums, art galleries, libraries, and buses—noted that many residents suffered from lung ailments and had come to Arizona for its healthy air. By the end of 1975, thirty-one states had approved legislation establishing or extending smoking restrictions. Minnesota's Clean Indoor Air Act, adopted in 1975, was the most comprehensive, restricting smoking to designated areas in all public places except bars.

The concept of nonsmokers' rights had transformed quiet resentment into vocal political action. As a Michigan legislator put it, "Few people . . . are able to argue against the belief that the ability to breathe smoke-free air is the kind of right that needs to be insured." A Nebraska legislator said, "Now when an individual asks me if I mind if he or she smokes, I say 'Yes.' I used to say 'No' to be polite. I think the law has helped a lot

ALL HANDS AT IT.

The Reverend George Trask's 1852 *Thoughts and Stories on Tobacco for American Lads* included this depiction of an entire family seduced by the Devil's weed. (Arents Collection, The New York Public Library)

_ Je ne comprends pas le plaisir qu'on peut avoir à fumer du tabac.....s'en bourrer le nez....à la bonne heure !.....

These irritated bystanders in a nineteenth-century French cartoon foreshadowed contemporary complaints about secondhand smoke. (Arents Collection, The New York Public Library)

The British "cigar mania" of the nineteenth century, like the recent fashion for stogies in the United States, prompted dismay among tobacco's opponents. (Arents Collection, The New York Public Library)

As this nineteenth-century English cartoon suggests, hostility toward smokers is not a new development. (Arents Collection, The New York Public Library)

The cigarette serpent ensnares an English dandy in an 1882 cartoon. (Corbis-Bettmann)

GVARDS
CAMBRIDGE
MARLBORO
DERBY
ASCOT

THE "SERPENT" CIGARETTE

Entitled "A Sermon Without Words," this 1906 American lithograph speaks for itself. (Library of Congress)

Samuel E. Creasey
1906

A Sermon Without Words.

STILL SMOKING

The ever-popular skull with a burning cigarette, featured in an 1885 van Gogh painting and a 1997 New York City taxi ad, appears in a 1910 American lithograph. (Corbis-Bettmann)

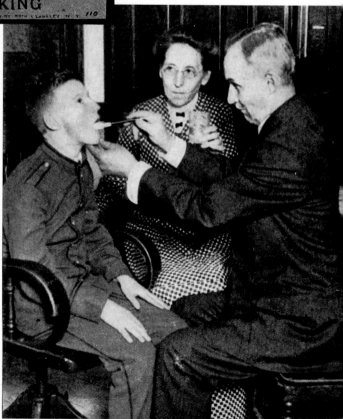

In this 1913 photograph, the Anti-Cigaret League's Lucy Page Gaston and Dr. D. H. Kress give a boy the silver nitrate treatment, intended to deter smoking. (General Research Division, The New York Public Library)

*On Which Side
of the Cigaret
Are You?*

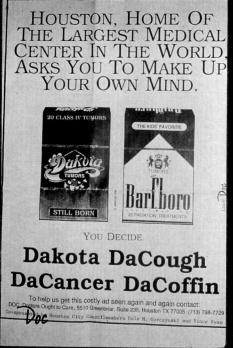

Carrie H. Livings Flatter asks young people a burning question in *Twelve Reliable Lessons on Cigarets*, published by the Anti-Cigaret Alliance of America in 1931. (Arents Collection, The New York Public Library)

Doctors Ought to Care (DOC) created this ad in 1990, when R. J. Reynolds announced plans to test-market Dakota, a new cigarette brand reportedly aimed at young, working-class women. (DOC)

A 1990 California Department of Health Services billboard explicitly ties tobacco to illegal drugs.

Trading cards produced by Doctors Ought to Care: C. Everett Koop meets the Garbage Pail Kids. (DOC)

An American Cancer Society billboard in Los Angeles tallies deaths attributed to smoking.

A New York City subway ad, sponsored by the Coalition for a Smoke-Free City, suggests that even casual exposure to second-hand smoke can have fatal consequences.

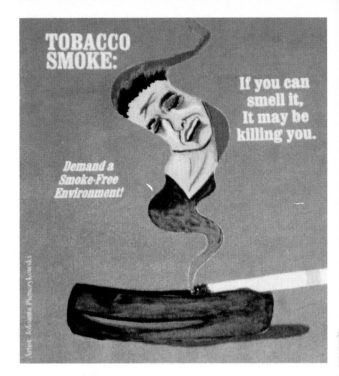

A New York City taxi ad, featuring the winner of a poster contest sponsored by SmokeFree Educational Services, mocks Virginia Slims and the brand's new slogan.

The Marlboro Man has some bad news in a 1997 billboard sponsored by the California Department of Health Services. (Neil Michel, Axiom Photo)

A 1997 California billboard suggests that smokers are guilty of homicidal negligence. (Neil Michel, Axiom Photo)

of people do the same thing."[30] Once legitimized, the anger of non-smokers who felt they had suffered too long in silence was a renewable resource. Each victory in restricting smoking established higher expectations, which in turn led to demands for more restrictions. As drug policy scholar Mark Kleiman has observed, "Nonsmokers seem to become more sensitive to cigarette smoke the less they encounter it."[31]

The cigarette companies recognized the threat posed by the non-smokers' rights movement. In a 1978 report, a polling company hired by the Tobacco Institute warned that the issue of "passive smoking" would be a potent weapon for tobacco's opponents. "What the smoker does to himself may be his business, but what the smoker does to the non-smoker is quite a different matter," the report said. "This we see as the most dangerous development to the viability of the tobacco industry that has yet occurred."[32]

THE LOCAL OPTION

The 1980s brought a second wave of smoking restrictions, mostly at the local level, prompted largely by growing anxiety about the health effects of secondhand smoke. During the previous decade such concerns had focused mainly on nonsmokers who were considered especially vulnerable, such as those with respiratory diseases. By the end of the '80s, however, it was widely accepted that secondhand smoke, dubbed environmental tobacco smoke (ETS) by public health specialists, could seriously harm otherwise healthy nonsmokers. Most people who objected to secondhand smoke were probably still concerned, first and foremost, about the immediate odor and discomfort. But as Koop observed in 1987, the possibility of grave long-term consequences made the demand for smoking bans seem more compelling. At the Seventh World Conference on Tobacco in 1990, Stanton A. Glantz, the University of California researcher who cofounded Californians for Nonsmokers' Rights, reflected on the importance of the health argument: "The main thing the science has done on the issue of ETS, in addition to help people like me pay mortgages, is it has legitimized the concern that people have that they don't like cigarette smoke. And that is a strong emotional force that needs to be harnessed and used."[33]

An early attempt to generate concern about ETS appeared in the May 2, 1980, issue of *Science.* James L. Repace, a physicist who worked for the Environmental Protection Agency, and Alfred H. Lowrey, a chemist at the Naval Research Laboratory, sampled air from various locations where people smoked—including bars, restaurants, and a bowling alley—and found significant levels of respirable suspended particles (material that can be inhaled). "Clearly," they concluded, "indoor air pollution from tobacco smoke presents a serious risk to the health of nonsmokers. Since the risk is involuntary, it deserves as much attention as outdoor air pollution."[34]

The following year two studies appeared to support the speculation that Repace and Lowrey had presented as fact. In one, Takeshi Hirayama, chief of epidemiology at the National Cancer Center Research Institute in Tokyo, tracked more than ninety thousand nonsmoking women for fourteen years and found that lung cancer was significantly more common among those married to smokers than among those married to nonsmokers. "These results indicate the possible importance of passive or indirect smoking as one of the causal factors of lung cancer," he wrote in the *British Medical Journal.*[35] In the other study, a team of researchers led by Dimitrios Trichopoulos, an epidemiologist at the University of Athens School of Medicine, interviewed 51 women with lung cancer and 163 other hospital patients about their own and their husbands' smoking habits. Looking at just the nonsmokers (40 and 149, respectively, in the two groups), they found that the patients married to smokers were significantly more likely to have lung cancer than single women or wives of nonsmokers. "This study has obvious limitations," they wrote in the *International Journal of Cancer,* "and is offered principally to suggest that further investigation of this issue be pressed."[36] A third study published in 1981, an analysis by Lawrence Garfinkel of American Cancer Society data for more than 175,000 women, found that "compared to nonsmoking women married to nonsmoking husbands, nonsmokers married to smoking husbands showed very little, if any, increased risk of lung cancer."[37]

Both Hirayama and Trichopoulos were tentative in their conclusions, and both studies were criticized on grounds of methodology and plausibility.[38] During the next decade and a half, researchers continued to investigate the possible link between ETS and lung cancer, producing more than forty additional epidemiological studies.[39] Several studies also looked for a connection between ETS and heart disease. Almost all of these studies compared nonsmoking wives of smokers to nonsmoking wives of nonsmokers, and they generally used a retrospective, case-control method, the approach taken by Trichopoulos. That is, they started by "matching" a group of lung cancer cases with a group of women who did not have lung cancer, rather than following subjects over time, as Hirayama did, to see who developed the disease. Most of these studies found a modest association between lung cancer and marriage to a smoker, and sometimes the association was statistically significant. But because the associations were weak, interpreting them was problematic.

Unlike the research on smoking and lung cancer, the ETS studies were not prompted by unexplained increases in disease. American men have been smoking cigarettes in large numbers since World War I, and by the 1950s most of them were exposing their wives to ETS. Yet lung cancer rates in women did not start rising substantially until decades after *they* had started smoking in large numbers.[40] In his 1981 article, which looked at lung cancer rates among nonsmokers in a study of U.S. veterans from 1954 to 1969 and in the ACS study from 1960 to 1972, Garfinkel concluded that "there was no evidence of any trend."[41] Data from national mortality surveys indicate that lung cancer rates among never-smoking women remained stable between the late 1950s and the mid-1980s.[42]

Despite the uncertainty, anti-smoking activists were quick to latch on to evidence suggesting that exposure to secondhand smoke could be fatal. In the April 1984 issue of the *Western Journal of Medicine,* Stanton Glantz suggested "What to Do Because Evidence Links Involuntary (Passive) Smoking with Lung Cancer." Although he conceded that there appeared to be "a genuine controversy" about the studies published in 1981, he nevertheless recommended "legislative efforts to protect non-smokers in the workplace and public places." He acknowledged that one goal of such laws is to "discourage smoking and help smokers who wish to quit."[43]

Glantz elaborated on that point at a 1986 anti-smoking conference: "Although the nonsmokers' rights movement concentrates on protecting the nonsmoker rather than on urging the smoker to quit for his or her own benefit, clean indoor air legislation reduces smoking because it undercuts the social support network for smoking by implicitly defining smoking as an antisocial act. Moreover, since the nonsmokers' rights movement speaks to the nonsmoking majority, it is dealing with an audience that is willing to hear—and act on—the message that secondhand smoke is dangerous." He advised activists to state that they were "not 'anti-smoker' but rather environmentalists concerned with clean indoor air for everyone." Said Glantz, "The issue should be framed in the rhetoric of the environment, toxic chemicals, and public health rather than the rhetoric of saving smokers from themselves or the cigarette companies."[44]

That strategy has been remarkably successful. In the early 1980s, Californians for Nonsmokers' Rights (CNR), which grew out of the failed campaigns for a statewide anti-smoking initiative in 1978 and 1980, started lobbying for smoking restrictions at the local level. In 1981 and 1982 several municipalities in California, including San Diego, adopted smoking ordinances. CNR's most conspicuous victory came in San Francisco, where voters approved an anti-smoking measure known as Proposition P in 1983. The proposition began as an ordinance that gave employees the right to demand a smoke-free workplace. After Mayor Dianne Feinstein signed the ordinance in June, a coalition that included tobacco companies and the local chamber of commerce announced a campaign to overturn the measure by submitting it to voters for approval. This effort was known as the "No on P" campaign (rather counterintuitively, since it was run by the people who had put the measure on the ballot). On the other side was San Franciscans for Local Control, an organization that included CNR, the local chapters of the American Cancer Society and the American Lung Association, the Sierra Club, and Common Cause. Although the tobacco industry spent more than $1.2 million on the campaign, Proposition P prevailed by twelve hundred votes.[45]

After the much-publicized victory in San Francisco, many other California municipalities, including Los Angeles, adopted smoking ordinances. Local restrictions proliferated in other states as well, often beginning in cities with a "progressive" reputation, such as Eugene, Brookline,

Seattle, and Aspen. By the end of 1985, more than a hundred municipalities had adopted smoking ordinances. Most were in California and almost a fifth were in Massachusetts, but a dozen other states were also represented, including Michigan, New York, South Dakota, and Texas.[46]

The nonsmokers' rights movement got a big boost in 1986, when both Surgeon General C. Everett Koop and the National Research Council, an arm of the National Academy of Sciences, declared that secondhand smoke was a serious health hazard. In *The Health Consequences of Involuntary Smoking,* Koop reviewed the epidemiological evidence and concluded that "involuntary smoking is a cause of disease, including lung cancer, in healthy nonsmokers." He also found that the children of smokers get respiratory infections and exhibit symptoms such as coughing and wheezing more often than the children of nonsmokers. To encourage movement toward "a smoke-free society," he emphasized that "the simple separation of smokers and nonsmokers within the same air space may reduce, but does not eliminate, the exposure of nonsmokers to environmental tobacco smoke." The NRC's Committee on Passive Smoking, which reviewed the literature at the request of the EPA and the Office on Smoking and Health, agreed that "considering the evidence as a whole, exposure to ETS increases the incidence of lung cancer in nonsmokers." Both Koop and the NRC reserved judgment on the possibility that ETS might cause cardiovascular disease or other kinds of cancer, saying more research was required to resolve those issues.[47]

The year after these two reports were released, Congress banned smoking on most domestic airline flights, and twenty states passed legislation restricting smoking. In a 1987 Gallup poll, 81 percent of respondents agreed that exposure to secondhand smoke is hazardous and 55 percent supported a complete ban on smoking in public places. The trend toward local restrictions accelerated dramatically. By the end of the decade some four hundred cities or counties—including New York, Chicago, Houston, and Washington, D.C.—had adopted smoking ordinances, covering more than a fifth of the U.S. population. All but a handful of states had smoking laws, generally less restrictive than the local measures. It also appears that most businesses, in response to legal requirements or the complaints of nonsmokers, had imposed smoking restrictions on their employees. In one survey, the share of companies restricting smoking rose from 54 percent in 1987 to 85 percent in 1992. Even more striking, the proportion that banned smoking completely rose from 7 percent to 34 percent.[48]

ZERO TOLERANCE

Smoking bans are the wave of the present. No longer content with simple segregation, advocates of nonsmokers' rights now insist that ETS be eliminated from all "public places," including stores, offices, factories, restaurants, stadiums, parks, bowling alleys, and even bars, which were scheduled to go smoke-free in California on January 1, 1998. To justify the new policy of zero tolerance, activists cite the EPA's decision to classify ETS as a "known human carcinogen." In its risk assessment, dated December 1992 but released in January 1993, the EPA estimated that exposure to ETS in the United States causes some three thousand cases of lung cancer each year. It also found that ETS affects the health of children by aggravating asthma, raising the incidence of fluid in the middle ear, and increasing the risk of lower respiratory tract infections such as bronchitis and pneumonia. Like the surgeon general and the NRC, the EPA did not draw any conclusions about ETS and heart disease, limiting its review to respiratory health effects.[49]

Since earlier drafts of the EPA report were released in May 1990 and May 1992, the classification of ETS as a known human carcinogen received extensive publicity well before the decision was finalized. The message that the public heard was summed up on a billboard in Los Angeles that I used to pass every day on the way to work: "Secondhand smoke kills." Advocates of smoking bans declared that it was no longer appropriate to balance the needs of smokers and nonsmokers; the time for compromise had passed. In a 1991 op-ed piece calling for smoking bans in outdoor stadiums, Ahron Leichtman compared smoking in the presence of others to spraying them with poison, slapping them, or spitting on them. "Would you sit idly by while the ballclub's management spoke to you about sprayers' rights, spitters' rights or slappers' rights?" he asked. "Would you calmly suggest these folks be placed in a separate section where they couldn't harm you? No, you'd probably want them arrested and put in jail. That's where people who commit assault and battery are sent."[50]

Recognizing the power of the EPA's pronouncement, Philip Morris, R. J. Reynolds, and groups representing tobacco growers and vendors challenged the risk assessment in federal court several months after it came out. They argued that the EPA's classification of ETS violated the Administrative Procedure Act and the due process clause of the Fifth Amendment by ignoring contrary data, using unscientific methods, and disregarding the agency's own guidelines for risk assessment. A year later U.S. District Judge William L. Osteen rejected the government's motion to dismiss the complaint, finding that the plaintiffs had standing to sue because the EPA's decision could reasonably be expected to have an impact on their economic interests.[51]

The industry had reason to be concerned. After the EPA tentatively called ETS a known human carcinogen in 1990, there was an immediate surge in strict local smoking ordinances: About forty cities, mostly in California, banned smoking in restaurants or workplaces between 1990 and 1992, compared to just two during the previous three years. By the end of 1992, the total number of local smoking ordinances had risen to more than 540.[52] In the wake of the EPA's final report in 1993, the Pentagon banned smoking indoors on all of its military bases, except for restaurants, recreational areas, and housing. San Francisco, Los Angeles, and New York banned smoking in restaurants. Maryland, Vermont, Washington, and California adopted laws or regulations prohibiting smoking in virtually all enclosed workplaces. The Occupational Safety and Health Administration proposed federal regulations that would impose the same rule nationwide. Representative Henry Waxman, the California Democrat who at the time chaired the House Subcommittee on Health and the Environment, introduced the Smoke-Free Environment Act, which would have banned smoking in almost every indoor location in the country except residences.[53] In June 1997, Waxman, Senator Durbin, and Senator Lautenberg introduced another Smoke-Free Environment Act, covering international flights as well as "all public and private buildings in which more than 10 people regularly enter." They also called upon President Clinton to ban smoking in all federal buildings by executive order, which he did two months later.[54] Under the nationwide tobacco settlement proposed that summer, the cigarette companies agreed to endorse a weaker version of Waxman's bill, exempting restaurants, bars, private clubs, hotel guest rooms, casinos, bingo parlors, tobacco merchants, and prisons.

The ostensible motivation for these restrictions was concern about the health effects of secondhand smoke. But, once again, they served a broader agenda. During the 1994 hearings on Waxman's bill, EPA administrator Carol Browner testified that the main benefit of a nationwide smoking ban would be its impact on smokers. "The reduction in smoker mortality due to smokers who quit, cut back, or do not start is estimated to range from about 33,000 to 99,000 lives per year," she said. Six former surgeons general, the *New York Times* reported, "echoed the theme that this simple measure could do more for the public health than any other bill in years."[55]

It's certainly plausible that people will smoke less as the number of places where they can do so shrinks. A 1996 paper published by the National Bureau of Economic Research estimated that workplace smoking bans reduce the prevalence of smoking among employees by about 5 percentage points and cut cigarette consumption among those who continue smoking by about 10 percent.[56] In a 1994 CNN/*Time* poll, 30 percent of smokers said they were smoking less because of restrictions on smoking in public places, and that percentage is likely to rise as the restrictions become more severe. The same poll found that 60 percent of smokers believed "increased restrictions on smoking in public places" were justified, while 39 percent felt "unjustly discriminated against as a smoker."[57] That is a substantial level of resentment, and it, too, will probably grow.

Beginning in the 1980s, nonsmokers' rights activists were countered by organizations with names like the Puffer Alliance and the United Smokers Association. Tobacco's opponents tend to dismiss such groups, noting that some of them receive funding and encouragement from cigarette companies. In 1989 Richard Durbin complained about industry efforts "to help militant smokers organize against local anti-smoking ordinances," saying, "The goal is to create what appears to be a grass-roots movement of smokers fighting for their civil rights."[58] But even this description presupposes the existence of "militant smokers," who surely are not an invention of the tobacco companies. Their grievances are just as sincere as those of nonsmokers, and it would be a mistake to pretend otherwise.

Sue Henderson has served as president of the Florida Smokers' Rights Association and as a spokeswoman for the United Smokers Association. A former Florida prosecutor, she was dismissed from her job after she protested a smoking ban that she said was "imposed without any accommodation, discussion, or any reasonableness at all" in response to the EPA's report. Forbidden to smoke even in her own office, she had to go outside for cigarettes, and she says her performance suffered as a result. "Although Ms. Henderson had once been a lawyer with some promise," a letter from the Florida attorney general's office said, "over the past six months, she's become very unproductive." The letter also described her as "generally obnoxious, harassing, vitriolic, and verbally abusive" after the ban was imposed. "I have been accused of being a puppet of the Tobacco Institute," Henderson said on CNN in 1994. "There are some people who would say this, but I think those people are just refusing to believe that people will speak out on things that are very compelling to them."[59]

The strong feelings of people like Sue Henderson are grounded in circumstances that can be readily observed. In nineteenth-century Berlin, smoking was prohibited on the street. In twentieth-century New York, the street is one of the few places where smoking is still allowed. An ordinance that took effect in April 1995 bans smoking in restaurants and offices, with minor exceptions (e.g., smoking is still permitted in restaurants with thirty-five or fewer seats, in bar areas, and at outdoor tables). So unless they want to spend the day in a bar, most smokers have to light up on the street—near the building where they work, on the way from the subway, while walking to lunch or a meeting. On a crowded sidewalk in the middle of the day, tobacco smoke is everywhere.

This phenomenon, which is becoming increasingly familiar in cities throughout the country, has provoked predictable complaints. As John Banzhaf told the *New York Times,* "All those smokers standing at the door, and all those butts sitting on the ground. People are tired of it."[60] Although Ahron Leichtman concedes that "the restriction on indoor smoking created the pollution right outside the building, where people hover," he says, "If you've got six people smoking around the entrance of a building and somebody has to walk through that cloud of smoke, even though it's outside, there is a degree of discomfort [or] harm."[61] In Davis and Palo Alto, California, smoking is prohibited within twenty feet of any building that is open to the public, which makes just about anywhere downtown off-limits. (Smokers can skirt the restriction if they keep walking.) In Bellaire, Texas, a suburb of Houston, smoking is banned in all public parks. Several other towns have adopted or are considering bans in outdoor recreation areas.

Direct regulation is not the only way to restrict smoking. In 1993 the attorneys general of fifteen states urged fast-food restaurants to ban smoking, citing the EPA report and expressing concern about the health of young customers and workers. In 1994 the National Restaurant Association complained that the EPA had sent letters to restaurateurs that asked them to sign a "Memorandum of Understanding" promising to ban smoking in exchange for an EPA certificate indicating their cooperation. The association's president said, "We are very concerned that the EPA—an agency with no jurisdiction over indoor air—should be taking it upon itself to get restaurateurs to sign a suspicious agreement regarding smoking policies in their establishments."[62]

Such friendly suggestions from prosecutors and federal regulators may be worrisome, but the threat of lawsuits is probably more intimidating. The year after the release of the EPA's report, thousands of businesses decided to ban smoking. One survey of U.S. and Canadian workplaces found that the share of buildings where smoking was prohibited rose from 42 percent in 1991 to 71 percent in 1994.[63] This trend was largely due to liability concerns, a factor the EPA was counting on when it issued its risk assessment, since the agency does not have the authority to regulate workplaces.[64]

Businesses that allow smoking have to worry about lawsuits by both customers and employees, who can use several strategies to get around the limits imposed by worker's compensation laws.[65] One of these is to sue under the Americans with Disabilities Act (ADA). The ADA, which took effect in July 1992, requires "reasonable accommodation" of customers and employees with disabilities. It did not take long for tobacco's opponents to realize that people who are especially sensitive to ETS

could be considered disabled. As the American Civil Liberties Union of
Southern California put it, "Second-hand smoke in the workplace, in
public transportation, and in public accommodations such as restaurants and shopping malls poses a significant health hazard to persons
with respiratory disabilities, depriving them of normal access to public
accommodations and the opportunity and ability to engage in gainful
employment."[66] A 1994 workshop in Ventura County, California,
cosponsored by the American Lung Association and the American Cancer Society, urged participants to demand smoking bans everywhere
they went, as a civil right guaranteed by the ADA. Writing in the *Saint
Louis University Public Law Review,* three attorneys with the Tobacco
Products Liability Project called the ADA "the most far-reaching tobacco control law yet."[67]

Three ADA cases filed in 1993 suggest why. In one, an asthmatic argued that the law required his employer, Virginia Electric and Power
Co., to prohibit smoking in the building where he worked. Before the
case went to trial, the company constructed separately ventilated smoking rooms and banned smoking everywhere else at its work sites. Agreeing that "the ADA protects Harmer from discrimination due to his disability," the judge concluded that the company's new policy (which
would be prohibitively expensive for most businesses) amounted to "reasonable accommodation." In Connecticut a woman with lupus and the
mothers of three children with asthma sued Burger King, McDonald's,
and Wendy's under the ADA, demanding that the chains ban smoking
in all of their restaurants nationwide. A Utah man with a genetic lung
disease sued two bowling alleys and eleven eateries, including five
Denny's restaurants, charging them with illegal discrimination under
the ADA. McDonald's, which in 1994 banned smoking at all its corpo-
rate-owned locations and urged franchisees to do likewise, saw the writing on the wall. As its attorneys noted in the Connecticut case, the
plaintiffs' legal theory, "if accepted, will effectively prohibit smoking just
about wherever people gather outside their homes. This prohibition
would include places that are smoke-filled virtually by definition—tav-
erns, nightclubs, faculty lounges and even tobacconist shops."[68]

In 1987 William McKinney pioneered another legal tactic for a special class of people seeking to avoid secondhand smoke. McKinney, a

murderer serving a life sentence in a Nevada state prison, filed a complaint arguing that forcing him to share a cell with a five-pack-a-day
smoker violated the Eighth Amendment's guarantee against cruel and
unusual punishment. He complained of nosebleeds, headaches, chest
pains, and lethargy. The trial court concluded that McKinney could not
show a causal connection between these symptoms and his exposure to
secondhand smoke, but the U.S. Court of Appeals for the Ninth Circuit
said the possibility of illness in the future should be considered. In 1993
the U.S. Supreme Court agreed that McKinney might have a constitutional claim, based on "an unreasonable risk of serious damage to his future health," and sent the case back to the trial court for consideration.[69]
By then, McKinney had been moved to a smoke-free cell in another
prison.

Even smoking at home, so far exempted from state and local regulations, can end up in the courts. "In a close custody dispute," says ASH's
John Banzhaf, "where you have two parents who have no other obvious
advantages or disadvantages . . . a factor which should be considered is
whether the child will be subjected to tobacco smoke." Judges have
begun to take Banzhaf's advice; he reports that custody has been denied
because of a parent's smoking in several cases. In 1994 a New Jersey
judge, responding to a father's complaint about his ex-wife's smoking, allowed her to retain custody of their children but ordered her to buy an air
purifier and to smoke only in her bedroom. That same year an article in
the *Marquette Law Review* argued that "parents who expose their children
to ETS should be viewed as committing child abuse. . . . A logical place
to eliminate ETS exposure is in the home, where children should be the
most protected."[70] Banzhaf does not go quite that far. "Where a parent
knows that the child is sensitive to it, where the child has exhibited serious symptoms from it in the past," he says, "then it seems to me that in
some situations some intervention is warranted." Banzhaf supports prohibiting smoking in vehicles carrying passengers under the age of sixteen,
a rule that was recently proposed by a state legislator in Pennsylvania. "It
seems to me," he says, "that the risks and problems of tobacco smoke,
particularly in a very small, enclosed situation like a car, are significant
enough to warrant the law saying that you should not do it."[71]

Action on Smoking and Health also urges apartment and condominium dwellers who are disturbed by their neighbors' tobacco smoke to take various steps and, "if all else fails, consider legal action."[72] In 1994 William and Valerie Pentony did more than consider it. The Dover, New Jersey, couple sued their downstairs neighbors, a sixty-one-year-old widow named Marie Conrad and her forty-two-year-old daughter, Mary, claiming that smoke from their cigarettes was seeping up through the floor. The Pentonys complained of nausea, coughing, sneezing, wheezing, and watery eyes. They said their clothes, rug, and cat smelled of smoke. They asked for a court order requiring the Conrads to smoke only between 9 A.M. and 4 P.M., when the Pentonys were at work. Superior Court Judge John M. Boyle suggested that the co-op board try to mediate a compromise instead. The Conrads got an air purifier and the board did repair work to seal the apartments, but the Pentonys were not satisfied. They dropped the suit nearly a year later, after the board agreed to pay them $6,100 (they had initially sought $45,000). "I consider them fanatics," Marie Conrad said midway through the dispute. "Years ago, we smoked with our babies in our laps. Now, all of a sudden, people think they get a whiff of smoke, they'll keel over."[73]

A WHIFF OF RISK

Well, what about it? How dangerous is this stuff, anyway? The honest answer is we don't exactly know. But it is safe to say that the hazards of secondhand smoke have been grossly exaggerated. ETS is certainly an irritant. It can induce tears, headaches, coughing, and nausea. It probably aggravates asthma and bronchitis, and it may increase the frequency of respiratory infections in young children.[74] On the other hand, the risk for kids exposed to ETS in the home, which the *Lancet* calls "unquantifiable and probably tiny," is hardly enough to justify a charge of child abuse.[75] When ASH claimed in one of its Internet reports that "smoking parents are killing their infants," John Banzhaf received a letter of rebuke from the Sudden Infant Death Syndrome Alliance, which emphasized that "*no direct causal relationship has been established*" between ETS and SIDS.[76] More generally, the evidence that secondhand smoke actually kills people is far less certain than you would guess from the confident assertions of public health officials and anti-smoking activists—

and, facile analogies notwithstanding, far less certain than the evidence that smoking causes fatal diseases.

But the evidence is just one of several factors shaping beliefs about secondhand smoke. In a fascinating survey of 1,461 scientists reported by the journal *Risk Analysis* in 1992, each respondent heard a brief summary of the evidence concerning radon, dioxin, or ETS. The substance was named in only half of the interviews. Although the summaries were otherwise identical, scientists who knew the name of the substance were more likely to consider it hazardous, and the effect was most pronounced in the case of ETS. When respondents knew they were being asked about ETS, 70 percent said it was a serious environmental health hazard and 85 percent said background exposure should prompt regulation. When ETS was called Substance X, by contrast, 33 percent of the scientists said the hazard was serious and 41 percent thought regulation was appropriate. Speculating on the source of this discrepancy, the researchers noted that opinions regarding ETS may be affected by knowledge about the risks of smoking.[77]

The idea that secondhand smoke is a deadly health hazard dovetails so well with the goal of discouraging smoking that tobacco's opponents generally have not been inclined to scrutinize it very closely. Nevertheless, several scientists who agree that discouraging smoking is important have warned that sound science should not be compromised for that purpose. On the subject of ETS they have observed a tendency to ignore subtleties, make questionable assumptions, minimize methodological problems, and gloss over the limitations of the data. "I just think a great deal more skepticism is in order," says Geoffrey Kabat, a cancer epidemiologist who served on the advisory panel that reviewed the EPA's report. "If these were data on something else—risk factors for ingrown toenails or something like that—people would look at it and say, 'Well, it's really not too impressive. . . . There's not that much there.' "[78]

Kabat, an assistant professor of preventive medicine at the State University of New York in Stony Brook, believes there is enough evidence about the health effects of ETS—that it aggravates respiratory conditions, for example—to justify banning smoking in public places. But he considers the evidence that ETS causes lung cancer much more equivocal, and he was troubled by the way the EPA approached the issue. "To all appearances," he writes, "the EPA decided in the late 1980s to classify 'environmental tobacco smoke' as a 'known human carcinogen.' Their view of their mission was to 'update' the reports issued by the Surgeon General and the NRC, which had reached the same conclusion in 1986. Thus, although the process of drafting the EPA report had the appearance of an independent, critical evaluation of the scientific evidence, with intensive scrutiny from a panel of non-EPA scientists assembled by the EPA's Scientific Advisory Board, in fact this was fundamentally a political exercise which involved marshaling a mountain of evidence to support a *predetermined* conclusion."[79]

Kabat, though in a minority on the advisory panel and in the public health community, is not the only scientist who has expressed concern that the case for a link between ETS and lung cancer has been overstated. The list of skeptics includes the eminent toxicologist Philippe Shubik, UCLA epidemiologist James Enstrom, Yale epidemiologist Alvan Feinstein, Stockholm University toxicologist Robert Nilsson, University of Chicago biostatistician John Bailar, and Michael Gough, a molecular biologist who served more than a decade as a senior associate and program manager in the U.S. Office of Technology Assessment. Weaknesses in the evidence have also been highlighted by reports from the Congressional Research Service and the Energy Department.[80] As my Author's Note indicates, some antismokers have tried to discredit critics of the case against ETS by implying that they are secretly in league with the cigarette companies. Not only does this sort of *ad hominem* attack carry no logical weight— whatever the motivation of the skeptics, their arguments have to be dealt with—but it is simply not credible that all of these reputable scientists and analysts are part of some grand conspiracy to create the illusion of a controversy.

All of the skeptics agree that smoking is bad for you, and some of them are vigorous critics of the tobacco industry. In the 1970s Shubik rebuked scientists employed by the cigarette companies for trying to cast doubt on the evidence that smoking is harmful. "You will go down in history denying facts well known to the scientific community," he said.[81] It is therefore especially noteworthy that in 1992 Shubik wrote a letter to the EPA's ETS advisory panel in which he said:

It has come to my attention that the EPA has adopted the view that ETS demonstrably poses a lung cancer hazard. While being absolutely opposed to cigarette smoking, an unequivocal human cancer hazard, I believe that adopting an official stand that the levels of carcinogens produced by ETS are established human carcinogens is not only unjustified but establishes a scientifically unsound principle.

Indeed, current smoking advocates might well use the unsound science inherent in this approach to undermine the association between cigarette smoking and lung cancer. Assuming that ETS is a human carcinogen necessitates the assumption that a single cigarette must be carcinogenic to a smoker, a demonstrably false assumption. . . . Let us not undermine the credibility of the best case in carcinogenesis even if the final aim is a laudable one.[82]

As Shubik's comments suggest, there is a big difference between smoking and exposure to ETS—so big that terms such as *passive smoking* and *involuntary smoking* are misleading. A smoker deeply inhales concentrated tobacco smoke directly from a cigarette, mainly through his mouth. A person exposed to ETS, by contrast, breathes air containing a highly diluted combination of sidestream smoke (from the cigarette's burning end) and exhaled mainstream smoke (from the filter end), mainly through his nose, which provides added filtration. ETS is so diluted that researchers sampling air in real-world situations have been able to detect only a small fraction of the many chemicals known to be present in mainstream smoke. The smoke not only disperses but ages—some of the compounds break down, while others cling to surfaces—so that no one knows what exactly is in the final mix. Nevertheless, ETS does include several carcinogens at detectable levels.

Researchers have used various methods to get some idea of how a nonsmoker's dose compares to a smoker's. In studies of cotinine, a nicotine metabolite, the levels in nonsmokers exposed to ETS have ranged between 0.1 percent and 2 percent of the levels in smokers.[83] On the basis of this measure, nonsmokers may absorb the nicotine equivalent of between 0.1 and 1 cigarette a day.[84] Repace and Lowrey have used a mathematical model—including estimates for ventilation, respiration, cigarette yields, smoking frequency, and "smoker density"—to calculate that a typical U.S. nonsmoker during the 1980s was exposed to 1.4 milligrams of tar and 0.14 milligram of nicotine a day.[85] By comparison, the official yield of a regular Marlboro is 16 milligrams of tar and 1.1 milligrams of nicotine.

Modest as Repace and Lowrey's estimates might seem, they are much higher than the levels found in two subsequent studies that used personal monitors—portable air pumps with filters—to measure the respirable suspended particles (RSP) and nicotine encountered by nonsmokers in the course of a day. Both studies measured solanesol, a marker for tobacco-related particulate matter, to estimate how much of the RSP should be attributed to ETS. In a 1994 study with about 250 British volunteers, researchers at Hazleton Europe, an independent laboratory, found that the median level of exposure was about 0.05 milligram of tar and 0.01 milligram of nicotine, while the most heavily exposed subjects inhaled something like 1.5 milligrams of tar and 0.17 milligram of nicotine.[86] In a 1995 study with about 1,600 volunteers from sixteen U.S. cities, a team led by Roger A. Jenkins of the Oak Ridge National Laboratory found that the median level of exposure for those reporting tobacco smoke at home, at work, or both was roughly 0.02 milligram of tar and 0.01 milligram of nicotine per day, while the most heavily exposed subjects were inhaling perhaps 0.8 milligram of tar and 0.1 milligram of nicotine.[87]

HOW MUCH IS TOO MUCH?

It's clear that the doses absorbed by nonsmokers are tiny compared to the doses absorbed by smokers. In terms of tar and nicotine, they probably amount to a small fraction of a cigarette per day, even for people who live or work with smokers. Is that enough to give you lung cancer? The EPA assumed it is. "The conclusive evidence of the dose-related lung carcinogenicity of [mainstream smoke] in active smokers, coupled with information on the chemical similarities of [mainstream smoke] and ETS and evidence of ETS uptake in nonsmokers," said the EPA report, "is sufficient *by itself* to establish ETS as a known human lung carcinogen."[88] In other words, if a lot of tobacco smoke causes cancer, so does a little. But in research on smoking and lung cancer, the lowest dose has typically been up to nine cigarettes a day; a few studies have found an effect among smokers of up to five cigarettes a day. No one has ever measured an increase in lung cancer among people smoking as little as one cigarette or less a day.

"There is an enormous leap of faith to think that we know anything about the smoke way down there," says Michael Gough, formerly with the U.S. Office of Technology Assessment and now director of science and risk studies at the Cato Institute. The belief that tobacco smoke can cause disease at very low levels is based on the widely held assumption that there is no threshold—that "there is no safe level of exposure to a cancer-causing substance," as a CDC fact sheet puts it. "Now we're getting into theology," says Gough, "to take a position on either side of that question. . . . There is a great deal of debate now about the idea of threshold. There are good people on both sides of it." And while scientists can offer arguments about whether a threshold might exist for a given substance, the issue is difficult to resolve empirically. We are, after all, talking about very low doses, so any effect would be correspondingly small—and therefore hard to detect. "If you do three dozen studies that show no increase at all," says Gough, "you can still say, 'Well, it's compatible with the risk that we predict.'"[89]

The controversy about the relationship between ETS and lung cancer stems mainly from the problems that scientists encounter when they try to determine whether an environmental agent has an effect at very low doses. First of all, statistical significance is elusive. In any study that compares a group exposed to a suspected risk factor with a control group, the luck of the draw may result in a difference between the two groups that does not reflect a difference between the populations the groups are supposed to represent. Researchers do statistical tests to account for the possibility of such a fluke. By convention, epidemiologists call a result significant when the probability that it occurred purely by chance is 5 percent or less. Even then, the true association—the one we would see if we could examine the entire population—is generally not known with much precision. Rather, the researchers can say they are 95 percent sure that the true association lies within a certain range, known as the confidence interval. The association is usually expressed as a ratio that compares the risk of disease in the exposed group to the risk in the nonexposed group. Epidemiologists tend to cite risk ratios in the middle of the confidence interval, but if the range includes 1.0 (representing no association), the result is not statistically significant. When, as in the case of ETS, any effect is likely to be small—and especially if the outcome is a rare disease, such as lung cancer in nonsmokers—it is difficult to collect samples large enough to show a statistically significant association.

Eighty percent of the epidemiological studies reviewed by the EPA did not find a statistically significant overall association between ETS and lung cancer, and none of the eleven U.S. studies did.[90] In an attempt to gain greater statistical power, the EPA pooled the results of the U.S. studies. This technique, known as meta-analysis, was originally developed for randomized clinical tests of drugs and other therapies. There is some controversy about using meta-analysis to detect small risks in data from observational research; critics say it tends to mask important differences and weaknesses in the underlying studies.[91] On the basis of its meta-analysis, the EPA estimated that nonsmoking wives of smokers are 1.19 times as likely to get lung cancer as nonsmoking wives of nonsmokers. In the meta-analysis the EPA used an unconventional confidence level of 90 percent—in effect doubling the odds that the association was spurious. The lower confidence level resulted from the use of a one-tailed test, a procedure that assumes away the possibility of a negative association (i.e., a significantly *lower* rate of lung cancer among the wives of smokers).

"That bothers me," says Kabat. "It is rather unusual to use a one-tailed test and a 90 percent confidence interval. The *Journal of the National Cancer Institute* requires authors to include a statement in the methods section that 'all statistical tests are two-tailed.' It's relaxing the standard, and it's especially suspicious since, as I remember it, if you use the 95 confidence interval, the 1.19 summary risk would not have been statistically significant."[92] According to the report, "the justification for this usage is based on the *a priori* hypothesis . . . that a positive association exists between exposure to ETS and lung cancer."[93] The idea is that ETS couldn't possibly be good for you; it just doesn't make sense that it would *reduce* the risk of lung cancer. Maybe so, but a negative association could still result from confounding variables or biases in the data.

In fact, several of the studies did find that lung cancer was less common among smokers' wives than among nonsmokers' wives, and in one the difference was statistically significant.[94]

Nevertheless, the use of a one-tailed test and the corresponding 90 percent confidence level with these data is at least arguably appropriate. It's harder to explain why the EPA used the conventional 95 percent confidence level in the first draft of its report and switched to the less rigorous standard later. "It's just a convention, the 5 percent, and they could have started off with 10 percent," says Gough. "They could have started with a one-tailed test rather than a two-tailed test. But it is suspicious when they switch, when an analysis goes one way, and they can change the rules and get it to go another way."[95] Furthermore, the EPA's review of thirty epidemiological studies obscured the fact that almost all of them used a 95 percent confidence level. Instead of presenting the results as they originally appeared, the EPA recalculated them using the less rigorous standard. As a 1994 report from the Congressional Research Service dryly noted, "It is unusual to return to a study after the fact, lower the required significance level, and declare its results to be supportive rather than unsupportive of the effect one's theory suggests should be present."[96]

Defenders of the EPA report have argued that the issue of statistical significance, which the tobacco industry emphasized in its challenge of the risk assessment, is a red herring designed "to confuse the public."[97] It's true that the case against ETS does not hinge on the EPA's choice of confidence level. But the decision suggests that the agency approached this issue as a prosecutor rather than a judge, trying to "fashion [an] indictment" of ETS, as an article in *Science* put it, even if that required "some fancy statistical footwork."[98] (The EPA reinforced the impression that the classification of ETS was a foregone conclusion by releasing the first draft of a guide to workplace smoking restrictions in June 1990, two and a half years before it officially declared ETS a hazard.) The EPA's statistical stretch also illustrates the point that however plausible it might seem that ETS could cause lung cancer, demonstrating that connection in the real world is very tricky. Even with the looser standard, the lower end of the confidence interval generated by the EPA's meta-analysis was 1.04, meaning the result was barely significant.[99]

An April 1996 literature review commissioned by several European tobacco companies cited about fifty epidemiological studies of ETS and
lung cancer, including seventeen conducted in the United States. Of
these, only eight (including one U.S. study) found statistically significant
overall associations between ETS and lung cancer. Of twenty studies that
considered the relationship between the amount a man smoked and his
wife's risk of lung cancer, seven found a statistically significant trend.[100]
This rather unimpressive track record is especially striking when we consider the widely recognized phenomenon of publication bias: Researchers
tend not to submit, and journals tend not to publish, articles that present
negative findings. This means that studies supporting the hypothesis that
ETS causes lung cancer are more likely to see print.[101]

For similar reasons, researchers tend to emphasize results that favor
the hypothesis while downplaying those that don't. "Epidemiologists
want positive findings," says Kabat. "Nobody wants to find no relationship. It's boring."[102] In one of the largest case-control studies, led by
Ross C. Brownson of the Missouri Department of Health, there was no
overall association between lung cancer and childhood, spousal, or
workplace exposure, and none of the subgroup results reported in the tables was statistically significant.[103] "Almost all of the findings he had
were consistent with [zero risk]," says UCLA epidemiologist James E.
Enstrom. "Yet in spite of that, he concluded that his research supported
everybody else's findings."[104] Brownson and his colleagues wrote, "Ours
and other recent studies suggest a small but consistent increased risk of
lung cancer from passive smoking."[105] Because of this statement, which
was included in the abstract, journalists who looked up the study mis-
takenly concluded that tobacco industry representatives were lying when
they said the Brownson study did not support the case against ETS.[106]

THE ROOT OF CAUSE

Even when an association is statistically significant, it does not in itself
prove a cause-and-effect relationship. The association could be due to
other factors that the researchers have not taken into account. That possibility is especially hard to rule out when the association is weak, as it is
in the case of ETS. The EPA estimated that a woman who lives with a

smoker is 1.19 times as likely to get lung cancer as a woman who doesn't. More recent data from the largest case-control study, led by Louisiana State University epidemiologist Elizabeth T. H. Fontham, indicate a risk ratio of 1.29.[107]

"In epidemiologic research," noted a 1994 press release from the National Cancer Institute, "relative risks of less than 2 are considered small and are usually difficult to interpret. Such increases may be due to chance, statistical bias, or effects of confounding factors that are sometimes not evident." The press release concerned a study reported in the *Journal of the National Cancer Institute* that found that women who have abortions are 1.5 times as likely to get breast cancer as women who don't. An editorial that accompanied the study said a 50 percent difference in risk "is small in epidemiologic terms and severely challenges our ability to distinguish if it reflects cause and effect or if it simply reflects bias." At least seven studies have found a statistically significant link between abortion and breast cancer, and a 1996 meta-analysis yielded a risk ratio of 1.3. In response, public health authorities, reporters, and even the researchers themselves have emphasized the uncertainties associated with small relative risks. Such caution is equally appropriate in discussions of ETS and lung cancer, but it is rarely seen—perhaps because the right to smoke, unlike the right to abortion, is not very fashionable in journalistic and public health circles.[108]

As the NCI noted, confounding variables are one source of uncertainty. Women who marry smokers may differ from women who marry nonsmokers in some way (other than ETS exposure) that affects lung cancer risk. For example, there is some evidence that diet, especially a deficiency of antioxidant vitamins and excessive fat, plays a significant role in lung cancer.[109] There is also evidence that smokers tend to eat poorer diets than nonsmokers and that their spouses tend to eat the same foods, in which case wives of smokers might get lung cancer more often even if ETS posed no risk.[110] A few studies, including Fontham's, have tried to take diet into account, but the methods of doing so are necessarily imprecise, relying largely on questionnaires.

In their more realistic moments, epidemiologists recognize that information gleaned from questionnaires or interviews is not always accurate. When people are asked if they eat their vegetables, how much fat they consume, how much they drink, and how often they exercise, their answers have to be taken with a grain of salt. And it's plausible that the less healthy their habits, the more likely they are to misremember or misrepresent their behavior. Ernst Wynder, the pioneering lung cancer researcher, remarked on the uncertain reliability of self-reports at a 1993 forum on ETS. "A big problem in interview studies is bias, because we depend on what an individual tells us," he observed. "Whatever it is, if it relates to human nature you have an inherent bias that is difficult to measure and therefore very difficult to control."[111]

Researchers cannot even be sure about the most important confounding variable of all: smoking. To determine the smoking status of lung cancer patients, researchers rely on reports from the subjects themselves or from proxies (usually relatives) if the subject has died; they may also check medical records. Since this information is not always accurate, some women classified as never-smokers may in fact be current or (more likely) former smokers and would therefore have a much higher risk of lung cancer. Since smokers are more likely to marry smokers than nonsmokers are, this sort of error introduces a systematic bias in favor of an association between ETS exposure and lung cancer. The problem of misclassification is widely recognized, but estimates of its impact vary. In 1986 the NRC estimated that misclassification could account for half or more of the observed elevation in lung cancer risk.[112] The EPA's adjustment for misclassification, on the other hand, had very little impact on its risk assessment.[113] In a 1995 report, the Congressional Research Service concluded that plausible levels of misclassification could entirely account for the observed association between ETS and lung cancer.[114]

Other factors that might contribute to the appearance of a causal link include recall bias (people with lung cancer may be more likely, because of their disease, to report ETS exposure) and proxy bias (information from proxies—used only for the subjects with lung cancer—is likely to be less accurate than information from the subjects themselves). As with confounding variables and misclassification, the true impact of these biases is not only unknown but unknowable. If we were dealing with a robust association—like the link between smoking and lung cancer, where the risk ratios range upward of 10—confounding and bias would not matter so much. But with risk ratios as low as 1.19 or 1.29, it may be impossible to rule out alternative explanations.

"The noise is going to be bigger than the signal in that area," says Enstrom. "You may never be able to resolve it."[115] Gough agrees. "If environmental tobacco smoke causes cancer," he says, "I'm convinced we'll never show it. It's just beneath the level of detection."[116]And Howard E. Rockette, a University of Pittsburgh biostatistician who served on the EPA's advisory panel, concedes that "simple arguments in regard to statistical power, model dependence of extrapolation, and the potential for confounding when estimating low risks make this, as well as other low-dose problems, unsolvable using current techniques."[117]

If the existence of a lung cancer risk from ETS is questionable, its impact is even more uncertain. Jan Stolwijk, the Yale epidemiologist who was vice chairman of the advisory committee, has said the panel tried to discourage the EPA from including a lung cancer death toll in its report. "There was a tendency or a desire on the part of EPA to do what I call the body count," he said at a scientific conference in 1993, "in other words, to actively attribute a certain number of lung cancer deaths to this kind of exposure. . . . We tried to be as discouraging of that particular effort as we knew how." To derive the body count from its estimate of the risk facing the wife of a smoker, the EPA had to make a series of controversial assumptions about the level of risk facing people in different situations, none of them based on direct evidence. The EPA found that varying just two of the parameters used in the calculation produced estimates ranging from 400 to 7,000. "With all the caveats in there, and the way it was derived," Stolwijk said, "it has not a very firm basis."[118]

Although some members clearly had reservations, the advisory panel unanimously approved the final version of the EPA's report. The vote can be explained by several factors. First, it is probably unrealistic to expect underpaid outside consultants to keep sending the EPA back to the drawing board until all of their objections have been adequately addressed. Second, with the exception of Kabat, the panelists apparently agreed that it was appropriate to classify ETS as a known human carcinogen. Finding the analogy between smoking and exposure to ETS more persuasive than the epidemiological data, they advised the EPA to play up that aspect of the argument. If they had doubts about the evidence of what ETS was doing in the real world, they may have decided that it was better to err on the side of caution, agreeing with Howard Rockette's argument that "it is unreasonable to subject people to low levels of established carcinogens simply because we have never demonstrated a statistically significant risk at low levels."[119]

Then, too, expressing skepticism about the case against ETS can be risky. "The tobacco industry for decades sort of denied the findings of epidemiologists, even though they were incredibly strong," Enstrom says. "Now it's like you can't agree with anything that the tobacco industry says, even if there might actually be some truth in it." He remembers receiving phone calls in 1994 from people who had seen his comments on ETS quoted in the press. The gist of their complaint was, "How can you possibly say something like that? It can be misused."[120] Gough recalls that after he publicly doubted that ETS causes lung cancer, Representative Henry Waxman, sponsor of the Smoke-Free Environment Act, wrote "very strong letters to the director of OTA, saying, 'What is Gough doing here?'"[121]

Members of the EPA's advisory panel were not immune to such pressures. In November 1990 the Associated Press reported that six of the sixteen panelists, including its chairman, had "ties to a tobacco industry research group." The AP was referring to the Center for Indoor Air Research, which is funded mainly by tobacco companies. Five of the panelists had advised or reviewed research proposals for the center, while a sixth had received one of its grants. The story added that a seventh panelist, Geoffrey Kabat, "had been recommended by Philip Morris," apparently because he and Ernst Wynder had conducted two case-control studies of ETS and lung cancer and had written about the limitations of the data.[122] In a subsequent editorial, entitled "Objectivity Up in Smoke," the *New York Times* questioned the credibility of all seven scientists and recommended that the panel be reconstituted.[123] Soon the committee's chairman, Morton Lippmann, was assuring the *Washington Post*: "It's not that I'm a tool of industry. I'm a bigger tool of government. I've been working for the EPA longer. I have more to lose by offending the EPA than industry."[124]

In this context anyone who questioned the case against ETS risked being portrayed as a tool of the cigarette companies—even if, like Kabat, he had never received a dime from them. "Painting people in that way reminds you of, 'Were you ever a member of the Communist Party?' " Kabat says. "I felt really put on the spot, because I did not want to be seen as a spokesman, giving grist to the tobacco lobby's mill. But I also felt that I had an ethical obligation to not let pass the kind of stuff that was going on. . . . I would guess that some people are chilled and won't speak up because it's not comfortable, and you don't want to be labeled. It was very unpleasant for me. In a way, it was a political game. It wasn't primarily about science."[125]

DON'T PANIC

Even if we accept the EPA's conclusion at face value, there is no cause for alarm. "The reality is that the risk of getting lung cancer from living with someone who smokes is really small," says Elizabeth Whelan, president of the American Council on Science and Health. "It seems to be there, but it's an extremely weak effect."[126] The EPA estimated that living with a smoker increases your risk of lung cancer by 19 percent. In contrast, smoking increases your risk of lung cancer by 1,000 percent or more. Despite this huge difference, tobacco's opponents sometimes imply that the risks of ETS exposure are comparable to the risks of smoking. A time line displayed at a symposium sponsored by the American Cancer Society listed the 1992 death of singer Mary Wells from throat cancer, describing her as "a former two-pack-a-day smoker who was subjected to years of second-hand smoke in nightclubs."[127] This sort of false equivalence distracts attention from the substantial hazards of smoking, the last thing the ACS should want to do.

Not only is the estimated risk from ETS small when compared to the risk from smoking, but it's small in absolute terms as well. The lifetime risk of lung cancer among nonsmokers is very low to begin with (less than 1 percent). If you increase that risk by 19 percent—or 29 percent, or even 100 percent—it's still quite low. On the basis of the EPA's risk ratio, an epidemiologist with the North Carolina health department estimated that a nonsmoking woman who lives with a smoker faces an ad-

ditional lung cancer risk of 6.5 in 10,000.[128] That would raise her lifetime risk from about 0.34 percent to about 0.41 percent. Based on
Fontham et al.'s risk ratio, a coauthor of that study came up with similar
figures.[129] And remember, these risk increases apply to people who live
with smokers for decades.

Despite all the workplace regulations that have been enacted or proposed, there is scant evidence that exposure to ETS on the job increases
the risk of lung cancer. Contrary to what the EPA and the Occupational Safety and Health Administration have assumed, the two recent
studies using personal monitors found that exposure at home is more
substantial than exposure at work for people who report both. In its
proposed smoking ban, OSHA relied on the Fontham study, one of
only two that had found a statistically significant association between
workplace exposure and lung cancer.[130] (Ross Brownson and his colleagues, whose large study was reported about the same time, found
that "in general, there was no elevated lung cancer risk associated with
passive smoke exposure in the workplace."[131]) Fontham et al. found
that women who reported workplace exposure were 1.39 times as likely
to get lung cancer as women who didn't, compared to a risk ratio of
1.29 for the wives of smokers.[132] But the researchers did not control for
other sources of exposure when they calculated these ratios. As a group,
people who report ETS exposure at work are probably more likely to
socialize and live with smokers as well. So leaving aside the weaknesses
shared by all the epidemiological studies of ETS, it is not correct to say
that Fontham et al.'s figure represents the increase in risk traceable to
exposure at work per se.

Yet a 1994 public service announcement produced by the CDC implied just that. Citing a figure from an earlier version of the Fontham
study, it said, "People exposed to secondhand smoke at work are 34%
more likely to get lung cancer. And you thought the long hours were
killing you." In addition to wrongly implying that Fontham and her
colleagues separately measured the impact of workplace exposure, the
commercial created the impression that the preliminary finding of a
single study with female subjects applied to all people for all time. "It's
very sad that epidemiology has been misused like this," says Enstrom.
"In the old days, you'd say something like, 'Smokers have 10 times the

risk of getting lung cancer compared to never-smokers,' and that was a ballpark figure. No one would ever think of saying '10.14 times the risk,' based on one particular study."[133]

In addition to employing false precision, public health messages have promoted the notion that casual exposure to ETS—say, sitting next to a smoker in a restaurant or on an international flight—is potentially deadly. According to a CDC fact sheet, the EPA "now states that exposure to secondhand smoke greatly increases the chances of developing lung cancer."[134] But 19 percent is hardly a "great" increase, either in epidemiological terms or from an individual's perspective, and the CDC gives no indication of how much exposure we're talking about. A TV ad sponsored by the California Department of Health Services with Proposition 99 money shows a smoker going about his day and declares that all thirty-seven people he encounters "will die a little, because they were forced to breathe the smoke from his cigarette." A California billboard offers a variation on that theme: "Mind if I smoke?" a man asks a woman. "Care if I die?" she replies. A New York City subway ad sponsored by the Coalition for a Smoke-Free City shows smoke curling up from a cigarette in an ashtray and warns, "If you can smell it, it may be killing you."

Contrary to the impression created by these messages, there is no evidence that occasional encounters with tobacco smoke pose a significant risk. Even Dimitrios Trichopoulos, who pioneered research in this area and firmly believes that prolonged exposure to ETS can cause lung cancer, thinks that things have gotten out of hand. "There is an exaggeration," says Trichopoulos, who now heads the epidemiology department at the Harvard School of Public Health. "The risk is probably higher than many of the other alleged risks that we discuss—pollutants, contaminants, you name it. But it is still a risk that is considerably lower than, for instance, [the risk posed by] lack of exercise, or exposure to real active smoking, or eating red meat, or drinking excessively." He adds, "I hate to have someone smoking next to me in a transatlantic trip, but this is mostly because I'm concerned about the offensive odor, rather than that the risk during these particular 10 hours would be anything that would be noticeable. . . . If you are careful in your life to avoid exposure to passive smoking, and you just came across someone, or you entered a restaurant with smokers, you are not going to have anything that will affect materially your life expectancy or your probability of getting lung cancer. It's different if you're continuously exposed."[135]

As if the prospect of getting lung cancer were not enough to scare people about secondhand smoke, the CDC offers other reasons to avoid it. According to a CDC fact sheet that urges people to make their homes smoke-free, "Even your pets will be happier. For example, secondhand smoke increases the risk of lung cancer in dogs."[136] Another fact sheet warns: "At high exposure levels, nicotine is a potent and potentially lethal poison. Secondhand smoke is the only source of nicotine in the air."[137] The implication seems to be that people should worry about dying of nicotine poisoning as a result of exposure to ETS. "At high levels, arsenic is a poison," says Michael Gough. "I don't know what the sources of arsenic are in the environment—there are some out there—but I don't worry about them. The first statement is true, and the second statement is true, but it doesn't say anything about the level of nicotine in the general environment being harmful. They should have been ashamed."[138]

The most common way of building on the alarm created by the EPA's report is to claim that secondhand smoke kills not three thousand but fifty thousand or more Americans a year. The original source for this estimate seems to be a 1988 paper in *Environment International*.[139] Most of the additional deaths are attributed to heart disease, but the evidence that ETS contributes to heart disease is even weaker than the evidence that it contributes to lung cancer. A 1996 article coauthored by Kyle Steenland, a scientist at the National Institute for Occupational Safety and Health who has produced a widely cited estimate for heart disease deaths due to ETS, conceded, "This association remains controversial."[140] There are relatively few studies, and they generally do a poor job of controlling for confounding variables, which are more important for heart disease than for lung cancer. Furthermore, the risk of coronary heart disease is only about twice as high in smokers as in nonsmokers (with a mortality risk about 70 percent higher), so it's not likely that a risk from ETS would be detectable even if it existed.[141] In that light, the risk ratios reported in some of the studies—1.5 or more—are highly implausible. A 1995 analysis of data from the American Cancer Society and the National Mortality Followback Survey found that ETS exposure was not associated with a higher risk of heart disease, and the authors argued that publication bias had created a misleading impression.[142]

Probably the strongest study to find a link between ETS and coronary heart disease was published by the American Heart Association journal *Circulation* in 1997. The researchers, led by Ichiro Kawachi of Harvard Medical School, found that women who said they were regularly exposed to secondhand smoke at home or work were nearly twice as likely to develop coronary heart disease as those who did not report exposure. The prospective study, which followed thirty-two thousand nurses for ten years, took into account several risk factors, including high blood pressure, diabetes, high cholesterol, lack of exercise, high fat consumption, and low vitamin E intake (all of which were more common among subjects reporting regular ETS exposure).[143]

Although Kawachi et al. found a significant difference in heart disease rates even after adjusting for these variables, they acknowledged, "Unknown confounding factors may have contributed to the observed excess risk."[144] Furthermore, since the researchers relied on self-reports to determine smoking history, diet, exercise habits, and other relevant characteristics, the results may have been biased by inaccurate information (from respondents who, for example, failed to identify themselves as ex-smokers or who fibbed about their poor diet and lack of exercise). Another weakness in the study is that subjects were asked about ETS exposure only once, at the beginning of the ten-year period. And while the total number of subjects was large, the number of heart attacks—152 (including twenty-five deaths), with only 17 (including three deaths) in the nonexposed group—was relatively small, which may help explain inconsistencies in the results: Although the disease rate was higher for subjects reporting regular exposure than for those reporting occasional exposure, women exposed at home *or* at work had a higher risk than women exposed in *both* settings, and risk did not increase with years of exposure at home. The overall elevation in risk was not statistically significant for women exposed only at home, only at work, or in both settings. Finally, given the huge difference in dose, it just doesn't make sense that exposure to secondhand smoke could pose risks comparable to those associated with smoking.

Although anti-smoking activists have sometimes ascribed the higher estimate of ETS deaths, including heart disease, to the surgeon general or the EPA, no federal agency has officially endorsed it. It's especially striking that the EPA did not include heart disease in its risk assessment, since that would have bolstered the case against ETS. Nevertheless, the estimate of fifty thousand or so deaths has been adopted by anti-smoking groups and the California Department of Health Services. "In California, if you listen to some of the public service announcements that are put out by the Department of Health Services, it's amazing," says Enstrom. "They're making announcements that there are 50,000 deaths a year caused by ETS, based on these extrapolations for cardiovascular disease. I mean, they're not even equivocating. . . . In many cases, I think there has been a big overreaction. All the laws have been passed based on the [claim] that this number of deaths is being caused by ETS."[145]

DESTROYING DIVERSITY

Does the exact death toll really matter? Whatever the true risk, many people would like to avoid it. And even if secondhand smoke doesn't kill people, it certainly irritates them. Isn't that enough of a justification for restrictions on smoking?

The real question is not whether there should be restrictions—there always have been—but who should impose them. Traditionally, decisions about where smoking should be allowed were left to millions of merchants and restaurateurs, hoteliers and taxi drivers, homeowners and apartment dwellers. The right to set smoking rules was one of the prerogatives you acquired when you purchased or rented a piece of property. Vestiges of this system remain. You still get to decide whether visitors may smoke in your living room, and you would probably object if the government tried to impose a particular policy on you. But on other kinds of private property, the owner's authority to regulate smoking has been steadily usurped by government. The doctrine of "nonsmokers' rights" holds that people who object to smoking are entitled to a "smoke-free environment" just about anywhere they might want to go.

This doctrine blurs the distinction between a place that is "public" because it is jointly owned by taxpayers, such as a courthouse or the Department of Motor Vehicles, and a place that is "public" because the owner chooses to let people walk in off the street, such as a store or a restaurant. The first kind of public place is operated by the government on behalf of taxpayers, and it seems perfectly appropriate for the government to restrict smoking in such locations, taking into account the interests of smokers as well as nonsmokers (both are taxpayers, after all) wherever possible. The second kind of public place is operated by entrepreneurs on their own behalf, and the better they are at serving the needs of their customers (who may include both smokers and nonsmokers), the more successful they will be. In a system based on property rights, freedom of contract, and freedom of association, a business's smoking policy is one of many factors that people consider when deciding where to shop, dine, or work. Those decisions, in turn, help shape the policy.

In the absence of government-imposed restrictions, businesses do not uniformly permit smokers to light up wherever they please. Some do, but others ban smoking or restrict it to particular areas. Other rules are possible: A restaurant might allow smoking only on certain nights, for example, or only when no one objects. The point is that competition for customers and employees leads to a diversity of arrangements. In this connection it is instructive to note that half of the nation's airlines, including all the major carriers, were already setting aside no-smoking sections by 1973, when the Civil Aeronautics Board started requiring them to do so.[146] If federal legislation had not preempted market forces in the late 1980s, some U.S. airlines might have responded to increasing complaints about secondhand smoke by improving ventilation, and others might have followed Northwest's smoke-free example. By 1997, U.S. airlines had voluntarily banned smoking on almost all international flights.[147] And while many employers have restricted smoking because of government regulation or fear of lawsuits, many others have done so in response to complaints from employees. That's a trend that would have continued as attitudes toward smoking evolved, with or without legal requirements.

To justify government intervention, anti-smokers often compare ETS exposure to assault. In a 1996 appearance on the Fox News Channel, Matthew Myers of the National Center for Tobacco-Free Kids likened someone who encounters tobacco smoke on the job to an employee who gets punched every time he goes to work.[148] Would we tell that employee to switch jobs if he didn't like getting punched? Yes—if he were a boxer. Since he has chosen an occupation that explicitly involves letting other people hit him, we do not consider him an assault victim every time he steps into the ring. Similarly, a bartender or a flight attendant on an airline that permits smoking knows that exposure to smoke is part of the job. Popular as the assault metaphor is, secondhand smoke is really more like loud music than a punch in the face. In certain contexts—when it disturbs people in other buildings, for example—loud music is a public nuisance. But when it's confined to a bar, dance club, or concert hall, it's just a feature of the establishment, one that some people will like and others will find annoying and uncomfortable. No one proposes to ban loud music in all "public places" to accommodate those who prefer quiet.

By stepping in and imposing the same smoking policy on everyone, the government destroys diversity—the potential to satisfy a wide variety of tastes and preferences, not just the majority's. If someone tried to open a large restaurant in New York City that catered exclusively to smokers, he would be breaking the law. The same is true of a domestic airline that let passengers light up and advertised itself as "smoker-friendly." Although I have no desire to eat in such a restaurant or fly on such an airline, I think it's a shame that no one can. In a free society it's especially troubling that tobacco's opponents seek to foreclose these options as a way of pressuring smokers into quitting. In a 1997 *Washington Post* article about businesses that try to accommodate smokers, an American Cancer Society spokesman objected to such flexibility. "Many people quit smoking because it's just plain socially unacceptable," he said. "Health risks didn't move them. . . . But the fact that they were social pariahs and not welcome in their own buildings did move them."[149]

When my wife and I moved to New York a few years ago, we took Interstate 15 out of Los Angeles, and our first stop was Las Vegas. I'd never been there before, and I was duly impressed by the neon signs, the garish architecture, and the poker machines near the rest rooms. But the most striking thing was the smoking. People were lighting up with abandon in the casinos, the shops, the restaurants, the hotels. No one was shooing them outside, ostentatiously waving the smoke away, or pointing in annoyance at NO SMOKING signs. (I don't remember seeing any.) After five years in aggressively healthy and increasingly smoke-free Los Angeles, it was like a breath of fresh air.

Chapter 6

TRY, TRY AGAIN

We're going to take the Marlboro Man to court.

—Florida Governor Lawton Chiles, 1994

LET'S MAKE A DEAL

"I, personally, am not a scientist," said Bennett S. LeBow, chairman of the Liggett Group's parent corporation. "But like all of you, I am aware of the many reports concerning the ill effects of cigarette smoking." That much sounded like the standard industry line. LeBow should have continued, "I honestly don't know whether smoking causes disease." But he deviated from that timeworn pose of uncertainty, saying, "We at Liggett know and acknowledge that, as the surgeon general and respected medical researchers have found, cigarette smoking causes health problems, including lung cancer, heart and vascular disease, and emphysema." LeBow also broke ranks with the tobacco industry on the subject of addiction: "We at Liggett . . . know and acknowledge that, as the surgeon general, the Food and Drug Administration, and respected medical researchers have found, nicotine is addictive."[1]

Why did Liggett decide to admit the obvious? More to the point, why had cigarette makers been doubting or denying it for more than four decades? To answer the first question is to answer the second. Liggett came clean as part of a settlement agreement, announced in March 1997, that promised to eliminate the threat of devastating legal liability. And that threat was the main reason why the tobacco companies had for so long continued—predictably, preposterously—to reserve judgment about the health risks of smoking while denying that cigarettes are addictive.

The Liggett settlement resolved suits by twenty-two states (others joined later) seeking reimbursement for the costs of treating smoking-related diseases under Medicaid. A companion agreement with plaintiffs' lawyers was aimed at settling hundreds of other pending suits, including class actions in several states. If upheld by the courts, the deal would also bar future lawsuits by smokers or their survivors.

In exchange for this blanket of protection, Liggett did not have to do much. Aside from conceding what everyone already knew, the company agreed to attach the warning "Smoking Is Addictive" to its cigarette packages and ads; to avoid cartoon characters in advertising and promotion; to refrain from challenging the Food and Drug Administration's tobacco regulations; to begin following some the agency's rules right away; and to assist the attorneys general and plaintiffs' lawyers with their actions against the other tobacco companies by providing documents and witnesses. Liggett did not admit any wrongdoing, and nothing in the settlement can be used against the company in court.

Liggett also agreed to contribute 25 percent of its pretax income for twenty-five years to a fund from which the states and other plaintiffs would be compensated. Based on Liggett's pretax income in 1995, that would amount to about $575,000 a year—not much to pay the states, the lawyers, and hundreds of thousands, if not millions, of potential class members. The company spent $10 million in 1996 just to defend these cases. Had it started losing, it could have been hit by damage awards totaling much more than that—something Liggett, a small company best known for the has-been brands L&M and Chesterfield, simply could not afford.[2]

The attorneys general warned that such easy terms would "not be offered to any other defendants," knowing that Liggett's competitors would covet the deal it got. The tobacco industry was facing an unprecedented legal assault, including state lawsuits, class actions, secondhand smoke claims, and hundreds of cases filed by individual smokers. In August 1996, for the first time ever, a jury had ordered a tobacco company to pay a smoker damages for a tobacco-related disease. A class action claiming injuries from secondhand smoke was scheduled for trial in June, followed by the first Medicaid lawsuit (Mississippi's) in July and a class action by smokers in September. The tobacco companies were starting to rethink their long-standing determination never to settle a case.

In March 1996, about a week after an initial agreement between Liggett and five states had been announced, the *Financial Times* of London broached the possibility of a comprehensive, industry-wide settlement with RJR-Nabisco CEO Steven F. Goldstone. "I don't know of a way," Goldstone replied, "but I do know that it isn't the kind of thing that the tobacco industry would try to obstruct, because we know that litigation is not good for our companies." He said the industry did not have "such a fight-to-the-death mentality that it would ignore eminently reasonable solutions."[3] After the expanded Liggett settlement was announced a year later, Philip Morris sent its own signal: "As we have said in the past, we will explore and discuss all reasonable measures that may be in the best interests of our shareholders, including a comprehensive legislative solution to smoking and health claims against the tobacco industry."[4]

By early April 1997, Philip Morris and R. J. Reynolds, negotiating on behalf of the industry, had begun secret talks (later revealed in the *Wall Street Journal*) with the attorneys general and plaintiffs' lawyers. Matthew Myers, vice president of the National Center for Tobacco-Free Kids, was also participating. And since a comprehensive settlement would require federal legislation, both President Clinton (brother-in-law of plaintiff's lawyer Hugh Rodham) and Senate Majority Leader Trent Lott (brother-in-law of plaintiff's lawyer Richard Scruggs) were kept apprised.

The details of the agreement, announced on June 20, amounted to a stunning capitulation by the industry. The companies agreed to shell out $368.5 billion over twenty-five years, money that would be used to pay the states and other plaintiffs, cover enforcement costs, and fund various "tobacco control" efforts, including smoking cessation programs and a $500-million-a-year anti-smoking ad campaign. They conceded the FDA's jurisdiction over tobacco products and accepted severe restrictions on advertising and promotion that went beyond what the agency had proposed, even though a federal judge had overturned that aspect of the FDA's regulations. They committed themselves to achieving sharp reductions in underage smoking, under the threat of hefty fines. They promised to back a federal ban on smoking in most nonresidential buildings. They agreed to big, new warning labels—saying, among other things, "Smoking can kill you" and "Cigarettes are addictive." They said they would disband the Tobacco Institute and the Council for Tobacco Research.

In exchange for these and other concessions, the companies would get out from under about forty state Medicaid lawsuits and a mass of private litigation, including class actions backed by a consortium of prominent law firms and hundreds of cases filed on behalf of individual smokers or their families. The deal called for limits on liability that would allow individual lawsuits while eliminating punitive damages for past conduct, banning future class actions, and capping yearly outlays. The accord also included limits on FDA authority: The agency could not order the elimination of nicotine from cigarettes for at least twelve years, and it would have to show that any restrictions on nicotine were technologically feasible, would reduce health risks, and would not lead to a significant black market in full-strength cigarettes.

Critics of the settlement proposal, which required congressional approval, were mainly concerned about the limits on liability and on the FDA's authority. They also complained about the penalties for missing the smoking reduction targets, which they said were inadequate; the tax deductibility of the industry's payments; the absence of money for the federal share of smokers' health coverage; the lack of a tobacco tax increase; and the windfall enjoyed by the plaintiffs' lawyers, who stood to receive the largest legal fees in history (totaling $2 billion to $18 billion under various proposals). While some critics, including the American Cancer Society, former FDA commissioner David Kessler, and former surgeon general C. Everett Koop, seemed prepared to endorse a deal if Congress addressed their concerns, others rejected the very idea of a settlement.

Even before the proposal was announced, John Banzhaf of Action on Smoking and Health was warning that neither the ambitious attorneys general, "motivated at least in part by political considerations," nor the greedy plaintiffs' lawyers, who "stand to make billions of dollars from any negotiated settlement with very little work," could be trusted to defend "the general public health and welfare."[5] Ahron Leichtman's Citizens for a Tobacco-Free Society launched a "No Immunity to Kill with Impunity" campaign aimed at sinking any settlement. "Every time we think we're dancing on this industry's grave," Minnesota Attorney General Hubert H. Humphrey III said two days before the accord was announced, "they have instead found a way to keep dancing on those of our loved ones." If the scheduled trials proceeded, he argued, more damning information would emerge, and the industry would be under greater pressure to compromise. "What's the rush?" he asked. "If we take just enough time to get it right, America can make the rules, and we won't have to trade away the rights of victims or the powers of the federal government to fashion a real solution." After the details of the accord were made public, Humphrey said, "I fear that this deal could be a tobacco bailout." He called it a "Trojan Camel."[6]

Other opponents of the deal similarly argued that time was on their side. In a June 19 letter to the American Cancer Society, the American Heart Association, the American Medical Association, and the National Center for Tobacco-Free Kids, Ralph Nader warned against "premature support for a settlement," saying, "Those involved in the negotiations and their close supporters have become invested in the negotiation process." He also implied that their judgment had been compromised by the lure of anti-smoking money. He held out the hope that "a host of new disclosures, initiatives, regulatory controls and lawsuits not yet contemplated" would force the "tobacco drug addiction companies" to give up more.[7]

Writing in the *Los Angeles Times* on June 23, longtime anti-smoking activist Stanton Glantz noted that tobacco stocks had gone up during the settlement talks. "The business community clearly thinks this deal is good for tobacco," he said. "And what is good for tobacco is bad for public health." Anticipating the results of continued litigation, Glantz predicted, "The tobacco industry will lose enough of these cases to be brought to its knees. At that point, the same stock market that has been bidding up tobacco stocks will force R. J. Reynolds, Philip Morris and the others out of the tobacco business." With the stocks plummeting, he said, the government should take over the tobacco business, shut down foreign operations, and "make plain cigarettes available . . . for smokers who can't quit."[8]

Both the hard-liners' fantasies of dictating terms to a vanquished enemy and the details of the settlement proposal itself demonstrated that the tobacco lawsuits were supposed to do more than allocate blame and money. They were a tool of social policy, a way of moving us further along the road to a smoke-free society. Even leaving aside industry concessions on matters such as advertising and FDA regulation, anti-smokers hoped that making the tobacco companies pay up would cut cigarette sales by forcing an increase in prices. In fact, the proposed deal explicitly required the companies to pass the cost on to their customers. Like smoking bans and cigarette taxes, the lawsuits ostensibly dealt with rights and compensation, but for true believers discouraging smoking was the main point. As Stanley M. Rosenblatt, a pioneer of the tobacco class action, had declared, "My goal is to destroy the industry and thereby save millions of lives."[9]

UNCOMPROMISING POSITION

The tobacco companies have always taken death threats from plaintiffs' lawyers seriously. The first tobacco lawsuit was filed in 1954, and cigarette makers have been fending off litigation ever since. Early on, it was clear that the industry faced potentially ruinous liability. If a plaintiff found a legal theory that a jury would buy and that an appeals court would uphold, the tobacco companies would soon be confronted by thousands of imitators, and each successful suit would encourage still more. The trickle would become a torrent and then a flood that would sweep the industry away. To ward off this terrifying prospect, the tobacco companies resolved never to settle a case and never to concede anything that might be helpful to the enemy. Hence the industry's notorious take-no-prisoners approach to litigation, which aimed to intimidate, exhaust, and bankrupt plaintiffs, preferably before they saw a courtroom.

The tobacco companies have faced more than a thousand product liability suits since the 1950s. Of the eight hundred or so that have been resolved, only about two dozen went to a jury, and until 1996 no smoker had ever been awarded damages for a tobacco-related disease. As an R. J. Reynolds attorney explained in a 1988 memo: "The aggressive posture we have taken regarding depositions and discovery in general continues to make these cases extremely burdensome and expensive for plaintiffs' lawyers, particularly sole practitioners. To paraphrase General Patton, the way we won these cases was not by spending all of [RJR's] money, but by making that other son of a bitch spend all of his."[10]

In 1992, when about fifty product liability cases were pending, the Advocacy Institute estimated that the industry was spending $600 million a year defending itself. *Time* reported that Liggett, Brown & Williamson, and Philip Morris spent as much as $75 million fighting one high-profile suit—*twenty-five times* what the plaintiffs laid out. "Spending far more to defeat each case than would be required to settle the case would make no economic sense," noted Richard Daynard, director of the Tobacco Products Liability Project at Northeastern University, "if the stakes were limited to that one case. Rather, what the industry fears—and must fear—is not writing checks to a few plaintiffs, but the public collapse of its reputation as being invulnerable to legal claims."[11]

Anxiety about liability was also the most important reason for the industry's refusal to admit that smoking causes disease. A leading tobacco defense attorney, David R. Hardy, summed up the industry's quandary in an August 1970 letter. Hardy, warning that indiscreet comments by industry scientists, including references to "biologically active" components of cigarette smoke and "the search for a safer cigarette," constituted "a real threat to . . . continued success in the defense of smoking and health litigation," wrote, "Of course, we would make every effort to 'explain' such statements if we were confronted with them during a trial, but I seriously doubt that the average juror would follow or accept the subtle distinctions and explanations we would be forced to urge." Such admissions by company employees, Hardy said, would suggest "actual knowledge on the part of the defendant that smoking is generally dangerous to health, that certain ingredients are dangerous to health and should be removed, or that smoking causes a particular disease. This would not only be evidence that would substantially prove a case against the defendant company for compensatory damages, but could be considered as evidence of willfulness or recklessness sufficient to support a claim for punitive damages."[12]

The desire to avoid the appearance of "actual knowledge" has driven industry employees to absurd extremes. In the 1950s, for example, researchers at BAT, Brown & Williamson's parent corporation in England, referred to cancer in writing as "ZEPHYR."[13] Even when they did not actually use code words, internal communications were usually circumspect on the issue of smoking and health, often parroting the industry's official position. But more than a few indiscretions have turned up in documents obtained during lawsuits or leaked to the press by whistle-blowers. While most of these gaffes could be explained away by creative lawyers (though probably not very convincingly), some directly contradicted the industry's public statements. In a much-cited 1963 memo, for example, Addison Yeaman, then Brown & Williamson's vice president and general counsel, stated flatly that "nicotine is addictive" and concluded, "We are, then, in the business of selling nicotine, an addictive drug effective in the release of stress mechanisms."[14] An R. J. Reynolds scientist conceded in a 1962 memo, "Obviously the amount of evidence accumulated to indict cigarette smoke as a health hazard is overwhelming. The evidence challenging such an indictment is scant."[15] Similarly, the minutes from a 1978 research conference sponsored by BAT include the following statements: "There has been no change in the scientific basis for the case against smoking. Additional evidence of smoke-dose-related incidence of some diseases associated with smoking has been published. But generally this has long ceased to be an area for scientific controversy."[16]

Beginning in the 1980s, lawyers suing tobacco companies used such behind-the-scenes remarks as evidence of a conspiracy to deceive the public. The irony, of course, is that the industry's posture of disbelief, which was supposed to protect it against liability, has instead invited lawsuits. But during the first wave of tobacco litigation, in the 1950s and '60s, disputing causation seemed to make perfect sense. At that stage, the argument that smokers know the risks associated with cigarettes was not as persuasive as it would later become, since definitive evidence of the link between smoking and fatal disease began to emerge only in the early '50s. By the same token, however, it was hard to argue that the tobacco companies could reasonably have foreseen that their products would cause lung cancer. Indeed, they maintained that the causal connection still had not been demonstrated conclusively. And, as always, the cigarette makers had superior resources, and therefore more endurance than their opponents. Of the ten cases that were reported during this period (others were dropped before producing recorded decisions), four were discontinued by the plaintiffs, three resulted in summary judgments for the defendants, and three ended in jury verdicts for the defendants. Tobacco liability did not seem to be a promising area for trial lawyers.

That perception eventually changed because of the revolution in product liability law that started toward the end of the first wave of litigation. Citing an imbalance in power between consumers and corporations, a group of influential legal scholars and judges rejected a contract model of product liability, which forbade fraud and required sellers to deliver what they promised. They proposed a broader understanding of a manufacturer's obligations based on the concept of defect. Under so-called strict liability, a consumer injured by a defective product could recover damages even without proving that the manufacturer had been dishonest or negligent. In theory, strict liability abolished the need to show fault. Instead of a compensation scheme for people who had been wronged, it would be a kind of insurance arrangement: Consumers would pay premiums, in the form of higher prices, and they would be "covered" in the event of a product-related mishap. Furthermore, the prospect of liability awards would encourage companies to design safer products. Given their resources and knowledge, advocates of strict liability reasoned, manufacturers were in the best position to prevent injuries. This was not a matter of justice so much as efficiency.

In practice, however, the concept of defectiveness included some sense of fault. A product could be defective, for example, because of a mistake in the manufacturing process or because it was not accompanied by appropriate warnings. Imposing liability for such failures implied that consumers had a right to expect better. The importance of consumer expectations is clear in the 1965 *Restatement (Second) of Torts*, which served as a legal model for most states. The *Restatement* says a manufacturer can be held liable for selling a product in a "defective condition unreasonably dangerous" to the consumer. It explains: "The article sold must be dangerous beyond that which would be contemplated by the ordinary consumer who purchases it, with the ordinary knowledge common to the community as to its characteristics. Good whiskey is not unreasonably dangerous merely because it will make some people drunk, and is especially dangerous to alcoholics; but bad whiskey, containing a dangerous amount of fusel oil, is unreasonably dangerous. *Good tobacco is not unreasonably dangerous merely because the effects of smoking may be harmful;* but tobacco containing something like marijuana may be unreasonably dangerous. Good butter is not unreasonably dangerous merely because, if such be the case, it deposits cholesterol in the arteries and leads to heart attacks; but bad butter, contaminated with poisonous fish oil, is unreasonably dangerous."[17]

Coming after a series of failed tobacco lawsuits, this explanation was not exactly encouraging for lawyers hoping to win damages from cigarette companies. It specifically cited tobacco as a product that is hazardous but not defective, and it implied that manufacturers could not be held liable for failing to warn consumers about commonly known risks. To prevail against the tobacco companies, it seemed, plaintiffs would have to define defectiveness in a way that did not depend on consumer expectations. Beginning in 1968, for example, courts had found that manufacturers could be held liable for failing to design a safer product. This approach seemed promising, since the tobacco companies had researched safety innovations without marketing them. Risk–utility analysis went even further than the idea of defective design. In 1983, for instance, the New Jersey Supreme Court found that a man who was injured when he dove into an above-ground swimming pool and slipped on its liner could recover damages from the manufacturer even without showing that a safer design was feasible. The court said a jury could decide that the pool was defective because its risks outweighed its utility.[18]

For an ambitious young New Jersey lawyer named Marc Z. Edell, these extensions of strict liability made tobacco litigation seem attractive. As a defense attorney in asbestos litigation, he had become familiar with tobacco's contribution to lung cancer. Although no one had ever been awarded damages from a tobacco company for a smoking-related disease, Edell thought the risk–utility test was a promising approach. If he could convince a jury that the substantial hazards of cigarettes out-weighed their benefits, he stood to make a nice profit and a name for himself. As he later put it, "I will not tell you it was for altruistic reasons, that we got together as a group of public interest lawyers who decided this was something that would benefit society."[19] Having decided that tobacco litigation would be a good investment of his time and energy, Edell needed a plaintiff. He heard about Rose Cipollone from a partner in his firm who was friendly with one of her doctors.

ROSE'S BAD HABIT

Growing up on the Lower East Side of Manhattan, Rose played dress-up with her sisters, donning ladies' clothing and rolling pieces of paper to simulate cigarettes. She began smoking in 1942, when she was sixteen. "I thought it was cool, as you would call it today, to smoke, and grown-up," she later recalled, "and I was going to be glamorous or beautiful." Bette Davis and Joan Crawford smoked in the movies she watched at the neighborhood Loews theater, and Hollywood stars touted cigarettes in the magazines she read. Rose picked Chesterfields, the brand endorsed by Tyrone Power, Rosalind Russell, and Yvonne De Carlo. At first she bought them one at a time at the local candy store. She smoked them in the girls' room at school, because she knew her mother—who consid-ered the habit "unladylike" and blamed tobacco for the stroke that had killed Rose's father—wouldn't approve. Within a few years Rose was smoking a pack and a half a day. As she put it, "I became addicted or I became hooked."[20]

When Rose started dating Antonio Cipollone in 1946, she warned him about her "bad habit," and he urged her to quit, something he would continue to do during their thirty-eight-year marriage. The Cipollones moved to Little Ferry, New Jersey, and began to raise a fam-ily. Rose, who never learned to drive, would send Tony out at night to buy cigarettes for her, and sometimes she ordered groceries she didn't re-ally need so she could have cigarettes delivered. "I had to smoke," she later said. "I would panic if I didn't have cigarettes around me." Tony promised her a fur coat as a reward for quitting. She kept smoking, and he bought her one anyway. During her first pregnancy, under pressure from Tony and her doctor, Rose smoked only occasionally. But during labor she went back to her usual rate, and she smoked throughout her two subsequent pregnancies. Tony and their children would show her newspaper and magazine articles about the hazards of smoking, and she would tell them to leave her alone. "She used to tell me that it hadn't been proved yet that it's harmful," Tony Cipollone recalled. Nor was Rose swayed by the advice of her favorite magazine, *Reader's Digest*, which eschewed tobacco advertising and had been publishing warnings about the dangers of cigarettes, including the widely read 1952 article "Cancer by the Carton," since 1924. "Through advertising," she said, "I was led to assume that they were safe and wouldn't harm me."[21]

That was indeed the not-so-subtle message of some cigarette ads that appeared in the '40s and '50s. The headline in a 1952 ad for Rose's first brand announced, NOSE, THROAT, AND ACCESSORY ORGANS NOT AD-VERSELY AFFECTED BY SMOKING CHESTERFIELDS. Ads for L&M, the fil-tered brand that she started smoking in 1955, carried the slogan "Just What the Doctor Ordered." (The doctor, it turned out, was Liggett & Myers's research director, who had a Ph.D. in chemistry.) But despite such reassurances, Rose knew that smoking was not good for her. She switched to filtered and low-yield brands—first L&M, later Virginia Slims, Parliament, and True—in an attempt to reduce the hazards. Re-calling her response when the Surgeon General's Advisory Committee concluded in 1964 that smoking caused cancer, she said, "I didn't want to hear it. I liked to smoke. It gave me something to do." Beginning in 1966, every pack Rose smoked carried a warning from the surgeon gen-eral. She later acknowledged that she understood that the warning meant "smoking was dangerous," though she insisted, "I didn't believe it." She said she felt "that if there was anything that dangerous, . . . the tobacco people wouldn't allow it and the government wouldn't let them do that." Still, when she developed a "smoker's cough" in the mid '60s, she became frightened: "I was making novenas, I was so scared that I was getting sick, and I used to make all kinds of promises to God if he didn't let me have cancer, that I wouldn't do this and I wouldn't do that."[22]

The prayers didn't work. In 1981 an X ray found a spot on Rose's right lung, and she underwent surgery in New York to remove a malig-nant tumor. She continued smoking. "I did it furtively," she said, "and I was afraid, and yet I was tempted."[23] Less than a year later, the cancer came back, and this time the entire lung was removed. After her second surgery, Rose finally stopped smoking. The cancer spread, and a tumor was removed from her adrenal gland the next year.

It was around this time, in the summer of 1983, that Marc Edell paid a visit. Despite the reputation of the tobacco industry's lawyers—who were known to drag out discovery endlessly, drown their opponents in paperwork, and conduct grueling depositions—Rose agreed to become Edell's client. On August 1, 1983, she and her husband filed suit in federal court against the Liggett Group (maker of the Chesterfield and L&M brands), Philip Morris (maker of Virginia Slims and Parliament), and Lorillard (maker of True). As amended, their complaint alleged that the cigarettes Rose had smoked were defective because their risks outweighed their benefits and because the manufacturers could have offered safer alternatives. The Cipollones also argued that the companies had failed to adequately warn her of their products' hazards and had in fact violated warranties of safety. Finally, they claimed that the companies had engaged in a conspiracy to misrepresent the hazards of smoking, suppress scientific evidence, and undermine health warnings, all with the intent of falsely reassuring their customers.

Rose Cipollone died the following year, at the age of fifty-eight, and her husband pursued the lawsuit on her behalf. During the four and a half years before the case went to trial, Edell and the two attorneys who worked with him scored an important victory, gaining access to hundreds of thousands of company documents, of which they ultimately introduced about three hundred into evidence. They also suffered two major setbacks. In 1986 the U.S. Court of Appeals for the Third Circuit ruled that the Federal Cigarette Labeling and Advertising Act of 1965 and the Public Health Cigarette Smoking Act of 1969, which were intended to establish a uniform national standard for cigarette warning labels, preempted claims that the warnings were inadequate.[24] The trial judge, H. Lee Sarokin, interpreted this decision to mean that the Cipollones could not pursue claims that hinged on the tobacco companies' advertising, promotional, or public relations activities after January 1, 1966, when the 1965 law took effect. Since Rose smoked only Liggett brands before the cutoff date, this decision let Philip Morris and Lorillard mostly off the hook. The year after the Third Circuit's ruling, responding to intense lobbying by the tobacco industry, the New Jersey legislature approved the Product Liability Act of 1987, which said a product could not be considered defective under a risk–benefit test if its hazards were common knowledge. Based on the legislative history, Sarokin concluded that the law applied retroactively, thereby eliminating what Edell had considered his most promising argument.

THE CONSPIRACY THEORY

During the trial of *Cipollone v. Liggett Group,* which began in February 1988, Edell presented testimony and documents concerning an experimental cigarette, containing palladium and magnesium nitrate, that Liggett had developed but never marketed. The company's researchers found that the additives dramatically reduced the carcinogenic activity of cigarette tars as measured by mouse skin tests. After spending $14 million on the project over a period of two decades or so, Liggett abandoned the palladium cigarette in the late 1970s, claiming there were too many unresolved questions about its health effects. Edell argued that the company was actually worried that a safer cigarette would indict its other products by implication and expose Liggett to liability. He maintained that if the company had marketed the palladium cigarette, Rose Cipollone might have switched to it and thereby reduced her risk of lung cancer. (This argument, which became a familiar feature of tobacco lawsuits, highlighted the industry's double bind: Offering a safer cigarette could invite litigation, and so could failing to do so.) Edell also showed the jury cigarette ads, which he said had implicitly or explicitly told Rose that smoking was safe, a message that undermined warnings from scientists and the government.

But the heart of the case was the charge that the tobacco companies had conspired to defraud the public by "creating doubt about the health charge without actually denying it," as Tobacco Institute vice president Fred Panzer described the industry's strategy in a 1972 memo.[25] Through the Tobacco Institute and the Council for Tobacco Research, Edell argued, the cigarette makers sought to perpetuate the notion that the scientific case against cigarettes remained open. They relentlessly criticized research and reports incriminating tobacco as a cause of disease while maintaining the pretense that they were aggressively seeking the truth. They steered industry money away from research that might find evidence of tobacco's hazards and sought to delay or prevent publication of such information.

In support of his conspiracy theory, Edell cited the first draft of a 1968 request for funding from Philip Morris scientists that alluded to a "gentleman's agreement" among the tobacco companies to avoid in-house research on the health hazards of smoking. Similarly, in a 1980 letter to Lorillard executive vice president Alexander W. Spears, Robert B. Seligman, vice president for research and development at Philip Morris USA, listed three "subjects to be avoided" in industry-funded research: "1. Developing new tests for carcinogenicity. 2. Attempt to relate human disease to smoking. 3. Conduct experiments which require large doses of carcinogen to show additive effects of smoking."[26]

This willful ignorance apparently had more to do with protecting the industry from liability than with hiding information from the public. As early as 1955, according to a report on a Liggett research conference cited by Edell, an official of Ecusta Corp., a maker of cigarette paper, "mentioned one big manufacturer of cigarettes whose people . . . at a high level . . . said they didn't want to be told certain factual knowledge because they wanted to be in a position to say they didn't know about these things."[27] Testimony by former Liggett president Milton E. Harrington, deposed by Edell in 1985, offered further evidence of this see-no-evil attitude: "I didn't think anything about smoking and health other than smoking was not harmful to you in any way," he said, explaining, "It didn't ever harm me." After the 1964 surgeon general's report, Harrington didn't investigate the matter further because, he said, "It wouldn't do any good anyway."[28]

Meanwhile, Edell charged, industry researchers privately conceded that smoking caused cancer. A 1961 memo from Arthur D. Little, a consulting firm that began doing research for Liggett in 1954, said that there were "biologically active materials present in cigarette tobacco" that were "cancer causing," "cancer promoting," and "poisonous."[29] In another 1961 memo, Philip Morris research director Helmut Wakeham noted that developing a "medically acceptable cigarette" would require "reduction of the general level of carcinogenic substances in smoke." He added, "Carcinogens are found in practically every class of compound in smoke," a circumstance that prohibited "complete solution of the problem."[30] In a 1970 letter to Tobacco Institute president Earle Clements, Wakeham suggested it might be time to be more candid about the hazards of smoking: "We may be able to emphasize the benefits of smoking without talking about the risks implied by the statistics. But we should be prepared to admit the possibility of some risk by being able at the same time to emphasize factually that benefits accompany the risk as they do in many other human pursuits."[31] James D. Mold, former assistant research director at Liggett, testified that by the early 1960s he was convinced that smoking caused cancer.[32]

For an industry that had managed to keep an open mind about the health effects of smoking despite overwhelming evidence, explaining away such indiscretions was not too hard. The defense attorneys said the remarks about carcinogenic effects referred to skin cancer in mice, and the industry had never conceded that such results can be extrapolated to lung cancer in humans. They said Liggett used the mouse test because everybody else seemed to think it was important, not because the company agreed it was a valid measure of tobacco's hazards. And even if some industry employees or contractors agreed that smoking was hazardous, the tobacco attorneys said, their beliefs did not amount to official policy (a point that was hard to deny).

In any case, said the industry's lawyers, Rose Cipollone had not been duped. She knew very well that smoking was (allegedly) bad for her, and she chose to do it anyway. Aside from the warning label on every pack of cigarettes she smoked from 1966 on, hundreds of articles on the health hazards of smoking appeared in periodicals that she and her husband regularly read. "This is a woman who did what she wanted to do," said Liggett attorney Donald J. Cohn. "Before she ever smoked a cigarette, she had been told by her mother that smoking killed her father. . . . She knew this bad habit was not good for her. . . . Given her personality, she could have stopped smoking if she wanted to. She did not want to. She could control her smoking. She never smoked in the bedroom. She knew what she was doing. She was an intelligent, strong-minded person. She prayed that she would not get lung cancer, but she continued to smoke."[33]

Edell countered this argument by presenting testimony that Rose was "severely dependent" on cigarettes. He cited the conclusions of a 1957 "motivation survey" of 750 heavy smokers conducted by Liggett's advertising agency: "It is clear that the average heavy smoker is afraid to give up smoking. The habit . . . has become such an integral part of their lives that many smokers say: 'I feel lost when I'm out of cigarettes,' many describe feelings of panic and inability to think, coordinate, or function normally without cigarettes. . . . The typical heavy smoker fears to lose the pleasures and psychological benefits that he realizes smoking affords him, and that he knows he needs. Thus, what smokers are really saying is: 'I wish I had never started to smoke . . . but now that it's got me, I know that I can't stop.'"[34] Edell also introduced into evidence the 1988 surgeon general's report on smoking, in which C. Everett Koop concluded that nicotine is "addicting in the same sense as are drugs such as heroin and cocaine."[35]

Edell's presentation apparently persuaded the judge. After his last witness, the defense submitted a routine motion to dismiss the plaintiff's case. Sarokin agreed to drop the claim that the cigarettes made by the defendants were defective because alternative designs were possible, since that count relied on speculation about how Rose Cipollone might have reacted to safer cigarettes. He also dismissed the claim that the cigarette companies had been negligent in failing to do "reasonable research" about the health hazards of smoking, because the connection of that failure to Rose's injury was unclear. Finally, he dropped Philip Morris and Lorillard from the failure-to-warn count, since Rose had smoked their brands only after the federally mandated warning labels started to appear. But instead of simply rejecting the rest of the motion, the judge made it clear that he sympathized with the thrust of the plaintiff's case.

Sarokin said the evidence offered by Edell "permits the jury to find a tobacco industry conspiracy, vast in its scope, devious in its purpose and devastating in its results." He said the jury could "reasonably conclude" that the tobacco companies conspired to deceive the public with "callous, wanton, willful and reckless disregard . . . for the illness and death it would cause"; "chose profits" over "the health and lives of the consumers"; and "deliberately and intentionally refuted, denied, suppressed and misrepresented facts regarding the dangers of smoking." He noted evidence that Rose Cipollone was "heavily dependent on tobacco and would grasp at any rationalization to continue, and that the cigarette companies provided that rationalization on a steady basis." The day after his ruling, the front-page headline in a local paper, the *Record,* read JUDGE FINDS CONSPIRACY BY TOBACCO FIRMS.[36]

THE VERDICT

After four months in the courtroom and nearly a week of deliberations, the six jurors rejected the conspiracy argument and every other charge, with two exceptions. They concluded that Liggett had not provided adequate warnings prior to 1966 and that its advertisements in the 1950s had offered what amounted to an express warranty of safety, which the company had breached. They found that Rose Cipollone was 80 percent responsible for her lung cancer, since she had chosen to smoke, and therefore awarded no damages in her name. But they did order Liggett to pay Tony Cipollone $400,000.

Since it was the first time a court had awarded damages for tobacco-related illness, the decision was big news, and the mixed verdict left plenty of room for spin. "The dam has been broken," declared Edell's associate Alan M. Darnell, "and the water behind is going to push out." But the defense team, also known as "the wall of flesh," noted that the modest award, which represented just a small share of the resources that had been spent to obtain it, was not likely to encourage more lawsuits. They dismissed it as "an expression of sympathy" likely to be overturned on appeal.[37]

Two years later it was. In January 1990, the U.S. Court of Appeals for the Third Circuit threw out the verdict and ordered a new trial to determine whether Rose Cipollone had actually relied on the warranty that the jury said Liggett's ads had offered. The court also concluded that, contrary to Sarokin's rulings, New Jersey's Product Liability Act of 1987 did not apply retroactively, so Edell could pursue the claim that cigarettes are defective because their risks outweigh their utility. A year later, the U.S. Supreme Court agreed to review the Third Circuit's pretrial decision that federal law had preempted claims about the adequacy of cigarette warnings from 1966 on. That interpretation had been echoed by four circuit courts, but the supreme courts of Minnesota and New Jersey had found otherwise.

In June 1992 the Supreme Court ruled that the 1965 act, which said that "no statement relating to smoking and health" other than the one specified by the statute "shall be required on any cigarette package," did not affect lawsuits arguing that cigarette makers had failed to provide adequate warnings. But the 1969 act used broader preemption language: "No requirement or prohibition based on smoking and health shall be imposed under State law with respect to the advertising or promotion of any cigarettes the packages of which are [lawfully] labeled." The Court concluded that the second law "preempted claims based on a failure to warn and the neutralization of federally mandated warnings to the extent that those claims rely on omissions or inclusions in respondents' advertising or promotions." But plaintiffs could still press claims based on warnings prior to November 1, 1970, when the 1969 law took effect, or based on theories of express warranty, intentional fraud and misrepresentation, or conspiracy.[38]

These post-verdict rulings left open several avenues of attack for a second trial. But Tony Cipollone had died by this time, and his son was carrying on in his stead. The law firms representing the Cipollone family, after devoting almost a decade and nearly $3 million to the case, had not earned a cent. Five months after the Supreme Court decision that the *New York Times* said "opened the door wide to damage suits by smokers against the cigarette industry,"[39] Edell and his associates dropped the case. A few days later Edell gave up three other tobacco lawsuits he had taken on. Despite his unprecedented achievement, the tobacco industry's dam was still holding.

Edell was not the only attorney who thought the tobacco companies might be vulnerable. In 1985, two years after Edell started *Cipollone,* celebrity lawyer Melvin Belli, who had participated in the first wave of tobacco litigation, filed a $100 million suit in Santa Barbara, California, on behalf of Mark Galbraith, a three-pack-a-day smoker who had died at sixty-nine. Of what, exactly, turned out to be a pivotal issue in the case. No autopsy had been performed, and the cause of death was said to be arteriosclerosis and pulmonary fibrosis, with lung cancer and emphysema contributing. The jury was not convinced that smoking was the

decisive factor in his death, and it seemed to agree with the defense that
Galbraith had in any case voluntarily assumed the risk. Like Rose Cipollone, he had continued smoking despite knowledge of the hazards and
repeated warnings from relatives.

The assumption-of-risk argument also apparently prevailed in the
case of Nathan Horton, a Mississippi smoker who died of lung cancer in
1987 at the age of fifty. After a hung jury resulted in a mistrial, the jury
in the second trial found for the plaintiff but awarded no damages. The
bizarre decision, reminiscent of the mixed verdict in *Cipollone,* was a
compromise between deadlocked jurors. It was especially striking because Mississippi law allows juries to award damages even when a plaintiff is found to be almost entirely responsible for his injury.

During this second wave of litigation, when nearly two hundred lawsuits were filed but none resulted in a sustained damage award, assumption of risk emerged as the tobacco industry's most reliable defense. The
attorneys who brought the suits, notes Stanford University law professor
Robert L. Rabin, "simply failed to grasp how intensely most jurors
would react to damage claims by individuals who were aware of the risks
associated with smoking and nonetheless chose to continue the activity
over a long period of time." The attorneys could (and did) argue that addiction to cigarettes meant that the decision to smoke was not truly voluntary. But jurors knew from everyday experience that quitting smoking, while often difficult, is hardly impossible. "In court," writes Rabin,
"the addiction expert can say at most only that quitting is often extremely hard to do. If the jury believes that a gap remains between commitment to a difficult personal sacrifice and extinction of free choice,
there is little that the expert can offer in rebuttal."[40]

THE THIRD WAVE

The third wave of litigation, which began just as the second was ending,
featured lawsuits that were designed, in one way or another, to overcome
the major obstacles encountered by previous efforts: the assumption-of-
risk defense, the preemption of failure-to-warn claims, and the intimidating resources of the tobacco industry. *Broin v. Philip Morris,* filed in
1991 by Miami attorney Stanley M. Rosenblatt, addressed all three of

these problems. Rosenblatt's innovation was to sue the tobacco companies on behalf of *nonsmokers*. *Broin* was a class action seeking compensation for illness among flight attendants exposed to secondhand smoke
on the job.

Patty Young, a flight attendant turned activist who testified in
favor of the 1989 airline smoking ban, helped kick off the case by
putting Norma Broin, a nonsmoker who developed lung cancer after
thirteen years as a flight attendant, in touch with Miami lawyer Peter
S. Schwedock, who introduced her to Rosenblatt. As plaintiffs, Broin
and the other flight attendants, who encountered tobacco smoke incidentally while earning a living, were much more sympathetic than
smokers. It wasn't clear how the preemption issue would be resolved,
but the surgeon general's warnings said nothing about secondhand
smoke, which was not labeled a serious health hazard until 1986. (At
the same time, of course, it was hard to argue that the tobacco companies should have known the risks.) And because this was a class action seeking billions of dollars in damages, the potential payoff would
amply reward Rosenblatt for sticking with the case.

On the other hand, since the evidence on secondhand smoke is not
nearly as weighty as the evidence on smoking and since the magnitude
of the apparent risk is much smaller, proving causation would be difficult. Dade County Circuit Judge Robert P. Kaye said he was "deeply
concerned about the issue of causation."[41] Even if Rosenblatt could convince a jury that exposure to secondhand smoke raises the risk of certain
diseases, it seemed impossible to establish causation and damages for all
of the flight attendants in one trial. Assuming damages could be established, apportioning them among the various cigarette manufacturers
might be tricky. Finally, jurors might wonder why the flight attendants
were suing the tobacco companies, who simply sold the product, rather
than the passengers who smoked it or the airlines that let them. Rosenblatt argued that the tobacco companies knew secondhand smoke was
hazardous yet failed to warn the airlines and "failed to design, manufacture, distribute, and sell a cigarette that would *not* pollute the immediate
environment of the smoker."[42]

Broin was not the only lawsuit against tobacco companies for injuries allegedly caused by secondhand smoke, but it was easily the

largest. Rosenblatt estimated that the class could include some sixty thousand flight attendants. (He later admitted this number was just "an educated guess"; as of October 1997, eight thousand flight attendants had applied for inclusion in the class, and it was not clear how many would qualify.[43]) Judge Kaye initially refused to let the case proceed as a class action. After an appeals court ordered a rehearing, he reversed his decision, certifying the class in December 1994 as "all nonsmoking flight attendants who are or have been employed by airlines based in the United States and are suffering from diseases and disorders caused by their exposure to secondhand cigarette smoke in airline cabins."[44] In their appeal of Kaye's decision, the tobacco companies argued, among other things, that a Florida court should not have nationwide jurisdiction. In January 1996, Florida's Third District Court of Appeals disagreed, allowing the case to proceed. "The odds are against us," Rosenblatt conceded after the ruling. "Most sophisticated lawyers think I'm a fool and think that the tobacco companies, with all their money and all their public relations and all their lawyers, are ultimately going to win."[45] But as he said when he filed the initial complaint, "This is a crusade, not a lawsuit."[46] Rosenblatt did not welcome the nationwide settlement talks. "I'm very disheartened and unhappy about the fact that our case is being used as leverage in these negotiations," he said.[47] After the deal was announced, however, Kaye ruled that *Broin* could still proceed, and the trial began in July 1997.

After three months of testimony, a settlement was announced. The tobacco companies agreed to donate $300 million for research on smoking-related diseases, to be dispensed by an institute named after Norma Broin. The plaintiffs' attorneys—Rosenblatt and his wife, Susan—would receive a breathtaking $49 million in fees and costs. But the flight attendants got nothing, aside from some procedural concessions that might help them prevail in individual lawsuits, and the tobacco companies did not acknowledge any health risks from secondhand smoke. It seemed that Rosenblatt's long shot had paid off (for him, anyway) mainly because the cigarette makers were worried that a verdict against them, even if ultimately overturned, would hurt the prospects for a nationwide settlement.

Rosenblatt was also handling a class action on behalf of smokers. The lead plaintiff was Howard A. Engle, a Florida pediatrician with asthma and emphysema who had been smoking for half a century. *Engle v. R. J. Reynolds* alleged that the tobacco companies conspired to addict smokers by manipulating nicotine levels in cigarettes. In October 1994, Dade County Circuit Judge Harold Solomon allowed the case to proceed as a class action representing "all United States citizens and residents, and their survivors, who have suffered, presently suffer or have died from diseases and medical conditions caused by their addiction to cigarettes that contain nicotine." Rosenblatt asked for $200 billion in compensatory and punitive damages, charging sale of defective products, negligence, fraud and misrepresentation, conspiracy, breach of implied and express warranties, and intentional infliction of emotional distress.[48]

In *Cipollone,* testimony about addiction served mainly to counter the assumption-of-risk argument, while the conspiracy theory focused on what the industry said about the health effects of smoking. In *Engle,* by contrast, addiction was the essence of the conspiracy charge, and Rosenblatt therefore emphasized the industry's ability to control the amount of nicotine delivered by each cigarette. Furthermore, because of numerous Brown & Williamson documents that were leaked to researchers and the press in 1994, he had additional examples of inconsistencies between the industry's public and private statements on the hazards and addictiveness of cigarettes. But the basic point remained the same: that industry spokesmen didn't really believe what they said. The jury in *Cipollone* did not think this amounted to fraud. Nor did it think that addiction trumped the assumption-of-risk defense, and cigarettes had not become more addictive since 1988. The really novel aspect of the case was that it made these charges in the context of a nationwide class action, with potential plaintiffs numbering in the tens of millions. In January 1996, Florida's Third District Court of Appeals ruled that the class would have to be limited to residents of the state, but that still left as many as three million potential members.[49] The trial was scheduled for February 1998.

Although the *Engle* class was the first to be certified, the case was eclipsed by what was dubbed "the largest class action in U.S. history." In March 1994 a group of about sixty law firms filed a federal lawsuit in New Orleans, seeking to represent current smokers plus everyone who had been addicted to nicotine during the previous half century, their estates, and their survivors. No one really knew how many people this represented; estimates ranged from fifty million to a hundred million. The lead plaintiff was Dianne A. Castano, widow of Peter Castano, a smoker who died of lung cancer in 1993 at the age of 47. *Castano v. American Tobacco* asked for punitive damages as well as compensation for economic loss and emotional distress. Unlike *Engle,* it did not seek damages for smoking-related illness, which would have entailed a causation inquiry for each plaintiff. But given the enormous number of plaintiffs, any payout would be in the billions—as much as $100 billion, according to one analyst.[50] The central theory in *Castano,* inspired by the furor over "nicotine manipulation" that had followed FDA commissioner David Kessler's move to regulate tobacco products (see chapter 7), was basically the same as in *Engle:* a conspiracy to hook smokers while deceiving the public about the addictiveness of cigarettes. "We will prove that the tobacco industry has conspired to catch you, hold you, and kill you," said Melvin Belli, back again to catch the third wave.[51] Said New Orleans attorney Wendell Gauthier, "They've conducted a masterful fraud."[52]

This fraud theory, designed to take advantage of the main opening left by the Supreme Court's ruling in *Cipollone,* was based on a rather implausible idea: that people did not realize smoking was addictive, despite centuries of lore about the difficulty of kicking the habit, and did not realize that tobacco companies controlled the level of nicotine in cigarettes, even though the yields of various brands had been advertised for decades. The main attraction of *Castano* was not the story it told but the fact that so many big-time law firms were cooperating, each contributing $100,000 a year, in an attempt to counter the tobacco industry's resources. Along with Gauthier and Belli (a.k.a. "the King of Torts"), the participating attorneys included such famously successful litigators as Stanley M. Chesley ("the Master of Disaster"), John P. Coale ("Bhopal Coale"), and Ronald L. Motley ("the Asbestos Avenger").

Some of them had personal motives. Gauthier, who helped get the case started, was a close friend of the Castanos. Coale said his father, a smoker, had emphysema. And Motley declared, "The tobacco companies killed my mother." Unlike Rosenblatt, however, they were not calling the lawsuit a crusade; it was clearly an investment. Given the huge size of the class, the lawyers stood to make much more money than any plaintiff could ever hope to recover. "Our biggest motivation is money," Gauthier conceded, "but we have our pride. The tobacco companies have made it so expensive to sue them that they've bankrupted a string of lawyers and tried to scare the plaintiffs' bar away from the courthouse." And lest anyone mistake *Castano* for a high-minded enterprise, Coale told the *New York Times:* "I am a pirate. . . . I have been described as an ambulance chaser, and I don't disagree."[53]

The aspect of *Castano* that made it so appealing to pirates and ambulances chasers—its enormous size, which implied a large payoff—was also a major weakness. From the outset U.S. District Judge Okla B. Jones worried that the case was too big to manage. In February 1995 he presented a tentative scheme for handling the lawsuit: The "core liability issues"—the charges of fraud, breach of warranty, intentional tort, negligence, strict liability, and violation of consumer protection statutes— would be addressed in the mass trial. But the issue of whether the plaintiffs had in fact suffered injury as a result of the defendants' conduct, including the question of whether they had actually relied on misrepresentations by the cigarette companies, would have to be determined in separate proceedings, where the companies could offer affirmative defenses such as assumption of risk. Claims for compensatory damages, including payments toward a "medical monitoring fund," would also have to be determined individually. The jury in the class action would, however, decide whether the tobacco companies' behavior was egregious enough to warrant punitive damages. If so, the jury would set a ratio for awarding punitive damages based on compensatory damages. On these terms, Jones certified a class consisting of "all nicotine-dependent persons in the United States," their estates, heirs, and survivors. A cigarette smoker would qualify if he had been diagnosed as nicotine-dependent or if he had continued smoking after being advised by a medical practitioner to quit.[54]

After Jones's decision, the *Castano* legal team started receiving calls from smokers eager to cash in. "More than 1,000 calls per day were logged from around the country," reported the *Times-Picayune,* "and that number is expected to top 50,000 daily when the case heats up."[55]

The buzz about *Castano* reached a crescendo in March 1996 when the Liggett Group broke ranks with the rest of the industry and agreed to settle the case. In exchange for being dropped from the list of defendants, the company agreed to reserve 5 percent of its pre-tax profits for a fund to help smokers quit and to withdraw its formal opposition to the pending FDA regulations. News of the decision prompted a spin-doctoring frenzy, with the industry and its opponents depicting the agreement as either a ho-hum financial maneuver or a stunning legal development.

In a sense, both were right. On the one hand, Liggett had broken one of the tobacco industry's cardinal rules: *Never settle.* At a time when the industry was facing more-formidable legal challenges than ever before, the company's concession made it look like the dam was finally starting to crack. On the other hand, the settlement was part of an attempt by Bennett S. LeBow, chairman of Liggett's parent, the Brooke Group Ltd., to take control of RJR-Nabisco. If LeBow succeeded in his bid for the company, the terms of the settlement would extend to R. J. Reynolds, making the merger more appealing to RJR-Nabisco's shareholders. But if LeBow failed (as he ultimately did), the settlement would apply only to Liggett, which accounted for just 2 percent of the cigarette market. Furthermore, Liggett admitted no wrongdoing, and the deal would be off if the other tobacco companies prevailed in *Castano.* Liggett was not even conceding that the FDA had jurisdiction over tobacco; it was just letting the other companies fight that battle. In short, it was a no-lose proposition for Liggett. Stanley Rosenblatt, for his part, was not impressed. "I think the settlement is outrageous," he said. "People are being asked to give up their right to sue for cancer in exchange for a lousy discount at a Smoke Enders course."[56]

Two months later, the merits of the Liggett settlement seemed moot. In May 1996 the U.S. Court of Appeals for the Fifth Circuit threw out Judge Jones's certification of the *Castano* class, finding that he had not adequately considered how variations in state law would affect the "core liability issues" that he said could be addressed in a mass trial. The court also noted that Jones had failed to explain how each plaintiff's claim of addiction would be assessed. Calling the conspiracy-to-addict theory "novel and wholly untested," it concluded that even without these errors the class certification could not stand, because "a mass tort cannot be properly certified without a prior track record of trials. . . . The collective wisdom of individual juries is necessary before the court commits the fate of an entire industry or, indeed, the fate of a class of millions, to a single jury."[57] Like King Kong, *Castano* was too damned big for its own good.

Castano's creators promised to persevere. "We will be filing class-action lawsuits in all 50 states, the District of Columbia, and Puerto Rico," declared John Coale.[58] The next day, they started moving toward that goal, filing a class action in Louisiana, home of the Castanos. Such lawsuits were eventually filed in about two dozen states. So now the big-shot lawyers whose main motivation was money were pursuing the same strategy as Stanley Rosenblatt, who said, "I'd be out of my mind if I said I was doing this for the money."[59] The state class actions, which sought to cover hundreds of thousands or millions of plaintiffs, avoided the problem of diverse liability rules, but many of the difficulties cited by the Fifth Circuit remained. Courts still had no track record of trials to draw upon for guidance. Each plaintiff had a unique history of tobacco use and reaction to industry statements. Damages would still have to be assessed individually. Recognizing these problems, U.S. District Judge Clarence C. Newcomer threw out a Pennsylvania class action in October 1997, a month before the case was sheduled for trial. "When the court looks down the road to determine how this class would be tried," he said, "it is obvious that the litigation is unmanageable as a class action and would ultimately splinter into individual issues, which would have to be tried separately."[60] Despite their weaknesses, the class actions had already helped bring the tobacco companies to the bargaining table.

PAYBACK TIME

With *Castano* out of the picture, the biggest litigation threat facing the tobacco industry was a spate of lawsuits seeking compensation for the cost of treating smoking-related diseases under public health insurance. This kind of case was pioneered by Mississippi Attorney General Mike Moore. Moore got the idea from a law school classmate, Michael T. Lewis, whose secretary's mother, a smoker, had just died of heart disease.

Lewis suggested that Mississippi could sue cigarette makers to recoup the Medicaid expenses of such patients. Moore put him in touch with another University of Mississippi alumnus, Richard Scruggs, who had done some tobacco work and would soon represent Merrell Williams, the former paralegal who leaked the Brown & Williamson documents. Working under a contingency-fee arrangement, Scruggs, Lewis, Don Barrett (who had handled the Nathan Horton case), and several other attorneys filed suit on behalf of Mississippi in May 1994. Moore said: "This lawsuit is premised on a simple notion: you caused the health crisis; you pay for it. The free ride is over. It's time these billionaire tobacco companies start paying what they rightfully owe to Mississippi taxpayers."[61]

The notion, however, really was not so simple. If manufacturers of products associated with disease and injury should pick up the Medicaid tab for their customers, there seemed to be no end of potential defendants. Under the same sort of reasoning, a state might sue manufacturers of alcoholic beverages, which can cause cirrhosis of the liver; of dairy products, which contribute to heart disease; of candy, which fosters tooth decay and obesity; and of such instruments of injury as cars, bicycles, skis, skateboards, and bathtubs.

The implications of this principle were especially clear in Florida, where the legislature approved a bill intended to help the state win such lawsuits. The Medicaid Third-Party Liability Act of 1994 built on a right the state already had to seek reimbursement from third parties who injured people covered by Medicaid. Under the principle of subrogation, the state, having covered a patient's medical expenses, had first claim on any damages he might recover. A 1990 law authorized the state, in pursuit of Medicaid compensation, to "institute, intervene in, or join any legal proceeding." The 1994 statute dramatically expanded the basis for such suits, so that the state could now recover damages from third parties who would not otherwise be liable—money that the people who were actually injured could not have obtained. Under the new law, the state did not even have to name individual Medicaid recipients. It could sue the manufacturer of an allegedly harmful product for the medical expenses of a group, and it could rely on statistical evidence instead of proving causation and damages in each case. The statute barred the assumption-of-risk argument and every other affirmative defense. It allowed courts to order damages on the basis of market share, without inquiring into the brands used by Medicaid patients. At the same time, it imposed joint and several liability—meaning that a single defendant could be forced to pay damages for an entire industry.[62]

The general counsel of Florida's Agency for Health Care Administration, which was charged with carrying out the law, summed it up this way: "The state can change the legal criteria for a suit, and that is what we have done." He was being modest. The changes set forth in the law did not simply improve the state's chances in litigation against the tobacco industry. If upheld in court, they made a victory almost a foregone conclusion. It would hardly have been worse for the tobacco companies if the legislature had simply ordered them to cough up so many millions of dollars; at least they would have saved on legal fees. In a stroke, the law eliminated the industry's most effective defenses. The state did not have to prove that a single case of illness was actually caused by a defendant's product, and the tobacco companies could not point out that people voluntarily choose to smoke. "The state does not buy that package of tobacco," explained Governor Lawton Chiles, "so we don't read the warning on the side. We just pay for the carnage."[63]

Since the law applied retroactively, businesses could be held liable for activities—making and selling cigarettes, for instance—that were perfectly legal at the time they were carried out. Furthermore, the law was worded so broadly (it did not actually mention tobacco) that it could be used to sue manufacturers and distributors of any product that contributes to disease or injury. In response to the alarm that the broad language generated within Florida's business community, Chiles insisted that he was only interested in suing the tobacco companies, and he suggested that the law could be changed to make that clear. He later issued an executive order saying that the statute should be applied exclusively to cigarette manufacturers, but this reassurance only served to emphasize that the state was targeting a particular industry for political reasons, stripping it of the legal protections that apply to other businesses. "We're going to take the Marlboro Man to court," Chiles gloated upon signing the bill.[64] Along the way, he was creating a tobacco exception to the principle of equal protection.

In opposing the law, the tobacco companies were joined by business groups such as the Associated Industries of Florida, which lobbied for repeal and filed a lawsuit challenging the statute on constitutional grounds. The prospects for repeal seemed promising at first. The *Wall Street Journal* reported that the law, which allowed the state to hire private attorneys to handle the litigation and pay them a percentage of any recovery, had been conceived by the Inner Circle, "an exclusive group of 100 personal-injury lawyers."[65] Drafted by Pensacola plaintiff's attorney Fredric G. Levin, a friend of Senate sponsor W. D. Childers, the bill was rushed through at the end of the legislative session without explanation or debate. It soon became clear that most of the legislators had not realized what they were voting for. The *St. Petersburg Times* said the law "is the product of offensive political trickery and its terms are dangerously broad. . . . In the long history of 'snookers,' as legislative argot defines such stunts, this is the worst."[66]

In 1995 an overwhelming majority of the legislature voted to repeal the Medicaid Third-Party Liability Act; the vote was 102 to 13 in the House, 32 to 7 in the Senate. Decrying heavy lobbying by the tobacco companies, Chiles vetoed the repeal legislation, declaring, "I will not allow the tobacco industry or its champions in Florida's capital to continue to wreak havoc on the health of our people."[67] During the next legislative session he ran TV and newspaper ads, aimed at discouraging an override attempt, that urged, "Don't let killer tobacco put a smokescreen on the truth."[68] Having expressed their anger at the way the law was passed, some legislators may have started to worry about appearing to be tools of the tobacco industry. Despite several attempts, opponents of the law failed to muster enough votes to override Chiles's veto.

The constitutional challenge fared somewhat better. In June 1995 Leon County Circuit Court Judge F. E. Steinmeyer agreed with the Associated Industries of Florida that the structure of the Agency for Health Care Administration (AHCA), the agency charged with filing suits under the Medicaid Third-Party Liability Act, violated Florida's constitution. He also agreed that the law's directives concerning the identification and grouping of Medicaid patients, application of the evidence code, and interpretation of common law theories impermissibly infringed on the authority of the courts. Finally, he ruled that the law could not be applied retroactively and could not revive claims already barred by time limits.[69]

A year later, acting on an expedited appeal, the Florida Supreme Court agreed that expired claims could not be brought back from the dead and that the act could apply only to Medicaid payments made after July 1, 1994, when the law took effect. It further ruled that the provision allowing the state to sue for the expenses of unnamed patients violated the right to due process because it prevented the defendants from challenging the legitimacy of the expenses. And it found that the state could not simultaneously apply both market-share liability and joint and several liability, since the two theories are "fundamentally incompatible." On the other hand, it concluded that the AHCA was constitutional and that the law did not violate the separation of powers doctrine. The court also rejected the argument that the law was unconstitutional on its face because it eliminated all affirmative defenses, although it emphasized that the application of the statute could still be challenged on due process grounds.[70]

In a dissent joined by two other members of the court, Judge Stephen Grimes noted that notwithstanding Chiles's tobacco-only executive order (which itself seemed to violate the right to equal protection of the laws), "the statute would apply to anyone who ever caused an injury to someone who was later treated for that injury by a Florida Medicaid provider." Grimes called attention to the anomaly created by this rule: The liability of a defendant would hinge not on the nature of his actions but on the medical coverage of the plaintiff. "A law that presumes to measure the liability of a party based on such a consideration is completely arbitrary and violates due process," he wrote. "Whether a claim is Medicaid-eligible has no more relevance in measuring whether a party may raise an affirmative defense than the question of whether [the injured party] has brown hair or blond hair." Since it treats similarly situated defendants differently, Grimes argued, such an arbitrary distinction violates the right to equal protection as well as the right to due process. "The State has arrogated to itself a right that no other plaintiff can claim," he noted. "The State's action in this respect is nothing more than a thinly veiled taking."[71]

Unfazed by such considerations, Governor Chiles pursued his money grab. In February 1995 the state filed suit in West Palm Beach County Circuit Court against twenty-one cigarette companies, along with consulting and public relations firms, seeking $1.4 billion in compensation for Medicaid payments during the previous five years. The suit asked for triple (punitive) damages, charging that the tobacco companies had misled the public about nicotine addiction, and requested a court order against advertising campaigns aimed at teenagers. "We are filing suit to protect the rights of Florida taxpayers," Chiles said, "and to protect future generations from falling victim to tobacco's cycle of death."[72] The state was represented by Richard Scruggs (who was also handling the Mississippi suit), Ronald Motley (one of the *Castano* attorneys), and eleven other lawyers, who stood to receive 25 percent of any award plus reimbursement of their expenses. By precluding recovery of Medicaid payments prior to July 1994, the Supreme Court's ruling made the case considerably less lucrative, but the attorneys' net take could still amount to hundreds of millions of dollars.

In addition to paying attorneys' fees, the Associated Industries of Florida noted, states that successfully sued tobacco companies would have to reimburse the federal government for its share of Medicaid spending. The organization cited a study by the Commonwealth Foundation of Virginia that concluded that the average state could expect to receive only about 15 percent of any judgment. The calculation used the average federal Medicaid share, 61 percent, and assumed that legal fees and internal costs would amount to about 25 percent of damages. The study found that states where the federal share is unusually high, including Mississippi, could actually lose money by pursuing this sort of litigation. On the other hand, the study showed that some states would see returns as high as twenty-five cents on the dollar, or roughly what the attorneys would make.[73]

With compensatory and punitive damage claims in the hundreds of millions or billions, this was nothing to sneeze at, and there seemed to be little danger in attacking America's most unpopular legal industry, especially with plenty of trial lawyers eager to help. By June 1997 more than three dozen states had followed the example set by Mississippi and Florida. The suits used various common-law and statutory theories, generally revolving around a conspiracy to deceive and addict smokers, often with the targeting of children thrown in for good measure. "We hope this lawsuit will be the straw that breaks Joe Camel's back," said Connecticut Attorney General Richard Blumenthal as he hopped on the money train.[74] In March 1996 Texas Attorney General Dan Morales filed a $4 billion suit in federal court citing the Racketeer Influenced and Corrupt Organizations Act, a statute aimed at organized crime. "The tobacco industry has violated the law for so long and in so many ways that it has become standard operating procedure," he said. "History will record the modern-day tobacco industry alongside the worst of civilization's evil empires."[75]

A couple of weeks before Morales compared the tobacco industry to Nazi Germany and the Soviet Union, five states—Mississippi, Florida, Louisiana, Massachusetts, and West Virginia—had agreed to drop the Liggett Group from their lawsuits. Liggett, which settled with the states about the same time it negotiated its way out of *Castano,* agreed to pay a total of $1 million immediately and $440,000 for each of the next nine years, plus 2.5 percent of its annual pre-tax profits during the next twenty-five years. It also agreed to set aside 5 percent of its pre-tax profits to reimburse states that joined the settlement later. Finally, without conceding any wrongdoing, it promised to help the states assemble evidence for use in their lawsuits.

About a year later, the deal was expanded to cover all twenty-two states (including Texas) that had brought lawsuits up to that point, and others joined the agreement as they filed suit. The payout was raised to 25 percent of pre-tax profits, and Liggett made some additional concessions, including its shocking confession about the hazards and addictiveness of smoking. It also said that other companies market their products to minors, a practice it condemned and promised to avoid.

Liggett's agreement to share its files prompted an immediate legal challenge from the other companies, which argued that records of consultation among their lawyers had to be kept confidential. But Liggett was hardly the only source of inside information. In addition to the Brown & Williamson documents and the evidence used in *Cipollone,* the states could draw on the testimony of several former industry employees who came forward in 1995 and 1996. Jeffrey Wigand, a former Brown & Williamson research director, said that company officials had privately conceded that nicotine was addictive, despite public statements to the contrary, and that cigarette manufacturers used a variety of techniques to control nicotine yields. Scientists who had worked at Philip Morris confirmed that nicotine control was an important part of the manufacturing process. Meanwhile, FDA chief David Kessler was emphasizing that point in his proposal to regulate cigarettes as "drug delivery systems." He said evidence from internal documents suggested "that cigarette vendors intend the obvious—that many people buy cigarettes to satisfy their nicotine addiction."[76]

But if all this was obvious, how could the tobacco companies be accused of concealing it? As with the private class actions, common knowledge of tobacco's addictiveness and the industry's ability to control nicotine yields suggested that the conspiracy described in state lawsuits was not very effective. The argument that the lawsuits were needed to compensate taxpayers also did not bear close scrutiny: At the same time that states were suing tobacco companies to pay for the cost of treating smoking-related disease, they were taxing smokers for the same reason. At the very least, it seemed only fair to deduct state cigarette tax revenue from the Medicaid bill. In response to the lawsuit in Texas, the cigarette companies noted that state sales and excise taxes on tobacco had yielded $815 million the previous year—nearly five times the state's estimate of smoking-related Medicaid expenses.[77] The industry was more reluctant to use another promising argument, since it hinged on tobacco's tendency to cause fatal diseases: Because smokers die earlier than nonsmokers, their Medicaid expenses are offset by savings on health care and Social Security later in life. The states could respond by noting that they pay much of the Medicaid bill, while the savings accrue to the federal government, which pays for Medicare and Social Security. But this seems more like an argument for revenue sharing than a rationale for suing the tobacco industry.

As with the class actions, however, the threat posed by the state lawsuits had more to do with their size and the resources behind them than the plausibility of their claims. In the summer of 1997, after the proposed national settlement was announced, the tobacco companies made separate deals with Mississippi and Florida, agreeing to pay them $3.4 billion and $11.3 billion, respectively, even if the broader arrangement

fell apart. In the Florida case the tobacco companies also agreed to eliminate cigarette ads near schools, at sporting events, and on public transportation; remove vending machines from locations accessible to minors; and spend $200 million on anti-smoking programs. By settling
with Mississippi and Florida, the industry avoided the first two Medicaid trials. The next two, in Texas and Minnesota, were expected to begin
in 1998.

UNREASONABLY DANGEROUS

Despite all the hoopla about the big class actions and the state lawsuits,
the first victory of the third wave came in a case filed on behalf of a single smoker. In August 1996 a jury in Jacksonville, Florida, told Brown
& Williamson to pay $500,000 to Grady Carter, a retired air traffic con-
troller with lung cancer, and $250,000 to his wife. It was the first time a
jury had awarded damages to a smoker for a tobacco-related disease.
Carter, who started smoking Lucky Strikes in 1947, switched to other
brands in 1972 and continued smoking, despite nagging from his family, until his cancer was diagnosed in 1991. "I am responsible," he conceded on the witness stand.[78] But his attorney, Norwood S. Wilner, argued that American Tobacco, which owned the Lucky Strike brand and
was acquired by Brown & Williamson in 1995, was also responsible because it had deliberately hooked Carter on a deadly product. After a
couple of weeks of testimony and two days of deliberations, the jury
concluded that cigarettes are unreasonably dangerous and that American
Tobacco had failed to adequately warn consumers about the dangers of
smoking. It awarded half the amount suggested by Wilner.

The jury saw several hundred pages of excerpts from the Brown &
Williamson documents, including Addison Yeaman's comments on nicotine, which highlighted the industry's dishonesty. "That really bothered
me," said one juror, "given that to this day, they argue the addiction
point." Another commented, "We wanted to send a message to the tobacco companies: We ain't going to take it no more."[79] Another important factor in the verdict was Florida's rule concerning comparative negligence, which (like Mississippi's) allows a partial damage award even when
the plaintiff is deemed mostly responsible for his injury. (Two weeks after

the *Carter* verdict, a smoker's family lost a case in Indiana, where a plain-tiff who is considered mostly responsible for his injury cannot recover damages.[80]) Wilner was taking advantage of the state's favorable legal cli-mate and its abundance of retirees. Before the *Carter* verdict, he had filed about 200 cases in Florida on behalf of individual smokers, including for-mer Winston model Alan Landers. At the end of August he filed another 125, along with 4 secondhand smoke cases and a class action naming nearly three hundred current and former smokers. (Stanley Rosenblatt expressed "puzzlement" at the apparent overlap with *Engle*.[81])

The verdict in Wilner's next case—which came in May 1997, during the nationwide settlement negotiations—lent support to those who ar-gued that the *Carter* award was an aberration rather than the start of a trend. Jean Connor, a Jacksonville bank branch manager, started smok-ing in 1961 as a teenager and died of lung cancer in 1995 at the age of forty-nine. In March 1995, six months before her death, her family filed a lawsuit against R. J. Reynolds, manufacturer of the Winston and Salem brands she had smoked for twenty years. During the trial, Wilner and cocounsel Ronald Motley (who also had a hand in *Castano* and the state lawsuits) offered the standard arguments: Reynolds had deceived consumers about the risks of smoking, and Connor had gotten hooked before she knew better. Reynolds's lawyer offered the standard defense: Connor was aware of the risks, and she could have quit if she really wanted to. (In fact, she *had* quit, two years before her death, so she could get a tummy-tuck operation, which the plastic surgeon would not perform unless she stopped smoking. She never smoked again.) The six-person jury, which included two social smokers and two ex-smokers, concluded that Reynolds was not liable in Connor's death.

The forewoman, a twenty-six-year-old former smoker who had quit without much difficulty, later explained the decision in the *Washington Post*. She said that the jurors recognized the company's duplicity in pri-vately acknowledging the hazards of smoking while publicly doubting them but that "Reynolds's actions did not negate the fact that the risks were widely known." In a deposition, Connor had admitted, "I knew smoking was hazardous to my health." She had also said that "the enjoy-ment outweighed the risks." The jurors were impressed, too, by the fact that "Connor was able to quit smoking on her first try."[82]

The *Connor* verdict was announced a little more than a week after a federal judge upheld the FDA's jurisdiction over cigarettes while denying it the authority to regulate tobacco advertising and promotion. That mixed ruling gave both sides in the settlement talks a reason to persevere: The industry could no longer hope for a quick win in the legal battle against FDA regulation, and the anti-smokers could no longer hope to get rid of Joe Camel billboards and Marlboro tote bags without the industry's cooperation. Similarly, the *Connor* verdict, combined with the memory of the *Carter* award, reminded both sides about the unpredictability of juries.

"I've referred to these suits all along as morality plays," Stanford University law professor Robert Rabin said after the *Carter* verdict. "The question is, who looks more irresponsible, and the industry has been very successful up to now in making the smokers look more irresponsible. But this tale that can be told from the Brown & Williamson documents is very likely to make some juries, not all, feel that the more culpable side now appears to be the industry side."[83]

If tobacco lawsuits are morality plays, what lesson do they teach? That it's wrong to blame others when we succumb to temptation? Or that it's wrong to put a stumbling block before the blind? Here is a smoker suffering from a terrible disease as a result of his own choices. There is the tobacco company cynically dancing around the truth to ward off liability and protect its profits. "Without the rationalizations," argues Richard Daynard, smokers "would have made earlier or more determined efforts to quit, and the industry was throwing them rationalizations."[84] One thing seems pretty clear, however: The tobacco companies didn't fool anyone who didn't want to be fooled. It would take a smoker's willing creation of disbelief to escape what has been common knowledge for decades (if not centuries), namely, that smoking is dangerous and hard to give up.

Juries have never been fond of tobacco companies, but until recently they recognized that cigarettes do not smoke themselves and they insisted that smokers should be responsible for their actions. That may be changing, and the *Carter* verdict is not the only sign. According to the Gallup poll, the proportion of Americans who say tobacco companies should be held legally responsible for smoking-related deaths rose from 13 percent in 1991 to 30 percent in 1996.[85]

A tobacco lawsuit is not just a morality play, of course. For those who dream of a smoke-free society, it is also a tool of public health. Ahron Leichtman argues that "massive damage awards and looming liability can drive up the price of cigarettes and drive down consumption, addiction and disease. Where proper regulation has been thwarted by the tobacco lobby, the courts can promote health and serve the public interest."[86] Other commentators call suing the tobacco companies "a cancer control strategy" and an example of "litigating for the public's health."[87]

While Stanley Rosenblatt and Stanton Glantz have declared their intention to destroy the tobacco industry, most liability advocates seem to assume that it will continue in some form. "I don't know anybody involved in litigation or in the tobacco control world who thinks that cold turkeying 40 to 50 million Americans is a good idea," says Daynard. "So that's not the purpose." He believes the industry should be "forced to pay to the extent that it can for the harm it does" and says, "Any back-of-the-envelope calculation is going to show that the industry simply cannot afford to pay for the harm it does, and therefore this will send it at least into Chapter 11, so that the companies that make cigarettes are likely to be successor companies."[88]

Daynard is wary of any tobacco deal that involves congressional intervention. "I think [the tobacco companies] would be willing to agree to almost anything if they thought they had a sure-fire way to kill the litigation," he says.[89] But if the cigarette companies actually had to undergo bankruptcy and reorganization, he believes, a more honest and responsible tobacco industry would emerge, one that would not dodge the health issue, pitch cigarettes to kids, or use pictures in its ads.

Even if the new tobacco companies did not engage in any questionable activities, their products would still cause disease. Under a system of absolute liability, which Daynard favors, they would have to pay for the costs associated with the unavoidable health effects of smoking. Daynard says the bill might amount to something like $6 a pack. He concedes that quadrupling the price of cigarettes would foster a black market but says he doesn't "envision that that would be a huge problem," especially since the legitimate companies would have a strong incentive to help curtail the activities of fly-by-night competitors.[90] At $8 or more a pack, not incidentally, cigarettes would be prohibitively expensive for many smokers. Like Kenneth Warner, who makes a similar argument for raising tobacco taxes, Daynard thinks higher prices would teach people the true costs of smoking.

Tobacco's opponents like to say that if the cigarette were introduced today, the government would never allow it on the market. They're right. In a sense, the cigarette is an anachronism, a relic from the age of *caveat emptor,* when people who sucked smoke into their lungs had to take responsibility for the consequences. Even the advent of strict liability did not completely erase that old-fashioned notion. In 1965 the *Restatement (Second) of Torts* declared that "good tobacco is not unreasonably dangerous." Three decades later—when the average cigarette is, if anything, somewhat safer—jurors are beginning to disagree, perhaps because the very concept of "good tobacco" seems like an oxymoron. Americans are increasingly coming to share the view, expressed by the Tennessee Supreme Court in 1898, that cigarettes "possess no virtue, but are inherently bad, bad only."[91] The puzzle that remains is why so many people continue to smoke them.

Chapter 7

LITTLE WHITE SLAVERS

In our times the use of tobacco is growing greatly and conquers men
with a certain secret pleasure, so that those who have once become
accustomed thereto can later hardly be restrained therefrom.

—Sir Francis Bacon, 1623

THE POWER OF ADDICTION

When the top executives of the seven largest U.S. tobacco companies
testified before the House Subcommittee on Health and the Environment in April 1994, the defining moment was an exchange between the
witnesses and Representative Ron Wyden, an Oregon Democrat and a
longtime critic of the industry.

"Do you believe nicotine is not addictive?" Wyden asked Philip Morris CEO William I. Campbell. He was not posing a question so much as
pushing a button that he knew would elicit a programmed response, like
Captain Kirk tricking a computer into self-destruction.

"I believe nicotine is not addictive, yes," came the inevitable reply.

"Mr. Johnston?" Wyden said, prompting James W. Johnston, the
CEO of R. J. Reynolds.

"Congressman, cigarettes and nicotine clearly do not meet the classic
definitions of addiction. There is no intoxication."

That rather terse and cryptic reply was a bit too detailed for Wyden.
"We'll take that as a no," he said, "and, again, time is short. If you can

just—I think each of you believes nicotine is not addictive. We just would like to have this for the record."

"I don't believe that nicotine or our products are addictive," said U.S. Tobacco president Joseph Taddeo.

"I believe nicotine is not addictive," said Liggett Group CEO Edward A. Horrigan.

"I believe that nicotine is not addictive," said Lorillard CEO Andrew Tisch.

"I believe that nicotine is not addictive," said Brown & Williamson CEO Thomas E. Sandefur.

"And I, too, believe that nicotine is not addictive," said American Tobacco CEO Donald S. Johnston, rounding out the list.[1]

This strange little ritual illustrated the power of addiction to cloud the minds of otherwise intelligent men. The concept is at once familiar and alien, commonsensical and arcane. In everyday usage, addiction is a habit that's hard to break, a strong attachment to a source of gratification. Nowadays we tend to assume that addiction is bad, a problem in need of a remedy. But as Thomas Szasz notes in his book *Ceremonial Chemistry*, this was not always the case: "Traditionally, the term 'addiction' has meant simply a strong inclination toward certain kinds of conduct, with little or no pejorative meaning attached to it. Thus, the *Oxford English Dictionary* offers such pre-twentieth-century examples of the use of this term as being addicted 'to civil affairs,' 'to useful reading,'—and also 'to bad habits.' . . . Until quite recently, then, the term 'addiction' was understood to refer to a habit, good or bad as the case might be, actually more often the former."[2] Even today, we speak of "news junkies," "chocoholics," and "football addicts," without meaning to imply that these people have problems.

Usually, however, addiction has a negative connotation—either because the addict himself considers his behavior harmful or because other people disapprove of it. Drug abuse is the most familiar example, but many other activities can qualify: gambling, sex, eating, jogging, shopping, even surfing the Internet.[3] Since anything that provides pleasure (or relief) can be the focus of an addiction, it is somewhat misleading to call a particular substance addictive. Certain chemicals are more popular than others, of course, and some are more likely to be used regularly. Yet most people who try substances that are considered addictive—including heroin and crack cocaine as well as nicotine—do not become regular users, and regular users often cut back or stop. On the other hand, many people who return to addiction do so after the physical effects of the substance, including withdrawal symptoms, have faded away. These observations suggest that addiction is a pattern of behavior, not a chemical reaction; that it resides in a person's relationship with a substance, not in the substance itself.

By contrast, the exchange between Wyden and the tobacco CEOs was colored by a drug-centered view of addiction. According to this model, which we might call voodoo pharmacology, powerful substances take control of people's behavior, turning them into chemical zombies. To say that smokers are addicted to cigarettes, then, means that they do not choose to smoke but are compelled to do so, that they are slaves to nicotine rather than independent moral agents. As Representative John Bryant, a Texas Democrat, put it during the hearing, "The fact of the matter is that you can't sit here today and say to us that people made a free choice to smoke if you also concede that once a person starts, they are addicted."[4] The CEOs agreed with Bryant, which is why they were so desperate to deny that smoking is a form of addiction.

In addition to the ever-present threat of litigation by smokers claiming that nicotine made them do it, the tobacco company executives were trying to ward off regulation by the Food and Drug Administration. They had been summoned to testify by Henry Waxman, the California Democrat who chaired the subcommittee, mainly because FDA commissioner David A. Kessler was suggesting that his agency might have jurisdiction over cigarettes. Kessler first publicly raised this possibility in a letter to Scott Ballin, then chairman of the Coalition on Smoking or Health. The coalition had petitioned the FDA to regulate low-yield cigarettes as drugs, arguing that such products were intended to reduce the risk of smoking-related disease. In a letter dated February 25, 1994, Kessler noted that the FDA had "traditionally refrained from asserting jurisdiction over most cigarette products." The only exceptions were brands whose manufacturers advertised specific health benefits, such as weight reduction. But contrary to the position taken by federal courts and by every one of his predecessors, Kessler suggested that the FDA might have the authority to regulate cigarettes even in the absence of such claims.[5]

This is how Kessler explained the reversal: "Evidence brought to our attention is accumulating that suggests that cigarette manufacturers may intend that their products contain nicotine to satisfy an addiction on the part of some of their customers. The possible inference that cigarette vendors intend cigarettes to achieve drug effects in some smokers is based on mounting evidence we have received that: (1) the nicotine ingredient in cigarettes is a powerfully addictive agent and (2) cigarette vendors control the levels of nicotine that satisfy this addiction." If so, he reasoned, a cigarette could be considered a drug under one of the definitions in the Food, Drug, and Cosmetic Act: "articles (other than food) intended to affect the structure or any function of the body of man or other animals."[6]

Although Kessler referred to "accumulating" and "mounting" evidence, the two premises of his argument had been widely acknowledged for many years. Nicotine was isolated and named (after sixteenth-century tobacco enthusiast Jean Nicot) in 1828, and its molecular formula was described in 1843. Researchers began studying its effects on the nervous system by 1889, and its importance as an incentive for smoking was taken for granted by the turn of the century. When James Barrie, author of *Peter Pan,* published a novel revolving around smoking in 1890, he titled it *My Lady Nicotine.* The role of nicotine in smoking was confirmed experimentally in 1942 when the British researcher Lennox M. Johnston found that injections of the drug soothed smokers' cravings. He concluded that "smoking tobacco is essentially a means of administering nicotine, just as smoking opium is a means of administering morphine."[7] Thousands of additional studies were published during the next half-century, along with numerous books and articles about nicotine addiction, many of them aimed at a popular audience. In a 1971 literature review, the British researcher M. A. Hamilton Russell observed, "If it were not for the nicotine in tobacco smoke people would be little more inclined to smoke cigarettes than they are to blow bubbles or light sparklers."[8] By 1994, therefore, it was a bit late to discover that smokers are fond of nicotine.

Nor was it news that tobacco companies controlled nicotine levels.

Several brands of denicotined cigarettes were introduced as early as the 1920s. (More recently, in 1991, Philip Morris launched Next and Merit DeNic, virtually nicotine-free brands that were attacked by the same anti-smoking groups that now complain cigarettes have too much nicotine in them.[9]) Claims of reduced tar and nicotine had been conspicuous since the 1950s, and the yields of each brand had been advertised, by agreement with the Federal Trade Commission, since 1971. The very idea of a consistent nicotine yield for a given brand implied control, which the manufacturers achieved through several methods, including filtration and dilution of the smoke, use of fillers such as reconstituted tobacco, and blending of different tobacco varieties and parts of the plant. As the journalist Richard Kluger observes in his tobacco history, *Ashes to Ashes,* "That manufacturers had been controlling or manipulating the amount of nicotine their customers ordinarily derived from their cigarettes had been known for forty years, ever since the introduction of filter tips, to students of the subject, and to any portion of the public that thought a moment about it."[10]

For anyone familiar with this history, and with centuries of reports about the difficulty of giving up smoking, Kessler's sudden discovery of nicotine addiction was puzzling. "It struck me that Kessler should get an Emmy, that Waxman should get an Emmy," says Alan Blum, founder of the anti-smoking group Doctors Ought to Care. "It's either extremely dishonest, or it's more than extremely naive."[11]

In any event, it was odd that Kessler put so much emphasis on addiction, a concept that is not even mentioned in the Food, Drug, and Cosmetic Act. Addictiveness, however defined, is neither a necessary nor a sufficient condition for FDA jurisdiction; under its drug authority, the agency regulates many substances that are not considered addictive, and it does not regulate some substances that are (e.g., caffeine, ethanol, heroin). The definition of *drug* on which Kessler relied says nothing about addiction; it refers to intended effects on the structure or functions of the body. It is well established by more than a century of research that nicotine has many effects on the body, some of which are desired by smokers and, presumably, intended by cigarette makers—who, after all, stay in business by paying attention to what their customers want. Once he had decided to rely on indirect evidence of manufacturer intent, Kessler could have simply noted that nicotine helps smokers stay slim by raising their metabolic rates or that it helps them stay alert by stimulating the production of neurotransmitters.

Emphasizing addiction did not make the case for FDA jurisdiction any more persuasive, but it did help delegitimize cigarettes, the people who smoke them, and the companies that make them. Employing the rhetoric of voodoo pharmacology, Kessler asserted, "Once they have started smoking regularly, most smokers are in effect deprived of the choice to stop smoking." He said the tobacco companies "may be controlling smokers' choice by controlling the levels of nicotine in their products in a manner that creates and sustains an addiction." He suggested that "it is a choice by cigarette companies to maintain addictive levels of nicotine in their cigarettes, rather than a choice by consumers to continue smoking, that in the end is driving the demand for cigarettes in this country."[12] By redefining a voluntary transaction—the purchase of cigarettes—as a coercive relationship, Kessler sought to deflect the argument that government has no business protecting smokers from themselves. If people smoke because they've been enthralled by the tobacco companies, perhaps the state has a duty to break the spell, to free the nicotine slaves. This argument, increasingly popular among tobacco's opponents, goes well beyond taxes, ad bans, and restrictions on smoking in public places. It offers a moral rationale for prohibition.

Tellingly, Kessler himself raised the possibility of a cigarette ban. If the FDA treated cigarettes like the other drugs it regulates, he noted, it would have to certify them as safe and effective. Cigarettes plainly are not safe, and it's not clear what it would mean to call them effective. Consequently, Kessler wrote in his letter to Scott Ballin, "a strict application of these provisions could mean, ultimately, removal from the market of tobacco products containing nicotine at levels that cause or satisfy addiction." Henry Waxman agreed, telling the *Los Angeles Times* that without action by Congress the FDA was "going to have only one option: ban cigarettes." Kessler expressed reservations about that prospect for practical reasons, not out of concern for the rights of smokers. "Given the widespread use of cigarettes and the prevalence of nicotine addiction," he said, "such a regulatory action could have dramatic effects on our society." He alluded to the impact of sudden withdrawal on tens of millions of smokers and the potential for a black market. "It is vital in this context that Congress provide clear direction to the agency," he concluded. "We intend therefore to work with Congress to resolve, once and for all, the regulatory status of cigarettes under the Food, Drug, and Cosmetic Act."13

Industry representatives cited this cautious language in arguing that Kessler's letter was no big deal. "We are surprised that this FDA letter is getting the attention it is," Tobacco Institute spokeswoman Brennan Dawson told the *New York Times*. "The bottom line of this letter is that the FDA won't act without further action from Congress. Nothing has happened."14

But something had. Kessler did not wait for the "clear direction" from Congress that he said was vital. Over the years members of Congress had unsuccessfully sponsored more than a dozen bills that would have given the FDA jurisdiction over cigarettes. The very introduction of such legislation indicated that tobacco's opponents in Congress did not think the FDA had the authority claimed by Kessler. The new Republican majority elected in November 1994 was even less likely to look favorably on the commissioner's foray into tobacco policy. So Kessler decided to "resolve the regulatory status of cigarettes" on his own. In August 1995 the FDA proposed sweeping restrictions on the advertising, promotion, and distribution of cigarettes and smokeless tobacco, ostensibly to discourage underage smoking. It was the most ambitious regulatory plan the tobacco industry had ever faced.

A CLEVER DEVICE

Calling cigarettes "drug delivery systems," the FDA claimed regulatory authority under the medical device provisions of the Food, Drug, and Cosmetic Act. It used basically the same reasoning as a 1977 petition from anti-smoking groups that was rejected by Donald Kennedy, then commissioner of the FDA. That petition had argued that a cigarette "is, after all, an instrument, apparatus, or contrivance designed to administer controlled amounts of nicotine and other substances to the smoker upon demand." Nearly two decades later, the FDA decided this approach made sense after all. The Food, Drug, and Cosmetic Act allows the agency to restrict the sale, distribution, or use of a medical device when "there cannot otherwise be reasonable assurance of safety and effectiveness." Leaving aside the puzzling question of effectiveness, this language implies that FDA regulations could provide reasonable assurance of safety—not a very plausible notion in the case of cigarettes. But since the device provisions let the FDA decide what's reasonable, they left some room to maneuver. As the FDA put it, "These device provisions authorize the agency to use the regulatory tools that most appropriately protect the public from unsafe or ineffective devices." By regulating cigarettes as medical devices rather than drugs, the FDA sought to avoid the strict safety and efficacy standards for drugs that cigarettes could not possibly meet.[15]

To gain this flexibility, however, the FDA had to put cigarettes in the same category as pacemakers, hearing aids, and orthopedic implants—an anomalous status for a recreational drug. In response to the FDA proposal, the Competitive Enterprise Institute, a free-market think tank, filed a tongue-in-cheek petition asking the agency to regulate coffee, tea, and caffeinated soft drinks as drug delivery devices. CEI noted that caffeine, like nicotine, has widely recognized "addictive, psychoactive, and other pharmacological effects." Furthermore, manufacturers of tea, coffee, and soft drinks control the level of caffeine in their products and could remove the drug entirely. "We do not claim that the risks of drinking these beverages are at all comparable to the risks of smoking," said CEI general counsel Sam Kazman, "and in our view FDA regulation of such beverages would produce no social benefit. Nonetheless, FDA's tobacco proposal sets out new criteria for classifying substances as drugs and devices, and these criteria are as applicable to caffeine as they are to nicotine. FDA has an obligation to apply these criteria evenhandedly."[16]

The tobacco companies challenged Kessler's reading of the Food, Drug, and Cosmetic Act in federal court. In his April 1997 response to the industry's motion for summary judgment, U.S. District Judge William L. Osteen noted that "FDA officials testified before congressional committees on numerous occasions that the agency lacked jurisdiction to regulate tobacco products" and that "members of Congress agreed with FDA's assertions that it lacked jurisdiction." But since Congress had defined both *drug* and *device* in broad terms, and since it had never explicitly forbidden the FDA to regulate tobacco products, Osteen concluded that the agency's new interpretation was reasonable. Legal experts thought there was a good chance this aspect of the ruling would be overturned on appeal; a decision was expected in late 1997. Even while upholding the FDA's jurisdiction, Osteen found that the "restricted device" provisions did not give it the authority to limit advertising and promotion, which was the main thrust of the agency's regulations.[17]

After Osteen's decision, the Associated Press reported that Representative Waxman "said the ruling could open the door to an outright ban."[18] Phil Schiliro, Waxman's press secretary, said his boss did not favor that outcome: "Congress won't let it happen. That creates a bigger problem than we have now." But though the FDA argued that the medical device provisions allow enough leeway to keep cigarettes on the market, Schiliro conceded that "reasonable people can disagree about whether they have the discretion or not. . . . You could see an argument where they would say, 'We have no choice but to ban this.' " In the end, he said, Congress would have to tell the FDA how to regulate cigarettes, which is what Waxman had maintained all along. The proposed nationwide liability settlement, which conceded FDA jurisdiction, recommended a separate category of medical devices especially for tobacco products—further evidence that they never really fit into the regulatory framework established by the Food, Drug, and Cosmetic Act.[19]

Whatever the ultimate scope of FDA authority, Kessler's anti-tobacco offensive had an immediate impact on public opinion. If he had voiced the suspicion that PepsiCo puts caffeine in Mountain Dew to "achieve drug effects" or that Anheuser-Busch brews Budweiser with alcohol-generating yeast for the same reason, he would have been greeted by yawns and blank stares. But even though he said he was only pointing out that "cigarette vendors intend the obvious,"[20] the news media treated nicotine control as a revelation. A story on ABC's *Day One,* broadcast three days after Kessler's letter to Ballin, set the tone for most of the press coverage. Correspondent John Martin said: "A lengthy *Day One* investigation has uncovered perhaps the tobacco industry's last best secret—how it artificially adds nicotine to cigarettes to keep people smoking and boost profits. The methods the cigarette companies use to control the [levels] of nicotine is something that has never before been disclosed to consumers or the government." Clifford Douglas, an anti-smoking activist, told Martin: "The public doesn't know that the industry manipulates nicotine, takes it out, puts it back in, uses it as if it were sugar being put into candy. They don't have a clue." Along with the general practice of "nicotine manipulation," *Day One* charged the tobacco companies with "spiking" or "fortifying" cigarettes.[21]

In response to the *Day One* story and a brief follow-up report, Philip Morris filed a $10 billion defamation lawsuit against ABC, insisting that it does not add extra nicotine to its cigarettes. On August 21, 1995, less than two weeks after Kessler announced his proposed tobacco regulations (finalized a year later), ABC publicly apologized to Philip Morris and agreed to pay the company's legal expenses, which reportedly amounted to $15 million. The network conceded that Philip Morris "does not add nicotine in any measurable amount from any outside source for any purpose in the course of its manufacturing process, and that its finished cigarettes contain less nicotine than is found in the natural tobacco from which they are made." The apology continued: "We now agree that we should not have reported that Philip Morris adds significant amounts of nicotine from outside sources. That was a mistake . . . for which we accept responsibility and which requires correction." But ABC added that "the principal focus of the reports was whether cigarette companies use the reconstituted tobacco process to control the levels of nicotine in cigarettes in order to keep people smoking. Philip Morris categorically denies that it does so. ABC thinks the reports speak for themselves on this issue."[22]

Shorn of the spiking charge, the *Day One* story consisted mainly of putting a negative spin on industry practices that have long been public knowledge. The cigarette companies have been using reconstituted tobacco—a sort of paper made from stems, leaf pieces, and tobacco dust—since the 1950s, and the process has been discussed in trade publications, medical journals, books, and government reports. To make reconstituted tobacco, cigarette companies soak the plant material in hot water, removing water-soluble components, including nicotine, from the fiber. After the water partly evaporates, the concentrated soluble matter is combined with flavorings, preservatives, and humectants. This mixture is applied to sheets made from tobacco fiber, which are dried,

cut into pieces, and added to the tobacco blend. Since stems have a relatively low nicotine content to begin with and since much of the nicotine
is lost during the process, reconstituted tobacco contains substantially
less nicotine than ordinary tobacco leaf. Other things being equal, therefore, the higher the proportion of reconstituted tobacco in a cigarette,
the lower its nicotine yield.

This hardly amounts to "spiking," but it is one method that cigarette
makers use to control nicotine levels (as well as reduce production
costs). Since they advertise brand-specific nicotine yields, the tobacco
companies can't very well deny that the way a cigarette is manufactured
determines the amount of nicotine it delivers (to smoking machines, at
least). "Do we do quality control to make sure that a Marlboro Light delivers, by the FTC testing method, the amount of nicotine that it says in
our ads?" asks Steven Parrish, senior vice president for corporate affairs
at Philip Morris Companies. "Yes. If that's the definition of control, we
certainly do quality control in that sense. But do we have somebody
there with a beaker of nicotine, making sure that the right amount of
nicotine is added in? No. And that was one of the problems I had with
the term *manipulate,* which has a very pejorative connotation to it."[23]

In particular, the term implied that the tobacco companies were
pulling a fast one on smokers by secretly addicting them. The companies
would say they were simply supplying what their customers want and expect: cigarettes with nicotine. But the sinister interpretation offered by
Day One stuck, partly because it was reinforced by government officials.
"That really bothered me when I heard that more nicotine was going in
to make sure that people were hooked," President Clinton said a few
weeks after the broadcast.[24] In his letter to Ballin, Kessler lent credence to
the spiking charge by saying, "It is our understanding that manufacturers
commonly add nicotine to cigarettes to deliver specific amounts of nicotine."[25] A call-out accompanying the *New York Times* story about
Kessler's letter asked, "Do cigarette makers boost nicotine levels to foster
addiction?"[26] A March 1994 story in *Newsweek* said, "The Food and
Drug Administration, prodded by a report on ABC's *Day One,* accused
[cigarette companies] of injecting products with extra nicotine."[27]

It was never exactly clear why smokers should care about "extra nicotine" so long as cigarette companies accurately advertised the yields of

their brands. In any case, Kessler's jurisdiction claim did not hinge on spiking. As he told the *Washington Post,* "it makes no difference for the purposes of the Food and Drug Administration" whether nicotine is added or occurs naturally. "Since manufacturers have the technology to remove nicotine from cigarettes," the *Post* reported, "leaving it in . . . might allow tobacco products to be classified as drugs."[28] Thus, even the *failure* to manipulate nicotine levels supported the case for regulation as Kessler had framed it. Since techniques to remove nicotine from cigarettes had been around for seventy years or more, it was not clear why it had taken the FDA so long to act.

What about the "mounting evidence"? According to *U.S. News & World Report,* Kessler was relying on "new evidence that nicotine is addictive and that the tobacco industry manipulates levels of the substance to keep smokers hooked." The magazine said Kessler had presented "a raft of new information" in his March 1994 congressional testimony.[29] But virtually all of the evidence Kessler cited—including research on the effects of nicotine, U.S. patents for techniques to control nicotine levels, data on tar and nicotine yields, trade journal excerpts, and a Philip Morris memo that was submitted in the *Cipollone* case—had been publicly available for years. Asked about this, FDA spokesman Jim O'Hara said, "The question is new information that is considered by the agency and is before the agency. That information has existed is not the question."[30] In other words, if the FDA doesn't acknowledge it, it isn't really there.

To be fair, some new information did emerge after Kessler started talking about regulating cigarettes. A former Philip Morris scientist testified in April 1994 that his research with rats on the reinforcing effects of nicotine had been shut down by his employer. In June 1994 Kessler testified about a high-nicotine strain of tobacco developed by Brown & Williamson for use in some of its low-tar brands. The notorious Brown & Williamson documents, first excerpted by the *New York Times* in May 1994, showed that tobacco executives privately acknowledged the psychoactive effects and addictiveness of nicotine. The insiders who came forward in 1995 and 1996, including former B&W research director Jeffrey Wigand, said such admissions were common within the industry, and they confirmed that the cigarette companies controlled nicotine delivery in various ways. None of these sources added anything important to the essential facts on which Kessler was basing his case for FDA jurisdiction: that nicotine is addictive and that tobacco companies control it. But journalists, like the trial lawyers, were enchanted by the idea of a shadowy conspiracy to keep smokers hooked. It seemed like a great exposé.

A BEWITCHING QUALITY

In truth, the addiction conspiracy was just a new twist on a very old story. Long before the modern cigarette was developed, people found the tobacco habit much easier to form than to break. In the early sixteenth century, Spanish settlers in the West Indies who were rebuked for smoking by Bishop Bartholomé de las Casas "replied that they found it impossible to give up." As the psychiatrist Jerome H. Jaffe noted in a 1977 monograph on smoking, "It is difficult to know how to interpret a statement to one's Bishop that a behavior of which he disapproves is beyond one's control."[31] But it seems clear that early smokers had a strong attachment to the weed that today would be described as an addiction.

In his *Counterblaste to Tobacco*, published in 1604, James I noted, "Many in this kingdome have had such a continuall use of taking this unsavorie smoke, as now they are not able to forbeare the same, no more than an olde drunkard can abide to be long sober, without falling into an incurable weakenesse and evill constitution. . . . And as no man likes strong headie drinks the first day . . . but by custome is piece and piece allured . . . so is not this the very case with of all the great takers of *Tobacco?* which therefore they themselves do attribute to a bewitching quality in it."[32] Sir Francis Bacon, the king's lord chancellor, observed, "In our times the use of tobacco is growing greatly and conquers men with a certain secret pleasure, so that those who have once become accustomed thereto can later hardly be restrained therefrom."[33]

Similar descriptions were recorded in other countries during the seventeenth and eighteenth centuries. Johann Michael Moscherosch called smokers "thralls to the tobacco fiend," while Cotton Mather dubbed them "*Slave*[s] to the *Pipe*." Fagon, court physician for Louis XIV, described the tobacco habit as "a fatal, insatiable necessity . . . a permanent epilepsy." In Bohemia, an observer reported, "The common people are so given up to the abuse that they imagine they cannot live

without several pipes of tobacco a day—thus squandering in these ne-
cessitous times the pennies they need for their daily bread." An account
from Nuremberg said, "Many a one becomes so used to the stuff that
he cannot be parted from it neither day nor night." The Jesuit priest
Jakob Balde cited "the smoking fellows of Northern Germany who live
only to smoke and cannot live without it." According to a witness in
Austria, "Although tobacco be not necessary for the sustenance of man,
yet have matters gone so far that many are of a mind that they would
rather lack bread than tobacco."[34]

During the ascendancy of snuff, it became apparent that tobacco addiction was not limited to smokers. Recall the Catholic Church's attempts to control the behavior of priests who were so dependent on the
powder that they sniffed it right before communion. After observing the
use of snuff in the court of Louis XIV (himself an opponent of tobacco),
Princess Elizabeth Charlotte of Orleans had this advice for her sister: "It
is better to take no snuff at all than a little; for it is certain that he who
takes a little will soon take much, and that is why they call it 'the enchanted herb,' for those who take it are so taken by it that they cannot
go without it; so take care of yourself, dear Louise!"[35]

In the United States, the physician Benjamin Rush argued, like James
I, that "the progress of habit in the use of Tobacco is exactly the same as
in the use of spirituous liquors."[36] As we saw in chapter 1, other temperance campaigners drew the same parallel. In 1853 a temperance group
awarded prizes for the best essays on "The Physical and Moral Effects of
the Use of Tobacco as a Luxury." One of the winners wrote: "The slave
of tobacco is seldom found reclaimable . . . I know full well the difficulty
of reclaiming the drunkard. But the tobacco drunkard is still less hope-
ful. I have, indeed, in the course of the last quarter of a century, met
with instances of entire emancipation, but they have been few and far
between." Another said: "Most emphatically does tobacco enslave its
votaries. . . . It is the uniform testimony of those who have attempted to
emancipate themselves from their attachment and bondage to tobacco,
that to break the chains in which they are bound, requires the earnest efforts of reason, conscience and the will."[37]

Although the difficulty of giving up tobacco had been observed for
hundreds of years, during the first half of this century scientists were re-

luctant to call smoking an addiction. This was partly because so many of
them smoked; people do not like to see themselves or their colleagues as
addicts. But it was also because their concept of addiction emphasized
the features of opiate use: stuporous intoxication, tolerance (a need for
escalating doses), and physical dependence (resulting in withdrawal
symptoms). By this standard, barbiturates are clearly addictive, but cocaine and amphetamines are not. Nor does nicotine seem to meet the requirements very well. Its psychoactive effects are subtle, and they do not
interfere with mental performance or hand–eye coordination. Smokers
do tend to increase their nicotine intake over time, but they eventually
reach a plateau where they remain indefinitely, usually at a pack or so a
day. And smokers often experience discomfort when they quit, but their
complaints are neither as dramatic nor as consistent as the symptoms of
opiate withdrawal.

The influence of the opiate model can be seen in remarks by Sir
Humphrey Rolleston, a British physician who chaired a drug policy
commission during the 1920s: "The Ministry of Health's Departmental
Committee on Morphine and Heroin Addiction (1926) defined an addict as 'a person who, not requiring the continued use of a drug for the
relief of symptoms of organic disease, has acquired, as a result of repeated administration, an overpowering desire for its continuance, and
in whom withdrawal of the drug leads to definite symptoms of physical
or mental distress or disorder.' That smoking produces a craving for
more when an attempt is made to give it up . . . is undoubted, but it can
seldom be accurately described as overpowering, and the effects of its
withdrawal, though there may be definite restlessness and instability,
cannot be compared to the physical distress caused by withdrawal in
morphine addicts. To regard tobacco as a drug of addiction may all be
very well in a humorous sense, but it is hardly accurate."[38]

The opiate model also shaped the conclusions of the 1964 surgeon
general's report, which relied on a definition of drug addiction formulated by the World Health Organization in 1957: "Drug addiction is a
state of periodic or chronic intoxication produced by repeated consumption of a drug (natural or synthetic). Its characteristics include: (1) an
overwhelming desire or need (compulsion) to continue taking the drug
and to obtain it by any means; (2) a tendency to increase the dose; (3) a

psychic (psychological) and generally a physical dependence on the effects of a drug; (4) detrimental effect on the individual and on society." By contrast, WHO defined "drug habituation" as "a condition resulting from the repeated consumption of a drug" and characterized by "(1) a desire (but not a compulsion) to continue taking a drug for the sense of well-being it engenders; (2) little or no tendency to increase the dose; (3) some degree of psychic dependence on the effects of the drug, but absence of physical dependence and hence of an abstinence syndrome; (4) detrimental effect, if any, primarily on the individual." The Surgeon General's Advisory Committee on Smoking and Health concluded that tobacco was "habituating" rather than "addicting."[39] As a subsequent surgeon general's report noted, "There was no question at the time of the 1964 Report that nicotine was the critical pharmacologic agent for tobacco use, but its role was then considered to be more similar to cocaine and amphetamines than to opiates and barbiturates."[40]

Within a decade WHO had abandoned the distinction between habituating and addicting drugs, along with the very term *addiction,* which it replaced with *drug dependence.* According to the new definition, as amended in 1993, drug dependence is "a cluster of physiological, behavioral and cognitive phenomena of variable intensity, in which the use of a psychoactive drug (or drugs) takes on a high priority. The necessary descriptive characteristics are a preoccupation with a desire to obtain and take the drug and persistent drug-taking behavior."[41] This rather amorphous concept plays down the notion of addictiveness, recognizing that any psychoactive substance can be the focus of drug dependence.

Even if smoking did not meet the old standard for addiction/dependence (and arguably it did), it clearly satisfied the new definition. During the 1970s the National Institute on Drug Abuse published monographs that treated smoking as a form of drug dependence, and the 1979 surgeon general's report called it "the prototypical substance-abuse dependency." In 1980 the American Psychiatric Association listed tobacco dependence as a "substance abuse disorder" in its *Diagnostic and Statistical Manual of Mental Disorders.* The 1988 surgeon general's report reviewed the literature on nicotine and concluded that cigarettes and other forms of tobacco are addictive because they contain nicotine and that "the processes that determine tobacco addiction are similar to those that determine addiction to drugs such as heroin and cocaine."[42]

The processes discussed by the 1988 report are almost exclusively pharmacological. The introduction acknowledges in passing that "psychological and social factors are also important influences on tobacco use," and scattered through the text are indications that such factors are crucial to understanding why people smoke. But the report is dominated by a drug-centered view of addiction. One of its major conclusions—that "nicotine is the drug in tobacco that causes addiction"—seems to leave no room for people's choices, motivations, or circumstances. Elsewhere we are told, "Drugs cause addiction by controlling the behavior of users"—a pretty succinct summary of voodoo pharmacology. In this model, the drugs are the actors and the people are their pawns. The report also treats addiction as a disease, assuring us that "tobacco use is a disorder that can be remedied through medical attention." The combination of compulsion and disease makes nicotine seem like some sort of extraterrestrial parasite, not unlike the creatures in Robert Heinlein's *The Puppet Masters*.[43]

CAN'T HELP MYSELF

Although it may sound like something out of science fiction, the concept of drug addiction as a compulsive disease goes back a couple of centuries. Tellingly, the original model for the irresistible, inevitably addictive drug was alcohol, which today is seen in quite a different light. The sociologist Harry G. Levine traced the shifting perceptions of habitual drunkenness in his seminal 1978 article, "The Discovery of Addiction." Levine noted that prior to the late eighteenth century "the assumption was that people drank and got drunk because they wanted to, and not because they 'had' to. In colonial thought, alcohol did not permanently disable the will; it was not addicting, and habitual drunkenness was not regarded as a disease. With very few exceptions, colonial Americans did not use a vocabulary of compulsion with regard to alcoholic beverages." Taking a lead from Benjamin Rush, the temperance movement redefined habitual drunkenness as "a progressive disease . . . the chief symptom of which is loss of control over drinking behavior, and whose only remedy is abstinence from all alcoholic beverages." Temperance activists (despite their name) argued that alcoholism followed naturally from moderate drinking. "Indeed," Levine wrote, "the idea that drugs are inherently addicting was first systematically worked out for alcohol and then extended to other substances. Long before opium was popularly accepted as addicting, alcohol was so regarded."[44]

During this century, in the face of undeniable evidence that the vast majority of drinkers do not become habitual drunkards, alcoholism was reconceived as an inherited handicap. According to this model, which had little empirical basis but gained wide acceptance, certain individuals are biologically predisposed to drunkenness and constitutionally incapable of moderation.[45] The redefinition of alcoholism, together with the repeal of alcohol prohibition in 1933, can be seen as a partial repudiation of voodoo pharmacology. Americans recognized that alcohol did not lead inexorably to alcoholism. It had to be combined with certain traits of the drinker—once viewed as moral failings, now recast as genetic defects.

But the notion that drugs themselves cause addiction persisted, especially with reference to opium and its derivatives. As the psychologist and addiction authority Stanton Peele notes, "narcotics, especially in the form of heroin, came to be seen in American society as the nonpareil drug of addiction—as leading inescapably from even the most casual contact to an intractable dependence, withdrawal from which was traumatic and unthinkable for the addict."[46] The image of the twitchy, sweaty heroin addict, desperate for a fix to ease the discomfort of withdrawal, became a staple of popular culture. Beginning with Harry J. Anslinger, who headed the federal Bureau of Narcotics from 1930 to 1962, government officials warned the American public that such a fate awaited anyone who dared fool around with opiates.

The reality was quite different. Government surveys consistently find that the vast majority of people who have tried heroin are not addicts. In the 1996 National Household Survey on Drug Abuse, 1.1 percent of respondents said they had used heroin at least once. Only 18 percent of them had used the drug in the previous year, while only 9 percent had done so in the previous month.[47] Since not everyone who has used heroin in the past month does so every day, only a fraction of this group could reasonably be described as addicts. It should be noted, however, that the Household Survey excludes groups, such as prisoners and the homeless, where illegal drug use is especially common. If drug users in these groups are more likely to be heavy users, which seems plausible, the addict-to-user ratio suggested by the survey data may be on the low side. (This variation in patterns of use, of course, also indicates that factors other than the drug itself play an important role in addiction.) But even if we adjust the survey data upward a bit, it's clear that heroin is not nearly so powerfully addictive as we have been led to believe—something to keep in mind when anti-smokers tell us, as a congressman did on CNN a few years ago, that "tobacco is as addictive as heroin."[48] The percentage of heroin users who are addicts seems to be roughly comparable to the percentage of drinkers who are alcoholics.[49]

Like heavy drinkers, heroin addicts can and do cut back or stop. One fascinating study tracked the experiences of veterans who had used heroin in Vietnam, where both the drug and reasons for taking it were abundant. Of the men who were addicted in Vietnam (defined by prolonged heavy use and severe withdrawal symptoms), half used heroin after coming home, but only 12 percent became addicted again. Half of these men underwent drug treatment, and after three years 47 percent of them were still addicted, compared to 17 percent of the men who were not treated. Although it's possible that the men who went through treatment were more dependent to begin with, these results clearly show that addicts can give up the drug on their own.[50] Even people who use heroin regularly for years tend to "mature out" by their mid-thirties.[51] There are not many middle-aged heroin addicts, and it's not because they all drop dead from AIDS or overdoses. It's because most of them stop using heroin. These findings fly in the face of conventional wisdom, which says heroin addiction can be overcome, if at all, only through professional treatment. The main reason for this perception is the belief that opiate withdrawal is intolerable, and addicts would do anything to avoid it. This notion is belied by the fact that heroin users who develop tolerance sometimes voluntarily stop taking the drug for a while so they can resume their habit at a lower dose and expense.[52] Although opiate withdrawal is not exactly pleasant—the symptoms can include fatigue, restlessness, perspiration, chills, teary eyes, a runny nose, diarrhea, nausea, and vomiting—the experience is typically no worse than the flu (unlike, for example, alcohol or barbiturate withdrawal, which can be fatal).[53]

Perhaps the most compelling evidence that pharmacology does not adequately explain narcotic addiction comes from patients treated for pain. Studies conducted during the last two decades have consistently found that patients who receive opioid painkillers rarely become addicted. In 1980 researchers at Boston University Medical Center reported that they had reviewed the records of 11,882 patients treated with narcotics in the hospital and found "only four cases of reasonably well documented addiction in patients who had no history of addiction."[54] A 1982 study of ten thousand burn victims who had received narcotic injections for weeks or months found no cases of drug abuse that could be attributed to pain treatment.[55] In a 1986 study of thirty-eight chronic pain patients who were treated with opioids for years, only two misused their medication, and both had histories of drug problems.[56]

Like heroin addicts, pain patients experience tolerance and physical dependence. Yet pain experts emphasize that such phenomena should not be confused with addiction, which requires a psychological component: a persistent desire to use the substance for its mind-altering effects. Critics have long complained that unreasonable fears about narcotic addiction discourage adequate pain treatment.[57] In 1989 Charles Schuster, then director of the National Institute on Drug Abuse, confessed, "We have been so effective in warning the medical establishment and the public in general about the inappropriate use of opiates that we have endowed these drugs with a mysterious power to enslave that is overrated."[58] Opiate addiction is the paradigmatic example of drug dependence. If the opiates do not have "a mysterious power to enslave," we should be skeptical when that property is attributed to other drugs, including nicotine.

TAKE IT OR LEAVE IT

During the 1996 presidential campaign, when Republican candidate Bob Dole dared to suggest that nicotine is not addictive for everyone, anti-smoking activists and the press reacted as if he had said the earth is flat. Yet while Dole spoke a bit loosely, the gist of his comments is plainly true. "To some people, smoking is addictive," he said during a visit to Kentucky in June. "To others, they can take it or leave it. Most people don't smoke at all." His take was similar in an interview that aired two weeks later on ABC: "My nonscientific view is that it's a habit. Some people who have tried it can quit easily. Others don't quit. So I guess it's addictive to some and not to others."[59]

Research confirms Dole's commonsensical view. According to the 1996 National Household Survey on Drug Abuse, 72 percent of Americans have smoked cigarettes at some time, but CDC data indicate that only about a third of them are now daily smokers.[60] Nicotine is clearly not irresistible. But these data do seem to support the idea that cigarettes are more addictive than heroin. That does not necessarily mean that nicotine is inherently more powerful. Since cigarettes are legal, they are much cheaper and easier to obtain. Unlike heroin, they can be consumed openly (except where smoking is prohibited), and their psychoactive effects are compatible with a wide range of activities. Consequently, former smokers are apt to be hit by urges more frequently (because they are used to smoking in many different contexts), and they can satisfy those urges more readily than former heroin users can. It would not be surprising, then, if some users of both drugs found it harder to give up cigarettes. In one survey, 57 percent of drug users entering a Canadian treatment program said giving up their problem substance (not necessarily heroin) would be easier than giving up cigarettes. In another survey, thirty-six heroin users entering treatment were asked to compare their strongest cigarette urge to their strongest heroin urge. Most said the heroin urge was stronger, but two said the cigarette urge was, and eleven rated the two urges about the same.[61]

The comparison between smoking and heroin addiction, which has become commonplace since the 1988 surgeon general's report, drives the tobacco companies crazy. They like to emphasize that smokers can work, drive, and engage in other everyday activities without a problem. This is probably what RJR CEO James W. Johnston had in mind when he told Representative Wyden, "There is no intoxication." But the fact that smokers do not stumble around in a stupor tells us nothing about the strength of their attachment to nicotine.

The tobacco companies are not alone in questioning the notion that cigarettes are as addictive as heroin. Writing in the *Wall Street Journal,* psychiatrist Sally Satel calls this claim "ridiculous." Says Satel,

"When cigarettes are temporarily unavailable, smokers—as lousy as they may feel without a cigarette—don't initiate a crazed effort to find their next 'fix.' In contrast, people addicted to heroin commonly lie, cheat or steal to get money to buy more, so distressing are the symptoms of heroin withdrawal."[62] It's true that smokers generally do not squander their savings, sell their bodies, steal car radios, or burglarize homes to support their habits. But that's because they don't have to. At a pack a day and $2 a pack, a year's supply of cigarettes costs $730. According to one estimate, the average heroin addict spends nearly $15,000 a year on his drug.[63] If tobacco were banned and smokers had to purchase cigarettes at black-market prices, many of them would also be driven to extreme measures. Smokers can afford to be blasé about their next cigarette because they know where to get it and how little it will cost.

In conditions of scarcity, smokers can seem just as desperate as a heroin addict looking for a fix. Recall the observations of James I and other critics of smoking who lived at a time when tobacco was much more expensive than it is today. Under such circumstances, they claimed, smokers would choose tobacco over food. Even allowing for the exaggeration of tobacco's opponents, that sounds like a pretty mean habit. The fact that seventeenth-century smokers would risk severe penalties, even death, in countries such as Turkey, Russia, and Japan also suggests a strong attachment. During the tobacco shortage in Germany after World War II, cigarettes served as currency. As one witness observed, "money was worthless, and you could get anything for tobacco." An account from the late 1940s reported that fifty kilograms of coal cost 14 cigarettes, one gram of gold cost 32, a pair of stockings cost 48, and a kilogram of coffee cost 160. "Cadging for cigarettes was a common practice in all strata of society," reports the German scholar Henner Hess. "People who, under different circumstances, would have felt disgust at such behavior, picked up butts, which were collected and then rolled into new cigarettes or smoked in pipes." In the POW camps, where conditions were harsher and there were fewer distractions, smokers were even more desperate, sometimes exchanging food rations for cigarettes.[64]

Satel suggests that such extreme drug-seeking behavior (in heroin addicts, at least) is evidence of severe withdrawal symptoms. The tobacco companies and their opponents also tend to emphasize withdrawal symptoms, arguing about how significant they are for smokers who quit. The American Psychiatric Association lists eight signs of nicotine withdrawal: dysphoric or depressed mood; insomnia; irritability, frustration, or anger; anxiety; difficulty concentrating; restlessness; decreased heart rate; and increased appetite or weight gain.[65] For tobacco's opponents, these symptoms are evidence of nicotine's lingering hold on smokers. For the cigarette companies, they are psychological reactions to the loss of an accustomed pleasure.

The emphasis on withdrawal symptoms reflects a drug-centered view of addiction. But as in the case of heroin, the evidence indicates that smoking is not simply a matter of pharmacology. According to the 1988 surgeon general's report, about one-fourth of smokers who try to quit "report no withdrawal at all," and for most withdrawal is not significant.[66] When they do occur, withdrawal symptoms generally peak during the first week and disappear within a month, yet former smokers commonly go back to the habit months and even years after quitting.[67] Furthermore, nicotine gum and patches are much safer methods of taking the drug, but smokers generally do not find them satisfying. According to several studies, nicotine gum reduces withdrawal symptoms without affecting the urge to smoke.[68] Success rates for smokers who rely on such products to quit are low. In the research reviewed by the 1988 surgeon general's report, 11 percent of smokers who used nicotine gum were still abstaining after a year, compared to 50 percent of those who underwent group hypnosis and 63 percent of cardiac patients who were advised by a doctor to quit.[69] A 1992 study of nicotine patch therapy reported in *Psychopharmacology* said the "overall lack of effect of nicotine patches on cigarette consumption is perhaps surprising and suggests that in regular smokers the lighting up of a cigarette is generally triggered by cues other than low plasma nicotine levels."[70]

SET AND SETTING

The limitations of the pharmacological model suggest that viewing cigarettes as "nicotine delivery devices" is rather simplistic. It is true in the same sense that beer is an "ethanol delivery device" or coffee is a "caffeine delivery device." People who consume these products do, after all, want the drug; alcohol-free beer and decaffeinated coffee are not nearly as popular as the real things. At the same time, however, beer and coffee drinkers enjoy the aroma, the taste, the feel, the sights and sounds associated with these beverages. They relish the rituals of pouring and serving. They look forward to the socializing that occurs around the coffee pot at work or at the local tavern.

The same is true of smoking. There's no question that nicotine is a remarkably useful and versatile drug—calming anxiety or boosting concentration, as needed, without impairing mental faculties—and that smoking is a very efficient way of getting it to the brain. But the smoking experience also involves the crinkling of the cellophane, the smoothness of the cylinder, the click of a lighter or the crack of a match, the smell and taste of the smoke, the way it feels in the mouth and throat, the sight of it rising into the air. Smoking may be associated with quiet companionship or lively conversation, relaxation or intense work, sex or solitude. Smokers make statements with their cigarettes about their readiness to take risks, their attitude toward authority, their membership in a group, their receptiveness to seduction.

All these elements and many more, different from person to person, define what it means to smoke. They make up what the psychiatrist Norman Zinberg called the "set and setting" of drug use: the expectations of the user, combined with the physical, social, and cultural environment. These factors interact with the pharmacology of a drug to shape the user's experience. A remarkable fact about marijuana, for example, is that people typically do not "get high" the first time they try the drug; they have to *learn* how to be high, and that condition can be exquisitely sensitive to unpleasant intrusions. Even (perhaps especially) in the case of potent mind-altering substances like LSD, set and setting are often decisive, making the difference between a good trip and a bad trip. For the veterans in the Vietnam study, the set and setting of the war created a desire for heroin that most of them did not feel upon returning to the United States. Similarly, narcotics serve a particular function for patients in pain, who usually do not even report euphoria; once they recover (assuming they do), they rarely continue to seek the drug. In the case of alcohol, personality traits and cultural expectations have a powerful impact on the observed effects of intoxication: whether the drinker becomes nasty or genial, buffoonish or entertaining, aggressive or withdrawn. Set and setting help explain why the level of violence associated with drinking differs widely across cultures.

Tobacco, like other drugs, has to be viewed in context. This means understanding the importance of culture, which explains why Native Americans reserved tobacco for special occasions while Westerners came to treat it as an all-purpose accompaniment to work and play. It means paying attention to the smoker's situation and state of mind, which help determine whether a cigarette sedates or stimulates. Most important, it means considering the role that smoking plays in people's lives. "The to-baccorectionist," complained a smoker in 1928, "says that we do not smoke for pleasure at all; but that the habit, once begun, is continued in order to avoid the discomfort and even the pain of going without a drug. He brands the supposed joy spurious, a hypnoidal resultant of partially paralyzed nerves."[71] To hear some of tobacco's opponents talk, people smoke because they're addicted, not because they like smoking or find it useful. But the truth is that smokers are addicted (i.e., have difficulty giving up the habit) *because* they like smoking or find it useful.

A smoker might depend on cigarettes to control stress, to stay slim, to keep focused at work, to fill idle time, to mingle at parties, even to define an identity. For most smokers, cigarettes probably serve several functions. Depending upon how important these functions are and whether the smoker can find good substitutes for cigarettes, quitting may be easy or difficult. The drug is the same in every instance, but the level of addiction is different. One evening I had dinner with a middle-aged couple, both of whom were former smokers. When the topic of this book came up, the man said quitting had been a breeze, while his wife said it was the hardest thing she'd ever done. During my research, I came across more than one writer who emphasized the difficulty of quitting even while conceding that he himself did not have much trouble doing so. This kind of disparity cannot be understood in pharmacological terms.

The psychological function of smoking helps explain even the most extreme cases of addiction, the ones that tobacco's opponents cite to demonstrate the enslaving power of nicotine. Anyone who has spent some time with anti-smoking activists has probably heard about people who keep smoking even after a heart attack, a cancer diagnosis, or the onset of emphysema symptoms. Especially memorable is the image of the patient who continues to imbibe through a hole in his throat after the removal of his cancerous larynx. Such smokers may reason (accurately or not) that the damage has already been done, and they may not want to linger on with a disabling disease in any case. More important, they may have come to rely on cigarettes to relieve anxiety, and they probably feel a stronger need for such solace than ever before. This is not to say that their behavior is necessarily rational, but it can be understood without reference to magical chemicals.

The psychologist Stanton Peele is fond of a rhetorical device that illustrates how smoking confounds common expectations about addiction. He asks his audience of drug specialists which habit is the hardest to quit. "Smoking" is always the most common answer. Then he asks those who have successfully quit this toughest of all drug addictions to raise their hands. A bunch of arms go up. Finally, he asks how many of the former smokers underwent professional treatment. All or nearly all the arms go down. Peele's demonstration is not scientific, but his results resemble those of national surveys. According to the CDC, there are about as many former smokers in this country as there are smokers, and some 90 percent of them gave up the habit on their own, usually by quitting abruptly.[72]

The stories such smokers tell illustrate the importance of firm resolve. One woman who called a radio show on which I appeared said she decided to quit shortly after the price of her favorite brand went up. She bought a carton at the supermarket, and on the way out she thought, "There must be a cheaper way to kill myself." She threw out the carton and never smoked another cigarette. Peele offers a similar anecdote about his Uncle Ozzie: "Ozzie, a union activist, smoked three packs a day and more from the age of eighteen until a fateful day when, in his forties, he went to lunch with his regular cronies. On this day in 1960, cigarette prices had gone up a nickel. As Ozzie put the extra coin in the machine, a co-worker said, 'Look at Oscar; why, if they raised the price of cigarettes to a dollar, he'd pay up. Those tobacco companies have him by the balls.' Ozzie looked at the man (so he told me later) and said, 'You're right. I'm going to quit.' His friend, who also smoked, then asked, 'Can I have your cigarettes?' Ozzie replied, 'What, and throw away the money I just spent?' After he smoked that pack, however, Ozzie never smoked again."[73] Peele observes that Ozzie, a shop steward, saw himself as an enemy of greedy capitalists and could not stand the idea that he was under their control.

Books offering advice on how to quit also emphasize the need for strong commitment (and persistence, since successful quitters often try several times). Given the ready availability of cigarettes and the plethora of environmental cues for lighting up, a smoker who is ambivalent about quitting is probably destined to fail. Invoking will power may seem facile, if not insensitive to the difficulties many smokers encounter when they try to quit. Will power may not be easy to summon, and if a smoker cannot find alternative ways of coping, it may not be enough. But it is essential, and the experiences of millions show it is possible.

As tobacco's opponents are fond of noting, most smokers tell pollsters they'd like to quit. In a 1996 Gallup poll, for example, 73 percent of smokers answered yes to the question "All things considered, would you like to give up smoking, or not?"[74] Interpreting such results calls to mind the excuse offered by Spanish settlers to Bishop Bartholomé de las Casas when he asked them why they indulged in such a disgusting habit. Some smokers may simply be giving pollsters the approved response: I'd like to quit, but I can't. In the current cultural environment, this is clearly the path of least resistance. Smokers may also be intimidated by all the talk about how difficult it is to quit. Treating addiction like an intractable illness may seem compassionate, but it ultimately hurts the people it is supposed to help by setting them up for failure.

Finally, smokers may be expressing their ambivalence about a habit that offers short-term benefits at the price of long-term risks. Their behavior demonstrates that they are still willing to accept this trade-off, but no doubt they would prefer to avoid the hazards. In *Smoking: Making the Risky Decision,* the economist W. Kip Viscusi notes that almost half of Los Angeles residents say they'd like to live elsewhere and that nearly a third of blue-collar workers say they'd like to leave their jobs.[75] The fact that these people stay where they are does not mean they are powerless to change their situations. Rather, it indicates that they are not prepared to bear the costs of making a change, including the benefits they would have to give up. "The claims of some heavy drinkers and smokers that they want to but cannot end their addictions," write University of Chicago economists Gary S. Becker and Kevin M. Murphy, "seem to us no different from the claims of single persons that they want to but are unable to marry or from the claims of disorganized persons who say they want to become better organized. What these claims mean is that a person will make certain changes—for example, marry or stop smoking—when he finds a way to raise long-term benefits sufficiently above the short-term costs of adjustment."[76]

This perspective may seem inappropriate for a behavior that is reputedly driven by unreasoning appetites. Indeed, for a long time economists treated addiction as an anomaly, immune to standard analyses of consumer behavior. But during the last two decades, "rational addiction" theory, developed by Becker, Murphy, and George Stigler, has had an important impact on the way economists look at smoking and other hard-to-break habits. In this model, the hallmark of addictive behavior is that past consumption influences current consumption. Roughly speaking, the more you consumed then, the more you consume now. A pharmacologist looking for the classic signs of addiction might see this pattern as evidence of reinforcement, tolerance, and withdrawal. The basic point is that addictions have a certain inertia; they tend to keep going. Not exactly a radical idea. But Stigler, Becker, and Murphy also argued that aside from this tendency addicts behave much like other consumers: They consider the future consequences of their actions, including the difficulty of quitting, and weigh costs against benefits. Their tastes and preferences are consistent and stable. Of course, their preferences may not seem reasonable to others. Addicts may focus on short-term benefits and attach relatively little weight to long-term costs. And they may ultimately regret their choices: Smokers who get lung cancer probably wish they had never smoked. But prior to the diagnosis, it was a risk they were prepared to tolerate.[77]

Most of tobacco's opponents would reject the notion that there could be anything rational about smoking. At the same time, however, they implicitly assume that smokers behave rationally. Anti-smokers lobby for higher cigarette taxes because they believe (correctly) that raising the price of cigarettes will lead smokers to cut back or stop. Some even favor continuing the federal government's tobacco price support program— which is opposed by libertarians, free-market conservatives, and anti-smoking groups such as the AMA—because they recognize that it keeps the cost of cigarettes higher than it would otherwise be.[78] Similarly, to-bacco's opponents support restrictions on smoking in the workplace largely because they believe that the inconvenience of having to leave the building for a cigarette will encourage smokers to quit. Such policies simply would not work unless smokers routinely weighed the costs of continuing to smoke. The very idea of educating the public about the health consequences of smoking, whether through warning labels, TV commercials, or pamphlets, assumes that such information will have an impact. And it has. The decline in the prevalence of smoking since the 1960s, from 43 percent to 25 percent, means that tens of millions of Americans have quit, while many millions more have chosen not to start—an unprecedented voluntary shift in drug use.

The people who continue to smoke are not oblivious to this trend and the reasons for it. But they have chosen not to join the march toward a smoke-free society. They may not attach as much weight to the long-term health risks as former smokers do, or they may find the habit more rewarding. Not surprisingly, surveys indicate that smokers, as a group, are less risk-averse than nonsmokers. They are less likely to wear seat belts, and they demand less compensation for dangerous work.[79] Research has also consistently found that extroverts—gregarious, aggressive, thrill-seeking individuals—are disproportionately attracted to smoking, per-haps for its stimulating effects, perhaps for its social aspects.[80]

Similar factors—tastes, attitudes toward risk, personality traits—help determine who uses any product or service. The choices that consumers make—paying $500 for a bottle of perfume, collecting commemorative plates, riding a motorcycle, jumping out of an airplane—often strike ob-servers as foolish, shortsighted, even potentially deadly. From an eco-nomic perspective, however, such judgments are irrelevant. If a choice makes sense within the context of a consumer's own tastes and prefer-ences, it is a rational act, no matter how crazy it might seem to others.

SICK, SICK, SICK

From an economic perspective, smoking can be perfectly rational. Public health specialists have a different perspective. For them, smoking is a dis-ease, not a choice. As a 1985 article in the *New York State Journal of Med-*

icine put it, "The cancer or the myocardial infarction or the emphysema are only signs of an underlying disease: chronic cigarette use."[81] Similarly, a 1986 editorial in the *Journal of the American Medical Association* declared, "Tobaccoism Is the Disease—Cancer Is the Sequela."[82] According to this model, smoking is something that happens to people, not something that people do. Furthermore, smoking is inherently undesirable; nobody in his right mind *wants* to be sick. According to the 1988 surgeon general's report, "The central and common element across all forms of drug dependence is that a psychoactive drug has come to control behavior to an extent that is considered detrimental to the individual or society."[83] The phrase "considered detrimental" is telling. Who decides?

Not the drug user. Smokers who reject "treatment," who insist they have no desire to stop, are said to be "in denial," a symptom of their compulsive disease. "Of those who profess to be happy about their smoking," wrote M. A. Hamilton Russell in 1971, "some are ignorant but the majority use face-saving psychological defence mechanisms such as 'rationalization' and 'denial' to avoid uncomfortable inconsistency between attitude and behavior."[84] The 1988 surgeon general's report cited "a reluctance to admit that one's behavior is largely controlled by a drug."[85] A radio show on which I appeared a couple of years ago received a call from a man who said it was his decision to smoke, he could stop if he wanted, and he would never think of blaming the cigarette companies for his habit. The host, a vociferous opponent of smoking, loudly berated the caller, trying to get him to admit that he was in fact a helpless victim of the tobacco industry. As the philosopher John C. Luik observes, there is a double standard at work here: "The self-reports of smokers who report that they are (1) rational and (2) choose to smoke are universally discounted as false, whilst the self-reports of other smokers who report that they wish to stop smoking, have tried to stop smoking but have been unable to stop smoking are accepted as true."[86]

To its opponents, smoking is not just a disease that impairs the victim's judgment. It is, as David Kessler put it, "a pediatric disease."[87] By this he meant that most smokers take up the habit before they turn 18. In the 1991 National Household Survey on Drug Abuse, 71 percent of smokers and former smokers in their thirties had started smoking daily by 18. The mean age at which they had first tried a cigarette was 14.5, and the mean age at which they had become daily smokers was 17.7.[88] According to data from the 1996 survey, the average age of people who started smoking daily in 1995 was 17.6.[89] This pattern has led tobacco's opponents to conclude that smoking is essentially a phenomenon of adolescence that people get locked into before they are old enough to know better. As the journalist Philip J. Hilts writes in his book *Smoke-screen,* "Smoking appeals to the very young not because of its nicotine, but chiefly for a number of social reasons—they need this product as a badge of daring and independence, and this is at least partly *because* it is dangerous and discouraged by authorities. Adults *do not* start smoking because that social motivation is not present; adults have already formed up their image of themselves, and found the necessary badges of independence and contrariness elsewhere."[90]

Hilts overstates his case. The Household Survey data indicate that more than a quarter of smokers start smoking daily after turning eighteen, though they may experiment with cigarettes before then. And while it may be true that the young are especially attracted to smoking, it is probably also true that people who are especially attracted to smoking tend to start young. If so, many of the same people would still smoke even if they could somehow be shielded from cigarettes until adulthood. Still, Hilts has a point. Smoking has special significance for adolescents, who are absorbed in defining themselves, usually by imitating others. Teenagers are much more likely to smoke if their siblings, friends, and acquaintances do, especially if the smokers are the same sex and slightly older.[91] Smoking is a handy technique for looking cool, fitting in, and rebelling—all at once.

The important symbolic role of smoking suggests that adults should proceed with caution in trying to steer kids away from cigarettes. When authority figures condemn smoking as reckless, obnoxious, and antisocial, they may inadvertently make it all the more appealing to some teenagers. In this connection, it's interesting to note that smoking among teenagers declined more or less steadily from the late 1970s until 1992, then rose for several years in a row. In one survey, the share of high school seniors who were daily smokers rose from 17.2 percent in 1992 to 21.6 percent in 1995. During the same period, the use of marijuana among teenagers also rose, following a fourteen-year decline.[92] Yet this group of teenagers had been bombarded by the most intense anti-tobacco and anti-pot propaganda in U.S. history. By telling these kids to "Just Say No," the schools, the media, and the government may have taught them a more useful lesson: how to offend adults.

The paradoxical nature of attempts to stop teenagers from smoking can be seen in a series of newspaper and magazine ads sponsored by the Campaign for Tobacco-Free Kids, an alliance of anti-smoking groups formed in 1995. The ads attacked politicians for accepting contributions from the tobacco industry and criticized cigarette companies for "marketing to children." Yet they were the only ads I'd ever seen that actually showed kids enjoying cigarettes and trying to look adult, often wearing clothing embossed with cigarette brand logos. The models appeared to be about eleven or twelve. Presumably, these photographs were intended to outrage parents and stir up support for the FDA's regulations. But they also created the impression that smoking by kids that young is common, when in fact 91 percent of eighth-graders do not report smoking so much as a cigarette a day, and reinforced the idea that smoking is a way to be cool and fit in.[93] If tobacco's opponents really believe that advertising has an important impact on underage smoking, the choice of such illustrations—which no cigarette company would ever dare use—is hard to understand.

In a less blatant way, restrictions on the advertising and promotion of cigarettes might also have the perverse effect of making these products more appealing. The attempt to shield kids not only from cigarettes but from *images* of cigarettes—even from articles of clothing carrying brand names—is bound to pique curiosity and foster rebellion. For teenagers, smoking already has the allure of the forbidden, and such restrictions enhance that attraction. So does the FDA rule requiring manufacturers to print "Nicotine-Delivery Device for Persons 18 or Older" on every pack. Emphasizing the difficulty of quitting, as the conspicuous "Cigarettes are addictive" label required by the proposed settlement would do, is also apt to backfire. For many adolescents, the idea of addiction is glamorous. It's a simple way to be complex.

Some anti-smoking activists have criticized the focus on underage smoking. "The anti-tobacco movement has careened off on this narrow path because they know it's noncontroversial," Stanton Glantz told the *New York Times*. "But it's probably counterproductive. A kid-centered program is doomed to fail." Glantz argues that such an approach plays into the hands of the tobacco companies, which insist that smoking is an adult habit. To underscore that message, the industry has lobbied for state laws forbidding cigarette sales to minors, distributed signs to retailers urging compliance, and taken out ads declaring that "kids should not smoke." Glantz complains that depicting smoking as an adult habit not only makes it more appealing to kids but lets the vast majority of smokers off the hook. "The best way to keep kids from smoking is to reduce tobacco consumption among everyone," he writes. "The message should not be 'we don't want kids to smoke'; it should be 'we want a smoke-free society.'"[94]

On the other hand, emphasizing children is an effective strategy for gaining support from people who might be uneasy about a broader assault on smoking. Every state already prohibits cigarette sales to minors, but the laws are laxly enforced. Merchants rarely ask for proof of age, and vending machines are often unsupervised. Teenagers generally can obtain cigarettes even more readily than beer. A natural response would be to enforce the existing laws, and pilot programs aimed at getting merchants to take the age rule more seriously, including fines and undercover investigations, have met with some success.[95] Such efforts were eclipsed by the FDA's plan, which transformed a bunch of boring local struggles into a dramatic national issue around which anti-smoking forces could rally.

Established in 1996, the Washington-based National Center for Tobacco-Free Kids, which grew out of the Campaign for Tobacco-Free Kids, attracted at least $32 million in funding for its first five years, mostly from the Robert Wood Johnson Foundation and the American Cancer Society. The center is also well positioned to claim a big chunk of the billions in "tobacco control" money offered by the proposed nationwide settlement agreement it helped negotiate. Despite its name, the organization's agenda is broad, including not only advertising and promotion but excise taxes, cigarette exports, and secondhand smoke. The center's president, publicist William D. Novelli, told the Louisville *Courier-Journal*, "What we have to do, basically, is delegitimize the tobacco industry. . . . They're the last of the evil empire."[96] In response to Glantz's criticism of the focus on kids, Matthew Myers—formerly with the Coalition on Smoking or Health and now the center's vice president—"denies that the National Center will shy away from issues that don't directly affect children."[97]

Similarly, the FDA's save-the-children mission reaches much further than the sixteen-year-old puffing away on the corner. David Kessler noted that smokers usually start as teenagers, when they are not mature enough to make such a decision, and he assumed—despite abundant evidence to the contrary—that nicotine addiction is inescapable. "Nicotine addiction is a pediatric disease that often begins at 12, 13, and 14, only to manifest itself at 16 and 17, when these children find they cannot quit," he said when the FDA released the final version of its regulations in August 1996. "By then our children have lost their freedom and face the prospect of lives shortened by terrible disease."[98] By calling smoking "a pediatric disease," Kessler implied that smokers who take up the habit as teenagers should be treated like children for the rest of their lives. The authority claimed by the FDA is correspondingly broad: to impose whatever restrictions it considers appropriate, ranging from product specifications (such as limits on nicotine content) to a complete ban. Ominously, the FDA promised to "take additional measures" if smoking by minors was not cut in half within seven years after the regulations went into effect—a goal that is not likely to be reached.[99]

The goal was incorporated into the proposed nationwide settlement, which said the tobacco companies would be fined unless daily smoking by high school seniors dropped by 30 percent after five years, 50 percent after seven years, and 60 percent after ten years. Since the baseline for these reductions was a ten-year average and since smoking by teenagers has been rising in recent years, the agreement actually required sharper reductions from current smoking levels than these percentages imply. For some, the targets were not ambitious enough. This was apparent at a June 1997 meeting of the Advisory Committee on Tobacco Policy and Public Health, a panel chaired by Kessler and C. Everett Koop, which reviewed the accord. "Some time short of year 10, we should come to 100 percent," said Robert Graham, executive vice president of the American Academy of Family Physicians. "This is an illegal activity. We do not believe that *anyone* underage should smoke or use tobacco products." John Banzhaf of Action on Smoking and Health agreed: "The tobacco industry does have total control over this. They can, through a system of licensing, bring down noncompliance to zero. . . . They can, by raising taxes, decrease the level to anything they want."[100]

Even if the chimerical goal of eliminating teenage smoking within a decade could be achieved, tobacco's opponents would not be satisfied. "The goal is not just to reduce childhood addiction to nicotine and to tobacco products," Mark Pertschuk of Americans for Nonsmokers' Rights reminded the Koop–Kessler committee. "It's also to reduce adult addiction to levels which are feasible." Michele Bloch of the American Medical Women's Association made the same point: "I would ask that in our own recommendations, in addition to putting youth as our top priority, we not tie our hands from working on reducing adult smoking through penalties, etc., when the time comes."[101]

It cannot be lost on Philip Morris et al. that Lucy Page Gaston's campaign for tobacco-free kids culminated in cigarette prohibition. Mentioning the possibility of a ban may seem alarmist, when Kessler and President Clinton have rejected that option as impractical, but prohibition has a logic of its own. Americans are learning to view smokers as addicts and the tobacco companies as drug dealers. "Gradually, but perceptibly," noted a 1988 editorial in the *Nation,* "the image of the tobacco companies is changing from rugged corporate citizens defending good old American libertarian values to that of an international drug cartel that maximizes its profits as callously as do the drug czars in Latin America."[102] The rhetoric of tobacco's opponents is designed to encourage this shift, transforming a familiar and accepted custom into something exotic and sinister. "A cigarette is essentially the crack cocaine form of nicotine delivery," says the addiction expert Jack Henningfield. Gregory Connolly, the Massachusetts public health official, says "tobacco extract" is "a drug called nicotine. It's a euphemism. It's like calling heroin 'poppy seed soil.' It's a drug, it's a drug, it's a drug."[103]

And what do Americans do with drugs? They wage war on them.

"Most adults view illegal drugs with scorn, and express disapproval (if not outrage) at their sale or use," wrote C. Everett Koop in his 1988 report on nicotine addiction. "This Nation has mobilized enormous resources to wage a war on drugs—illicit drugs. We should also give priority to the one addiction that is killing more than 300,000 Americans a year."[104] Koop was right to think that we can learn a lot from the war on drugs about efforts to discourage smoking. Unfortunately, he drew the wrong lesson.

Chapter 8

DOCTOR'S ORDERS

*Hygiene is the corruption of medicine by morality. It is impossible to
find a hygienist who does not debase his theory of the healthful with
a theory of the virtuous. The whole hygienic art, indeed, resolves
itself into an ethical exhortation. This brings it, at the end, into
diametrical conflict with medicine proper. The true aim of medicine
is not to make men virtuous; it is to safeguard and rescue them from
the consequences of their vices. The physician does not preach
repentance; he offers absolution.*

—H. L. Mencken, *Prejudices: Third Series,* 1922

DRUG HABITS

Philip Morris is not only the nation's leading manufacturer of cigarettes. It
is also, through its Miller and Maxwell House brands, a major producer of
beer and coffee. Yet Philip Morris gives money to a propaganda campaign
called the Partnership for a Drug-Free America.[1] Clearly, a drug-free
America is the last thing Philip Morris wants to see. But the company's executives understand that legal, socially accepted drugs are not *really* drugs.
Conversely, when people start comparing your product to heroin and cocaine, social acceptance is waning and legal restrictions may follow.

Best, then, to maintain the pretense that tobacco is not a drug, especially since it does not measure up very well against other psychoactive
substances. Judging by the share of experimenters who become regular
users—a somewhat misleading but commonly used index—tobacco is

more addictive than any other recreational drug. Recall that in the 1996 National Household Survey on Drug Abuse, 9 percent of the people who had tried heroin reported using it in the previous month. The figure was about the same for nonmedical use of prescription stimulants and slightly lower (just under 8 percent) for cocaine. Even for crack cocaine—which is considered more addictive because it's smoked, providing a faster, more intense, shorter high—the proportion was only about 14 percent. By contrast, 40 percent of the people who had ever smoked cigarettes said they had done so in the previous month.[2]

For most drugs, past-month use should not be equated with addiction. To take a familiar example: If someone has ever consumed alcohol, he has probably had a drink in the last month. But in the 1996 Household Survey only about 1 in 10 past-month drinkers reported heavy alcohol use, defined as five or more drinks during the same session on five or more of the previous thirty days. Moderation is the rule for illegal drugs as well. In a 1993 survey of young adults, for example, only 7 percent of past-month cocaine users were daily users. Tobacco is an exception to this pattern: A large majority of people who smoke cigarettes do so every day, averaging more than one per waking hour.[3]

Judging by the share of users who die from its effects, tobacco is also far more hazardous than any other recreational drug. Based on CDC figures, the annual tobacco-related death rate among current and former smokers is about 440 per 100,000.[4] The CDC puts the death toll for alcohol (including accidents, suicides, and homicides) at about 100,000 a year, roughly 100 deaths per 100,000 drinkers.[5] In a 1989 paper, Cato Institute policy analyst James Ostrowski estimated that the death rates per 100,000 users for heroin and cocaine were 80 and 4, respectively.[6] Even allowing for a high level of uncertainty in all of these estimates, it's clear that tobacco kills its aficionados more efficiently than any other popular intoxicant. This is really not so surprising. The most serious side effect of long-term opiate use—assuming an uncontaminated supply, reliable doses, clean injection equipment, and no drug mixing—is usually constipation. Cocaine overdoses have been implicated in heart attacks, but fatal reactions are rare.[7] By contrast, smokers regularly expose their tissues to hundreds of toxins, including numerous carcinogens. As a result, a fair proportion of them suffer major organ damage.

Tobacco's main advantage is its compatibility with the requirements of everyday life. Although they're under the influence of a drug throughout their waking hours, smokers function normally. In a sense, this is also tobacco's main disadvantage, since it encourages people to smoke frequently, thereby running a substantial risk of disease. Paradoxically, the mildness or "transparency" of nicotine's psychoactive effects is one of the factors that make it seem more addictive than other drugs. People who are always under the influence of alcohol, marijuana, heroin, or cocaine are much less likely than smokers to lead productive, respectable lives. On the other hand, people who use these drugs generally do not use them all the time, precisely because it's hard to get anything done if you're constantly drunk or high. Thus, the typical pot smoker can meet his obligations as well as the typical tobacco smoker, because he smokes occasionally. For the same reason, he faces much less serious health hazards, even though he inhales similar combustion products. Indeed, there is no credible evidence that marijuana has ever killed anyone.[8]

So here we have Philip Morris, purveyor of the most dangerous recreational drug, helping to finance messages that warn people away from one of the least dangerous. To compound the irony, the anti-pot ads from the Partnership for a Drug-Free America use arguments that would be familiar to early anti-cigarette propagandists such as Lucy Page Gaston and Henry Ford: It makes you stupid; it turns teenagers into ne'er-do-wells and juvenile delinquents; it ruins academic performance, stifles ambition, impairs efficiency at work, and leads to the use of other drugs. The music is the same; only the weeds have changed.

Philip Morris, of course, is simply conforming to the distinctions enshrined in our drug laws, which have little to do with the relative hazards of psychoactive substances. The company's inconsistency reflects the confusion and hypocrisy of a country in which a politician who drinks coffee in the morning, smokes cigarettes throughout the day, and enjoys a cocktail after work can condemn drug use in the strongest possible terms, calling for its forcible suppression, and elicit applause rather than laughter. For someone who believes, as I do, that the government has no business telling adults what chemicals they may ingest, citing the inconsistency of U.S. drug policy is risky. There are, after all, two ways to correct the inconsistency: by legalizing the currently proscribed drugs or by proscribing the currently legal ones. If tobacco really is worse than heroin—and in some ways it clearly is—why not ban tobacco? Assuming that the government has a duty to protect people from dangerous, addictive substances, it seems like a logical step.

Yet President Clinton and Food and Drug Administration commissioner David Kessler insisted that FDA regulation was not a prelude to prohibition. More generally, anti-smoking politicians and activists almost uniformly agree that a cigarette ban would be impractical, "given the widespread use of cigarettes and the prevalence of nicotine addiction."[9] That consensus is based on hard experience. History and economics tell us that attempts to prevent the use of psychoactive products lead to smuggling, high prices, uncertain quality, greater health hazards, violence, theft, official corruption, disrespect for the law, and the erosion of civil liberties. Although scholars disagree about the extent of these effects, the general pattern is clear, and it's the most important thing to keep in mind as we contemplate the future of tobacco policy in the United States.

THE IGNOBLE EXPERIMENT

For Americans, the folly of prohibition is most vividly illustrated by the experience with the Eighteenth Amendment, which banned the manufacture, sale, transportation, import, and export of alcoholic beverages from January 1920 until its repeal in December 1933. The amendment revived the alcohol ban that Congress had imposed temporarily during World War I and extended the reach of a policy pioneered by the states, nearly half of which had adopted prohibition by 1916. States were banning cigarettes around the same time—the temperance movement, since the days of Benjamin Rush, had condemned tobacco almost as vociferously as alcohol. Indeed, activists such as Billy Sunday hoped for a Nineteenth Amendment that would do for tobacco what the Eighteenth Amendment did for alcohol. Given the results of alcohol prohibition, the country was fortunate that Sunday never got his wish.

The Volstead Act, which implemented the Eighteenth Amendment, helped usher in modern organized crime by creating an illegal, risky, highly profitable business. The economist Irving Fisher estimated that the price of beer rose eightfold between 1916 and 1928, while the prices of brandy and gin rose fourfold and sixfold, respectively.[10] Operating outside the legal system, suppliers of alcohol used violence to settle disputes, enforce contracts, and defend their market share. Gangster murders became frequent events in major cities and a familiar theme in the movies. The economist Milton Friedman, a senior fellow at the Hoover Institution, has noted that the U.S. homicide rate, which began climbing in 1910, rose throughout Prohibition, peaking the year of repeal. It then fell dramatically and remained low during the 1940s and '50s, except for an increase during World War II. (Crime rates tend to rise during wars; most of the pre-Prohibition increase in homicide occurred during World War I.) Friedman also looked at the rate of imprisonment, which rose sharply from 1926 (the first year for which data were available) until 1931.[11]

Official corruption was another conspicuous feature of alcohol prohibition, a fact reflected in the image of Eliot Ness's Chicago task force (later portrayed in *The Untouchables*), Prohibition agents who were considered unusual because they *weren't* on the take. The artificial profits created by the Volstead Act gave criminals an incentive and the means to bribe law enforcement officers. Since supplying alcohol was a victimless crime, cops were both more inclined to look the other way (if not actively participate) and less likely to be caught when they did. The Wickersham Commission, appointed by President Hoover to evaluate the effectiveness of Prohibition, cited evidence of widespread corruption at every level of government. "There have been other eras of corruption," the commission's 1931 report said. "But the present regime of corruption in connection with the liquor traffic is operating in a new and larger field and is more extensive."[12]

Along with corruption, opposition by millions of drinkers undermined respect for the Volstead Act and for the law in general. As H. L. Mencken observed, "The national government is trying to enforce a law which, in the opinion of millions of otherwise docile citizens, invades their inalienable rights, and they accordingly refuse to obey it."[13] Although alcohol consumption fell during the early years of Prohibition, continuing a trend that had started a few years earlier, it soon began to rebound. Similarly, the incidence of cirrhosis of the liver, which had fallen dramatically since 1903, dropped in the first year of Prohibition but then rose steadily through the '20s.[14]

John P. Morgan, a professor of pharmacology at the City University of New York Medical School, suggests that this increase in cirrhosis may be partly explained by a shift from beer and wine to liquor during Prohibition. Given high prices and the risks of apprehension, both suppliers and drinkers were attracted to more potent beverages, which were more compact and offered more bang for the buck. Drinkers also tended to consume more in one sitting, since availability was iffy, and the ambience at underground taverns (speakeasies) encouraged excess. Without the protection afforded by open competition and the threat of legal liability, buyers of illicit alcoholic beverages risked blindness, paralysis, and death from adulterants (such as methanol) and contaminants. In the early 1930s, some fifty thousand people were permanently paralyzed after drinking an adulterated Jamaican ginger extract ("jake") that was designed to provide beverage alcohol on the sly.[15]

Nearly fourteen years of experience taught Americans that alcohol prohibition was not nearly as effective as promised and that it caused a host of unintended consequences, making life noticeably less pleasant and more dangerous for drinkers and teetotalers alike. A growing number of Americans, including prominent academics, judges, journalists, and politicians, have reached a similar conclusion about the prohibition of other psychoactive chemicals.

As with alcohol, the prohibition of drugs such as marijuana, heroin, and cocaine has enriched and strengthened criminal organizations, from the Cali Cartel to the Bloods and Crips of Los Angeles. John Morgan estimates that prohibition has raised the price of cocaine twentyfold or more.[16] In Europe, where heroin is legally sold for some purposes, the drug can cost more than forty times as much on the black market.[17] According to one estimate, cannabis is more than a hundred times as expensive as it would be if it were legal.[18] Such multiples represent the risk premium that drug dealers can earn because of prohibition. No one really knows how much money Americans spend on illegal drugs, but a 1986 report from the President's Commission on Organized Crime estimated the total was perhaps $50 billion a year. This is roughly the rev-

enue of the domestic tobacco industry, which has more than three times
as many customers.[19]

Black-market violence leads to hundreds of deaths each year, and
today's drug suppliers are far more indiscriminate than Al Capone's
thugs, killing bystanders with alarming frequency. Contrary to popular
myth, "drug-related homicides" are generally *not* crimes committed
under the influence of a drug. An analysis of crack-related homicides in
New York City found that 85 percent grew out of black-market disputes, while about 7 percent occurred during crimes committed to support a crack habit. Only one homicide out of 118 involved a perpetrator
who was high on crack. Despite crack's reputation as a drug that fosters
violence, the association between alcohol intoxication and homicide is
actually stronger. The same study also looked at a broader sample of all
drug-related homicides and found that alcohol was involved in 68 percent of the cases where a drug's psychoactive effects seemed to have
helped precipitate the crime.[20]

In addition to assaults and homicides, prohibition fosters property
crime, since the artificially inflated prices of illegal drugs lead some
heavy users to support their habits through theft. Research has found
that crimes committed by heroin users rise dramatically when they are
taking the drug every day rather than occasionally or not at all. Other
studies indicate that property crime increases with the price of heroin
and with the intensity of enforcement efforts.[21]

From New York to Los Angeles, scandals involving cops who take
bribes, sell drugs, commit perjury, plant evidence, and rob suspects
show that prohibition continues to corrupt law enforcement officials.[22] The credibility of the criminal justice system is further eroded
by the arrest and imprisonment of people who are guilty of nothing
other than possessing certain substances or selling them to willing
buyers. In 1996 state and local law enforcement agencies arrested 1.5
million Americans for drug offenses, up more than 100 percent since
1984. Three-quarters of these arrests were for possession (unlike the
Volstead Act, our current drug laws target users as well as sellers), and
more than two-fifths of the cases involved marijuana.[23] Largely because of the war on drugs, the number of Americans behind bars has
more the tripled since 1980, reaching 1.6 million in 1995. About one

in four were drug law violators, compared to fewer than one in 10 a decade and a half earlier.[24]

With the proliferation of mandatory minimum sentences, penalties have also increased. The average drug sentence more than tripled between 1988 and 1993, from two to seven years.[25] Under federal law, a few rocks of crack or tabs of LSD will put a first-time offender away for five years without parole, and a large enough quantity of marijuana can result in the death penalty.[26] Under Michigan law, possession of more than 650 grams (about a pound and a half) of cocaine triggers a mandatory life sentence. In 1991 the U.S. Supreme Court upheld that penalty against a challenge by a defendant who had been caught with 672.5 grams in his car, finding that the sentence was not disproportionate enough to violate the Eighth Amendment's prohibition of cruel and unusual punishment.[27]

More arrests and longer sentences for drug offenses have contributed to overcrowding in prisons throughout the country. In 1993 the average prison system was operating at 15 percent over designed capacity. Overcrowding has led to the early release of predatory criminals, giving them more time to steal, rob, rape, and kill. The cost of incapacitating such offenders is high—ranging from about $20,000 a year in the federal system to about $58,000 in New York City—but the cost of letting them go is far higher: According to one estimate, a career criminal at large can cause hundreds of thousands of dollars in damage each year. Using scarce resources to lock up drug dealers makes even less sense when you realize that such arrests have no lasting impact on the drug trade. As the journalist Joshua Wolf Shenk observes, "Putting a murderer in jail means one less murderer on the street. Putting a drug dealer in jail means a job opening."[28]

In addition to harsh prison sentences, U.S. courts have endorsed invasions of privacy and other violations of property rights, all in the name of preventing people from ingesting certain chemicals.[29] Among other things, the U.S. Supreme Court has ruled that a search warrant can be granted based on information from an anonymous (and perhaps nonexistent) informant;[30] that evidence obtained with an invalid search warrant can be used in court so long as the police acted in "good faith";[31] that police do not need a warrant to search a privately owned field, de-

264

FOR YOUR OWN GOOD

spite a locked gate and a NO TRESPASSING sign, or to monitor homes and backyards from low-flying helicopters;[32] that drug agents may use dogs to inspect luggage without probable cause;[33] that police may search the interiors of cars, including closed containers, without a warrant;[34] and that police who stop a car for a traffic violation can ask the driver for permission to search without informing him that he is free to go.[35] The Court has also approved government-mandated drug testing without suspicion for railroad workers, Customs Service employees, and student athletes.[36]

Not only can the police search your property based on little or no evidence of wrongdoing; they can take it, too. After initially expressing some reservations, the Supreme Court has upheld the practice of civil forfeiture, in which the government confiscates property that it believes can be linked to a crime without having to show that the owner participated in the offense or even knew about it.[37] In most federal forfeitures, the owner is never even charged with a crime. Civil forfeiture has been applied to a variety of crimes, but the biggest impetus has come from the war on drugs. Since law enforcement agencies receive a share of the booty, the prospect of forfeiture helps determine their targets. In 1992 California millionaire Donald Scott was killed during a drug raid that turned up empty; prior to the raid, sheriff's deputies had researched the value of Scott's house and property.[38]

As with alcohol prohibition, the war on drugs makes "controlled substances" more dangerous. Inflated prices and the need for concealment encourage higher potency, favoring crack over coca beverages, heroin over opium. And like consumers of illicit rotgut during the 1920s and '30s, buyers of the currently illegal drugs are rarely sure of what they're getting. Potency and additives vary widely, leading to overdoses and poisoning. In a 1989 Cato Institute paper, James Ostrowski estimated that the lack of quality control leads to 2,400 deaths a year.[39] Laws limiting access to needles and syringes encourage the sharing of injection equipment, which spreads AIDS, hepatitis, and other diseases. Dirty needles are believed to account for one in four U.S. AIDS cases, representing thousands of deaths each year.[40] Mark Kleiman, a drug policy scholar who supports heroin prohibition, concedes that "perhaps if the AIDS epidemic had been foreknown, a convincing argument could have been made that an increase in heroin addiction as a result of one or another form of legal availability would have been more than compensated for by the reduction in HIV transmission."[41] Prohibition not only impedes the use of existing safety measures, it discourages innovations, such as coca gum or marijuana vaporizers, that would reduce the risks associated with drug use. Without a legal system to protect brand names and punish fraud, drug dealers have little incentive to offer safety improvements, and their customers have little reason to believe they will work as claimed.

PSSST. WANNA CIGARETTE?

Given the consequences of prohibitions past and present, it's not hard to picture an America where tobacco is banned: The guy in Washington Square Park muttering "Smoke, weed" is selling tobacco. Smugglers from the south are carrying cigarettes more often than cocaine. The drug dealers shooting at each other in Bedford-Stuyvesant and South Central L.A. are competing to offer their customers a nicotine fix. The addict stealing your car radio or burglarizing your home is a smoker. Emergency rooms across the country are treating smokers poisoned by adulterants.

Adding tobacco to the list of proscribed substances would presumably require more cops, more prosecutors, more judges, and more prison cells. Federal, state, and local governments already spend more than $30 billion a year to enforce the drug laws, not including prison costs.[42] To the extent that taxpayers resisted additional expenditures, the cost would be felt in less attention to crimes against people and property, more-crowded courts, and more early releases of burglars, muggers, rapists, and murderers.

A ban would increase the price of tobacco dramatically, though exactly how much is hard to say. During the postwar tobacco shortage in Germany, domestic cigarettes on the black market sold for sixteen to twenty-two times the price of a legal cigarette purchased with a ration coupon; imported cigarettes cost even more.[43] About forty-eight million American adults are current (mostly daily) smokers, more than four times the number who report using any of the illicit drugs in the last month.[44] A ban would probably convince some smokers to quit, but history suggests most would keep smoking. Boston University economist Jeffrey A. Miron and MIT economist Jeffrey Zwiebel estimate that alcohol consumption dropped after passage of the Volstead Act to between 20 and 40 percent of the pre-Prohibition level, then rebounded to between 60 and 70 percent.[45] If anything, smokers are more attached to tobacco than drinkers are to alcohol. Even if we assume that prohibition would cut demand for tobacco in half, the illicit market would be bigger than the market for all other illegal drugs combined. That's a conspicuous business opportunity for enterprising criminals.

If you think the legal tobacco industry is sinister, imagine the sort of people who will be attracted to the business after prohibition. They will be aggressive risk-takers with no compunction about breaking the law or using violence to settle disputes. They will have experience in smuggling, deception, and bribery. And they will be fighting each other for shares of a very lucrative business. The violence that occurred after Canada sharply raised cigarette taxes in 1989 and 1991 (see chapter 4) gives a hint of what happens when a government invites criminals to take over the tobacco business. A new black market also creates new temptations for the police. During the German cigarette shortage, the criminologist Henner Hess reports, "bribery and corruption of law enforcement were common."[46]

The high price of cigarettes will force smokers to reduce other expenditures or seek extra income. Some will resort to begging, theft, or prostitution. Hess notes that Germany's cigarette shortage "produced symptoms of withdrawal, desperate seeking behavior, a readiness to sacrifice a lot for the drug, and even moral degradation." In addition to shelling out a lot more for cigarettes, smokers will face the familiar hazards of a black market. They will not know if the product is adulterated or contaminated, and they will have no recourse if they are cheated. In postwar Germany, Hess observes, smokers who bought black-market cigarettes had "no way to hold the seller responsible by appealing to the law. . . . Often enough they ended up with cigarettes that contained sawdust instead of tobacco or tobacco mixed with side-shoots or other harmful ingredients."[47] Illegal suppliers will have little incentive to offer low-tar or otherwise safer cigarettes. Smokers will have to consume their drug on the sly, which will be difficult for people accustomed to smoking a pack or two a day. Every time they buy, carry, store, or smoke cigarettes, they will risk fines, arrest, humiliation, imprisonment, and property forfeiture. Tens of millions of smokers will suddenly start to identify with all those potheads and heroin addicts they once despised.

Tobacco's opponents have considered this prospect, and flinched. The leaders of the anti-smoking movement are, I think, sincere when they say they do not want to ban tobacco—for now. As smoking declines and becomes increasingly concentrated in lower socioeconomic groups, prohibition may not be so unthinkable anymore. The consequences of creating a big black market certainly seem unacceptable, but the American public has been perfectly willing to accept such consequences for the last eight decades, since the passage of the Harrison Narcotics Act in 1914. We have been living with prohibition for so long that we can't imagine living without it.

For critics of the war on drugs, the attitudes expressed by many of tobacco's opponents are worrisome. The FDA's authority was such a contentious issue in the debate over a nationwide liability settlement mainly because some anti-smokers have suggested that the tobacco companies should be forced to gradually eliminate nicotine from their cigarettes. This proposal makes little sense from a public health standpoint, since it would lead people to smoke more, and face higher risks, for a given dose of nicotine. Similarly, if your goal is to reduce disease, you should applaud low-tar cigarettes and Eclipse-like contraptions as safety improvements instead of attacking them because they might encourage people to keep smoking. But if your goal is to stamp out the use of a particular drug, making the activity safer is counterproductive. That is why drug warriors condemn needle exchange programs for "sending the wrong message." By the same logic, supporters of alcohol prohibition should have welcomed the fifty thousand cases of paralysis caused by ginger jake. Prohibitionists are also reluctant to concede that different forms of a drug pose different levels of risk, that chewing coca leaves or drinking coca tea is not tantamount to smoking crack. The same attitude is displayed by anti-smoking activists who insist that "tobacco is tobacco," even though pipes, cigars, and (especially) smokeless tobacco do not pose anything approaching the hazards that cigarettes do.

Most important, prohibitionists seem blind to the benefits of psychoactive substances, to the reasons humans have always liked them so much. Prohibitionists believe in the enslaving power of chemicals as firmly as medieval peasants believed in demonic possession. This belief, which simultaneously anthropomorphizes the drug and dehumanizes the drug user, animated people like George Trask and Lucy Page Gaston, who railed against demon rum as well as the Devil's weed. Today it animates people like C. Everett Koop and David Kessler, who talk as if tobacco were irresistible and inescapable.

THE NEW EPIDEMICS

Koop and Kessler, of course, claim to be acting in the name of public health, seeking to cure rather than punish. The public health approach, which penalizes and restricts drug users through taxes and regulation instead of the criminal justice system, is often presented as a more humane alternative to the war on drugs. Public health supposedly treats drug use like a disease to be controlled rather than a crime to be deterred. Yet many of its prescriptions are aimed at making life difficult for the drug user so he will stop misbehaving. In practice, the main function of the disease metaphor is to banish the notion that the drug user's choices and desires should matter. A happy, productive, well-adjusted drug user is still sick, still part of an epidemic, even though he doesn't realize it. Alternatively, he is an asymptomatic carrier, spreading misery to others by setting a bad example. Either way, he has to be isolated and cured, whether he likes it or not.

The public health approach does not preclude prohibition. Protecting public health was, after all, the official justification (cited by judges, if not by sanitarians) for cigarette bans in Tennessee and other states early in this century, and more recently it has been the rationale for removing products such as cyclamates and breast implants from the market. Furthermore, the heavy taxation, ruinous lawsuits, advertising bans, and product restrictions favored by many anti-smokers can have much the same impact as prohibition by raising prices, discouraging innovation, and preventing the sale of products that people want to buy. And while the techniques of the public health specialists are usually milder than the techniques of the drug warriors, their ambitions are much grander: not just a smoke-free society or a drug-free America, but a nation in which no one takes foolish risks or trades longevity for pleasure.

Public health used to mean keeping statistics, imposing quarantines, requiring vaccination of children, providing purified water, building sewer systems, inspecting restaurants, regulating emissions from factories, and reviewing drugs for safety. Nowadays it means, among other things, banning cigarette ads, raising alcohol taxes, restricting gun ownership, forcing people to buckle their seat belts, and making illegal drug users choose between prison and "treatment." In the past, public health officials could argue that they were protecting people from external threats: carriers of contagious diseases, fumes from the local glue factory, contaminated water, food poisoning, dangerous quack remedies. By contrast, the new enemies of public health come from within; the aim is to protect people from themselves rather than each other.

Treating risky behavior like a contagious disease invites endless meddling. The same arguments that are commonly used to justify the government's efforts to discourage smoking can easily be applied to overeating, for example. If smoking is a compulsive disease, so is obesity. It carries substantial health risks, and people who are fat generally don't want to be. They find it difficult to lose weight, and when they do succeed they often relapse. When deprived of food, they suffer cravings, depression, anxiety, and other withdrawal symptoms.

Sure enough, the headline of a March 1985 article in *Science* announced, "Obesity Declared a Disease." The article summarized a report by a National Institutes of Health panel that found that "the obese are prone to a wide variety of diseases, including hypertension, adult-onset diabetes, hypercholesterolemia, hypertriglyceridemia, heart disease, cancer, gall stones, arthritis, and gout." It quoted the panel's chairman, Jules Hirsch: "We found that there are multiple health hazards at what to me are surprisingly low levels of obesity. Obesity, therefore, is a disease."[48]

More recently, the "epidemic of obesity" has been trumpeted repeatedly on the front page of the *New York Times*. The first story, which appeared in July 1994, was prompted by a study from the National Center for Health Statistics that found the share of American adults who are obese increased from a quarter to a third between 1980 and 1991. "The government is not doing enough," complained Philip R. Lee, assistant HHS secretary. "We don't have a coherent, across-the-board policy." The second story, published in September 1995, reported on a *New England Journal of Medicine* study that found gaining as little as eleven to eighteen pounds was associated with a higher risk of heart disease—or, as the headline on the jump page put it, EVEN MODERATE WEIGHT GAINS CAN BE DEADLY. The study attributed three hundred thousand deaths a year to obesity, including one-third of cancer deaths and most deaths from cardiovascular disease. The lead researcher, JoAnn E. Manson, said, "It won't be long before obesity surpasses cigarette smoking as a cause of death in this country."[49]

In his book *The Fat of the Land*, journalist Michael Fumento argues that obesity, defined as being 20 percent or more above one's appropriate weight, is only part of the problem. According to a 1996 survey, 74 percent of Americans exceed the weight range recommended for optimal health. "So instead of talking about a third of Americans being at risk because of being overweight," he writes, "we really should be talking about somewhere around *three fourths*."[50]

If, as Philip R. Lee recommended, the government decides to do more about obesity—the second most important preventable cause of death in this country, soon to be the first—what would "a coherent, across-the-board policy" look like? As early as June 1975, in its *Forward Plan for Health,* the U.S. Public Health Service was suggesting "strong regulations to control the advertisement of food products, especially those of high sugar content or little nutritional value."[51] But surely we can do better than that. A tax on fatty foods would help cover the cost of obesity-related illness and disability, while deterring overconsumption of ice cream and steak.

Lest you think this proposal merely facetious, it has been offered, apparently in all seriousness, by at least one economist, who wrote: "It is somewhat ironic that the government discourages smoking and drinking through taxation, yet when it comes to the major cause of death—heart disease—and its spiraling health-care costs, politicians let us eat with impunity. . . . It is time to rethink the extent to which we allow people to impose their negative behavior on those of us who watch our weight, exercise and try to be as healthy as possible."[52]

Kelly Brownell, a professor of psychology at Yale University who directs the school's Center for Eating and Weight Disorders, has also suggested a fat tax, along with subsidies for healthy foods. "A militant attitude is warranted here," he told the *New Haven Register*. "We're infuriated at tobacco companies for enticing kids to smoke, so we don't want Joe Camel on billboards. Is it any different to have Ronald McDonald asking kids to eat foods that are bad for them?"[53]

Of course, a tax on fatty foods would be paid by the lean as well as the chunky. It might be more fair and efficient to tax people for every pound over their ideal weight. Such a market-based system would make the obese realize the costs they impose on society and give them an incentive to slim down.

If this idea strikes most people as ridiculous, it's not because the plan is impractical. In several states, people have to bring their cars to an approved garage for periodic emissions testing; there's no logistical reason why they could not also be required to weigh in at an approved doctor's office, say, once a year, reporting the results to the Internal Revenue Service for tax assessment. Though feasible, the fat tax is ridiculous because it's an odious intrusion by the state into matters that should remain private. Even if obesity is apt to shorten your life, most Americans would (I hope) agree, that's your business, not the government's. Yet many of the same Americans believe not only that the state should take an interest in whether people smoke but that it should apply pressure to make them stop, including fines (a.k.a. tobacco taxes), tax-supported nagging, and bans on smoking in the workplace.

In a 1997 talk show appearance, New York City lung surgeon William Cahan, a prominent critic of the tobacco industry, explained the rationale for such policies: "People who are making decisions for themselves don't always come up with the right answer."[54] Since they believe that smoking is inherently irrational, tobacco's opponents tend to assume that smokers are stupid, ignorant, crazy, or helpless—though they rarely say so in such blunt terms. They understandably prefer to focus on the evil tobacco companies, portraying smokers as their victims. Yet there is a palpable undercurrent of hostility toward smokers who refuse to get with the program. On two occasions while working on this book, I was sitting at a (smoke-free) table with a group that in-

cluded both a smoker and a busybody who took it upon himself to be-
rate the smoker for his unhealthy habit. In both cases, the smoker, con-
strained by politeness, offered only the mildest of objections, and no one
intervened on his behalf. Imagine what the reaction would have been if,
instead of a smoker, the meddler had zeroed in on a chubby diner, warning him about the perils of overeating and lack of exercise. I suspect that
the other diners would have been appalled, and the target, in turn,
would have been more likely to offer the appropriate response: *Mind
your own damned business.* It seems we have special license to pick on
smokers as a way of demonstrating our moral superiority. As one smoker
put it, responding to a proposed ban on smoking at the beach in
Carmel, New York, "If you're a smoker these days, the world tries to
make you feel like you're dirt."[55]

In response to this hostile environment, many smokers have re-
treated to a subculture that celebrates the pleasures of smoking and
mocks the self-righteousness of tobacco's opponents. Yet the anti-
smokers still cannot leave them alone. When I subscribed to a couple
of Internet newsgroups for smokers, I found that the discussions were
often interrupted by unprovoked harangues about the evils of smoking. On the World Wide Web, the Smoker's Home Page opens with a
caveat: "WARNING! This page may be hazardous to anti-smokers' blood
pressure. Quitting now may greatly reduce your chances of moral outrage." As if to demonstrate the need for such a warning, a 1997 report
from the Washington-based Center for Media Education noted with
horror that "the site has a hip rebellious tone, and avidly promotes
smokers' rights. . . . The topics . . . are very pro-smoking, with no attempt to balance the presentation of the issues." More generally, the
report complained that a "pervasive online Smoking-Is-Cool culture
has emerged on the World Wide Web which runs contrary to the prevailing attitude among most Americans about smoking and health."
As if that were not bad enough, the authors noted, "In this entire
study not a single Surgeon General's warning was found on any tobacco site." The report recommended several remedies, including congressional hearings, investigations by regulatory agencies, and "effective government oversight."[56]

These self-appointed Web watchdogs, who cannot abide any devia-

tion from "prevailing attitude[s]" about smoking, may be upset by the
avid promotion of "smokers' rights," but the concept really does not
pose much of a threat to the crusade for a smoke-free society. If smokers
assert their "right" to light up, nonsmokers can always assert their
"right" to a smoke-free environment. The government will step in to resolve the conflict, and it will do so in favor of the majority. Furthermore,
"smokers' rights," as interpreted by the tobacco companies and the
ACLU, can ride roughshod over freedom of contract by forbidding employers or insurers to treat smokers differently from nonsmokers. The
concept implies that smokers have special rights by virtue of their habit,
when in fact they have the same rights as other individuals. They have a
right to control what goes into their bodies. They have a right to purchase a product from a willing seller, without paying a fine because
someone else thinks the product is sinful. They have a right to use the
product in any place where their host does not object. They have a right
to see messages about the product from the manufacturer. They have a
right to buy and wear whatever clothing they like (including clothing
embossed with certain brand names or characters), even if it offends
powerful people. These rights are not trivial, and we should hesitate before saying they can be overridden for the sake of "public health," which
can easily become an all-purpose excuse.

Because the public health field developed in response to deadly
threats that spread from person to person and place to place, its practitioners are used to dictating from on high. Writing in 1879, U.S. Army
surgeon John S. Billings put it this way: "All admit that the State should
extend special protection to those who are incapable of judging of their
own best interests, or of taking care of themselves, such as the insane,
persons of feeble intellect, or children; and we have seen that in sanitary
matters the public at large are thus incompetent."[57] Billings was defending traditional public health measures aimed at preventing the spread of
infectious diseases and controlling hazards such as toxic fumes. It's reasonable to expect that such measures will be welcomed by the intended
beneficiaries, once they understand the aim. The same cannot be said of
public health's new targets. Even after the public is informed about the
relevant hazards (and assuming the information is accurate), many people will continue to smoke, drink, take illegal drugs, eat fatty foods, buy

guns, speed, eschew seat belts and motorcycle helmets, and otherwise behave in ways frowned upon by the public health establishment. This is not because they misunderstood; it's because, for the sake of pleasure, utility, or convenience, they are prepared to accept the risks. When public health experts assume these decisions are wrong, they are indeed treating adults like incompetent children.

One such expert, writing in the *New England Journal of Medicine* two decades ago, declared, "The real malpractice problem in this country today is not the one described on the front pages of daily newspapers but rather the malpractice that people are performing on themselves and each other—It is a crime to commit suicide quickly. However, to kill oneself slowly by means of an unhealthy life style is readily condoned and even encouraged."[58] The article prompted a response from Robert F. Meenan, a professor at the University of California School of Medicine in San Francisco, who observed: "Health professionals are trained to supply the individual with medical facts and opinions. However, they have no personal attributes, knowledge, or training that qualifies them to dictate the preferences of others. Nevertheless, doctors generally assume that the high priority that they place on health should be shared by others. They find it hard to accept that some people may opt for a brief, intense existence full of unhealthy practices. Such individuals are pejoratively labeled 'noncompliant' and pressures are applied on them to reorder their priorities."[59]

The dangers of basing government policy on this attitude are clear, especially given the broad concerns of the public health movement. According to John J. Hanlon's *Public Health Administration and Practice,* "Public health is dedicated to the common attainment of the highest levels of physical, mental, and social well-being and longevity consistent with available knowledge and resources at a given time and place."[60] The textbook *Principles of Community Health* tells us, "The most widely accepted definition of individual health is that of the World Health Organization: 'Health is a state of complete physical, mental, and social well-being and not merely the absence of disease or infirmity.'"[61] A government empowered to maximize health is a totalitarian government.

In response to such fears, the public health establishment argues that government intervention is justified because individual decisions about risk affect other people. "Motorcyclists often contend that helmet laws infringe on personal liberties," noted Surgeon General Julius Richmond's 1979 report *Healthy People*, "and opponents of mandatory [helmet] laws argue that since other people usually are not endangered, the individual motorcyclist should be allowed personal responsibility for risk. But the high cost of disabling and fatal injuries, the burden on families, and the demands on medical care resources are borne by society as a whole."[62] This line of reasoning, which is also used to justify taxes on tobacco and alcohol, implies that all resources—including not just taxpayer-funded welfare and health care but private savings, insurance coverage, and charity—are part of a common pool owned by "society as a whole" and guarded by the government.

As Meenan noted in the *New England Journal of Medicine*, "Virtually all aspects of life style could be said to have an effect on the health or well-being of society, and the decision [could then be] reached that personal health choices should be closely regulated."[63] Writing eighteen years later in the same journal, Faith T. Fitzgerald, a professor at the University of California, Davis, Medical Center, observed: "Both health care providers and the commonweal now have a vested interest in certain forms of behavior, previously considered a person's private business, if the behavior impairs a person's 'health.' Certain failures of self-care have become, in a sense, crimes against society, because society has to pay for their consequences. . . . In effect, we have said that people owe it to society to stop misbehaving, and we use illness as evidence of misbehavior."[64]

Most public health practitioners would presumably recoil at the full implications of the argument that government should override individual decisions affecting health because such decisions have an impact on "society as a whole." C. Everett Koop, for his part, seems completely untroubled. "I think that the government has a perfect right to influence personal behavior to the best of its ability if it is for the welfare of the individual and the community as a whole," he writes. This is paternalistic tyranny in its purest form, arrogating to government the authority to judge "the welfare of the individual" and elevating "the community as a whole" above mere people. Ignoring the distinction between self-regarding behavior and behavior that threatens others, Koop compares efforts

to discourage smoking and other risky behavior to mandatory vaccination of schoolchildren and laws against assault.[65]

While Koop may simply be confused, some defenders of the public
health movement explicitly recognize that its aims are fundamentally
collectivist and cannot be reconciled with the American tradition of limited government. In 1975 Dan E. Beauchamp, then an assistant professor of public health at the University of North Carolina, presented a
paper at the annual meeting of the American Public Health Association
in which he argued that "the radical individualism inherent in the market model" is the biggest obstacle to improving public health. "The his-
toric dream of public health that preventable death and disability ought
to be minimized is a dream of social justice," Beauchamp said. "We are
far from recognizing the principle that death and disability are collective
problems and that all persons are entitled to health protection." He rejected "the ultimately arbitrary distinction between voluntary and involuntary hazards" and complained that "the primary duty to avert disease
and injury still rests with the individual." Beauchamp called upon public health practitioners to challenge "the powerful sway market-justice
holds over our imagination, granting fundamental freedom to all individuals to be left alone."[66]

Of all the risk factors for disease and injury, it seems, freedom is the
most pernicious. And you thought it was smoking.

TEN MYTHS OF THE
ANTI-SMOKING MOVEMENT

1. *The tobacco companies hid the truth about the hazards and addictiveness of cigarettes from the American public.* Industry double-talk notwithstanding, warnings about the health risks of smoking go back hundreds of years. James I, in his 1604 *Counterblaste to Tobacco,* called smoking "a custome lothsome to the eye, hatefull to the Nose, harmefull to the braine, danger-ous to the Lungs." In every generation, tobacco's opponents have echoed him, attributing a long list of maladies to smoking (see chapter 1). Persua-sive scientific evidence of tobacco's hazards, which began to emerge in the early 1930s, has received widespread attention since the '50s (see chapter 2). Likewise, the difficulty of giving up the tobacco habit has been com-mon knowledge for centuries (see chapter 7). Sir Francis Bacon, lord chancellor under James I, observed, "In our times the use of tobacco is growing greatly and conquers men with a certain secret pleasure, so that those who have once become accustomed thereto can later hardly be re-strained therefrom." The seventeenth-century polemicist Johann Michael Moscherosch called smokers "thralls to the tobacco fiend," while Cotton Mather dubbed them "*Slave*[s] to the *Pipe.*" Fagon, court physician to Louis XIV, described the tobacco habit as "a fatal, insatiable necessity . . . a permanent epilepsy."

2. *"Tobacco is tobacco."* Although all tobacco products pose some health risks, cigarettes are by far the most hazardous. Cigars and pipes are con-

siderably less dangerous. Research by the American Cancer Society found that "death rates were far higher in cigarette smokers than in non-smokers," while "cigar smokers had somewhat higher death rates than nonsmokers" and "there was little difference between the death rates of pipe smokers and the death rates of men who never smoked regularly." By one measure, smokeless tobacco is 98 percent safer than cigarettes. (See chapter 2.)

3. *People smoke because of advertising.* There is remarkably little evidence that advertising plays an important role in getting people to smoke, as opposed to getting them to smoke a particular brand. The 1989 surgeon general's report conceded that "there is no scientifically rigorous study available to the public that provides a definitive answer to the basic question of whether advertising and promotion increase the level of tobacco consumption. Given the complexity of the issue, none is likely to be forthcoming in the foreseeable future." The 1994 report, which focused on underage smoking, also acknowledged the "lack of definitive literature." None of the widely publicized studies that have appeared in recent years, including the much-hyped research on Joe Camel, actually measured the impact of advertising on a teenager's propensity to smoke. (See chapter 3.)

4. *Smoking imposes costs on society.* Because smokers tend to die earlier than nonsmokers, the costs of treating tobacco-related illness are balanced, and probably outweighed, by savings on Social Security, nursing home stays, and medical care in old age. Every analysis that takes such long-term savings into account, including reports from the RAND Corporation, the Congressional Research Service, and Harvard economist W. Kip Viscusi, concludes that "social cost" cannot justify raising cigarette taxes. (See chapter 4.)

5. *Secondhand smoke poses a grave threat to bystanders.* The evidence concerning the health effects of secondhand smoke is not nearly as conclusive as the evidence concerning the health effects of smoking. The research suggests that people who live with smokers for decades may face a slightly higher risk of lung cancer. According to one esti-

mate, a nonsmoking woman who lives with a smoker faces an additional lung cancer risk of 6.5 in 10,000, which would raise her lifetime risk from about 0.34 percent to about 0.41 percent. Studies of secondhand smoke and heart disease, including the results from the Harvard Nurses Study published in 1997, report more dramatic increases in disease rates—so dramatic, in fact, that they are biologically implausible, suggesting risks comparable to those faced by smokers, despite the much lower doses involved. In any case, there is *no* evidence that casual exposure to secondhand smoke has any impact on your life expectancy. (See chapter 5.)

6. *If secondhand smoke really is dangerous, smoking ought to be banned everywhere, except in private residences.* Since almost all of the epidemiological evidence about the health effects of secondhand smoke relates to long-term exposure in the home, the fact that this is the one place exempted from current and proposed smoking bans suggests a residual concern for property rights. Yet business owners have property rights, too. If the government respected their right to establish rules about smoking on their own property, potential employees and customers could take such policies into account when deciding where to work or which businesses to patronize. Whether secondhand smoke is a health hazard or merely a nuisance, such a voluntary system is the most appropriate way to deal with the conflicting demands of smokers and nonsmokers, since it allows for diversity and competition, rather than simply imposing the will of the majority on everyone. (See chapter 5.)

7. *States have a right to demand compensation from tobacco companies for the costs of treating smoking-related diseases under Medicaid.* This claim ignores the long-term savings traceable to smoking (see Myth 4) and the tobacco taxes smokers already pay to cover the costs they supposedly impose on others. Furthermore, by the same logic, states could sue the manufacturer of any product associated with disease or injury, including alcoholic beverages, fatty foods, candy, firearms, swimming pools, bathtubs, skateboards, and automobiles. The makers (and consumers) of such products should not be blamed because politicians decided to pay for health care with taxpayers' money. (See chapter 6.)

8. *The tobacco companies have been secretly manipulating the nicotine in cigarettes to keep smokers hooked.* Nicotine control was never a secret. Several brands of denicotined cigarettes were introduced as early as the 1920s. Claims of reduced tar and nicotine have been conspicuous since the 1950s, and the yields of each brand have been advertised since 1971. The very idea of a consistent nicotine yield for a given brand implies control, which cigarette manufacturers achieve through a variety of methods that have long been discussed in trade journals, books, and government reports. (See chapter 7.)

9. *Smoking is "a pediatric disease."* Although most smokers start as teenagers, the vast majority are, in fact, adults. And while it raises the risk of certain illnesses, smoking itself is a behavior—something people choose to do—not a disease. As then-surgeon general C. Everett Koop noted in his 1984 speech calling for "a smoke-free society," smoking "is a voluntary act: one does not have to smoke if one does not want to." (See chapter 7.)

10. *Once people have started smoking, nicotine addiction prevents them from stopping.* This is so contrary to everyday experience that it's amazing politicians and anti-smoking activists can say it with a straight face. In fact, there are about as many former smokers in this country as there are smokers, and almost all gave up the habit on their own, without formal treatment—usually by quitting cold turkey. (See chapter 7.)

NOTES

Author's Note

1. In fiscal year 1996, Philip Morris Companies gave $25,000 to the Reason Foundation and bought $6,766 in ads from *Reason*. The foundation's total budget was about $4 million.
2. Stanton A. Glantz, letter to the editor, *Globe and Mail*, December 11, 1996.
3. Philip J. Hilts, *Smokescreen: The Truth Behind the Tobacco Industry Cover-Up*, Reading, Mass.: Addison-Wesley, 1996, p. 106.
4. *Afternoon Edition*, NewsTalk Television, January 10, 1995.
5. Scott Ballin, "Tobacco Tax Argument Scorched," *Wall Street Journal*, August 17, 1994, p. A13. Gary S. Becker and Michael S. Grossman, "Smoking Out Red Herrings," *Wall Street Journal*, August 29, 1994, p. A11.
6. Glantz, letter to the editor.
7. Majority Staff of the House Subcommittee on Health and the Environment, "The Tobacco Industry's Misinformation Campaign," *ETS Facts*, July 22, 1994, p. 2.
8. See, e.g., Jon Cohen, "Tobacco Money Lights Up a Debate," *Science*, 272 (April 26, 1996), pp. 488–494.

Introduction. Without a Doubt

1. U.S. Department of Health, Education, and Welfare, *Smoking and Health: Report of the Advisory Committee to the Surgeon General of the Public Health Service*, U.S. Public Health Service, Center for Disease Control, 1964, p. 33.
2. *The Steve Kane Show*, WFTL, Ft. Lauderdale, Florida, December 27, 1995.
3. Ibid.
4. Ibid.
5. John Stuart Mill, *On Liberty*, Indianapolis: Bobbs-Merrill, 1956 (originally published in 1859), p. 13.
6. Interview with Alan Blum, May 14, 1996.
7. James Bennett, "Anti-Smoker Presses Shea Billboard Battle," *New York Times*, April 26, 1993, p. B3.

8. David Satcher and Michael Eriksen, "The Paradox of Tobacco Control," *Journal of the American Medical Association,* 271:8 (February 23, 1994), p. 627.

9. Interview with Scott Ballin, Fall 1990.

10. Christopher Hitchens, "Smoke and Mirrors," *Vanity Fair,* October 1994, pp. 88–95.

11. Florence King, "I'd Rather Smoke Than Kiss," *National Review,* July 9, 1990, pp. 32–36.

12. Nader Mousavizadeh, "Washington Diarist," *New Republic,* September 18 & 25, 1995, p. 58.

13. Julie DeFalco and Adam Lieberman, "A Libertarian E-Mail Exchange on Smoking," *Priorities,* 9:2 (1997), pp. 23–24.

14. Interview with David Brenton, fall 1990.

15. Interview with Ballin.

16. Interview with Anne Wortham, fall 1990.

17. Hitchens, "Smoke and Mirrors," p. 95.

18. *Crossfire,* CNN, March 10, 1994.

19. Associated Press, "Absent Cigarette Sparks Debate Over Stamp," *New York Times,* September 18, 1994, p. A27.

20. Bruce Horovitz, "Activists' Ads Focus Fire Where There's Smoke," *Los Angeles Times,* February 3, 1993, p. D2.

21. Raymond Hernandez, "Hyde Park Ponders Symbol of Its Most Famous Smoker," *New York Times,* July 29, 1995, p. A1.

22. Charles Paul Freund, "Those Hellhounds-of-Censorship Blues," *Washington Post,* September 25, 1994, p. C3.

23. Byron J. Bailey, "Tobaccoism Is the Disease: Cancer Is the Sequela," *Journal of the American Medical Association,* 255:14 (April 11, 1986), p. 1923.

24. William H. Foege, "The Growing Brown Plague," *Journal of the American Medical Association,* 264:12 (September 26, 1990), p. 1580.

25. Louis Sullivan, "An Opportunity to Oppose: Physicians' Role in the Campaign Against Tobacco," *Journal of the American Medical Association,* 264:12 (September 26, 1990), pp. 1581–1582.

26. Stanton Glantz, "What Deal? We Got Suckered," *Los Angeles Times,* June 23, 1997, p. B5.

27. Philip J. Hilts, *Smokescreen: The Truth Behind the Tobacco Industry Cover-Up,* Reading, Mass.: Addison-Wesley, 1996, pp. 216–217.

28. Barnaby J. Feder, "Texas Joins Other States in Suing Tobacco Industry," *New York Times,* March 29, 1996, p. B9.

29. Shankar Vedantam, "Antismoking Campaign Often Invokes Moral Terms," *Philadelphia Inquirer,* August 24, 1996, p. A8.

30. Dennis L. Breo, "Kicking Butts," *Journal of the American Medical Association,* 270:16 (October 27, 1993), p. 1978.

31. U.S. Centers for Disease Control and Prevention, "Smoking Prevalence Among U.S. Adults," April 24, 1996. "Cigarette Smoking Among Adults—United States, 1994," *Morbidity and Mortality Weekly Report,* July 12, 1996, p. 588.

32. Interview with Charles Paul Freund, January 6, 1997.

33. Susan Steinberg, "Smoke Rings," *Los Angeles Times,* June 15, 1995, p. J14. Sheryl Gay Stolberg, "Cigar Fad Reported to Be Recruiting Legions of Teen-Agers," *New York Times,* May 23, 1997, p. A24.

34. Suein L. Hwang, "FDA Seeks to Mount Attack on Smoking by Minors That Could Mean Regulation," *Wall Street Journal,* July 13, 1995, p. A1.

Chapter 1. From Devil's Weed to Soldier's Friend

1. Egon C. Corti, *A History of Smoking,* London: George Harrap, 1931, p. 50.

2. Ibid., pp. 41–42.

3. Ibid., pp. 42–43.

4. James I, *A Counterblaste to Tobacco,* London: English Reprints, 1870 (originally published in 1604), p. 100.

5. Ibid., p. 110.

6. Ibid., p. 112.

7. Victor G. Kiernan, *Tobacco: A History,* London: Hutchinson Radius, 1991, p. 22.

8. Cotton Mather, *Manuductio ad Ministerium,* Boston, 1726 (emphasis in original).

9. Corti, *History of Smoking,* pp. 111–112.

10. Ibid., p. 119.

11. Jordan Goodman, *Tobacco in History: The Cultures of Dependence,* New York: Routledge, 1993, p. 69.

12. Kiernan, *Tobacco: A History,* p. 23.

13. Corti, *History of Smoking,* p. 141.

14. Goodman, *Tobacco in History,* p. 191.

15. Corti, *History of Smoking,* pp. 185–186.

16. Kiernan, *Tobacco: A History,* p. 27.

17. Corti, *History of Smoking,* p. 232.

18. Benjamin Rush, *Essays, Moral, Political and Philosophical,* Philadelphia, 1798, pp. 264, 270.

19. *Journal of Health,* September 23, 1829, pp. 37–38.

20. J. Smyth Rogers, *An Essay on Tobacco,* New York: How & Bates, 1836, pp. 66–67 (emphasis in original).

21. Ibid., p. 61.

22. Ibid., pp. 58, 66.

23. *Anti-Tobacco Journal,* November 1859, p. 2.

24. *Anti-Tobacco Journal,* July and August 1860, p. 135.

25. *Anti-Tobacco Journal,* November 1859, p. 5.

26. *Anti-Tobacco Journal,* January 1860.

27. George Trask, *Thoughts and Stories on Tobacco for American Lads; or Uncle Toby's Anti-Tobacco Advice to His Nephew Billy Bruce,* Boston, 1852, p. 30.

28. *Anti-Tobacco Journal,* July and August 1860, p. 135.

29. Ronald J. Troyer and Gerald E. Markle, *Cigarettes: The Battle over Smoking,* New Brunswick, N.J.: Rutgers University Press, 1983, p. 34.

30. Quoted in Gordon L. Dillow, "Thank You for Not Smoking: The Hundred-Year

War Against the Cigarette," *American Heritage,* February/March 1981, pp. 94–107.

31. Ibid., p. 101.
32. Troyer and Markle, *Cigarettes: The Battle over Smoking,* p. 34.
33. Charles Bulkley Hubbell, "The Cigaret Habit: A New Peril," *Independent,* February 18, 1904, pp. 375–378.
34. Dillow, "Thank You for Not Smoking," p. 102.
35. Troyer and Markle, *Cigarettes: The Battle over Smoking,* p. 34. Rivka Widerman, "Tobacco Is a Dirty Weed. Have We Ever Liked It? A Look at Nineteenth Century Anti-Cigarette Legislation," *Loyola Law Review,* 38 (1992), pp. 387–423.
36. Goodman, *Tobacco in History,* p. 120.
37. *Austin v. Tennessee,* 179 U.S. 343 (1900).
38. Winfield S. Hall, ed., *Tobacco: The Cigarette: Why It Is Especially Objectionable,* Chicago: Anti-Cigarette League, 1900, pp. 20–21.
39. Albert F. Blaisdell, *Our Bodies and How We Live,* New York: Ginn and Company, 1910, pp. 239, 241.
40. Charles B. Towns, "The Injury of Tobacco and Its Relation to Other Drug Habits," *Century Magazine,* March 1912, p. 768.
41. Dillow, "Thank You for Not Smoking," p. 103.
42. Henry Ford, ed., *The Case Against the Little White Slaver,* Detroit, 1914, p. 3.
43. Ibid., p. 5.
44. Towns, "The Injury of Tobacco," pp. 769–772.
45. Troyer and Markle, *Cigarettes: The Battle over Smoking,* p. 39.
46. Towns, "The Injury of Tobacco," p. 772 (emphasis in original).
47. "Incidents and Effects of Smoking," *Harper's Weekly,* February 27, 1904, p. 314.
48. "Refuges for Non-Smokers," *Literary Digest,* November 22, 1924, p. 28.
49. "Cigarettes," *Harper's Weekly,* August 12, 1905, p. 1148.
50. Dillow, "Thank You for Not Smoking," p. 105.
51. Rush, *Essays, Moral, Political and Philosophical,* p. 264.
52. Richard Klein, *Cigarettes Are Sublime,* Durham, N.C.: Duke University Press, 1993, p. 139.
53. Corti, *History of Smoking,* p. 264.
54. *Harper's Weekly,* July 7, 1900, p. 631.
55. Dillow, "Thank You for Not Smoking," p. 103.
56. "The Cigarette and Its Users," *Harper's Weekly,* September 17, 1910, p. 25.
57. "Smoking," *The Atlantic Monthly,* April 1916, p. 574.
58. Goodman, *Tobacco in History,* p. 106.
59. Ibid., pp. 107–108.
60. Harry Burke, "Women Cigarette Fiends," *Ladies' Home Journal,* June 1922, p. 19.
61. Dillow, "Thank You for Not Smoking," p. 105.
62. "Lucy Page Gaston, Reformer, Is Dead," *New York Times,* August 21, 1924, p. 11.
63. Troyer and Markle, *Cigarettes: The Battle over Smoking,* p. 47.
64. Carl Avery Werner, "The Triumph of the Cigarette," *American Mercury,* December 1925, pp. 415–421.

65. Science Service, "Cigarette Tar in Cancer," *Scientific American*, April 1933, pp. 245–246.

Chapter 2. Appropriate Remedial Action

1. Marjorie Hunter, "Smoking Banned at News Parley," *New York Times*, January 12, 1964, p. 66.
2. U.S. Department of Health, Education, and Welfare, *Smoking and Health: Report of the Advisory Committee to the Surgeon General of the Public Health Service*, U.S. Public Health Service, Center for Disease Control, 1964, pp. 28–40.
3. Elizabeth M. Whelan, *A Smoking Gun: How the Tobacco Industry Gets Away with Murder*, Philadelphia: George F. Stickley, 1984, p. ix.
4. Barry J. Ford, *Smokescreen: A Guide to the Personal Risks and Global Effects of the Cigarette Habit*, North Perth, Australia: Halcyon Press, 1994, p. 30.
5. U.S. Census Bureau, *Historical Statistics of the United States, Colonial Times to 1970*, 1975, p. 55. *Statistical Abstract of the United States*, 114 (1994), p. 87.
6. Ford, *Smokescreen*, p. 30. "Mortality Trends for Selected Smoking-Related Cancers and Breast Cancers—United States, 1950–1990," *Morbidity and Mortality Weekly Report*, November 12, 1993, pp. 857–866.
7. Alton Ochsner et al., "Bronchogenic Carcinoma: Its Frequency, Diagnosis, and Early Treatment," *Journal of the American Medical Association*, 148:9 (March 1, 1952), pp. 691–697.
8. Raymond Pearl, "Tobacco Smoking and Longevity," *Science*, 87 (1938), pp. 216–217.
9. Quoted in C. Barr Taylor and Joel D. Killen, *The Facts About Smoking*, Yonkers, N.Y.: Consumer Reports Books, 1991, p. 10.
10. Robert H. Feldt, "The Truth About Tobacco," *American Mercury*, September 1943, pp. 272–278.
11. U.S. Centers for Disease Control and Prevention, "Total and Per Capita Manufactured Cigarette Consumption," January 10, 1994.
12. U.S. Centers for Disease Control and Prevention, "Smoking Prevalence Among U.S. Adults," April 24, 1996.
13. Ernst L. Wynder and Evarts A. Graham, "Tobacco Smoke as a Possible Etiologic Factor in Bronchiogenic Carcinoma: A Study of Six Hundred and Eighty-Four Proved Cases," *Journal of the American Medical Association*, 143 (May 27, 1950), pp. 329–336. The study was supported by the American Cancer Society.
14. "Smoke Cloud Obscures Bad Effect of Smoking," *New York Times*, October 25, 1951, p. 35.
15. Richard Doll and A. Bradford Hill, "A Study of the Aetiology of Carcinoma of the Lung," *British Medical Journal*, December 13, 1952, pp. 1271–1286.
16. "Deadly Weed?" *New York Times*, December 13, 1953, p. D2.
17. "Lung Cancer Rise Is Laid to Smoking," *New York Times*, December 9, 1953, p. 16.
18. Lawrence E. Davies, "Cigarettes Found to Raise Death Rate in Men 50 to 70," *New York Times*, June 22, 1954, p. 1.

19. "Cancer Aide Testifies," *New York Times,* April 30, 1953, p. 34.

20. "TV: Cigarettes and Cancer," *New York Times,* June 1, 1955, p. 67.

21. "Cigarette Concern Scouts Cancer Link," *New York Times,* November 27, 1953, p. 29.

22. *Life,* September 26, 1949.

23. *Life,* December 1, 1952.

24. "Cigarette Concern Scouts Cancer Link," *New York Times,* November 27, 1953, p. 29.

25. "Tobacco Industry, Upset by Link to Cancer, Starts Own Research," *New York Times,* January 4, 1954, p. 1.

26. Quoted in Larry C. White, *Merchants of Death: The American Tobacco Industry,* New York: Beech Tree Books, 1988, pp. 32–33.

27. Jon Cohen, "Tobacco Money Lights Up a Debate," *Science,* 272 (April 26, 1996), pp. 488–494.

28. Alix M. Freedman and Laurie P. Cohen, "How Cigarette Makers Keep Health Question 'Open' Year After Year," *Wall Street Journal,* February 11, 1993, p. A1.

29. "AMA Report Hits Smoking," *Washington Post,* August 6, 1978, p. A9.

30. Stanton A. Glantz et al., *The Cigarette Papers,* Berkeley: University of California Press, 1996, p. 25.

31. *Life,* December 7, 1951, p. 54.

32. White, *Merchants of Death,* p. 35.

33. Jordan Goodman, *Tobacco in History: The Cultures of Dependence,* New York: Routledge, 1993, pp. 109–110.

34. *Life,* December 7, 1957, p. 137.

35. "Industry to Make Cigarette Report," *New York Times,* March 31, 1954, p. 55.

36. White, *Merchants of Death,* p. 188.

37. U.S. Department of Health and Human Services, *Reducing the Health Consequences of Smoking: 25 Years of Progress/A Report of the Surgeon General,* U.S. Public Health Service, Centers for Disease Control, Office on Smoking and Health, 1989, pp. 5–6.

38. "State Cigarette Use Rises After Decline," *New York Times,* April 9, 1964, p. 1.

39. U.S. Centers for Disease Control and Prevention, "Total and Per Capita Manufactured Cigarette Consumption," January 10, 1994 and "Smoking Prevalence Among U.S. Adults," April 24, 1996.

40. Testimony before the House Subcommittee on Health and the Environment, April 14, 1994.

41. "Attorney General/Tobacco Industry Settlement," June 20, 1997, pp. 1, 9.

42. Barry Meier, "Chief of R. J. Reynolds Says Smoking Has Role in Cancer," *New York Times,* August 23, 1997, p. A7.

43. Interview with Michael York, October 11, 1995. Elizabeth Gleick, "Tobacco Blues," *Time,* March 11, 1996, p. 54.

44. *Talk Back Live,* CNN, May 6, 1997.

45. HHS, *Reducing the Health Consequences of Smoking,* pp. 150–151, 153.

46. Ibid., pp. 158–161.

47. "Cigarette Smoking-Attributable Mortality and Years of Potential Life Lost—

United States, 1990," *Morbidity and Mortality Weekly Report*, August 27, 1993, pp. 645–652.

48. Whelan, *A Smoking Gun*, pp. xiii–xiv (italics removed).

49. White, *Merchants of Death*, pp. 17, 240.

50. Louis Sullivan, "An Opportunity to Oppose: Physicians' Role in the Campaign Against Tobacco," *Journal of the American Medical Association*, 264:12 (September 26, 1990), pp. 1581–1582.

51. William H. Foege, "The Growing Brown Plague," *Journal of the American Medical Association*, 264:12 (September 26, 1990), p. 1580.

52. R. T. Ravenholt, "Tobacco's Impact on Twentieth-Century U.S. Mortality Patterns," *American Journal of Preventive Medicine*, 1 (1985), pp. 4–17.

53. David Cox et al., "Estimation of Risk from Observations of Humans," in *Risk: Analysis, Perception, and Management*, London: The Royal Society, pp. 67–87.

54. Theodor Sterling et al., "Risk Attribution and Tobacco-Related Deaths," *American Journal of Epidemiology*, 138:2 (1993), pp. 128–139. The paper notes that the authors "have in the past received support from Tobacco Industry sources."

55. Richard D. Lyons, "Califano in Drive to End Smoking; Calls Habit 'Slow-Motion Suicide,'" *New York Times*, January 12, 1978, p. A12.

56. Joseph A. Califano Jr., *Governing America: An Insider's Report from the Cabinet and the White House*, New York: Simon & Schuster, 1981, p. 182.

57. Lyons, "Califano in Drive to End Smoking," p. A12.

58. Blythe Babyak, "Califano's Cigarette Campaign: All Smoke and No Fire," *Washington Monthly*, July/August 1978, pp. 32–36.

59. Edward B. Black, "Rx for Califano," *New York Times*, May 7, 1978, p. IV-22.

60. Califano, *Governing America*, p. 187. Tom Mathews, "Crusading at HEW," *Newsweek*, May 29, 1978, p. 23.

61. Terence Smith, "Carter Replaces Bell, Blumenthal, Califano; Miller Goes to Treasury," *New York Times*, July 20, 1979, p. A1.

62. Fred Barbash, "A Delighted President Goes Politicking," *Washington Post*, August 6, 1978, p. A1.

63. Matthews, "Crusading at HEW," p. 23. Eliot Marshall, "Califano Exits HEW in Classic Form," *Science*, 205:17 (August 1979), p. 669.

64. C. Everett Koop, "A Smoke-Free Society by the Year 2000," *New York State Journal of Medicine*, July 1985, pp. 290–292.

65. Irvin Molotsky, "Q&A: Dr. C. Everett Koop, Surgeon General," *New York Times*, December 13, 1985, p. B10.

66. C. Everett Koop, "Non-Smokers: Time to Clear the Air," *Reader's Digest*, April 1987, pp. 110–113. C. Everett Koop, *Koop: The Memoirs of America's Family Doctor*, New York: Random House, 1991, p. 180.

67. "Pursuing the Smoke-Free Dream," *New York Times*, September 28, 1984, p. A30.

68. "Surgeon General Nominee to Target Smoking, AIDS, Drugs & Alcohol," *Alcoholism & Drug Abuse Week*, February 14, 1990, p. 7. (Antonia Novello "pledged to maintain the momentum toward a 'smoke-free society,'" noting "some progress in this effort" but expressing concern that smoking was declining more slowly

among women than among men.) "Survey of Smoking-Prevention Efforts in Elementary Schools—Washington State, 1989," *Morbidity and Mortality Weekly Report,* November 9, 1990, p. 801. ("To achieve the Surgeon General's challenge of a smoke-free society by the year 2000, the initiation of smoking must be prevented in school-age children.")

69. White, *Merchants of Death,* p. 11.
70. Carol Wallace, "C. Everett Koop," *People,* April 21, 1986, p. 91.
71. Koop, *Koop: The Memoirs of America's Family Doctor,* p. 149.
72. Ibid., p. 165.
73. Wallace, "C. Everett Koop," p. 91.
74. Carl L. Anderson et al., *Community Health,* 3rd ed., St. Louis: Mosby, 1978, p. 173.
75. C. Everett Koop, testimony before the House Subcommittee on Health and the Environment, August 1, 1986.
76. R. T. Ravenholt, "Tobacco's Global Death March," *Population and Development Review,* 16 (1990), pp. 213–240.
77. Carl E. Bartecchi et al., "The Global Tobacco Epidemic," *Scientific American,* May 1995, pp. 44–51.
78. Albert H. Buck, ed., *A Treatise on Hygiene and Public Health,* New York: Arno Press, 1977 (originally published 1879), pp. 3–4.
79. Jack Smolensky, *Principles of Community Health,* Philadelphia: W. B. Saunders, 1977, p. iii.
80. Daniel M. Wilner et al., *Introduction to Public Health,* New York: Macmillan, 1978, pp. 5–6 (italics in original).
81. *Journal of the American Public Health Association,* 1 (1911), pp. 4, 102, 282, 293.
82. *American Journal of Public Health,* 85 (1995), pp. 67, 96, 145, 921.
83. Buck, *A Treatise on Hygiene and Public Health,* p. 269.
84. Elizabeth W. Etheridge, *Sentinel for Health: A History of the Centers for Disease Control,* Berkeley: University of California Press, 1992, p. 282.
85. U.S. Department of Health, Education, and Welfare, *Healthy People: The Surgeon General's Report on Health Promotion and Disease Prevention,* U.S. Public Health Service, 1979, p. 1-9.
86. Ibid., p. 11-22.
87. Ronald J. Troyer and Gerald E. Markle, *Cigarettes: The Battle over Smoking,* New Brunswick, N.J.: Rutgers University Press, 1983, p. 73.
88. Allan M. Brandt, "The Cigarette, Risk, and American Culture," *Daedalus,* Fall 1990, pp. 155–176.
89. Whelan, *A Smoking Gun,* p. ix.
90. Jane E. Brody, "Smoking Foe Sees Anti-Cigarette Trend," *New York Times,* April 7, 1971, p. 24.
91. HHS, *Reducing the Health Consequences of Smoking,* pp. 179–204. The 1985 figures are from the National Health Interview Survey. In 1987—when the questions were preceded by the doubt-inducing statement, "People have differing beliefs about the relationship between smoking and health"—the survey yielded less agreement: 89, 77, and 77 percent, respectively.

92. Correspondence with Kenneth Warner, February 11, 1996.

93. Elizabeth Whelan, "The Tobacco Cartel's Most Valuable Asset: Societal Complacency," *Priorities*, 7:2 (1995), pp. 4–5.

94. W. Kip Viscusi, *Smoking: Making the Risky Decision*, New York: Oxford University Press, 1992, pp. 61–78.

95. HHS, *Reducing the Health Consequences of Smoking*, p. 11.

96. Viscusi, *Smoking: Making the Risky Decision*, pp. 79–81.

97. Koop, "A Smoke-Free Society by the Year 2000," p. 290.

98. "Public Health Focus: Effectiveness of Smoking-Control Strategies," *Morbidity and Mortality Weekly Report*, September 4, 1992, pp. 645–653.

99. U.S. Department of Health and Human Services, *The Health Consequences of Smoking: Nicotine Addiction: A Report of the Surgeon General*, U.S. Public Health Service, Centers for Disease Control, Office on Smoking and Health, 1988, p. 466.

100. Richard Klein, *Cigarettes Are Sublime*, Durham, N.C.: Duke University Press, 1993, p. ix.

101. Egon C. Corti, *A History of Smoking*, London: George G. Harrap & Co., 1931, pp. 41–42.

102. Interview with Elizabeth Whelan, October 12, 1995.

103. HHS, *Reducing the Health Consequences of Smoking*, p. v.

104. Richard Peto et al., *Mortality from Smoking in Developed Countries, 1950–2000: Indirect Estimates from National Vital Statistics*, New York: Oxford University Press, 1994.

105. "Cigarette Smoking-Attributable Mortality and Years of Potential Life Lost—United States, 1990," *Morbidity and Mortality Weekly Report*, August 27, 1993, pp. 645–652.

106. In *The Costs of Poor Health Habits* (Cambridge, Mass.: Harvard University Press, 1991), Willard G. Manning and his colleagues at the RAND Corporation estimate that smoking "reduces the life expectancy of a 20-year-old by about 4.3 years," which is near the midpoint of this range.

107. HHS, *The Health Consequences of Smoking: Nicotine Addiction*, p. i.

108. U.S. Federal Trade Commission, *Federal Trade Commission Report to Congress for 1993*, 1995, pp. 21–23.

109. Whelan, *A Smoking Gun*, p. 95.

110. John H. Allan, "Tobacco Institute Says Report 'Is Not Final Chapter' in Debate Over Health Issue," *New York Times*, January 12, 1964, p. 66.

111. Gio B. Gori, "Low-Risk Cigarettes: A Prescription," *Science*, 194 (1976), pp. 1243–1246.

112. Gio B. Gori and Cornelius J. Lynch, "Toward Less Hazardous Cigarettes: Current Advances," *Journal of the American Medical Association*, 240:12 (September 12, 1978), pp. 1255–1259.

113. Greg Otolski, "Cigarette Firms Found Unlikely Ally in Adversary," (Louisville) *Courier-Journal*, August 11, 1994, p. A1.

114. Victor Cohn, "Some Cigarettes Now 'Tolerable,' Doctor Says," *Washington Post*, August 10, 1978, p. A1 (italics added).

115. Victor Cohn, "Health Officials Challenge Report on Cigarette Use," *Washington Post,* August 11, 1978, p. A1 (all quotes but Richmond). Califano, *Governing America,* p. 193 (Richmond quote).

116. E. Cuyler Hammond, "Matched Groups Analysis Method," *National Cancer Institute Monographs,* 67 (1985), pp. 157–160.

117. Oscar Auerbach et al., "Changes in Bronchial Epithelium in Relation to Cigarette Smoking, 1955–1960 vs. 1970–1977," *New England Journal of Medicine,* 300:8 (February 22, 1979), pp. 381–386.

118. HHS, *Reducing the Health Consequences of Smoking,* p. 183.

119. G. H. Miller, "The 'Less Hazardous' Cigarette: A Deadly Delusion," *New York State Journal of Medicine,* July 1985, pp. 313–317.

120. See, e.g., Neal J. Benowitz et al., "Smokers of Low-Yield Cigarettes Do Not Consume Less Nicotine," *New England Journal of Medicine,* 309 (1983), pp. 139–142. The study was supported by grants from the National Institute on Drug Abuse.

121. Alison Stephen et al., "Estimating the Extent of Compensatory Smoking," in N. Wald and P. Froggatt, eds., *Nicotine, Smoking and the Low Tar Programme,* New York: Oxford University Press, 1989, pp. 100–115.

122. Miller, "The 'Less Hazardous' Cigarette," pp. 316–317.

123. "Attorney General/Tobacco Industry Settlement," June 20, 1997, p. 14.

124. Philip J. Hilts, "Little Smoke, Little Tar, but Full Dose of Nicotine," *New York Times,* November 27, 1994, p. 1.

125. Don Colburn, " 'Cleaner,' But Is It Safer?" *Washington Post,* September 6, 1988, p. Z6.

126. Ibid.

127. Malcolm Gladwell, " 'Smokeless' Cigarette Shows Tobacco Industry Dilemma," *Washington Post,* March 2, 1989, p. E1.

128. John Slade, "Re-Inventing the Cigarette: Innovation in the Cigarette Industry," *Priorities,* Summer 1990, pp. 5–9.

129. HHS, *Reducing the Health Consequences of Smoking,* p. 134.

130. E. Cuyler Hammond and Daniel Horn, "Smoking and Death Rates: Report on Forty-Four Months of Follow-up of 187,783 Men," *Journal of the American Medical Association,* 166 (1958), pp. 1294–1308.

131. E. Cuyler Hammond, "Smoking in Relation to Mortality and Morbidity: Findings in First Thirty-Four Months of Follow-Up in a Prospective Study Started in 1959," *Journal of the National Cancer Institute,* 32 (1964), pp. 1161–1188.

132. Edward M. Brecher et al., *Licit and Illicit Drugs,* Boston: Little, Brown & Co., 1972, p. 241.

133. Barry Stimmel et al., *The Facts About Drug Use,* Yonkers, N.Y.: Consumer Reports Books, 1991, p. 218.

134. Sheryl Gay Stolberg, "Cigar Fad Reported to Be Recruiting Legions of Teen-Agers," *New York Times,* May 23, 1997, p. A24.

135. Brecher et al., *Licit and Illicit Drugs,* pp. 241–242.

136. Stimmel et al., *The Facts About Drug Use,* pp. 216–218.

137. U.S. Department of Health and Human Services, *The Health Consequences of*

Using Smokeless Tobacco: A Report of the Advisory Committee to the Surgeon General, U.S. Public Health Service, 1986.

138. Brad Rodu, *For Smokers Only: How Smokeless Tobacco Can Save Your Life,* New York: Sulzburger & Graham, 1995, pp. 130–131 (italics removed).

139. Ibid., pp. 133, 10 (italics in original).

140. Jay Reeves, "Researcher Drawing Fire for Smokeless-Tobacco Theories," *State* (Columbia, S.C.), p. B5. Connolly has recommended heavier taxation of smokeless tobacco, not only to discourage adolescent use but also to deter smokers from switching. See "Taxing Other Tobacco Products" in *World Smoking and Health,* 19:1 (1994), pp. 13–14.

141. Sample letter to the editor accompanying letter to AAOMS members from Barbara N. Moles, associate executive director of the organization, 1994.

142. Julie A. Jacob, "Smokeless Advice 'Irresponsible,'" *ADA News,* October 3, 1994, p. 18.

143. Ibid.

144. Interview with Brad Rodu, April 16, 1996.

145. In a November 14, 1994, letter to ADA official James Marshall, AAOMP president Bruce F. Barker said, "It is not the role of the AAOMP to make public statements in support of or in disagreement with any individual research that has been appropriately reviewed and approved by institutional review boards at universities or other research facilities."

146. Brad Rodu and Philip Cole, "Tobacco-Related Mortality," *Nature,* 370 (July 21, 1994), p. 184.

147. Draft statement from the NCI Press Office, July 19, 1994.

148. Letter from John R. Durant, vice president for health affairs at UAB, to Harold Varmus, director of the National Institutes of Health, July 22, 1994.

149. Letter from IRB chairman Russell Cunningham to J. Thomas Puglisi, chief of the Compliance Oversight Branch in the OPRR's Division of Human Subject Protections, September 1, 1994.

150. Interview with Rodu.

151. *Day One,* ABC, February 28, 1994.

152. Corti, *A History of Smoking,* p. 112.

Chapter 3. Coughing Cowboys

1. Fred Feretti, "Now That TV Has Given Up Smoking," *New York Times,* January 3, 1971, p. IV-3.

2. Ibid. Thomas Whiteside, "Annals of Advertising: Cutting Down," *New Yorker,* December 19, 1970, pp. 42–95.

3. John Kenneth Galbraith, *The Affluent Society,* Boston: Houghton Mifflin, 1984 (originally published in 1958), pp. 129–130, 232.

4. Vance Packard, *The Hidden Persuaders,* New York: David McKay, 1957.

5. *Capital Broadcasting Co. v. John Mitchell,* 333 F. Supp. 582 (1971).

6. Eileen Shanahan, "U.S. Plans Curbs on Cigarette Ads," *New York Times,* January 14, 1964, p. 1.

7. Peter Bart, "Cigarette Makers Adopt an Industry Code for Ads," *New York Times,* April 28, 1964, p. A1.

8. Edith Evans Asbury, "PTA Asks Curb on Cigarette TV Ads," *New York Times,* May 25, 1967, p. 95.

9. James E. Roper, "The Man Behind the Ban on Cigarette Commercials," *Reader's Digest,* March 1971, pp. 213–218.

10 Interview with John Banzhaf, February 23, 1996.

11 Ibid.

12. Eileen Shanahan, "Radio-TV Warnings on Smoking Ordered," *New York Times,* June 3, 1967, p. 1.

13. Interview with John Banzhaf.

14. Whiteside, "Annals of Advertising," p. 55.

15. John D. Morris, "Lawyer to Challenge Tobacco Industry," *New York Times,* March 24, 1969, p. 18.

16. Elizabeth B. Drew, "The Cigarette Companies Would Rather Fight Than Switch," *New York Times Magazine,* May 4, 1969, p. 131.

17. Whiteside, "Annals of Advertising," p. 50.

18. Interview with John Banzhaf.

19. Courtney Leatherman, "You Want Their Attention? Sue!" *Chronicle of Higher Education,* February 10, 1995, p. A5.

20. Robert E. Dallos, "Perry Mason's TV Foe, Dead of Cancer, Left Antismoking Film," *New York Times,* September 13, 1968, p. 55.

21. Kenneth E. Warner, "Clearing the Airwaves: The Cigarette Ad Ban Revisited," *Policy Analysis,* Fall 1979, pp. 435–450.

22. U.S. Centers for Disease Control and Prevention, "Total and Per Capita Manufactured Cigarette Consumption," January 10, 1994.

23. U.S. Centers for Disease Control and Prevention, "Smoking Prevalence Among U.S. Adults," April 24, 1996.

24. Warner, "Clearing the Airwaves," p. 438.

25. See, e.g., *National Broadcasting Co. v. United States,* 319 U.S. 190 (1942).

26. Interview with John Banzhaf.

27. John F. Banzhaf, "Ban on Smoking Ads," *New York Times,* July 21, 1969.

28. Warner, "Clearing the Airwaves," p. 435.

29. U.S. Federal Trade Commission, *Federal Trade Commission Report to Congress for 1993,* 1995, pp. 18–19.

30. "Cancer Unit Urges All Cigarette Ads in Nation Be Ended," *New York Times,* October 19, 1967, p. 94.

31. *Federal Register,* 61:168 (August 28, 1996), pp. 44616–44618.

32. *Coyne Beahm v. FDA, American Advertising Federation v. Kessler, U.S. Tobacco v. FDA,* and *National Association of Convenience Stores v. Kessler,* Memorandum Opinion, Judge William L. Osteen, U.S. District Court for the Middle District of North Carolina, April 25, 1997. "Attorney General/Tobacco Industry Settlement," June 20, 1997, pp. 8–9.

33. Larry C. White, *Merchants of Death: The American Tobacco Industry,* New York: Beech Tree Books, 1988, p. 159.

34. Interview with Elizabeth Whelan, October 12, 1995.

35. Ellen Goodman, "Tobacco Industry's Smoke Draws Her Fire," *Philadelphia Inquirer,* June 30, 1992, p. A11.

36. Secretary of Health and Human Services Louis Sullivan, quoted in John E. Gallagher, "Under Fire from All Sides," *Time,* March 5, 1990, p. 41.

37. Elizabeth M. Whelan, *A Smoking Gun: How the Tobacco Industry Gets Away with Murder,* Philadelphia: George F. Stickley Co., 1984, p. xvi.

38. White, *Merchants of Death,* pp. 17, 240.

39. Interview with Peggy Carter, February 1996.

40. Erik Brady, "The Face-Off: Free Ads vs. Fair Promotion," *USA Today,* March 28, 1990, p. A1.

41. Jason DeParle, "Warning: Sports Stars May Be Hazardous to Your Health," *Washington Monthly,* September 1989, pp. 34–49.

42. Ben Wildavsky, "Tilting at Billboards," *New Republic,* August 20 & 27, 1990, pp. 19–20.

43. Bob Secter, "Billboard Battle: Priest Pleads Moral Right to Deface Ads," *Los Angeles Times,* August 16, 1990, p. A5.

44. Jacob Sullum, "Smoke and Mirrors," *Reason,* February 1991, p. 30.

45. Wildavsky, "Tilting at Billboards," p. 20.

46. Jordan Goodman, *Tobacco in History: The Cultures of Dependence,* New York: Routledge, 1993, p. 100.

47. Courtland Milloy, "Tobacco-Touting Cartoons," *Washington Post,* May 9, 1991, p. C3.

48. According to data from the Monitoring the Future project at the University of Michigan, the share of high school seniors who had smoked daily in the previous month dropped from 18.7 percent in 1987 to 17.2 percent in 1992. In the National Household Survey on Drug Abuse, the share of 12-to-17-year-olds who had smoked cigarettes at all in the previous month dropped from 22.7 percent in 1988 to 18.4 percent in 1992.

49. Dissent of Commissioner Roscoe B. Starek III, quoted in an FTC press release, May 28, 1997.

50. Paul M. Fischer et al., "Brand Logo Recognition by Children Aged 3 to 6 Years," *Journal of the American Medical Association,* 266:22 (December 11, 1991), pp. 3145–3148. The study was supported by grants from Doctors Ought to Care and the American Cancer Society.

51. Richard Mizerski, "The Relationship Between Cartoon Trade Character Recognition and Attitude Toward Product Category in Young Children," *Journal of Marketing,* 59:4 (Fall 1995), p. 58. The research was funded by R. J. Reynolds.

52. Joseph R. DiFranza et al., "RJR Nabisco's Cartoon Camel Promotes Camel Cigarettes to Children," *Journal of the American Medical Association,* 255:22 (December 11, 1991), pp. 3149–3153. The study was supported by grants from the University of Massachusetts Medical Center, the Massachusetts chapter of the American Cancer Society, and Doctors Ought to Care.

53. The comparison is problematic in any case. The pre-1989 surveys were drawn

from different populations, and the samples included seventh- and eighth-graders as well as high school students.

54. "Changes in the Cigarette Brand Preferences of Adolescent Smokers—United States, 1989–1993," *Morbidity and Mortality Weekly Report,* 43:32 (August 19, 1994), pp. 577–581.

55. Among males, 25 percent of the 12-to-17-year-olds preferred Camels, compared to 13 percent of 18-to-24-year-olds. Among females, the shares were 22 percent and 6 percent, respectively.

56. John P. Pierce et al., "Does Tobacco Advertising Target Young People to Start Smoking?: Evidence from California," *Journal of the American Medical Association,* 266:22 (December 11, 1991), pp. 3154–3158. The study was funded by the Tobacco Control Section of the California Department of Health Services. The comparison of the U.S. and California data is questionable, since the two surveys involved different populations and brand preferences are known to vary from one region to another.

57. Doug Levy, "Philip Morris Polled Teens in Early '70s," *USA Today,* November 22, 1996, p. B1.

58. *Peter Jennings Reporting,* ABC, June 20, 1996.

59. Fischer et al., "Brand Logo Recognition by Children," p. 3145.

60. DiFranza et al., "RJR Nabisco's Cartoon Camel," p. 3152.

61. Pierce et al., "Does Tobacco Advertising Target Young People," p. 3154.

62. Claude R. Martin Jr., "Ethical Advertising Research Standards: Three Case Studies," *Journal of Advertising,* 23:3 (September 1994), p. 17.

63. Joe B. Tye et al., "Tobacco Advertising and Consumption: Evidence of a Causal Relationship," *Journal of Public Health Policy,* Winter 1987, pp. 492–508.

64. Correspondence with Peggy Carter, February 9, 1996.

65. Gerard B. Hastings et al., "Children, Smoking, and Advertising: The Evidence Is There for Those Who Wish to See It," *International Journal of Advertising,* 13:2 (March 1994), p. 195.

66. Michael Schudson, "Symbols and Smokers: Advertising, Health Messages, and Public Policy," in Robert L. Rabin and Stephen D. Sugarman, eds., *Smoking Policy: Law, Politics, and Culture,* New York: Oxford University Press, 1993, p. 211.

67. Ibid., p. 213.

68. Nicola Evans et al., "Influence of Tobacco Marketing and Exposure to Smokers on Adolescent Susceptibility to Smoking," *Journal of the National Cancer Institute,* 87:20 (October 18, 1995), pp. 1538–1545. The research was supported in part by the California Department of Health Services, the Robert Wood Johnson Foundation, and the American Heart Association.

69. Philip J. Hilts, "Ads Linked to Smoking by Children," *New York Times,* October 18, 1995, p. B9.

70. Delores King, "Studies Link Tobacco Marketing to Smoking Among the Young," *Boston Globe,* October 18, 1995, p. 10.

71. Associated Press, "Cigarette Ads Strongest Influence on Young Smokers, Study Reports," *Charleston* (W. Va.) *Gazette,* October 18, 1995, p. A11.

72. Sullum, "Smoke and Mirrors," p. 31.

73. U.S. Department of Health and Human Services, *Reducing the Health Conse-quences of Smoking: 25 Years of Progress/A Report of the Surgeon General,* U.S. Pub-lic Health Service, Centers for Disease Control, Office on Smoking and Health, 1989, pp. 516–517.

74. U.S. Department of Health and Human Services, *Preventing Tobacco Use Among Young People: A Report of the Surgeon General,* U.S. Public Health Service, Centers for Disease Control and Prevention, Office on Smoking and Health, 1994, p. 188.

75. HHS, *Reducing the Health Consequences of Smoking,* p. 517.

76. HHS, *Preventing Tobacco Use Among Young People,* p. 195.

77. Schudson, "Symbols and Smokers," pp. 209, 217, 221.

78. Interview with Elizabeth Whelan.

79. See, e.g., Kenneth E. Warner et al., "Cigarette Advertising and Coverage of the Hazards of Smoking: A Statistical Analysis," *New England Journal of Medicine,* 326:5 (January 30, 1992), pp. 305–309, and Larry White and Elizabeth M. Whe-lan, "How Well Do American Magazines Cover the Health Hazards of Smok-ing?," *ACSH News and Views,* May/June 1986.

80. Jean J. Boddewyn, "Cigarette Advertising Bans and Smoking: The Flawed Policy Connection," *International Journal of Advertising,* 13:4 (1994), pp. 311–332.

81. White, *Merchants of Death,* p. 170.

82. Amitai Etzioni, "Has the ACLU Lost Its Mind?" *Washington Monthly,* October 1994, pp. 9–11.

83. 316 U.S. 52 (1942).

84. 425 U.S. 748 (1976).

85. 447 U.S. 557 (1980).

86. 478 U.S. 328 (1986).

87. "Should Cigarette Ads Be Outlawed?," *New York Times,* February 22, 1987, p. E9.

88. *City of Cincinnati v. Discovery Network,* 113 S.Ct. 1505 (1993).

89. *Robert E. Rubin v. Coors Brewing Co.,* 114 S.Ct. 2671 (1995).

90. *44 Liquormart v. Rhode Island,* #94–1140 (1996). In 1997, on the other hand, the Court declined to hear a challenge to Baltimore's bans on alcohol and cigarette billboards in residential neighborhoods.

91. Alex Kozinski and Stuart Banner, "Who's Afraid of Commercial Speech?" *Virginia Law Review,* 76:4 (May 1990), pp. 627–653.

92. Two of these ads used articles I had written for the *Wall Street Journal* and *Forbes MediaCritic.* See Author's Note.

93. Floyd Abrams, "R. J. Reynolds vs. the Government: A Chilling Effect on Corpo-rate Speech," *New York Times,* July 6, 1986, p. III-2.

94. J. B. Wilkinson et al., "Reader Categorization of a Controversial Communication: Advertisement Versus Editorial," *Journal of Public Policy & Marketing,* 14:2 (Fall 1995), p. 245.

95. *Capital Broadcasting v. Mitchell,* 333 F. Supp. 582 (1971).

96. John C. Luik, "Tobacco Advertising Bans and the Dark Face of Government Pater-nalism," *International Journal of Advertising,* 12:4 (September 22, 1993), p. 303.

97. G. Pierre Goad, "Canada's Tobacco-Ad Ban Is Overturned by Judge," *Wall Street Journal,* July 29, 1991, p. B1. In 1996 the Canadian Parliament tried again, approving severe restrictions on advertising that stopped short of a complete ban.

98. *Red Lion Broadcasting v. FCC,* 395 U.S. 367 (1969).

99. Brian R. Flay, "Mass Media and Smoking Cessation: A Critical Review," *American Journal of Public Health,* 77:2 (February 1987), pp. 153–160.

100. Ahron Leichtman, "The Top Ten Ways to Attack the Tobacco Industry and Win the War Against Smoking," *Saint Louis University Public Law Review,* 13:2 (1994), pp. 729–747.

101. *Miami Herald Publishing Co. v. Tornillo,* 418 U.S. 241 (1974).

102. Dennis L. Breo, "Kicking Butts," *Journal of the American Medical Association,* 270:16 (October 27, 1993), p. 1978. Interview with Alan Blum, May 14, 1996.

103. Breo, "Kicking Butts."

104. California Board of Equalization and U.S Department of Agriculture. The California data are reported by fiscal year. For 1988, I averaged the figures for 1987–88 and 1988–89; for 1994, I averaged the figures for 1993–94 and 1994–95.

105. These figures, from the California Board of Equalization, are for total taxable purchases.

106. Andrea Adelson, "Is Anybody Getting the Picture?" *New York Times,* July 17, 1997, p. B1.

107. Paul Jacobs, "Some TV Stations Drop Anti-Smoking Ad," *Los Angeles Times,* October 14, 1994, p. B4.

108. California Department of Health Services press release, March 20, 1997.

109. Lori Dorfman and Lawrence Wallack, "Advertising Health: The Case for Counter-Ads," *Public Health Reports,* 108:6 (November 1993), p. 716.

110. Mike Brown, "Smoking's New Opponent Is Armed with Big Budget," (Louisville) *Courier-Journal,* December 30, 1996, p. A1. John Schwartz, "Group Targets Tobacco Use Among Youth," *Washington Post,* February 12, 1996, p. A17.

111. Dorfman and Wallack, "Advertising Health."

Chapter 4. Vice Charge

1. U.S. Centers for Disease Control and Prevention, "Total and Per Capita Manufactured Cigarette Consumption," January 10, 1994.

2. Jonathan Fuerbringer, "Reagan Said to Shift in Favor of 16 Cent Cigarette Tax," *New York Times,* January 28, 1986, p. A12 (revenue estimate).

3. David A. Stockman, *The Triumph of Politics: How the Reagan Revolution Failed,* New York: Harper & Row, 1986, p. 356.

4. Kenneth E. Warner, "Cigarette Taxation: Doing Good by Doing Well," *Journal of Public Health Policy,* September 1984, pp. 312–319.

5. Michael F. Jacobson, "Raise the Taxes on Alcohol and Tobacco," *Christian Science Monitor,* February 16, 1982, p. 26.

6. Ellen Goodman, "This Tax Saves Lives," *Washington Post,* September 17, 1985, p. A23.

7. "Make Smokers Pay the Price," *New York Times,* July 30, 1986, p. A22.

8. Stockman, *The Triumph of Politics,* p. 346.

9. Judith Egerton, "Tax-Increase Idea Riles Liquor, Tobacco Interests," Louisville *Courier-Journal,* November 30, 1989, p. B12.

10. Mary McGrory, "Darman's Honeymoon Hearing," *Washington Post,* January 22, 1989, p. D1.

11. Egerton, "Tax-Increase Idea."

12. Dan Balz and John E. Yang, "Bush Abandons Campaign Pledge, Calls for New Taxes," *Washington Post,* June 27, 1990, p. A1.

13. Mike Brown, "Budget Cutters Plan to Boost Cigarette Tax," Louisville *Courier-Journal,* September 20, 1990, p. A1. Susan F. Rasky, "Accord to Reduce Spending and Raise Taxes Is Reached," *New York Times,* October 1, 1990, p. A1.

14. Richard McGowan, *Business, Politics, and Cigarettes: Multiple Levels, Multiple Agendas,* Westport, Conn.: Quorum Books, 1995, p. 11.

15. "5-Cent Rise Asked in Cigarette Tax," *New York Times,* January 8, 1964, p. A14.

16. Jacobson, "Raise the Taxes on Alcohol and Tobacco."

17. "Raise Cigarette Prices, Save Lives," *New York Times,* August 28, 1989.

18. Viveca Novak, "Kicking the Habits," *National Journal,* April 17, 1993, p. 912.

19. Michael Wines, "Rally in Capital Protests Rise in Smoking Tax," *New York Times,* March 10, 1994, p. A8.

20. Andrew Mollison and Jeff Nesmith, "Tobacco Industry Fighting for Its Life," *Atlanta Journal and Constitution,* June 11, 1994, p. A12.

21. Ronald Smothers, "Tobacco Country Is Quaking Over Cigarette Tax Proposal," *New York Times,* March 22, 1993, p. A1.

22. The Tobacco Institute, *The Tax Burden on Tobacco: Historical Compilation, Volume 31, 1996,* Washington, D.C.: The Tobacco Institute, 1997, p. 9.

23. Ibid., p. 9.

24. Ibid., pp. vii–viii. In addition to the state and federal governments, hundreds of counties and municipalities tax cigarettes, and many jurisdictions impose general sales taxes as well.

25. Since 1990 the money has been channeled into the general fund.

26. In 1993 the California legislature increased the tax by another two cents a pack to pay for breast cancer research and detection.

27. "Tobacco Industry Fights Anti-Smoking Tax Plan," *New York Times,* October 25, 1992, p. A21. Jonathan Sidener, "Millions Spent to Fight Tobacco Tax," *Arizona Republic,* October 15, 1994, p. A1.

28. John Schmeltzer, "Foundation Gives Cash to Raise Tobacco Taxes," *Salt Lake Tribune,* August 16, 1994, p. D5.

29. The Tobacco Institute.

30. David Kay Johnston, "Anti-Tobacco Groups Push for Higher Cigarette Taxes," *New York Times,* April 3, 1997, p. A18.

31 California Board of Equalization and CDC (1994). The comparison between 1988 and 1989 somewhat overstates the impact of the tax hike, since smokers stocked up before the increase took effect and some probably started buying out-of-state or black-market cigarettes afterward.

32. McGowan, *Business, Politics, and Cigarettes*, pp. 84–86.

33. W. Kip Viscusi, *Smoking: Making the Risky Decision*, New York: Oxford University Press, 1992, pp. 101–109.

34. U.S. Department of Health and Human Services, *Smoking and Health in the Americas: A 1992 Report of the Surgeon General*, U.S. Public Health Service, Centers for Disease Control, Office on Smoking and Health, 1992, pp. 129–131.

35. Quoted in Goodman, "This Tax Saves Lives."

36. Testimony of Lynne D. Richardson before the House Ways and Means Committee, November 19, 1993.

37. Judith Egerton, "Tobacco Industry Braces for Impact If Tax Rises," Louisville *Courier-Journal*, May 27, 1990, p. E1.

38. Kenneth J. Garcia, "In Effect Tomorrow, Cigarette Tax Sparks Rush to Stock Up," *Los Angeles Times*, December 31, 1988, p. A1.

39. Greg Otolski, "Farm Bureau Leads Kentucky Attack on Tobacco Taxes," Louisville *Courier-Journal*, September 24, 1993, p. D10.

40. W. Kip Viscusi, "Cigarette Taxation and the Social Consequences of Smoking," National Bureau of Economic Research, Working Paper #4891, October 1994, pp. 11–14.

41. Warner, "Cigarette Taxation," p. 315.

42. J. Paul Leigh, "Cigarette Taxes—Regressive or Progressive?" *Western Journal of Medicine*, 150:4 (April 1989), p. 467.

43. Quoted in Goodman, "This Tax Saves Lives."

44. Jane G. Gravelle and Dennis Zimmerman, *Cigarette Taxes to Fund Health Care Reform: An Economic Analysis*, Congressional Research Service, 1994, p. iii.

45. Quoted in Goodman, "This Tax Saves Lives."

46. Jack Nicholl, "Perspective on Smoking: Bans Alone Won't Win the War," *Los Angeles Times*, June 25, 1993, p. B7.

47. Coalition on Smoking or Health, "Saving Lives and Raising Revenue: The Case for Major State and Federal Tobacco Tax Increases," February 1995, p. 7.

48. Interview with Elizabeth Whelan, October 12, 1995.

49. Interview with John Banzhaf, February 23, 1996.

50. Interview with Elizabeth Whelan.

51. Richard W. Ault et al., "Smoking and Absenteeism," *Applied Economics*, 23 (1991), 743–754.

52. J. Paul Leigh, "Smoking, Self-Selection, and Absenteeism," *Quarterly Review of Economics and Finance*, 35:4 (December 22, 1995), p. 365. The study was supported by a grant from the Tobacco-Related Disease Research Program at the University of California, Berkeley.

53. Thomas C. Schelling, "Economics and Cigarettes," *Preventive Medicine*, 15 (1986), pp. 549–560.

54. Barbara C. Lippiatt, "Measuring Medical Cost and Life Expectancy Impacts of Changes in Cigarette Sales," *Preventive Medicine*, 19:5 (September 1990), pp. 515–532.

55. Thomas A. Hodgson, "Cigarette Smoking and Lifetime Medical Expenditures," *Milbank Quarterly*, 76:1 (1992), pp. 81–125.

56. Jan J. Barendregt et al., "The Health Care Costs of Smoking," *New England Journal of Medicine,* 337:15 (October 9, 1997), pp. 1052–1057. The study was supported by the Dutch Ministry of Health.

57. Coalition on Smoking or Health, "Saving Lives and Raising Revenue," pp. 8–9.

58. OTA assistant director Clyde Behney and senior analyst Maria Hewitt, testimony before the House Ways and Means Committee, November 18, 1993.

59. Coalition on Smoking or Health, "Saving Lives and Raising Revenue," p. 8.

60. Behney and Hewitt testimony before the House Ways and Means Committee.

61. The discount rate represents the time value of money, the fact that $100 today is worth more than the promise of $100 a year from now (even without inflation), because $100 today can be invested for a year longer. When future savings (e.g., lower Social Security outlays) are compared to current costs (e.g., treatment of smoking-related diseases), they have to be discounted.

62. Willard G. Manning et al., "The Taxes of Sin: Do Smokers and Drinkers Pay Their Way?" *Journal of the American Medical Association,* 261:11 (March 17, 1989), pp. 1604–1609.

63. The Tobacco Institute, *The Tax Burden on Tobacco,* p. 113.

64. The Tobacco Institute, *The Tax Burden on Tobacco,* p. 124. To update medical and nursing-home costs, the CRS used the medical services price index, which is higher than the consumer price index.

65. Gravelle and Zimmerman, *Cigarette Taxes to Fund Health Care Reform,* pp. 5, 7, 9.

66. Viscusi, "Cigarette Taxation and the Social Consequences of Smoking," pp. 31–33, 47, 49.

67. John H. Knowles, "The Struggle to Stay Healthy," *Time,* August 9, 1976, pp. 60–62.

68. John H. Knowles, "The Responsibility of the Individual," *Daedalus,* Winter 1977, pp. 57–80.

69. Gravelle and Zimmerman, *Cigarette Taxes to Fund Health Care Reform,* p. 32.

70. Jeffrey E. Harris, testimony before the House Ways and Means Committee, November 18, 1993.

71. James I, *A Counterblaste to Tobacco,* London: English Reprints, 1870 (originally published in 1604), p. 110.

72. Harris, testimony before the House Ways and Means Committee.

73. The Tobacco Institute, *The Tax Burden on Tobacco,* p. vii.

74. McGowan, *Business, Politics, and Cigarettes,* pp. 104–107.

75. Patrick Fleenor, "The Effect of Excise Tax Differentials on the Interstate Smuggling and Cross-Border Sales of Cigarettes in the United States," Background Paper #16, Washington, D.C.: Tax Foundation, October 1996, p. 1.

76. Ibid., p. 1.

77. Lindquist Avey MacDonald Baskerville, *Cigarette Smuggling in the State of Michigan,* 1995, pp. 18–20. The report was commissioned by the National Coalition Against Crime and Tobacco Contraband, a group of cigarette manufacturers and sellers.

78. Ibid., pp. 27–29, 33–35.

79. Lindquist Avey MacDonald Baskerville, *Cigarette Smuggling in the United States,* 1994, pp. 1, 22. Like the 1995 study, this report was commissioned by the Na-

tional Coalition Against Crime and Tobacco Contraband. Ed Carson, "Tobacco Road," *Reason,* March 1995, pp. 36–38.

80. Clyde Farnsworth, "Canada Cuts Cigarette Taxes to Fight Smuggling," *New York Times,* February 9, 1994, p. A3.

81. See, e.g., Mary Williams Walsh, "Smokes Schemes," *Los Angeles Times,* September 9, 1991, p. E6.

82. Lindquist Avey MacDonald Baskerville, *Cigarette Smuggling in the United States,* 1994, p. 39.

83. Clyde H. Farnsworth, "In Dodge City East, Cigarette Wars," *New York Times,* January 1, 1994, p. A4.

84. C. Gray, "Tobacco-Tax Rollback May End the Smuggling, but What Will Happen to Our Health?" *Canadian Medical Association Journal,* 150:8 (April 15, 1994), pp. 1295–1296.

85. Carson, "Tobacco Road," p. 36.

86. Lindquist Avey MacDonald Baskerville, *Cigarette Smuggling in the United States,* 1994, pp. 30–31. In 1996 the Canadian Parliament and four provincial governments approved new, less dramatic, increases in tobacco taxes.

87. The National Institute on Drug Abuse estimated that 336,000 Americans used cocaine daily in 1990. The CDC estimated that 46,000,000 Americans smoked cigarettes daily in 1991.

Chapter 5. Smoke Alarm

1. Ron Scherer, "Smoking Ban Is Durbin's Crusade," *Christian Science Monitor,* October 20, 1989, p. 7.

2. Myron Levin, "Fuse Lit for New Anti-Smoking Fight," *Los Angeles Times,* January 31, 1989, p. I1.

3. Interview with Ahron Leichtman, June 7, 1996.

4. Ibid.

5. Ron Scherer, "In-Flight Smoking Under Fire," *Christian Science Monitor,* September 30, 1987, p. 1.

6. Marlene Cimons, "Study May Bring Smoking Ban on Planes," *Los Angeles Times,* January 15, 1987, p. I19.

7. Associated Press, "House Passes Ban on Smoking on Flights of 2 Hours or Less," *New York Times,* July 15, 1987, p. A25.

8. Interview with Ahron Leichtman.

9. Richard J. Durbin, "Let's Clear the Air—Aloft," *Christian Science Monitor,* December 17, 1987, p. 13.

10. Mike Brown, "Panel Approves Permanent Ban on Smoking on All U.S. Flights," Louisville *Courier-Journal,* September 8, 1989, p. A1.

11. Walter V. Robinson, "Accord on Airline Smoking Ban," *Boston Globe,* October 17, 1989, p. 1.

12. "Hazardous on Airliners, Too," *Los Angeles Times,* November 1, 1987, p. V-4.

13. Associated Press, "House Votes to Extend Ban on Smoking to Almost All Domestic Airline Flights," *Los Angeles Times,* November 1, 1989, p. A28.

14. Ahron Leichtman, "Let's Press On with Public-Smoking Bans," *USA Today*, November 7, 1989, p. A10.

15. Martha M. Hamilton, "Federal Ban on Airline Smoking Set," *Washington Post*, December 30, 1987, p. F3.

16. James I, *A Counterblaste to Tobacco*, London: English Reprints, 1870 (originally published in 1604), pp. 111–112.

17. Victor G. Kiernan, *Tobacco: A History*, London: Hutchinson Radius, 1991, p. 27.

18. "Incidents and Effects of Smoking," *Harper's Weekly*, February 27, 1904, p. 314.

19. Ronald J. Troyer and Gerald E. Markle, *Cigarettes: The Battle over Smoking*, New Brunswick, N.J.: Rutgers University Press, 1983, p. 39.

20. Charles B. Towns, "The Injury of Tobacco and Its Relation to Other Drug Habits," *Century Magazine*, March 1912, p. 772.

21. Albert F. Blaisdell, *Our Bodies and How We Live*, New York: Ginn and Company, 1910, p. 240.

22. Towns, "The Injury of Tobacco," pp. 771–772.

23. "A Ban on Public Smoking?" *Newsweek*, January 25, 1971, pp. 90–91.

24. Harold M. Schmeck, "U.S. Study Warns Cigarettes Imperil Nonsmokers, Too," *New York Times*, January 11, 1972, p. 1.

25. "Even If You Don't Light Up," *New York Times*, January 16, 1972, p. IV- 7.

26. John F. Banzhaf III, "Please Put Your Cigarette Out; the Smoke Is Killing Me!" *Today's Health*, April 1972, pp. 38–40.

27. Max Wiener, "Non-Smokers, Arise!," *Reader's Digest*, November 1972, pp. 249–254.

28. Banzhaf, "Please Put Your Cigarette Out," p. 40.

29. Wiener, "Non-Smokers, Arise!" pp. 253–254.

30. "No Smoking—Some States Mean It," *U.S. News & World Report*, October 20, 1975, p. 45.

31. Mark A. R. Kleiman, *Against Excess: Drug Policy for Results*, New York: Basic Books, 1992, p. 322.

32. The Roper Organization, "A Study of Public Attitudes Toward Cigarette Smoking and the Tobacco Industry in 1978," May 1978.

33. Representative Thomas J. Bliley Jr. (R., Va.), statement before the House Subcommittee on Health and the Environment, July 21, 1993, pp. 25–26.

34. James L. Repace and Alfred H. Lowrey, "Indoor Air Pollution, Tobacco Smoke, and Public Health," *Science*, 208 (May 2, 1980), pp. 464–472. The study was sponsored by the Prince George's Environmental Coalition.

35. Takeshi Hirayama, "Non-Smoking Wives of Heavy Smokers Have a Higher Risk of Lung Cancer: A Study from Japan," *British Medical Journal*, 282 (January 17, 1981), pp. 183–185. The study was supported by a cancer research grant from the Japanese Ministry of Health and Welfare.

36. Dimitrios Trichopoulos et al., "Lung Cancer and Passive Smoking," *International Journal of Cancer*, 27 (1981), pp. 1–4. The study was supported by grants from the Greek Ministry of Social Services and the U.S. National Cancer Institute.

37. Lawrence Garfinkel, "Time Trends in Lung Cancer Mortality Among Nonsmok-

ers and a Note on Passive Smoking," *Journal of the National Cancer Institute,* 66:6 (June 1981), pp. 1061–1066.

38. For criticism of the Hirayama study, see the letters section of the *British Medical Journal,* April 25, 1981 (pp. 1393–1394), October 3, 1981 (pp. 914–917), and November 28, 1981 (pp. 1464–1466). For criticism of the Trichopoulos study, see Peter N. Lee, *Environmental Tobacco Smoke and Mortality,* Basel, Switzerland: Karger, 1992, pp. 64–65.

39. Jeffrey R. Idle et al., *Environmental Tobacco Smoke and Lung Cancer: Report of a European Working Group,* Trondheim, Norway: European Working Group, 1996, Table 5. The report was commissioned by several European tobacco companies.

40. "Mortality Trends for Selected Smoking-Related Cancers and Breast Cancer— United States, 1950–1990," *Morbidity and Mortality Weekly Report,* 42:44 (November 12, 1993), pp. 857, 863–866.

41. Garfinkel, "Time Trends in Lung Cancer Mortality," p. 1061.

42. James E. Enstrom, "Rising Lung Cancer Mortality Among Nonsmokers," *Journal of the National Cancer Institute,* 62:4 (April 1979), pp. 755–760, Table 2, and Enstrom's unpublished analysis of data from the 1986 National Mortality Followback Survey, Table 4.

43. Stanton A. Glantz, "What to Do Because Evidence Links Involuntary (Passive) Smoking with Lung Cancer," *Western Journal of Medicine,* 140:4 (April 1994), pp. 636–637.

44. Stanton A. Glantz, "Achieving a Smokefree Society," *Circulation,* 76:4 (October 1987), pp. 746–752 (originally presented at the Tobacco Free Young America by the Year 2000 conference in October 1986).

45. Peter Hanauer, "Proposition P: Anatomy of a Nonsmokers' Rights Ordinance," *New York State Journal of Medicine,* July 1985, pp. 369–374.

46. Mark Pertschuk and Donald R. Shopland, eds., *Major Local Smoking Ordinances in the United States,* Berkeley: Americans for Nonsmokers' Rights, September 1989, pp. 9–18.

47. U.S. Department of Health and Human Services, *The Health Consequences of Involuntary Smoking: A Report of the Surgeon General,* U.S. Public Health Service, Centers for Disease Control, Office on Smoking and Health, 1986. National Research Council, *Environmental Tobacco Smoke: Measuring Exposures and Assessing Health Effects,* Washington, D.C.: National Academy Press, 1986.

48. Pertschuk and Shopland, *Major Local Smoking Ordinances in the United States,* pp. v–vi, 1–4. N. A. Lang, "Last Gasp: Workplace Smokers Near Extinction," *Management Review,* 81:2 (February 1992), pp. 33–36.

49. U.S. Environmental Protection Agency, *Respiratory Health Effects of Passive Smoking: Lung Cancer and Other Disorders,* EPA, 1992.

50. Ahron Leichtman, "Unhealthy Haze Spoils Game," *USA Today,* June 12, 1991, p. C10.

51. *Flue-Cured Tobacco Cooperative Stabilization Corp. v. U.S. Environmental Protection Agency,* Memorandum Opinion of Judge Willam L. Osteen, U.S. District Court for the Middle District of North Carolina, July 20, 1994.

52. U.S. Department of Health and Human Services, *Major Local Tobacco Control

Ordinances in the United States, U.S. Public Health Service, National Institutes of Health, National Cancer Institute, 1993, pp. 8–11.

53. Both the proposed OSHA regulations and Waxman's bill allowed smoking in special rooms with separate ventilation systems, but this option would be prohibitively expensive in most cases.

54. Press release from the office of Frank Lautenberg, June 3, 1997.

55. Carol M. Browner, testimony before the House Subcommittee on Health and the Environment, February 7, 1994. Philip J. Hilts, "Smoking Ban Wins Clinton's Support," *New York Times,* February 8, 1994, p. A16.

56. William N. Evans et al., "Do Workplace Smoking Bans Reduce Smoking?" National Bureau of Economic Research, Working Paper #5567, May 1996.

57. Poll conducted by the Gallup Organization for CNN and *Time,* March 1994.

58. Richard J. Durbin, "The Tobacco Industry's Smokescreen," *Christian Science Monitor,* August 16, 1989, p. 18.

59. *Sonya Live,* CNN, February 1, 1994.

60. Sam Howe Verhovek, "As Indoor Fights Smolder, Combatants in Smoking Wars Take Battle Outdoors," *New York Times,* May 5, 1996, p. A14.

61. Interview with Ahron Leichtman.

62. National Restaurant Association press release, October 4, 1994.

63. Survey by Gelb Consulting Group for the International Facility Management Association, Houston (conducted June-July 1994).

64. Edward Flesenthal, "EPA Report Sparks Antismoking Plans: Plaintiffs' Suits May Prod Firms to Bar Smoking," *Wall Street Journal,* January 7, 1993, p. B1.

65. Katherine A. Young, "Environmental Tobacco Smoke and Employees," *Cornell Hotel & Restaurant Administration Quarterly,* 38:1 (February 1997), p. 36.

66. ACLU of Southern California, "Protection of the Rights of Persons with Respiratory Disabilities," Policy Statement #307, March 18, 1992.

67. Mark A. Gottlieb et al., "Second-Hand Smoke and the ADA: Ensuring Access for People with Breathing and Heart Disorders," *St. Louis University Public Law Review,* 13:2 (1994), pp. 635–644.

68. Ibid., pp. 642–644.

69. *Helling v. McKinney,* 113 S. Ct. 2475 (1993).

70. Jon D. Anderson, "Parental Smoking: A Form of Child Abuse?" *Marquette Law Review,* 77 (1994), pp. 360–384.

71. Interview with John Banzhaf, February 23, 1996.

72. Action on Smoking and Health, "Smoking Problems in Condominiums and Apartment Buildings."

73. Peggy Wright, "Dover Non-Smokers Seek Deal in Lawsuit Against Neighbors," *Morris County (N.J.) Daily Record,* May 2, 1994, p. A8. Lawrence Ragonese, "Apartment Neighbors Settle Smoke Lawsuit," *New Jersey Star Ledger,* March 3, 1995.

74. For a summary of possible effects on children, see Anne Charlton, "Children and Passive Smoking: A Review," *Journal of Family Practice,* 38:3 (March 1994), pp. 267–277; the review was funded by the British Cancer Research Campaign. For a critique of the evidence, see Brian N. Blakley and Joan E. Blakley, "Smoking and

Middle Ear Disease: Are They Related?" *Otolaryngology—Head and Neck Surgery,* 112 (March 1995), pp. 441–446.

75. "Is Health a Moral Responsibility?" *Lancet,* 347 (May 4, 1996), p. 1197.

76. Letter from Phipps Y. Cohe, national public affairs director of the Sudden Infant Death Syndrome Alliance, to John F. Banzhaf, December 4, 1996 (emphasis in original).

77. George L. Carlo et al., "The Interplay of Science, Values, and Experiences Among Scientists Asked to Evaluate the Hazards of Dioxin, Radon, and Environmental Tobacco Smoke," *Risk Analysis,* 12:1 (1992), pp. 37–43.

78. Interview with Geoffrey Kabat, May 15, 1996.

79. Geoffrey Kabat, "The Science, Politics, and Psychology of Cancer Risks," unpublished manuscript, November 10, 1995, p. 12 (emphasis in original).

80. The relevant CRS reports are Jane G. Gravelle and Dennis Zimmerman, *Cigarette Taxes to Fund Health Care Reform: An Economic Analysis,* March 8, 1994, and C. Stephen Redhead and Richard E. Rowberg, *Environmental Tobacco Smoke and Lung Cancer Risk,* November 14, 1995. The Energy Department report, prepared by Regulatory Impact Analysis Project Inc., is *Choices in Risk Assessment: The Role of Science in the Environmental Risk Management Process,* 1994; ETS is discussed in the chapter on workplace indoor air quality. Also see Alvan R. Feinstein, "Justice, Science and the 'Bad Guys,'" *Toxicologic Pathology,* 20:2 (1992), pp. 289–305, and Robert Nilsson, "Environmental Tobacco Smoke and Lung Cancer: A Reappraisal," *Ecotoxicology and Environmental Safety,* 34 (1996), pp. 2–17.

81. Stanton A. Glantz et al., *The Cigarette Papers,* Berkeley: University of California Press, 1996, p. 157.

82. Letter from Philippe Shubik to the Indoor Air Quality and Total Human Exposure Committee, July 18, 1992.

83. EPA, *Respiratory Health Effects of Passive Smoking,* p. 3-46.

84. HHS, *The Health Consequences of Involuntary Smoking,* pp. 25–26.

85. James L. Repace and Alfred H. Lowrey, "A Quantitative Estimate of Nonsmokers' Lung Cancer Risk from Passive Smoking," *Environment International,* 11 (1985), pp. 3–22. James L. Repace and Alfred H. Lowrey, "An Enforceable Indoor Air Quality Standard for Environmental Tobacco Smoke in the Workplace," *Risk Analysis,* 13 (1993), pp. 463–475.

86. Keith Phillips et al., "Assessment of Personal Exposures to Environmental Tobacco Smoke in British Nonsmokers," *Environment International,* 20:6 (1994), pp. 693–712. The study was supported by a grant from the Center for Indoor Air Research, which is funded mainly by tobacco companies.

87. Roger A. Jenkins et al., "Exposure to Environmental Tobacco Smoke in Sixteen Cities in the United States as Determined by Personal Breathing Zone Air Sampling," *Journal of Exposure Analysis and Environmental Epidemiology,* 6:4 (1996), pp. 473–502. The study was supported by a grant from the Center for Indoor Air Research, which is funded mainly by tobacco companies. Roger Jenkins supplied some additional calculations in an interview.

88. EPA, *Respiratory Health Effects of Passive Smoking,* pp. 1-2–1-3 (italics added).

89. Interview with Michael Gough, June 10, 1996. CDC, "Facts About Secondhand Smoke."

90. Gary L. Huber et al., "Smoke and Mirrors: The EPA's Flawed Study of Environmental Tobacco Smoke and Cancer," *Regulation,* 16:3 (1993), pp. 44–54. Gary L. Huber et al., "Passive Smoking: How Great a Hazard?" *Consumers' Research,* July 1991, pp. 10–15, 33–34.

91. See, e.g., Samuel Shapiro, "Meta-analysis/Smeta-analysis," *American Journal of Epidemiology,* 140:9 (November 1, 1994), pp. 771–778, and Samuel Shapiro, "Is Meta-Analysis a Valid Approach to the Evaluation of Small Effects in Observational Studies?" *Journal of Clinical Epidemiology,* 50:3 (1997), pp. 223–229.

92. Interview with Geoffrey Kabat.

93. EPA, *Respiratory Health Effects of Passive Smoking,* p. 5-2.

94. Huber et al., "Passive Smoking," p. 15.

95. Interview with Michael Gough.

96. Gravelle and Zimmerman, *Cigarette Taxes to Fund Health Care Reform,* p. 47.

97. Jerry E. Bishop, "Statisticians Occupy Front Lines in Battle Over Passive Smoking," *Wall Street Journal,* July 28, 1993, p. B1.

98. Richard Stone, "Bad News on Second-Hand Smoke," *Science,* 257 (July 31, 1992), p. 607.

99. EPA, *Respiratory Health Effects of Passive Smoking,* p. 1-10.

100. Idle et al., *Environmental Tobacco Smoke and Lung Cancer,* Tables 5, 8, and 9.

101. See, e.g., J. P. Vanderbrouke, "Passive Smoking and Lung Cancer: A Publication Bias?" *British Medical Journal,* 296 (1988), pp. 391–392.

102. Interview with Geoffrey Kabat.

103. Ross C. Brownson et al., "Passive Smoking and Lung Cancer in Nonsmoking Women," *American Journal of Public Health,* 82:11 (November 1992), pp. 1525–1530. The study was supported by the National Cancer Institute.

104. Interview with James Enstrom, June 6, 1996.

105. Brownson et al., "Passive Smoking and Lung Cancer in Nonsmoking Women," p. 1525.

106. See, e.g., Eben Shapiro, "Passive-Smoke Ruling Sparks Industry Suit," *Wall Street Journal,* June 23, 1993, p. B1, and Philip J. Hilts, *Smokescreen: The Truth Behind the Tobacco Industry Cover-up,* Reading, Mass.: Addison-Wesley, 1996, p. 106.

107. Elizabeth T. H. Fontham et al., "Environmental Tobacco Smoke and Lung Cancer in Nonsmoking Women: A Multicenter Study," *Journal of the American Medical Association,* 271:22 (June 8, 1994), pp. 1752–1759. The study was supported by grants from the National Cancer Institute, the Louisiana Cancer and Lung Trust Fund Board, and the Louisiana State University Stanley S. Scott Cancer Center.

108. National Cancer Institute, "Abortion and Possible Risk for Breast Cancer: Analysis and Inconsistencies," October 26, 1994. Janet R. Daling et al., "Risk of Breast Cancer Among Young Women: Relationship to Induced Abortion," *Journal of the National Cancer Institute,* 88 (November 2, 1994), pp. 1584–1592. Lynn Rosenberg, "Induced Abortion and Breast Cancer: More Scientific Data Are Needed,"

Journal of the National Cancer Institute, 88 (November 2, 1994), pp. 1569–1570. The meta-analysis is presented in Joel Brind et al., "Induced Abortion as an Independent Risk Factor for Breast Cancer: A Comprehensive Review and Meta-Analysis," *Journal of Epidemiology and Community Health,* 50 (1996), pp. 481–496. Also see Marilie D. Gammon et al., "Abortion and the Risk of Breast Cancer: Is There a Believable Association?" *Journal of the American Medical Association,* 275:4 (January 24/31, 1996), pp. 321–322, and Karin B. Michels and Walter C. Willett, "Does Induced or Spontaneous Abortion Affect the Risk of Breast Cancer?" *Epidemiology,* 7:5 (September 1996), pp. 521–528.

109. For a summary of the evidence, see Tim Byers, "Diet as a Factor in the Etiology and Prevention of Lung Cancer," in Jonathan N. Samet, ed., *Epidemiology of Lung Cancer,* New York: Dekker, 1994, pp. 335–352. On the role of fat, see M. C. R. Alavanja et al., "Saturated Fat Intake and Lung Cancer Risk Among Nonsmoking Women," *Journal of the National Cancer Institute,* 85:23 (December 1, 1993), pp. 1906–1916, and the editorial by Laurence N. Kolonel in the same issue, pp. 1886–1887.

110. See, e.g., Genevieve Matanowski et al., "Characteristics of Nonsmoking Women in NHANES I and NHANES I Epidemiologic Follow-up Study with Exposure to Spouses Who Smoke," *American Journal of Epidemiology,* 142:2 (1995), pp. 149–156. The study was supported by a grant from the Center for Indoor Air Research, which is funded mainly by tobacco companies.

111. Transcript of the Annual Summer Meeting of the Toxicology Forum, July 12–16, 1993, pp. 309–311.

112. NRC, *Environmental Tobacco Smoke,* pp. 234–240.

113. EPA, *Respiratory Health Effects of Passive Smoking,* pp. 5-26–5-27.

114. Redhead and Rowberg, *Environmental Tobacco Smoke and Lung Cancer Risk,* pp. 36–38, 40–42.

115 Interview with James Enstrom.

116. Interview with Michael Gough.

117. Howard E. Rockette, "What Evidence Is Needed to Link Lung Cancer and Second-Hand Smoke?" *Chance: New Directions for Statistics and Computing,* 6:4 (Fall 1993), pp. 15–18.

118. The Toxicology Forum, pp. 316–317.

119. Rockette, "What Evidence Is Needed to Link Lung Cancer and Second-Hand Smoke?" p. 18.

120. Interview with James Enstrom.

121. Interview with Michael Gough.

122. Associated Press, "6 Members of Panel on Smoking Have Ties to Tobacco Group," *New York Times,* November 10, 1990, p. 9.

123. "Objectivity Up in Smoke," *New York Times,* November 21, 1990.

124. Michael Weisskopf, "EPA Puzzles Over How to Assure Smoking Panel's Independence," *Washington Post,* November 23, 1990, p. A29.

125. Interview with Geoffrey Kabat.

126. Interview with Elizabeth Whelan, October 12, 1995.

127. ACS symposium on tobacco advertising, New York, March 26, 1996.

128. Peter D. Morris, "Lifetime Excess Risk of Death from Lung Cancer for a U.S. Female Never-Smoker Exposed to Environmental Tobacco Smoke," *Environmental Research,* 68 (1995), pp. 3–9.

129. Donald F. Austin, quoted in Daniel Seligman, "The 30% Solution," *Fortune,* July 11, 1994, pp. 177–178.

130. The other study found a positive association only in male subjects (in the female subjects, the association was negative, though not statistically significant). The sample was very small (twenty-five cases and twenty-five controls), and there is some question whether the result really was statistically significant. Geoffrey C. Kabat and Ernst L. Wynder, "Lung Cancer in Nonsmokers," *Cancer,* 53 (1984), pp. 1214–1221. Also see Lee, *Environmental Tobacco Smoke and Mortality,* pp. 47–48, 117–118.

131. Brownson et al., "Passive Smoking and Lung Cancer in Nonsmoking Women," p. 1527.

132. Fontham et al., "Environmental Tobacco Smoke and Lung Cancer in Nonsmoking Women," p. 1752.

133. Interview with James Enstrom.

134. CDC, "Secondhand Smoke in the Workplace."

135. Interview with Dimitrios Trichopoulos, June 7, 1996.

136. CDC, "Secondhand Smoke in Your Home."

137. CDC, "Facts About Secondhand Smoke."

138. Interview with Michael Gough.

139. A. Judson Wells, "An Estimate of Adult Mortality in the United States from Passive Smoking," *Environment International,* 14:3 (1988), pp. 249–265.

140. Kyle Steenland et al., "Environmental Tobacco Smoke and Coronary Heart Disease in the American Cancer Society CPS-II Cohort," *Circulation,* 94:4 (August 15, 1996), pp. 622–628.

141. U.S. Department of Health and Human Services, *The Health Consequences of Smoking: Cardiovascular Disease: A Report of the Surgeon General,* U.S. Public Health Service, Office on Smoking and Health, 1983, p. 7.

142. Maurice E. LeVois and Maxwell W. Layard, "Publication Bias in the Environmental Tobacco Smoke/Coronary Heart Disease Epidemiologic Literature," *Regulatory Toxicology and Pharmacology,* 21 (1995), pp. 184–191. The study was supported by funding from Philip Morris. Steenland et al., "Environmental Tobacco Smoke and Coronary Heart Disease," using a different selection of ACS data and slicing it differently, found a modest, barely significant increase in risk for men.

143. Ichiro Kawachi et al., "A Prospective Study of Passive Smoking and Coronary Heart Disease," *Circulation,* 95:10 (May 20, 1997), pp. 2374–2379.

144. Ibid., p. 2377.

145. Interview with James Enstrom.

146. Banzhaf, "Please Put Your Cigarette Out," p. 40. Donald R. Shopland, "Chronology of Select Major Events in the History of the Battle to Protect Nonsmokers from Environmental Tobacco Smoke," National Cancer Institute, 1993, p. 2.

147. "Smokers Get Dealt a Final Blow by United and American," *Best Fares,* July 3, 1997.

148. *The Cavuto Business Report,* Fox News Channel, November 21, 1996.

149. Lois Romano, "Lightening Up," *Washington Post,* September 22, 1997, p. A1.

Chapter 6. Try, Try Again

1. "Attorneys General Settlement Agreement," March 20, 1997.

2. Barry Meier, "Tobacco Deal Would Restrict Plaintiff Claims," *New York Times,* March 24, 1997, p. A1.

3. Reuters, "RJR Nabisco Asks 'What If?,'" *New York Times,* March 22, 1996, p. D4.

4. Philip Morris USA press release, March 20, 1997.

5. ASH press release, May 7, 1997.

6. Hubert H. Humphrey III, remarks before the Advisory Committee on Tobacco Policy and Public Health, June 18, 1997. John M. Broder and Barry Meier, "High Hurdles Still Confront Tobacco Pact," *New York Times,* June 22, 1997, p. A1. John M. Broder, "Senator Seeks Tobacco Data," *New York Times,* July 17, 1997, p. A20.

7. Letter from Ralph Nader to Matthew Myers, George Dessart, David A. Ness, and Lonnie Bristow, June 19, 1997.

8. Stanton Glantz, "What Deal? We Got Suckered," *Los Angeles Times,* June 23, 1997, p. B5.

9. Barnaby J. Feder, "Industry Split by Major Deal in Tobacco Suit," *New York Times,* March 14, 1996, p. 1.

10. Memo from J. Michael Jordan, counsel for R. J. Reynolds, April 29, 1988, quoted in *Haines v. Liggett Group,* 814 F. Supp. 414 (1993).

11. Richard A. Daynard, "Catastrophe Theory and Tobacco Litigation," *Tobacco Control,* 3 (1994), pp. 59–64.

12. Stanton A. Glantz et al., *The Cigarette Papers,* Berkeley: University of California Press, 1996, pp. 268–271.

13. Ibid., pp. 109–110.

14. Ibid., p. 15.

15. "Jacksonville Lawyer Touts Memo; Tobacco Stocks Fall," *Florida Times-Union,* March 14, 1997, p. A1.

16. Glantz et al., *The Cigarette Papers,* p. 19.

17. *Restatement (Second) of Torts,* Section 402A, Comment (i) (1965) (emphasis added).

18. *O'Brien v. Muskin Corp.,* 94 N.J. 169, 463 A.2d 298 (1983).

19. Daniel LeDuc, "Lawyer Behind the Suit Says Case Made Difference," *Philadelphia Inquirer,* November 6, 1992, p. A24.

20. Paula Span, "The War Over a Smoker's Death," *Washington Post,* May 27, 1988, p. B1. Donald Janson, "The Husband of a Smoker Testifies on Her Death from Lung Cancer," *New York Times,* April 7, 1988, p. B4. The quotations are drawn from Rose Cipollone's 1984 deposition.

21. Ibid.

22. Ibid. and Donald Janson, "Cigarette Maker Blameless in Death, Lawyer Says," *New York Times,* June 2, 1988, p. B2.

23. Span, "The War Over a Smoker's Death."

24. *Cipollone v. Liggett Group,* 789 F.2d 181 (1986).

25. Donald Janson, "Cancer Victim's Lawyer Sees Tobacco Conspiracy," *New York Times,* June 7, 1988, p. B2.

26. Morton Mintz, "Pact Barring Cancer Study Disclosed," *Washington Post,* May 20, 1988, p. D11.

27. Ibid.

28. Associated Press, "L&M View of Smoking's Dangers Recounted," Bergen County *Record,* February 18, 1988, p. A9.

29. Janson, "The Husband of a Smoker Testifies."

30. John Riley, "Smoking-Risk Evidence," *Newsday,* February 5, 1988, p.2.

31. Morton Mintz, "Tobacco Trial Lawyer Focuses on Deleted Risk Information," *Washington Post,* February 24, 1988, p. F3.

32. Richard A. Daynard and Laurie Morin, "The *Cipollone* Documents," *Trial,* November 1988, pp. 50–55.

33. Janson, "Cigarette Maker Blameless in Death, Lawyer Says."

34. Morton Mintz, "Ad Agency's Study Cites Strong Dependency of Smokers," *Washington Post,* March 9, 1988, p. F3.

35. U.S. Department of Health and Human Services, *The Health Consequences of Smoking: Nicotine Addiction: A Report of the Surgeon General,* U.S. Public Health Service, Centers for Disease Control, Office on Smoking and Health, 1988, p. vi.

36. Morton Mintz, "Judge Says Tobacco Industry Hid Risks," *Washington Post,* April 22, 1988, p. A1. Morton Mintz, "Cigarette Companies Lose Plea for Mistrial in Smoker-Death Case," *Washington Post,* April 23, 1988, p. B1.

37. Daniel LeDuc, "$400,000 Is Awarded in Smoking Suit," *Philadelphia Inquirer,* June 14, 1988, p. A1.

38. *Cipollone v. Liggett Group,* 112 S.Ct. 2608 (1992).

39. Linda Greenhouse, "Court Opens Way for Damage Suits Over Cigarettes," *New York Times,* June 25, 1992, p. A1.

40. Robert L. Rabin, "A Sociolegal History of the Tobacco Tort Litigation," *Stanford Law Review,* 44 (April 1992), pp. 853–878.

41. Glen Collins, "Air Crews Can Sue on Smoke," *New York Times,* December 14, 1994, p. D1.

42. Richard A. Daynard and Edward L. Sweda Jr., "Redressing Injuries from Secondhand Smoke," *Trial,* March 1992, pp. 50–53.

43. Ann Davis and Milo Geyelin, "Secondhand Smoke Accord Remains Hazy," *Wall Street Journal,* October 16, 1997, p. B12.

44. Collins, "Air Crews Can Sue on Smoke."

45. Sheryl Stolberg, "Leading the Air War on Cigarettes," *Los Angeles Times,* February 15, 1996, p. A1.

46. Andrew Blum, "Passive Smoking Targeted," *National Law Journal,* November 18, 1991, p. 16.

47. *Nightline,* ABC, June 19, 1997.

48. *Engle v. R. J. Reynolds,* Amended Class Action Complaint.

49. Glenn Collins, "Class Suit on Tobacco Illness Can Go to Trial in Florida," *New York Times,* February 1, 1996, p. D4.

50. Glenn Collins, "Legal Titans Square Off in Big Tobacco Lawsuit," *New York Times,* December 15, 1994 (citing Gary Black, a tobacco analyst with Sanford C. Bernstein & Company), p. D2.

51. Kent Price, "Lawsuit Filed on Behalf of Nicotine-Addicted," *Philadelphia Inquirer,* March 31, 1994, p. A17.

52. Maria Mallory, "These Days, Where There's Smoke, There's a Lawsuit," *Business Week,* June 6, 1994, p. 36.

53 Glenn Collins, "A Tobacco Case's Legal Buccaneers," *New York Times,* March 6, 1995, p. D1.

54. *Castano v. American Tobacco,* Order by Judge Okla B. Jones, U.S. District Court for the Eastern District of Louisiana, February 17, 1995.

55. Jeffrey Meitrodt, "Tobacco Lawsuit Phones Smoking," New Orleans *Times-Picayune,* February 25, 1995, p. A1.

56. Feder, "Industry Split by Major Deal in Tobacco Suit."

57. *Castano v. American Tobacco,* 84 F.3d 734 (May 23, 1996).

58. Glenn Collins, "Huge Tobacco Lawsuit Is Thrown Out on Appeal," *New York Times,* May 24, 1996, p. A1.

59. Glenn Collins, "2 Lawyers Carry On Tobacco Suits," *New York Times,* June 6, 1996, p. D4.

60. Milo Geyelin, "Judge Rejects Pennsylvania Lawsuit," *Wall Street Journal,* October 20, 1997, p. B12.

61. Michael Janofsky, "Mississippi Seeks Damages from Tobacco Companies," *New York Times,* May 24, 1994, p. A12.

62. *Agency for Health Care Administration v. Associated Industries of Florida,* Supreme Court of Florida, June 27, 1996.

63. Larry Rohter, "Florida Prepares New Basis to Sue Tobacco Industry," *New York Times,* May 27, 1994, p. A1.

64. Ibid.

65. Junda Woo, "Tobacco Firms Face Greater Health Liability," *Wall Street Journal,* May 3, 1994, p. A3.

66. "Good Intent, Bad Bill," *St . Petersburg Times,* May 6, 1994, p. A16.

67. Michael Griffin, "Chiles Vetoes Tobacco Law Repeal," *Orlando Sentinel,* June 16, 1995, p. C1.

68. John Kennedy, "Chiles Will Use TV Ads in Fight to Keep Anti-Tobacco Law," *Orlando Sentinel Tribune,* March 8, 1996, p. D6.

69. *Associated Industries of Florida v. Agency for Health Care Administration,* Final Order and Declaratory Judgment, Judge F. E. Steinmeyer, Leon County Circuit Court, June 26, 1995.

70. *Agency for Health Care Administration v. Associated Industries of Florida,* Supreme Court of Florida, June 27, 1996.

71. Ibid.

72. Adam Yeomans, "Florida Governor Sues Tobacco Companies," *Philadelphia Inquirer,* February 22, 1995, p. A2.

73. John E. Berthoud, "The Economic Consequences of Medicaid Litigation," Commonwealth Foundation of Virginia, July 11, 1994.

74. Associated Press, "Maryland and Connecticut Join States Seeking Tobacco Money," *New York Times,* May 2, 1996, p. A20.

75. Barnaby J. Feder, "Texas Joins Other States in Suing Tobacco Industry," *New York Times,* March 29, 1996, p. B9.

76. Letter from FDA commissioner David A. Kessler to Scott D. Ballin, chairman of the Coalition on Smoking or Health, February 25, 1994.

77. Stuart Eskenazi, "State's Revenue from Tobacco Taxes Exceeds Estimated Costs of Illnesses," *Austin American Statesman,* May 21, 1996, p. A1.

78. June D. Bell, "Smoker Tells Jury of His Quest to Quit," *Florida Times-Union,* August 1, 1996, p. A1.

79. June D. Bell, "Tobacco Jury: Message to Industry," *Florida Times-Union,* August 15, 1996, p. A1.

80. Glenn Collins, "Cigarette Makers Win Verdict in Suit by a Smoker's Family," *New York Times,* August 24, 1996, p. A8.

81. Stephanie Desmon, "Tobacco Retailers Targeted," *Florida Times-Union,* August 31, 1996, p. A1.

82. Laura T. Barrow, "Why My Jury Let R. J. Reynolds Off," *Washington Post,* May 25, 1997, p. C1. Donald P. Baker, "Jury Deliberates Smoker's Lawsuit," *Washington Post,* May 3, 1997, p. A18.

83. Myron Levin, "Former Smoker Wins Pivotal Tobacco Case," *Los Angeles Times,* August 10, 1996, p. A1.

84. Interview with Richard A. Daynard, August 7, 1996.

85. The Gallup Organization.

86. Ahron Leichtman, "The Top Ten Ways to Attack the Tobacco Industry and Win the War Against Smoking," *Saint Louis University Public Law Review,* 13:2 (1994), pp. 729–747.

87. Richard A. Daynard, "Tobacco Liability Litigation as a Cancer Control Strategy," *Journal of the National Cancer Institute,* 80:1 (March 2, 1988), pp. 9–13. Stephen P. Teret, "Litigating for the Public's Health," *American Journal of Public Health,* 76:8 (August 1986), pp. 1027–1029.

88. Interview with Richard Daynard.

89. Ibid.

90. Ibid.

91. Jordan Goodman, *Tobacco in History: The Cultures of Dependence,* New York: Routledge, 1993, p. 120.

Chapter 7. Little White Slavers

1. Hearing of the House Subcommittee on Health and the Environment, April 14, 1994.

2. Thomas Szasz, *Ceremonial Chemistry,* rev. ed. Holmes Beach, Fla.: Learning Publications, 1985, p. 6.

3. See, e.g., Molly O'Neill, "The Lure and Addiction of Life on Line," *New York Times,* March 8, 1995, p. C1.

4. Hearing of the House Subcommittee on Health and the Environment, April 14, 1994.

5. Letter from FDA commissioner David A. Kessler to Scott D. Ballin, chairman of the Coalition on Smoking or Health, February 25, 1994.

6. Ibid.

7. L. M. Johnston, "Tobacco Smoking and Nicotine," *Lancet,* 2 (1942), p. 742.

8. M. A. Hamilton Russell, "Cigarette Smoking: Natural History of a Dependence Disorder," *British Journal of Medical Psychology,* 44 (1971), pp. 1–16.

9. Charging that ads for Next made implicit health claims, the Coalition on Smoking or Health asked the FDA to regulate the new brand as a drug, which would have kept it off the market. See, e.g., "Coalition: No-Nicotine Cigarettes Are Drugs," *Alcoholism & Drug Abuse Week,* April 10, 1991, p. 4.

10. Richard Kluger, *Ashes to Ashes: America's Hundred-Year Cigarette War, the Public Health, and the Unabashed Triumph of Philip Morris,* New York: Alfred A. Knopf, 1996, p. 742 .

11. Interview with Alan Blum, May 14, 1996.

12. David A. Kessler, testimony before the House Subcommittee on Health and the Environment, March 25, 1994.

13. Letter from Kessler to Ballin. Edwin Chen, "In Shift, FDA Says It Could Classify Nicotine as a Drug," *Los Angeles Times,* February 26, 1994, p. A1.

14. Philip J. Hilts, "Agency Considers Treating Tobacco As Addictive Drug," *New York Times,* February 26, 1994, p. A1.

15. *Federal Register,* 60:155 (August 11, 1995), pp. 41346–41352. Petition by Action on Smoking and Health et al. to the FDA, May 26, 1977.

16. CEI petition and press release, October 25, 1995.

17. *Coyne Beahm v. FDA, American Advertising Federation v. Kessler, U.S. Tobacco v. FDA,* and *National Association of Convenience Stores v. Kessler,* Memorandum Opinion, Judge William L. Osteen, U.S. District Court for the Middle District of North Carolina, April 25, 1997.

18. Estes Thompson, "Tobacco Can Be Regulated, but Not the Ads, Judge Rules," *Charleston* (W. Va.) *Gazette,* April 26, 1997, p. A1.

19. Interview with Phil Schiliro, May 14, 1997. "Attorney General/Tobacco Industry Settlement," June 20, 1997, p. 13.

20. Letter from Kessler to Ballin.

21. *Day One,* ABC, February 28, 1994. *Philip Morris v. ABC,* Motion for Judgment, Circuit Court for the City of Richmond, March 24, 1994, p. 6.

22. ABC statement (reprinted in Philip Morris ad), *New York Times,* August 25, 1995, p. A15.

23. Interview with Steven Parrish, October 11, 1995.

24. *Philip Morris v. ABC,* Motion for Judgment, p. 4.

25. Letter from Kessler to Ballin.

26. Hilts, "Agency Considers Treating Tobacco as Addictive Drug."

27. Nancy Hass, "Fighting and Switching," *Newsweek,* March 21, 1994, p. 52.

28. John Schwartz, "Kessler Tells Committee FDA May Act to Regulate Tobacco Products' Content," *Washington Post,* March 26, 1994, p. A3.

29. Shannon Brownlee, "Should Cigarettes Be Outlawed?" *U.S. News & World Report,* April 18, 1994, pp. 32–36.

30. Interview with Jim O'Hara, October 1995.

31. Jerome H. Jaffe, "Tobacco Use as a Mental Disorder," *NIDA Monographs,* 1977, pp. 202–217.

32. James I, *A Counterblaste to Tobacco,* London: English Reprints, 1870 (originally published in 1604), pp. 109–110.

33. Egon C. Corti, *A History of Smoking,* London: George G. Harrap & Co., 1931, p. 94.

34. Ibid., pp. 111, 186, 116, 117, 118–119, 157. Cotton Mather, *Manuductio ad Ministerium,* Boston, 1726.

35. Corti, *A History of Smoking,* p. 182.

36. Benjamin Rush, *Essays, Literary, Moral and Philosophical,* Philadelphia, 1798, p. 264.

37. Jaffe, "Tobacco Use as a Mental Disorder," p. 206.

38. Ibid., pp. 207–208.

39. John C. Luik, " 'I Can't Help Myself': Addiction as Ideology," *Human Psychopharmacology,* 11 (1996), pp. S21–S32.

40. U.S. Department of Health and Human Services, *The Health Consequences of Smoking: Nicotine Addiction: A Report of the Surgeon General,* U.S. Public Health Service, Centers for Disease Control, Office on Smoking and Health, 1988, p. 10.

41. Luik, " 'I Can't Help Myself,' " p. S24.

42. HHS, *The Health Consequences of Smoking,* pp. iii, 9–13.

43. Ibid., pp. i, 6, 9, 267.

44. Harry G. Levine, "The Discovery of Addiction," *Journal of Studies on Alcohol,* 39:1 (1978), pp. 143–173.

45. For a critique of the disease model, see Herbert Fingarette, *Heavy Drinking: The Myth of Alcoholism As a Disease,* Berkeley: University of California Press, 1988.

46. Stanton Peele, "Addiction as a Cultural Concept," *Annals of the New York Academy of Sciences,* 602 (1990), pp. 205–220.

47. U.S. Department of Health and Human Services, *Preliminary Results from the 1996 National Household Survey on Drug Abuse,* U.S. Public Health Service, Substance Abuse and Mental Health Services Administration, 1997, p. 62.

48. Mike Synar, *Crossfire,* CNN, March 10, 1994.

49. Estimates for the share of drinkers who are "problem drinkers," including alcoholics, range from 5 to 10 percent.

50. L. N. Robins et al., "Vietnam Veterans Three Years After Vietnam: How Our Study Changed Our View of Heroin," *Yearbook of Substance Use and Abuse,* 2 (1980), pp. 213–230. The research was funded by the U.S. Public Health Service.

51. Charles Winick, "The Life Cycle of the Narcotic Addict and of Addiction," *Bulletin on Narcotics,* 16:1 (January-March 1964), pp. 1–11.

52. Steven B. Duke and Albert C. Gross, *America's Longest War: Rethinking Our Tragic Crusade Against Drugs,* New York: G. P. Putnam's Sons, 1993, p. 61.

53. Arthur B. Light and Edward G. Torrance, "Opiate Addiction, VI: The Effects of Abrupt Withdrawal Followed by Readministration of Morphine in Human Ad-

dicts, with Special Reference to the Composition of the Blood, the Circulation and the Metabolism," *Archives of Internal Medicine,* 44 (1929), pp. 1–16. Andrew Weil and Winifred Rosen, *From Chocolate to Morphine: Everything You Need to Know About Mind-Altering Drugs,* New York: Houghton Mifflin, 1993, p. 85.

54. Jane Porter and Hershel Jick, "Addiction Rare in Patients Treated with Narcotics," *New England Journal of Medicine,* 302:2 (January 10, 1980).

55. Samuel Perry and George Heidrich, "Management of Pain During Debridement: A Survey of U.S. Burn Units," *Pain,* 13 (1982), pp. 267–280.

56. Russell K. Portenoy and Kathleen M. Foley, "Chronic Use of Opioid Analgesics in Non-Malignant Pain: Report of 38 Cases," *Pain,* 25 (1986), pp. 171–186.

57. See, e.g., Richard M. Marks and Edward J. Sachar, "Undertreatment of Medical Inpatients with Narcotic Analgesics," *Annals of Internal Medicine,* 78:2 (February 1973), pp. 173–181; Marcia Angell, "The Quality of Mercy," *New England Journal of Medicine,* 306:2 (January 14, 1982), pp. 98–99; John P. Morgan, "American Opiophobia: Customary Underutilization of Opioid Analgesics," in Barry Stimmel, ed., *Controversies in Alcoholism and Substance Abuse,* Binghamton, N.Y.: Haworth Press, 1986. For a summary of the issue, see Jacob Sullum, "No Relief in Sight," *Reason,* January 1997, pp. 22–28.

58. Charles R. Schuster, "Does Treatment of Cancer Pain with Narcotics Produce Junkies?" in C. S. Hess Jr. and W. S. Fields, eds., *Drug Treatment of Cancer Pain in a Drug-Oriented Society,* New York: Raven, 1989, p. 2

59. Associated Press, June 14, 1996. *Peter Jennings Reporting,* ABC, June 27, 1996.

60. HHS, *Preliminary Results from the 1996 National Household Survey on Drug Abuse,* p. 57. U.S. Centers for Disease Control and Prevention, "Smoking Prevalence Among U.S. Adults," April 24, 1996. The Household Survey data are for respondents twelve and older, while the CDC data are for adults (eighteen and older). If anything, this difference would tend to exaggerate the "addictiveness" of cigarettes.

61. Lynn T. Kozlowski et al., "Comparing Tobacco Cigarette Dependence with Other Drug Dependencies," *Journal of the American Medical Association,* 261:6 (February 10, 1989), pp. 898–901. In the first survey, the problem drug was not specified.

62. Sally Satel, "Where There's Smoke, There's Ire," *Wall Street Journal,* July 16, 1996, p. A10.

63. Mark A. R. Kleiman, *Against Excess: Drug Policy for Results,* New York: Basic Books, 1991, p. 370.

64. Henner Hess, "The Other Prohibition: The Cigarette Crisis in Post-War Germany," paper presented at the 47th Annual Conference of the American Society of Criminology, November 1995, pp. 6, 10, 14–17.

65. American Psychiatric Association, *Diagnostic and Statistical Manual of Mental Disorders,* 4th ed., Washington, D.C.: APA, pp. 244–245.

66. HHS, *The Health Consequences of Smoking: Nicotine Addiction,* p. 200.

67. C. Barr Taylor and Joel D. Killen, *The Facts About Smoking,* Yonkers, N.Y.: Consumer Reports Books, 1991, p. 35.

68. HHS, *The Health Consequences of Smoking: Nicotine Addiction,* pp. 208–209, 472.

69. Ibid., pp. 489–490.

70. J. Foulds et al., "Effect of Transdermal Nicotine Patches on Cigarette Smoking: A Double Blind Crossover Study," *Psychopharmacology,* 106:3 (1992), pp. 421–427.

71. A. E. Hamilton, "Killing Lady Nicotine," *North American Review,* April 1928, pp. 465–468.

72. "Effectiveness of Smoking-Control Strategies—United States," *Morbidity and Mortality Weekly Report,* 41:35 (September 4, 1992), pp. 645–647.

73. Stanton Peele, *Diseasing of America: Addiction Treatment Out of Control,* Lexington, Mass.: Lexington Books, 1989, p. 189.

74. Gallup poll, May 9–12, 1996.

75. W. Kip Viscusi, *Smoking: Making the Risky Decision,* New York: Oxford University Press, 1992, p. 120.

76. Gary S. Becker and Kevin M. Murphy, "A Theory of Rational Addiction," *Journal of Political Economy,* 96 (August 1988), pp. 675–700.

77. Ibid. and George J. Stigler and Gary S. Becker, "De Gustibus Non Est Disputandum," *American Economic Review,* 67 (March 1977), pp. 76–90.

78. See, e.g., Larry C. White, *Merchants of Death: The American Tobacco Industry,* New York: Beech Tree Books, 1988, p. 55.

79. U.S. Department of Health and Human Services, *Reducing the Health Consequences of Smoking: 25 Years of Progress/A Report of the Surgeon General,* U.S. Public Health Service, Centers for Disease Control, Office on Smoking and Health, 1989, p. 139. Viscusi, *Smoking: Making the Risky Decision,* pp. 112–115.

80. David Krogh, *Smoking: The Artificial Passion,* New York: W. H. Freeman & Co., 1991, pp. 99–114.

81. John D. Slade, "A Disease Model of Cigarette Use," *New York State Journal of Medicine,* July 1985, pp. 294–297.

82. Byron J. Bailey, "Tobaccoism Is the Disease—Cancer is the Sequela," *Journal of the American Medical Association,* 255:14 (April 11, 1986), p. 1923.

83. HHS, *The Health Consequences of Smoking: Nicotine Addiction,* pp. 248–249.

84. Russell, "Cigarette Smoking: Natural History of a Dependence Disorder," p. 3.

85. HHS, *The Health Consequences of Smoking: Nicotine Addiction,* p. v.

86. Luik, " 'I Can't Help Myself,' " p. S26.

87. Suein L. Hwang et al., "FDA Seeks to Mount Attack on Smoking by Minors That Could Mean Regulation," *Wall Street Journal,* July 13, 1995, p. A1.

88. U.S. Department of Health and Human Services, *Preventing Tobacco Use Among Young People: A Report of the Surgeon General,* U.S. Public Health Service, Centers for Disease Control and Prevention, Office on Smoking and Health, 1994, p. 67.

89. HHS, *Preliminary Results from the 1996 National Household Survey on Drug Abuse,* p. 105.

90. Philip J. Hilts, *Smokescreen: The Truth Behind the Tobacco Industry Cover-up,* Reading, Mass.: Addison-Wesley, 1996, p. 76 (emphasis in original).

91. Teenage Attitudes and Practices Survey, CDC, 1989.

92. The same basic trends were found in both the National Household Survey on Drug Abuse, which is overseen by the Substance Abuse and Mental Health Services Administration, and the Monitoring the Future Project, a survey commissioned by the National Institute on Drug Abuse and conducted by the Institute

for Social Research at the University of Michigan. The figures for daily cigarette smoking come from the Monitoring the Future survey.

93. U.S. Department of Health and Human Services. *National Survey Results on Drug Use from the Monitoring the Future Study, 1975–1995, Volume I: Secondary School Students,* U.S. Public Health Service, National Institutes of Health, National Institute on Drug Abuse, 1996, p. 71.

94. Barnaby J. Feder, "Critics Call Anti-Smoking Drive Misdirected," *New York Times,* April 1, 1996, p. A12. Stanton A. Glantz, "Preventing Tobacco Use: The Youth Access Trap," *American Journal of Public Health,* 86:2 (February 1996), pp. 156–158.

95. See, e.g., Barnaby J. Feder, "Battle on Youth Smoking Brings Hope and Caution," *New York Times,* November 29, 1996, p. A1.

96. Mike Brown, "Smoking's New Opponent Is Armed with Big Budget," *Louisville Courier-Journal,* December 30, 1996, p. A1.

97. Benjamin Wittes, "Anti-Tobacco Group Not Just Blowing Smoke," *Miami Daily Business Review,* July 8, 1996, p. A1.

98. FDA press release, August 23, 1996, p. 3.

99. *Federal Register,* 60:155 (August 11, 1995), p. 41314.

100. Meeting of the Advisory Committee on Tobacco Policy and Public Health, June 25, 1997.

101. Ibid.

102. "Nicotine Fit," *Nation,* June 4, 1988, pp. 775–776.

103. *Day One,* ABC, February 28, 1994.

104. HHS, *The Health Consequences of Smoking: Nicotine Addiction,* p. vi.

Chapter 8. Doctor's Orders

1. Financial supporters of the Partnership for a Drug-Free America have also included R. J. Reynolds, American Brands (maker of Lucky Strike cigarettes and Jim Beam whiskey), and Anheuser-Busch, as well as several pharmaceutical companies. See Cynthia Cotts, "Hard Sell in the Drug War," *Nation,* March 9, 1992, pp. 300–302.

2. U.S. Department of Health and Human Services, *Preliminary Results from the 1996 National Household Survey on Drug Abuse,* U.S. Public Health Service, Substance Abuse and Mental Health Services Administration, 1997, pp. 57, 61.

3. Ibid., p. 61. U.S. Department of Health and Human Services, *National Survey Results on Drug Use from the Monitoring the Future Study, 1975–1994, Volume II: College Students and Young Adults,* U.S. Public Health Service, National Institutes of Health, National Institute on Drug Abuse, 1996, pp. 84–85. "Cigarette Smoking Among Adults—United States, 1992," *Morbidity and Mortality Weekly Report,* May 20, 1994, pp. 342–346.

4. The number of smoker deaths attributed to smoking (about four hundred thousand) is drawn from "Cigarette Smoking-Attributable Mortality and Years of Potential Life Lost—United States, 1990," *Morbidity and Mortality Weekly Report,* August 27, 1993, pp. 645–649. The number of current and former adult smokers

(about ninety million) is drawn from "Cigarette Smoking Among Adults—United States, 1991," *Morbidity and Mortality Weekly Report,* April 2, 1993, pp. 230–233.

5. "Alcohol Related Mortality and Years of Potential Life Lost—United States, 1987," *Morbidity and Mortality Weekly Report,* March 23, 1990, p. 175. According to the National Household Survey on Drug Abuse, the number of "current" (past-month) drinkers was about 109 million in 1988, roughly the same as in 1995.

6. James Ostrowski, "Thinking About Drug Legalization," Cato Institute Policy Analysis #121, May 25, 1989, p. 47. Starting with data from the Drug Abuse Warning Network, Ostrowski excluded suicides and discounted the number of deaths attributed to illegal drugs by 80 percent to account for the effects of prohibition, including contamination and uncertain doses.

7. On the health effects of cocaine and heroin, see Steven B. Duke and Albert C. Gross, *America's Longest War: Rethinking Our Tragic Crusade Against Drugs,* New York: G. P. Putnam's Sons, 1993, pp. 62–64, 70–73, and Andrew Weil and Winifred Rosen, *From Chocolate to Morphine: Everything You Need to Know About Mind-Altering Drugs,* rev. ed., New York: Houghton Mifflin, 1993, pp. 44–47, 81–92.

8. In the 1994 Monitoring the Future Study, only about 20 percent of past-month marijuana users smoked the drug daily—which, like daily drinking, is not necessarily excessive or irresponsible. On the health effects of marijuana use, see Lynn Zimmer and John P. Morgan, *Marijuana Myths, Marijuana Facts,* New York: The Lindesmith Center, 1997, and Lester Grinspoon and James Bakalar, *Marihuana: The Forbidden Medicine,* New Haven, Conn.: Yale University Press, 1993.

9. Letter from FDA commissioner David A. Kessler to Scott D. Ballin, chairman of the Coalition on Smoking or Health, February 25, 1994.

10. Mark Thornton, *The Economics of Prohibition,* Salt Lake City: University of Utah Press, 1991, p. 102.

11. Milton Friedman, "The War We Are Losing," in Melvyn B. Krauss and Edward P. Lazear, eds., *Searching for Alternatives: Drug-Control Policy in the United States,* Stanford, Calif.: Hoover Institution Press, 1991, pp. 53–67.

12. Thornton, *The Economics of Prohibition,* p. 134.

13. Kenneth D. Rose, *American Women and the Repeal of Prohibition,* New York: New York University Press, 1996, p. 53.

14. Jeffrey A. Miron and Jeffrey Zwiebel, "Alcohol Consumption During Prohibition," *AEA Papers and Proceedings,* 81:2 (May 1991), pp. 242–247.

15. John P. Morgan, "Prohibition Is Perverse Policy," in Melvyn B. Krauss and Edward P. Lazear, eds., *Searching for Alternatives: Drug-Control Policy in the United States,* Stanford, Calif.: Hoover Institution Press, 1991, pp. 405–423.

16. Ibid., p. 410.

17. Henner Hess, "The Other Prohibition: The Cigarette Crisis in Post-War Germany," paper presented at the 47th Annual Conference of the American Society of Criminology, November 1995, p. 10.

18. Dale Gieringer, "Economics of Cannabis Legalization," paper presented at the Seventh International Conference on Drug Policy Reform, November 1993.

19. Wharton Econometric Forecasting Associates, *The Impact: Organized Crime Today*, Washington, D.C.: President's Commission on Organized Crime, 1986. The 1996 National Household Survey on Drug Abuse reported about seventy-nine million past-year consumers of cigarettes and smokeless tobacco, compared to about twenty-three million past-year consumers of illegal drugs.

20. Paul J. Goldstein et al., "Crack and Homicide in New York City, 1988: A Conceptually Based Event Analysis," *Contemporary Drug Problems*, 16:4 (Winter 1989), pp. 651–687.

21. Duke and Gross, *America's Longest War*, pp. 65, 73, 108–110. Jeffrey A. Miron and Jeffrey Zwiebel, "The Economic Case Against Drug Prohibition," *Journal of Economic Perspectives*, 9:4 (Fall 1995), pp. 175–192. Bruce L. Benson and David W. Rasmussen, "Illicit Drugs and Crime," Independent Institute Policy Report, 1996, pp. 25–32.

22. See, e.g., Richard L. Berke, "Corruption in Drug Agency Called Crippler of Inquiries and Morale," *New York Times*, December 17, 1989, p. A1, and Clifford Krauss, "Police Charged in Drug Sting in New York," *New York Times*, April 16, 1994, p. A1.

23. U.S. Department of Justice, *Crime in the United States 1996*, Federal Bureau of Investigation, 1997, pp. 213–214.

24. "Drug Prohibition and the U.S. Prison System," The Lindesmith Center, February 1996. U.S. Department of Justice, *Drugs and Crime Facts*, Bureau of Justice Statistics, 1994.

25. David B. Kopel, "Prison Blues: How America's Foolish Sentencing Policies Endanger Public Safety," Cato Institute Policy Analysis #208, May 17, 1994, p. 6.

26. U.S. Sentencing Guidelines. The death penalty for certain nonviolent marijuana offenses is authorized by 18 USC 3591 (b) (1).

27. *Harmelin v. Michigan*, 111 S.Ct. 2680 (1991).

28. Kopel, "Prison Blues," pp. 3, 5, 6. Benson and Rasmussen, "Illicit Drugs and Crime," pp. 33–35. Joshua Wolf Shenk, "The Phony Drug War," *Nation*, September 23, 1996, p. 11.

29. See, e.g., Duke and Gross, *America's Longest War*, pp. 122–145, and Steven Wisotsky, "A Society of Suspects: The War on Drugs and Civil Liberties," Cato Institute Policy Analysis #180, October 2, 1992.

30. *Illinois v. Gates*, 103 S.Ct. 2317 (1983).

31. *United States v. Leon*, 104 S.Ct. 3405 (1984).

32. *Oliver v. United States*, 104 S.Ct. 1735 (1984). *Florida v. Riley*, 109 S.Ct. 693 (1989).

33. *United States v. Place*, 462 U.S. 606 (1983).

34. *California v. Acevedo*, 111 S.Ct. 1982 (1991).

35. *Ohio v. Robinette*, No. 95–891 (1996).

36. *Skinner v. Railway Labor Executives' Association*, 109 S.Ct. 1402 (1989). *National Treasury Employees Union v. Von Raab*, 109 S.Ct. 1384 (1989). *Vernonia School District v. Acton*, 115 S.Ct. 2386 (1995).

37. See, e.g., *Austin v. United States*, 113 S.Ct. 2801 (1993), holding that forfeiture is subject to the Eighth Amendment's excessive fines clause, and *United States v.*

James Daniel Good Real Property, 114 S.Ct. 492 (1993), holding that the Fifth Amendment's due process clause generally requires the government to notify the owner before seizing real estate. By contrast, in *Bennis v. Michigan,* #94–8729 (1996), the Court upheld the forfeiture of a car used to solicit prostitution, even though the co-owner had no knowledge of the offense.

38. Richard Miniter, "Ill-Gotten Gains," *Reason,* August/September 1993, pp. 32–37.

39. Ostrowski, "Thinking About Drug Legalization," p. 15.

40. Denise Paone et al., "Syringe Exchange: HIV Prevention, Key Findings, and Future Directions," *International Journal of Addictions,* 30:12 (1995), pp. 1647–1683. In 1989 Ostrowski attributed thirty-five hundred AIDS deaths a year to needle sharing.

41. Kleiman, *Against Excess,* p. 361.

42. Peter Reuter, "Rebalancing the Drug Control Budget: A Shadow Play," *Drug Policy Analysis Bulletin,* January 1997, pp. 2–3.

43. Hess, "The Other Prohibition," p. 10.

44. "Cigarette Smoking Among Adults—United States, 1992, and Changes in the Definition of Current Cigarette Smoking," *Morbidity and Mortality Weekly Report,* May 20, 1994, pp. 342–346. HHS, *Preliminary Results from the 1996 National Household Survey on Drug Abuse,* pp. 54, 60, 67 (12- to 17-year-olds subtracted).

45. Miron and Zwiebel, "Alcohol Consumption During Prohibition."

46. Hess, "The Other Prohibition," p. 11.

47. Ibid., pp. 11, 15.

48. Gina Kolata, "Obesity Declared a Disease," *Science,* March 1, 1985, p. 1019.

49. Marian Burros, "Despite Awareness of Risks, More in U.S. Are Getting Fat," *New York Times,* July 17, 1995, p. A1. Jane E. Brody, "Moderate Wait Gain Risky for Women, A Study Warns," *New York Times,* September 14, 1995, p. A1.

50. Michael Fumento, *The Fat of the Land: The Obesity Epidemic and How Overweight Americans Can Help Themselves,* New York: Viking, 1997, pp. 30–31 (italics in original).

51. U.S. Department of Health, Education, and Welfare, *Forward Plan for Health, FY 1977–81,* U.S. Public Health Service, 1975, p. 104.

52. Jack Chambless and Sarah C. McAlister, "Eating with Impunity," *Orlando Sentinel,* December 23, 1996, p. G1.

53. Abram Katz, "Tax Fatty Foods, Yale Prof Offers," *New Haven Register,* July 7, 1997, p. A1.

54. *Talk Back Live,* CNN, March 20, 1997.

55. "In One Town, No-Smoking Area May Be the Beach," *New York Times,* May 21, 1997, p. B5.

56. Wendy Swallow Williams et al., *Alcohol and Tobacco on the Web: New Threats to Youth,* Washington, D.C.: Center for Media Education, 1997, pp. 18–19, 24.

57. Introduction to Albert H. Buck, ed., *A Treatise on Hygiene and Public Health,* New York: Arno Press, 1977 (originally published in 1879), p. 38.

58. Leon S. White, "How to Improve the Public's Health," *New England Journal of Medicine,* 293:15 (October 9, 1975), pp. 773–774.

59. Robert F. Meenan, "Improving the Public's Health: Some Further Reflections," *New England Journal of Medicine,* 294:1 (January 1, 1976), pp. 45–46.

60. John J. Hanlon, *Public Health Administration and Practice,* St. Louis: Mosby, 1974.

61. Jack Smolensky, *Principles of Community Health,* Philadelphia: W. B. Saunders Co., 1977, p. 5.

62. U.S. Department of Health, Education, and Welfare, *Healthy People: The Surgeon General's Report on Health Promotion and Disease Prevention,* U.S. Public Health Service, 1979, p. 9-20.

63. Meenan, "Improving the Public's Health," p. 45.

64. Faith T. Fitzgerald, "The Tyranny of Health," *New England Journal of Medicine,* 331:3 (July 21, 1994), pp. 196–198.

65. C. Everett Koop, "C. Everett Koop: A Surgeon General Speaks," *Priorities,* 8:2 (1996), p. 25.

66. Dan E. Beauchamp, "Public Health as Social Justice," *Inquiry,* 13 (March 1976), pp. 3–14.

BIBLIOGRAPHY

Anderson, Carl L., Richard F. Morton, and Lawrence W. Green. *Community Health*. St. Louis: Mosby, 1978.

Barrie, James M. *My Lady Nicotine*. Chicago: Rand, McNally, 1891 (originally published in 1890 by Hodder and Stoughton, London).

Blaisdell, Albert F. *Our Bodies and How We Live*. Boston: Ginn, 1910.

Boaz, David, ed. *The Crisis in Drug Prohibition*. Washington: Cato Institute, 1990.

Brecher, Edward M. and the Editors of *Consumer Reports*. *Licit and Illicit Drugs*. Boston: Little, Brown, 1972.

Buck, Albert Henry, ed. *A Treatise on Hygiene and Public Health*. New York: Arno Press, 1977 (originally published in 1879).

Buckley, Christopher. *Thank You for Smoking*. New York: Random House, 1994.

Califano, Joseph A., Jr. *Governing America: An Insider's Report from the White House and the Cabinet*. New York: Simon & Schuster, 1981.

Corti, Egon C. *A History of Smoking*. London: George Harrap, 1931.

Davison, Alvin. *The Human Body and Health*. New York: American Book Co., 1908.

Duke, Steven B. and Albert C. Gross. *America's Longest War: Rethinking Our Tragic Crusade Against Drugs*. New York: G. P. Putnam's Sons, 1993.

Etheridge, Elizabeth W. *Sentinel for Health: A History of the Centers for Disease Control*. Berkeley: University of California Press, 1992.

Fingarette, Herbert. *Heavy Drinking: The Myth of Alcoholism as a Disease*. Berkeley: University of California Press, 1988.

Ferguson, Tom. *The No-Nag, No-Guilt, Do-It-Your-Own-Way Guide to Quitting Smoking*. New York: Ballantine Books, 1987.

Ford, Barry J. *Smokescreen: A Guide to the Personal Risks and Global Effects of the Cigarette Habit*. North Perth, Australia: Halcyon Press, 1994.

Ford, Henry, ed. *The Case Against the Little White Slaver.* Detroit, 1914.

Fumento, Michael. *The Fat of the Land: The Obesity Epidemic and How Overweight Americans Can Help Themselves.* New York: Viking, 1997.

Gahagan, Dolly D. *Switch Down and Quit: What the Cigarette Companies Don't Want You to Know About Smoking.* Berkeley, Calif.: Ten Speed Press, 1987.

Galbraith, John Kenneth. *The Affluent Society.* Boston: Houghton Mifflin, 1984 (originally published in 1958).

Glantz, Stanton A., John Slade, Lisa A. Bero, Peter Hanauer, and Deborah E. Barnes. *The Cigarette Papers.* Berkeley: University of California Press, 1996.

Goodman, Jordan. *Tobacco in History: The Cultures of Dependence.* New York: Routledge, 1993.

Gottsegen, Jack J. *Tobacco: A Study of Its Consumption in the United States.* New York: Pitman, 1940.

Gravelle, Jane G. and Dennis Zimmerman. *Cigarette Taxes to Fund Health Care Reform: An Economic Analysis.* Congressional Research Service, 1994.

Grinspoon, Lester and James B. Bakalar. *Marihuana: The Forbidden Medicine.* New Haven: Yale University Press, 1993.

Hall, Winfield S., ed. *Tobacco: The Cigarette: Why It Is Especially Objectionable.* Chicago: Anti-Cigarette League, 1900.

Hilts, Philip J. *Smokescreen: The Truth Behind the Tobacco Industry Cover-up.* Reading, Mass.: Addison-Wesley, 1996.

Huber, Peter W. *Liability: The Legal Revolution and Its Consequences.* New York: Basic Books, 1990.

Idle, Jeffrey R., J. Benítez, H. E. Krokan, P. H. M. Lohman, M. Roberfroid, and A. Springall. *Environmental Tobacco Smoke and Lung Cancer: An Evaluation of the Risk.* Trondheim, Norway: European Working Group, 1996.

James I. *A Counterblaste to Tobacco.* London: English Reprints, 1870 (originally published in 1604).

Jarvik, M. E. et al., eds. *Research on Smoking Behavior.* U.S. Department of Health, Education, and Welfare, 1977.

Jewitt, Frances Gulick. *Good Health.* Boston: Ginn, 1906.

Kiernan, Victor G. *Tobacco: A History.* London: Hutchinson, 1991.

Kleiman, Mark A. R. *Against Excess: Drug Policy for Results.* New York: Basic Books, 1992.

Klein, Richard. *Cigarettes Are Sublime.* Durham, N.C.: Duke University Press, 1993.

Kluger, Richard. *Ashes to Ashes: America's Hundred-Year Cigarette War, the Public Health, and the Unabashed Triumph of Philip Morris.* New York: Alfred A. Knopf, 1996.

Koop, C. Everett. *Koop: The Memoirs of America's Family Doctor.* New York: Random House, 1991.

Krauss, Melvyn B. and Edward P. Lazear, eds. *Searching for Alternatives: Drug-Control Policy in the United States.* Stanford, Calif.: Hoover Institution Press, 1991.

Krogh, David. *Smoking: The Artificial Passion.* New York: W. H. Freeman, 1991.

Krumholz, Harlan M. and Robert H. Phillips. *No If's And's or Butts: The Smoker's Guide to Quitting.* Garden City Park, N.Y.: Avery Publishing Group, 1993.

Lee, Peter N. *Environmental Tobacco Smoke and Mortality.* Basel, Switzerland: Karger, 1992.

London, William L., Elizabeth M. Whelan, and Andrea Golaine Case, eds. *Cigarettes: What the Warning Label Doesn't Tell You.* New York: American Council on Science and Health, 1996.

McGowan, Richard. *Business, Politics, and Cigarettes: Multiple Levels, Multiple Agendas.* Westport, Conn.: Quorum, 1995.

Manning, Willard G., Emmett B. Keeler, Joseph P. Newhouse, Elizabeth M. Sloss, and Jeffrey Wasserman. *The Costs of Poor Health Habits: A RAND Study.* Cambridge, Mass.: Harvard University Press, 1991.

Mather, Cotton. *Manuductio ad Ministerium.* Boston, 1726.

Musto, David F. *The American Disease: Origins of Narcotics Control.* Rev. ed. New York: Oxford University Press, 1987.

National Research Council. *Environmental Tobacco Smoke: Measuring Exposures and Assessing Health Effects.* Washington, D.C.: National Academy Press, 1986.

Packard, Vance. *The Hidden Persuaders.* New York: David McKay, 1957.

Peele, Stanton. *Diseasing of America: Addiction Treatment Out of Control.* Lexington, Mass.: Lexington Books, 1989.

Pertschuk, Mark and Donald R. Shopland. *Major Local Smoking Ordinances in the United States.* Berkeley, Calif.: Americans for Nonsmokers' Rights, 1989.

Petrone, Gerard. *Tobacco Advertising: The Great Seduction.* Atglen, Pa.: Schiffer Publishing, 1996.

Rabin, Robert L. and Steven D. Sugarman, eds. *Smoking Policy: Law, Politics, and Culture.* New York: Oxford University Press, 1993.

Redhead, C. Stephen and Richard E. Rowberg. *Environmental Tobacco Smoke and Lung Cancer Risk.* Congressional Research Service, 1995.

Regulatory Impact Analysis Project Inc. *Choices in Risk Assessment: The Role of Science Policy in the Environmental Risk Management Process.* Washington, D.C.: RIAP (prepared for Sandia National Laboratories, U.S. Department of Energy), 1994.

Rodu, Brad. *For Smokers Only: How Smokeless Tobacco Can Save Your Life.* New York: Sulzburger & Graham, 1995.

Rogers, J. Smyth. *An Essay on Tobacco.* New York: Howe & Bates, 1836.

Rose, Kenneth D. *American Women and the Repeal of Prohibition.* New York: New York University Press, 1996.

Rudgely, Richard. *Essential Substances: A Cultural History of Intoxicants in Society.* New York: Kodansha International, 1993.

Rush, Benjamin. *Essays, Moral, Political and Philosophical.* Philadelphia, 1798.

Samet, Jonathan N., ed. *Epidemiology of Lung Cancer.* New York: Dekker, 1994.

Schivelbusch, Wolfgang. *Tastes of Paradise: A Social History of Spices, Stimulants, and Intoxicants.* New York: Random House, 1992.

Siegel, Ronald K. *Intoxication: Life in Pursuit of Artificial Paradise.* New York: E. P. Dutton, 1989.

Skrabanek, Petr. *The Death of Humane Medicine and the Rise of Coercive Healthism.* London: The Social Affairs Unit, 1994.

Smolensky, Jack. *Principles of Community Health.* Philadelphia: W. B. Saunders, 1977.

Stimmel, Barry and the Editors of *Consumer Reports. The Facts about Drug Use.* Yonkers, N.Y.: Consumer Reports Books, 1991.

Stockman, David A. *The Triumph of Politics: How the Reagan Revolution Failed.* New York: Harper & Row, 1986.

Szasz, Thomas. *Ceremonial Chemistry.* Rev. ed. Holmes Beach, Fla.: Learning Publications, 1985.

Taylor, C. Barr and Joel D. Killen. *The Facts About Smoking.* Yonkers, N.Y.: Consumer Reports Books, 1991.

Thornton, Mark. *The Economics of Prohibition.* Salt Lake City: University of Utah Press, 1991.

Tobacco Institute. *The Tax Burden on Tobacco: Historical Compilation, Volume 31, 1996.* Washington, D.C.: Tobacco Institute, 1997.

Tollison, Robert D. and Richard E. Wagner. *The Economics of Smoking.* Boston: Kluwer Academic, 1992.

Tollison, Robert D. and Richard E. Wagner. *Smoking and the State: Social Costs, Rent Seeking, and Public Policy.* Lexington, Mass.: Lexington Books, 1988.

Trask, George. *Thoughts and Stories on Tobacco for American Lads; or Uncle Toby's Anti-Tobacco Advice to His Nephew Billy Bruce.* Boston, 1852.

Troyer, Ronald J. and Gerald E. Markle. *Cigarettes: The Battle over Smoking.* New Brunswick, N.J.: Rutgers University Press, 1983.

U.S. Department of Health, Education, and Welfare. *Forward Plan for Health, FY 1977–81.* U.S. Public Health Service, 1975.

U.S. Department of Health, Education and Welfare. *Healthy People: The Surgeon General's Report on Health Promotion and Disease Prevention.* U.S. Public Health Service, 1979.

U.S. Department of Health, Education, and Welfare. *Smoking and Health: Report of the Advisory Committee to the Surgeon General of the Public Health Service.* U.S. Public Health Service, Center for Disease Control, 1964.

U.S. Department of Health and Human Services. *The Health Benefits of Smoking Cessation: A Report of the Surgeon General.* U.S. Public Health Service, Centers for Disease Control, Office on Smoking and Health, 1990.

U.S. Department of Health and Human Services. *The Health Consequences of Involuntary Smoking: A Report of the Surgeon General.* U.S. Public Health Service, Centers for Disease Control, Office on Smoking and Health, 1986.

U.S. Department of Health and Human Services. *The Health Conse-*

quences of Smoking: Cardiovascular Disease/A Report of the Surgeon General. U.S. Public Health Service, Office on Smoking and Health, 1983.

U.S. Department of Health and Human Services. The Health Consequences of Smoking: Nicotine Addiction/A Report of the Surgeon General. U.S. Public Health Service, Centers for Disease Control, Office on Smoking and Health, 1988.

U.S. Department of Health and Human Services. The Health Consequences of Smoking for Women: A Report of the Surgeon General. U.S. Public Health Service, Office on Smoking and Health, 1980.

U.S. Department of Health and Human Services. The Health Consequences of Using Smokeless Tobacco: A Report of the Advisory Committee to the Surgeon General, U.S. Public Health Service, 1986.

U.S. Department of Health and Human Services. Major Local Tobacco Control Ordinances in the United States. U.S. Public Health Service, National Institutes of Health, National Cancer Institute, 1993.

U.S. Department of Health and Human Services. National Survey Results on Drug Use from the Monitoring the Future Study, 1975–1995, Volume I: Secondary School Students. U.S. Public Health Service, National Institutes of Health, National Institute on Drug Abuse, 1996.

U.S. Department of Health and Human Services. National Survey Results on Drug Use from the Monitoring the Future Study, 1975–1994, Volume II: College Students and Young Adults. U.S. Public Health Service, National Institutes of Health, National Institute on Drug Abuse, 1996.

U.S. Department of Health and Human Services. Preliminary Results from the 1996 National Household Survey on Drug Abuse. U.S. Public Health Service, Substance Abuse and Mental Health Services Administration, 1997.

U.S. Department of Health and Human Services. Preventing Tobacco Use Among Young People: A Report of the Surgeon General. U.S. Public Health Service, Centers for Disease Control and Prevention, Office on Smoking and Health, 1994.

U.S. Department of Health and Human Services. Reducing the Health Consequences of Smoking: 25 Years of Progress/A Report of the Surgeon General. U.S. Public Health Service, Centers for Disease Control, Office on Smoking and Health, 1989.

U.S. Department of Health and Human Services. *Smoking and Health in the Americas.* U.S. Public Health Service, Centers for Disease Control, Office on Smoking and Health, 1992.

U.S. Department of Justice. *Crime in the United States 1996.* Federal Bureau of Investigation, 1997.

U.S. Department of Justice. *Drug and Crime Facts.* Bureau of Justice Statistics, 1994.

U.S. Environmental Protection Agency. *The Costs and Benefits of Smoking Restrictions: An Assessment of the Smoke-Free Environment Act of 1993.* EPA, 1994.

U.S. Environmental Protection Agency. *Respiratory Health Effects of Passive Smoking: Lung Cancer and Other Disorders.* EPA, 1992.

U.S. Federal Trade Commission. *Federal Trade Commission Report to Congress for 1993 Pursuant to the Federal Cigarette Labeling and Advertising Act.* FTC, 1995.

Viscusi, W. Kip. *Smoking: Making the Risky Decision.* New York: Oxford University Press, 1992.

Wald, N. and P. Froggatt, eds. *Nicotine, Smoking and the Low Tar Programme.* New York: Oxford University Press, 1989.

Weil, Andrew and Winifred Rosen. *From Chocolate to Morphine: Everything You Need to Know about Mind-Altering Drugs.* New York: Houghton Mifflin, 1993.

Whelan, Elizabeth M. *A Smoking Gun: How the Tobacco Industry Gets Away with Murder.* Philadelphia: George F. Stockley, 1984.

White, Larry C. *Merchants of Death: The American Tobacco Industry.* New York: Beech Tree Books, 1988.

Williams, Wendy S., Kathryn Montgomery, and Shelley Pasnik. *Alcohol and Tobacco on the Web: New Threats to Youth.* Washington, D.C.: Center for Media Education, 1997.

Wilner, Daniel M., Rosabelle Price Walkley, and Edward J. O'Neill. *Introduction to Public Health.* New York: Macmillan, 1978.

Zimmer, Lynn and John P. Morgan. *Marijuana Myths, Marijuana Facts.* New York: The Lindesmith Center, 1997.

Zinberg, Norman E. *Drug, Set and Setting: The Basis for Controlled Intoxicant Use.* New Haven: Yale University Press, 1984.

ACKNOWLEDGMENTS

I should first thank my agent, Glen Hartley, who suggested this project and put me in touch with The Free Press. In thinking about the threat to liberty posed by an expansive interpretation of public health, I relied heavily on the insights of Thomas Szasz, whose prescient warnings about the disease model are more relevant today than ever, and Petr Skrabanek, whose witty and erudite book *The Death of Humane Medicine and the Rise of Coercive Healthism* deserves much wider circulation. Several people were especially helpful during the research phase. Ethan Nadelmann at the Lindesmith Center, Elizabeth Whelan at the American Council on Science and Health, Kenneth Warner at the University of Michigan, Susan Lucius at the American Heart Association, Tom Borelli at Philip Morris, Tom Lauria at the Tobacco Institute, and the staff of the rare books section at the New York Public Library answered questions, suggested references, and provided research material. Many readers of my work in *Reason, National Review,* and elsewhere sent me useful articles; they are too numerous to list, but I would be remiss if I didn't mention Martha Perske. *Reason* interns Marc Levin, Cosmo Wenman, Jamie Plummer, and Helen Gao assisted with library research. Virginia Postrel, Nick Gillespie, Rick Newcombe, David Booth, Jean Boddewyn, Marc Roston, Steve Postrel, Dwight Lee, Geoffrey Kabat, James Enstrom, Roger Jenkins, Walter Olson, Peter Huber, and Stanton Peele reviewed some or all of the manuscript and provided valuable advice. At The Free Press, Adam Bellow and David Bernstein helped sharpen the manuscript, while Chad Conway guided me through the production process. Finally, *Reason* art director Barbara Burch and Eric Solberg of Doctors Ought to Care helped me gather illustrations on a tight schedule and a shoestring budget.

INDEX

Abrams, Floyd, 111
Action on Smoking and Health (ASH), xii,
    86–87, 90, 128, 139, 145, 158–59,
    184, 254
Addiction, 7, 11, 13, 22, 24, 28, 67,
    127–28, 220–57, 277, 280
    in *Carter* case, 215
    in *Cipollone* case, 191, 197, 200, 203, 204
    in *Connor* case, 216
    disease model of, 236, 248–49
    in *Engle* case, 203
    and FDA regulation, 214, 223–25
    historical perspective on, 232–37
    individual variations and, 237–42
    set and setting in, 242–44
    tobacco companies on, 181, 188, 215,
        220–21, 240, 241–42
    withdrawal symptoms in, 238–39, 241–42
Adler, Isaac, 42
Advertising and promotion (tobacco), 12,
    13, 28, 36, 48, 51, 82–112, 191, 192:
    see also Anti-smoking ads
    ban advocated for, 92
    ban on broadcast advertising, 77, 82–83,
        90–91, 92, 108, 111
    and blacks, 95–96
    and children, 28, 58, 61, 85, 91, 92–93,
        96–101, 105–107, 108, 116–17, 251
    cost of, 92
    fairness doctrine and broadcast advertis-
        ing, 85–87, 110, 112–13
    freedom of speech and, 86, 90, 107–112,
        113
    impact on smoking of, 96–107, 278
    industry code for, 84–85
    restrictions on, 12, 92–93, 183–84, 268
    and target marketing, 95–96
    tobacco company settlement and, 12, 93,
        183–84
    and women, 36, 95, 96, 104
Advisory Committee on Tobacco Policy and
    Public Health, 253
Advocacy Institute, 122, 187

Affluent Society, The (Galbraith), 83
Airline smoking ban, 138–42, 146, 151,
    153, 178
Alaska, 125
Alcohol, 243–44, 257, 258, 262
    prohibition of, 37, 237, 259–61, 266, 267
    temperance movement and, 24–25, 26,
        30, 37, 69, 233, 236–37
American Anti-Tobacco Society, 25
American Cancer Society (ACS), xiv, 6, 46,
    47, 55, 64, 65, 76, 125, 157, 252, 278
    public service announcements, 88–89, 92
    safer cigarettes and, 68, 72
    secondhand smoke and, 149, 150, 172,
        176, 179
    tobacco company settlement and, 184, 185
American Civil Liberties Union (ACLU),
    107–108, 157, 273
American Council on Science and Health,
    56, 66, 75, 93, 128, 172
American Heart Association (AHA), 6, 92,
    113, 176, 185
American Lung Association (ALA), 6, 59,
    75, 92, 150, 157
American Medical Association (AMA), 9,
    70, 74, 92, 97, 122, 185, 247
American Psychiatric Association, 235, 242
American Public Health Association, 62,
    92, 276
Americans for Nonsmokers' Rights, xi, 146,
    254
Americans with Disabilities Act, 156–57
American Tobacco Company, 27, 47–48,
    49, 215, 221: see also *Carter* case; *Cas-
    tano v. American Tobacco*
Anatomy of Melancholy, The (Burton), 18
Annis, Edward R., 70
Anslinger, Harry J., 237
Anti-Cigarette League of America, 30
Anti-smoking ads, 3, 12, 65, 83, 88–91,
    112–18, 125, 173–75, 177, 251
Anti-Tobacco Journal, 25–27
Arizona, 115, 125, 146

Arkansas, 37, 125
Arthur D. Little, 195
Ashes to Ashes (Kluger), 224
Associated Industries of Florida, 210, 212
Asthma, 152, 157, 159, 203
Auerbach, Oscar, 72
Ault, Richard W., 129
Austin v. Tennessee, 30–31

Bacon, Sir Francis, 220, 232, 277
Bailar, John C., 161
Balance of Truth, The (Chelebi), 20–21
Balde, Jakob, 20, 57, 233
Ballin, Scott, xii–xiii, 6, 16, 222, 225, 228, 230
Band of Hope Pledge, 26
Banner, Stuart, 109–10
Banzhaf, John F., III, xii, 85–88, 90, 91, 96, 128, 137, 145, 146, 155, 158, 159, 184–85, 254
Barrett, Don, 208
Barrie, James, 223
Beauchamp, Dan E., 276
Becker, Gary S., xiii, 246–47
Belli, Melvin, 199, 204
Belshe, S. Kimberly, 116
Benedict XIII, Pope, 23
Benson & Hedges, 10, 71
Bergin, Kevin, 8
Bible, Geoffrey, 55
Billings, John S., 61–62, 273
Blacks and smoking, 95–96
Blaisdell, Alfred F., 143–44
Bloch, Michele, 254
Blum, Alan, 5, 113–14, 224
Blumenthal, Richard, 213
Boddewyn, Jean J., 107
Bonsack, James, 27
Boyle, John M., 159
Brain damage (as an effect of smoking), 18, 25, 31–32, 258
Brandt, Allan M., 65
Brenton, David, 7
Bristow, Lonnie, 9–10
British-American Tobacco (BAT), 27, 188
Broin v. Philip Morris, 200–202
Bronchitis, 41, 52, 113, 159: see also Chronic obstructive lung disease
Brooke Group Ltd., 206
Brownell, Kelly, 271
Browner, Carol, 154
Brownson, Ross C., 167, 173
Brown & Williamson, 50, 95, 187, 188, 203, 208, 213–14, 215, 217, 221, 231: see also *Carter* case
Bryant, John, 222
Buckley, Christopher, 7
Bull Durham, 97
Burger King, 157
Burney, Leroy, 52
Burton, Robert, 18
Bush, George, 120–21
Butts, Calvin O., III, 95

Cahan, William, 271
Caldwell, Michael, 8
Califano, Joseph A., Jr., 57–59, 61, 63, 72, 77
California, 112–13, 115–16, 124–25, 126, 136, 150–51, 152, 153, 156, 177
Californians for Nonsmokers' Rights (CNR), xi, 146, 147, 150
Camel, 36, 48
Campaign for Tobacco-Free Kids, 251, 252
Campbell, William, 54, 220
Canada, 112, 136–37, 266
Cancer, 17, 24, 26, 41, 42, 52, 54, 55, 72, 78, 151, 244–45: see also Lung cancer
Capri, 95
Carlton, 69, 71
Carter, Jimmy, 57, 58–59
Carter, Peggy, 94
Carter case, 215–16, 217
Casas, Bartholomé de las, 17, 232, 246
Castano v. American Tobacco, 203–207, 212, 213, 216
Cato Institute, 164, 257
Center for Indoor Air Research, 171
Center for Science in the Public Interest, 24, 120
Centers for Disease Control and Prevention, U.S. (CDC), 6, 56, 63–64, 68, 77, 99, 130, 173, 174, 175, 240, 245, 257
Central Hudson Gas & Electric Corp. v. Public Service Commission, 108
Ceremonial Chemistry (Szasz), 221
Chabot, Jean-Jude, 112
Chelebi, Katib, 20–21
Cherner, Joseph W., 5–6, 8, 114
Chesley, Stanley M., 204
Chesterfield, 36, 48, 182, 192, 193
Chicago Anti-Cigarette League, 29, 30, 31
Childers, W. D., 210
Children, 12, 13, 28–29, 124, 128
    addiction and, 249–54, 280
    advertising and, 28, 85, 91, 92–93, 96–101, 105–107, 108, 116–17, 251

secondhand smoke and, 151, 158, 159–60
   tobacco taxes and, 128, 254
Chiles, Lawton, 181, 209, 210, 211–12
Chretien, Jean, 137
Chronic obstructive lung disease, 55, 56, 72
Cigarette Labeling and Advertising Act of
   1965, 53, 90, 193
Cigarettes Are Sublime (Klein), 35, 67
Cigars, 11–12, 17, 23, 28, 29, 69, 76–77,
   277–78
Cipollone, Rose, 191–94, 196–98, 200
Cipollone v. Liggett Group, 191–99, 203,
   204, 213, 231
Citizens Against Tobacco Smoke (CATS),
   138, 139
Citizens for a Tobacco-Free Society, 113,
   142, 185
Class action lawsuits, 182–83, 184, 200–207:
   see also *Broin v. Philip Morris*; *Castano v.
   American Tobacco*; *Engle v. R.J. Reynolds*
Clean Indoor Air Act (Minn.), 146
Clean Life Pledge, 30
Clements, Earle, 196
Clinton, Bill, 83, 98, 108, 110, 122–23,
   126, 133, 153, 183, 230, 254, 259
Coale, John P., 204, 205, 207
Coalition for a Smoke-Free City, 174
Coalition on Smoking or Health, xii, 6, 16,
   61, 74, 75, 97, 122, 126, 128, 130,
   140, 222, 253
Cocaine, 22, 257, 258, 261, 262, 263
Cohn, Donald J., 196
Cole, Philip, 79
Colorado, 125
Commercial speech, 108–112
Common Cause, 150
Competitive Enterprise Institute (CEI), 227
Comprehensive Smoking Education Act of
   1984, 53
Confidence intervals, 164–66
Confounding variables, 56–57, 168–69,
   175, 176
Congressional Research Service (CRS), 127,
   131–32, 133, 161, 166, 169, 278
Connecticut, 19, 124, 213
Connolly, Gregory, 78, 80, 254
Connor case, 216–17
Conrad, Marie, 159
Consumers Union, 76–77
Corti, Egon C., 18, 24
Council for Tobacco Research (CTR), 49,
   54, 184, 194
Counterblaste to Tobacco, A (James I),

17–18, 143, 232, 277

Dakota, 95, 114
Darman, Richard, 120
Darnell, Alan M., 198
Dawson, Brennan, 226
Daynard, Richard, 187, 217, 218–19
Day One, 228–29, 230
Deaths, smoking-related, 55–57, 67–68, 257
DeFalco, Julie, 6–7
Denicotined cigarettes, 224, 280
Denny's restaurants, 157
DeParle, Jason, 94–95
*Diagnostic and Statistical Manual of Mental
   Disorders* (DSM), 235
DiFranza, Joseph R., 99, 101
Disease model of smoking, 61–64, 248–49,
   268–76, 280
Doctors Ought to Care (DOC), 113–14, 224
Dole, Bob, 239–40
Doll, Richard, 45–46
Donahue, Daniel, 55
Dorfman, Lori, 117
Douglas, Clifford, 229
Drew, Elizabeth, 87
Drug-free America, 256, 258, 269
Drug prohibition, 261–65
Drugs: see specific drugs
Drunkenness (as an effect of smoking),
   24–25, 26, 32
Duke, James B., 27, 28
Durbin, Richard J., 138, 140, 141, 142,
   153, 154

Eclipse, 74–75, 267
Edell, Marc Z., 190–91, 193, 194–95, 197,
   198, 199
Edison, Thomas, 32
Eighteenth Amendment, 259
Eighth Amendment, 158, 263
Elizabeth Charlotte, Princess, 233
Emphysema, 2, 6, 41, 53, 54, 57, 65, 66,
   113, 203, 244: see also Chronic ob-
   structive lung disease
Engle v. R.J. Reynolds, 203, 204, 216
Enstrom, James E., 161, 167, 170, 171,
   173–74, 177
Environmental Protection Agency (EPA), xi,
   xiii, 148, 151, 152–53, 154, 155, 156,
   161–62, 163–64, 165, 166, 167–68,
   169, 170–73, 174, 175, 177
Environmental tobacco smoke (ETS): see
   Secondhand smoke

Eriksen, Michael, 6, 77
Etzioni, Amitai, 107
Eve, 95

Fagon, 22, 232, 277
Fairness doctrine, 85–88, 110, 112–13
Fat of the Land, The (Fumento), 270
Federal Communications Commission
    (FCC), 85–86, 88, 90, 110, 112–13
Federal Trade Commission (FTC), 53, 69–70,
    73, 84, 90, 91, 97–98, 110–11, 224
Feinstein, Alvan, xiii, 161
Feinstein, Dianne, 150
Ferdinand III, Emperor, 20
Fifth Amendment, 153
Filter-tipped cigarettes, 50–51
First Amendment, 86, 90, 107–108, 109,
    110, 111, 113: see also Freedom of
    speech
Fischer, Paul M., 98, 100–101
Fisher, Irving, 259–60
Fitzgerald, Faith T., 275
Flay, Brian R., 113
Flight attendants' lawsuit, 200–202
Florida, 158, 208–212, 213, 214–16
Florida Smokers' Rights Association, 155
Foege, William H., 56
Fontham, Elizabeth T. H., 168, 173
Food and Drug Administration (FDA), 10,
    12, 74, 251, 252, 253, 259
    advertising and, 92–93, 108, 109
    regulation of tobacco by, 182, 183–84,
        186, 206, 217, 222–23, 224–28,
        230–31, 232, 267
Food, Drug, and Cosmetic Act, 223, 224,
    226–28
Ford, Henry, 32, 48, 143, 258
*For Smokers Only: How Smokeless Tobacco
    Can Save Your Life* (Rodu), 78
Forward Plan for Health, 270
Freedom of speech, 107–112: see also First
    Amendment
Freund, Charles Paul, 8, 10–11
Friedman, Milton, 260
F.S. Kinney and Company, 27
Fumento, Michael, 270

Galbraith, John Kenneth, 83
Galbraith, Mark, 199–200
Garfinkel, Lawrence, 148, 149
Gaston, Lucy Page, 29–30, 37–38, 61, 143,
    254, 258, 268
Gauthier, Wendell, 204, 205

Geller, Henry, 86
Glantz, Stanton A., xi, xii, 9, 102, 147,
    149–50, 185, 218, 252, 253
Goldstone, Steven F., 55, 183
Goodman, Ellen, 93, 120
Gori, Gio Batta, 70–72, 73, 78
Gough, Michael, 161, 164, 166, 170, 171,
    175
Graham, Evarts A., 44–45, 46, 47
Graham, Robert, 253–54
Gray, Herb, 137
Grimes, Stephen, 211
Grossman, Michael, xiii
Group Against Smokers' Pollution (GASP),
    139, 146

Hahn, Paul M., 47–48, 49
Hammond, E. Cuyler, 46, 47, 72, 87
Hanlon, John J., 274
Hardy, David R., 187–88
Harries, Benjamin R., 37
Harrington, Milton E., 195
Harris, Jeffrey, 133–34
Harrison Narcotics Act, 267
Harvard Institute for the Study of Smoking
    Behavior and Policy, 75, 106, 129
Harvard Nurses Study, 176–77, 279
Hawaii, 125
Hazleton Europe, 163
*Health Consequences of Involuntary Smoking,
    The*, 140, 151
Healthy People, 63, 64, 275
Heart disease
    secondhand smoke and, 149, 151,
        175–77, 279
    smoking and, 2, 31, 41, 46, 52, 53, 55,
        56, 57, 65, 66, 70, 72, 110–11, 113,
        176–77
Heinlein, Robert, 236
Heller, John R., 47
Helmar's, 36
Helms, Jesse, 140
Henderson, Sue, 155
Henningfield, Jack, 254
Heroin, 237–39, 240–41, 242, 243, 257,
    258, 261, 262
Hess, Henner, 241, 266
Hidden Persuaders, The (Packard), 83
Hill, A. Bradford, 45–46
Hilts, Philip J., xi–xii, 9, 250
Hirayama, Takeshi, 148, 149
Hirsch, Jules, 269
Hitchcock, Jan, 75

Hitchens, Christopher, 6
Hitler, Adolf, 8
Holleb, Arthur, 72
Homicide, 260, 262
Hooks, Benjamin, 96
Hoover, Herbert, 260
Horn, Daniel, 46, 47, 65, 87
Horrigan, Edward A., 221
Horton, Nathan, 200, 208
House Subcommittee on Health and the
    Environment, xiii, 54, 220–21
Howard, Ron, 8
Hubbell, Charles B., 28–29, 42–43
Huber, Gary, xiii
Humphrey, Hubert H., III, 185
Hunt, Jim, 58

Idaho, 37
Indiana, 34, 135
Indians (Native Americans), 15, 17–18, 23,
    244
Innocent X, Pope, 20, 23
Interagency Council on Smoking and
    Health, 144
International Anti-Cigarette League, 30, 37
Internet, 272–73
Introduction to Public Health, 62
Iowa, 30, 37

Jacobson, Michael F., 120, 121
Jaffe, Jerome H., 232
James I, King, 17–19, 35, 42, 48, 121, 134,
    143, 232, 233, 241, 277
Jenkins, Roger A., 163
Jerez, Rodrigo de, 15–16
Joe Camel, 83, 96–101, 102, 217, 278
Johnson, Lyndon, 121
Johnson, Robert, 7–8
Johnson, Samuel, 23, 143
Johnston, Donald S., 221
Johnston, James W., 54, 116, 220, 240
Johnston, Lennox M., 223
Jones, Okla B., 205, 206
Jordan, David Starr, 32
Journal of the American Medical Association
    (*JAMA*), 6, 9, 44, 45, 56, 71, 73,
    97–100, 131, 249
Journal of the National Cancer Institute, 105,
    168

Kabat, Geoffrey, 160–61, 165, 167, 170,
    171, 172
Kansas, 37–38

Kawachi, Ichiro, 176
Kaye, Robert P., 201, 202
Kazman, Sam, 227
Kennedy, Donald, 226
Kennedy, John F., 40–41
Kent, 51
Kentucky, 135
Kessler, David A., 13, 100, 184, 204, 214,
    222–23, 224–25, 227, 228, 230–31,
    232, 249, 253, 254, 259, 268
King, Florence, 6
Kleiman, Mark, 147
Klein, Richard, 35, 67
Kluger, Richard, 224
Knowles, John H., 133
Kool, 95
Koop, C. Everett, 9, 59–61, 67, 77, 140,
    147, 151, 184, 197, 253, 254, 255,
    268, 275–76, 280
Kozinski, Alex, 109–10
Kurland, Philip B., 109

Lambert, Samuel, 36–37
Landers, Alan, 2–3, 4, 9, 216
Lautenberg, Frank, 141, 142, 153
Lawsuits, 10, 53–54, 181–219: see also spe-
    cific lawsuits
    assumption-of-risk argument in, 188,
        196, 200, 203, 216, 217, 219
    class actions, 182–83, 184, 200–207
    by individual smokers or their relatives,
        191–200, 215–19
    raising secondhand smoke claims,
        156–59, 182–83, 200–202
    by states, 182, 183, 184, 207–215, 279
    strict liability in, 189–91, 193, 194, 198,
        219
LeBow, Bennett S., 181, 206
Lee, Philip R., 270
Leichtman, Ahron, 113, 138–41, 142, 146,
    152–53, 155–56, 185, 218
Leigh, J. Paul, 129
Levin, Fredric G., 210
Levin, Morton L., 45
Levine, Harry G., 236–37
Lewis, Michael T., 207–208
Life expectancy, 42, 66–67, 68, 78
Liggett Group, 54, 55, 100, 181–83, 187,
    193–94, 196–98, 206, 213, 221: see
    also *Cipollone v. Liggett Group*
Liggett & Myers, 27, 48, 50, 192
Lippmann, Morton, 171
Little, Clarence Cook, 54

L&M, 50, 182, 192, 193
Long, Gerald H., 51
Lorillard, 27, 36, 48, 50, 54, 193–94, 195, 197, 221
Lott, Trent, 183
Louisiana, 213
Louis XIII, King, 21
Louis XIV, King, 22, 232, 233, 277
Lowrey, Alfred H., 148, 162–63
Low-yield cigarettes, 50–51, 69–72, 73, 224, 266
LSD, 243, 263
Lucky 100s, 71
Lucky Strike, 36, 215
Luik, John C., 249
Lung cancer
    secondhand smoke and, 140, 148, 149, 151, 152, 160–75, 201, 278–79
    smoking and, 2–3, 38–39, 41–43, 44–47, 49, 50, 52, 53, 55, 56, 57, 65, 66, 70, 72, 76, 88–89
Lynch, Cornelius J., 71, 73

Maine, 125
Manning, Willard G., 131
Manson, JoAnn E., 270
Marijuana, 32, 243, 250–51, 258, 261, 263, 265
Marlboro, 5, 36, 50, 83, 89, 99–100, 163, 217
Marlboro Man, 82, 181, 209
Martin, James, 120
Martin, John, 228–29
Martin, Steve, 144
Maryland, 153
Massachusetts, 19, 115, 125, 134, 135, 151, 213
Massachusetts Tobacco Control Program, 78
Mather, Cotton, 19, 232, 277
McArthur, Douglas, 44
McDonald's, 157
McGowan, Richard, 125–26, 134–35
McKinney, William, 157–58
McNally, William D., 43, 46
Mecklenburg, Robert, 78–79
Medicaid, 133, 279
Medicaid lawsuits, 182, 183, 184, 207–215, 279
Medicaid Third-Party Liability Act of 1994 (Fla.), 208–211
Medicare, 131, 133
Meenan, Robert F., 274, 275
Mencken, H. L., 256, 260

Merchants of Death (White), 56, 107
Merit DeNic, 224
Merryman, Walker, 121
Meta-analysis, 165, 166, 168
Mexico, 136
Michael, Czar, 21
Michigan, 124, 135, 151, 263
Mikva, Abner, 108
Mill, John Stuart, 4
Milloy, Courtland, 97
Minnesota, 34, 124, 146, 199, 215
Miron, Jeffrey A., 266
Mississippi, 183, 200, 207–208, 212, 213, 214–15
Misty, 95
Mohammed IV, 21
Mold, James D., 196
Monardes, Nicolò, 17
Moore, Mike, 207–208
Moral corruption (as an effect of smoking), 19, 26, 28–29, 33, 80
Morales, Daniel, 9, 213
Morgan, John P., 261
Moscherosch, Johann Michael, 15, 19–20, 81, 232, 277
Motley, Ronald L., 204, 212, 216
Mousavizadeh, Nader, 6
Mulcahey, Katie, 35
Müller, F. H., 43
Multiple Risk Factor Intervention Trial (MR FIT), 110–11
Murad IV, Sultan, 20–21
Murphy, Kevin M., 246–47
Murrow, Edward R., 47
Myers, Matthew, 75, 179, 183, 253
My Lady Nicotine (Barrie), 223

Nader, Ralph, 87, 146, 185
Napoleon III, Emperor, 21
National Academy of Sciences, 151
National Anti-Cigarette League, 30, 37–38
National Cancer Institute (NCI), xiii–xiv, 47, 70, 71, 79–80, 168
National Center for Tobacco-Free Kids, 9–10, 13, 83, 117, 179, 183, 185, 252–53
National Clearinghouse for Smoking and Health, 57–58, 65
National Congress of Parents and Teachers, 85
National Household Survey on Drug Abuse, 237–38, 240, 249–50, 257
National Institute on Drug Abuse, 235, 239
National Institutes of Health, 79–80

National Mortality Followback Survey, 176
National Research Council (NRC), 140,
	151, 152, 169
Nebraska, 37
Nelson, Gaylord, 121
Ness, Eliot, 260
Newcomer, Clarence C., 207
New England Journal of Medicine, 78, 130,
	270, 274, 275
New Hampshire, 125, 134
New Jersey, 198, 199
New York, 135, 151, 153
New York Anti-Tobacco Society, 25
Next, 224
Nicholl, Jack, 128
Nicot, Jean, 17, 223
Nicotine, 17, 69, 70, 73, 74, 75, 77, 78, 80,
	175, 181, 184, 188, 203, 204, 220–43,
	259, 265, 267: see also Addiction;
	Low-yield cigarettes
	cigarettes as delivery devices for, 226–28,
		242
	control of levels, 203, 204, 223–24,
		228–32, 280
	pharmacologic effects of, 44, 224–225
Nilsson, Robert, 161
Non-Smokers Protective League of America,
	33, 143
Nonsmokers' rights, 33, 87, 139, 142–43,
	143–47, 150, 157, 178, 273: see also
	Smokers' rights
North Carolina, 124, 135, 140
North Dakota, 30
Novelli, William D., 252–53
Novello, Antonia, 97
Now, 69

Obesity, 269–71
Occupational Safety and Health Adminis-
	tration (OSHA), 153, 173
Ochsner, Alton, 43, 47
O'Hara, Jim, 231
Ohio, 135
Oklahoma, 30, 34
Old Gold, 48
Oliver, Daniel, 111
Opiates, 237–39, 257
Oregon, 125, 134–35
Organized crime, 135, 137, 259, 261
Osteen, William L., 93, 153, 227–28
Ostrowski, James, 257
Our Bodies and How We Live (Blaisdell),
	31–32, 143–44

Oviedo y Valdes, Fernandez de, 16–17, 67

Packard, Vance, 83
Palladium cigarettes, 194
Panzer, Fred, 194
Parliament, 192, 193
Parrish, Steven, 230
Partnership for a Drug-Free America, 256,
	258
Pauly, John, 75
Pearl, Raymond, 43
Pease, Charles G., 33, 143, 144
Pediatric disease label, 13, 249, 253, 280
Peele, Stanton, 237, 245–46
Pentagon, 153
Pentony, William and Valerie, 159
Pepples, Ernest, 50
Per capita cigarette consumption, 27–28,
	44, 51, 52, 89–90, 91, 115, 119, 121
Pershing, John J., 35, 44
Pertschuk, Mark, 254
Peter the Great, 21
Pfleger, Michael, 95–96
Philip Morris, xi, xii, xiii, 27, 36, 50, 54,
	94, 187, 224, 230, 256, 258
	advertising and, 100, 103, 110
	Broin case and, 200–202
	Cipollone case and, 193–94, 195, 197, 231
	defamation lawsuit filed by, 229
	secondhand smoke issue and, 153
	settlement agreement and, 183
	on smoking addictiveness, 214, 220
	on smoking hazards, 51, 55
Pierce, John P., 99–100, 101, 105
Pipes, 22, 23, 28, 29, 69, 76–77, 277–78
*Posadas de Puerto Rico Associates v. Tourism
	Company of Puerto Rico*, 109
Pregnancy, smoking and, 49, 53
Premier, 74, 75
Price, John Wiley, 95
Principles of Community Health, 62, 274
Product Liability Act of 1987 (N.J.), 194, 198
Prohibition
	of alcohol, 37, 237, 259–61, 266, 267
	and civil liberties, 259, 263–64
	and corruption, 259, 260, 262, 266
	and crime, 259, 260, 262, 265, 266
	of drugs, 261–65
	and prices, 259–60, 261, 265
	and quality, 259, 261, 264–65, 266
	of tobacco or cigarettes, 10, 19, 20–21,
		30–31, 34, 37–38, 225–26, 228,
		254–55, 265–67, 268

Proposition 99 (Calif.), 115–16, 124–25, 126, 127, 174
Proposition P (San Francisco), 150
Proxy bias, 169
Public Health Administration and Practice (Hanlon), 274
Public Health Cigarette Smoking Act of 1969, 53, 91, 193
Public health model, 12–13, 61–64, 68, 76, 127, 268–71, 273–76
Public service announcements (PSAs): see Anti-smoking ads
Puffer Alliance, 154
Puritans, 19

Question 1 (Mass.), 125

Rabin, Robert L., 200, 217
Racketeer Influenced and Corrupt Organizations Act, 213
Ralph Nader Health Research Group, 72
RAND Corporation, 131, 132, 278
Rational addiction theory, 247
Ravenholt, R. T., 56
Reader's Digest, 47, 192
Reagan, Ronald, 60, 119, 120, 140
Reason magazine/Reason Foundation, xi, xii
Recall bias, 169
Reconstituted tobacco, 224, 229–30
Redford, Robert, 8
Repace, James L., 148, 162–63
Restatement (Second) of Torts, 189–90, 219
Restaurant smoking bans, 11, 37, 153–54, 156, 157, 179
Rhode Island, 125
Richelieu, Cardinal, 21, 121
Richmond, Julius, 63, 72, 275
Risk ratios, 165, 168, 170, 173, 174, 176
R.J. Reynolds, xi, 27, 36, 50, 54, 74, 75, 94, 187
  advertising and, 95, 97, 98, 99, 100, 102, 103, 110–11, 114
  Connor case and, 216–17
  defamation suit threatened by, 116
  Engle case and, 203
  secondhand smoke issue and, 153
  settlement agreement and, 183
  on smoking addictiveness, 188, 220
  on smoking hazards, 48, 51, 55
RJR-Nabisco, 55, 183, 206
Robert Wood Johnson Foundation, 125, 252
Rockette, Howard E., 170, 171
Rodham, Hugh, 183

Rodu, Brad, 77–80
Rogers, J. Smyth, 25, 32
Rolleston, Sir Humphrey, 234
Roosevelt, Franklin D., 8
Rose, Charlie, 58, 122
Rosenblatt, Stanley M., 186, 200–203, 204, 206, 207, 216, 218
Rush, Benjamin, 24–25, 32, 35, 233, 236, 259
Russell, M. A. Hamilton, 223, 249

Safer cigarettes, 68–76, 190, 194, 266, 267
Salem, 216
Sandefur, Thomas E., 221
San Franciscans for Local Control, 150
Sarokin, H. Lee, 193, 194, 197–98
Satcher, David, 6
Satel, Sally, 240–41
Schelling, Thomas C., 106, 129–30
Schiliro, Phil, 228
Schivelbusch, Wolfgang, 23
Schudson, Michael, 104, 106
Schuster, Charles, 239
Schwedock, Peter S., 201
Scruggs, Richard, 183, 208, 212
Secondhand smoke, xi, xiii, 11, 13, 18, 33–34, 116, 131–32, 138–80, 278–79: see also *Broin v. Philip Morris*
  cause-and-effect relationship in, 163–72, 278
  and children, 151, 158, 159–60
  dose absorption of, 162–63
  federal restrictions on, 12, 57, 138–42, 153–54, 184
  health consequences of, 140, 148–49, 151, 152, 159–77, 278–79
  historical perspective on, 33–34, 143–44
  lawsuits based on, 156–59, 182–83, 200–202
  local restrictions on, 33, 139, 144, 146, 147–52, 153, 155, 179
  magnitude of lung cancer risk associated with, 165, 168, 170, 172–74, 278–79
  state restrictions on, 37, 146–47, 151, 152, 153
Seligman, Robert B., 195
Shenk, Joshua Wolf, 263
Shubik, Philippe, 161–62
Sierra Club, 150
Slade, John, 75
SmokeFree Educational Services, 5–6, 8, 114
Smoke-Free Environment Act, 153, 171
Smoke-free society, 3–4, 5, 13, 59–60, 143,

151, 186, 252, 269, 280
Smokeless tobacco, 15, 27, 29, 69, 77–80, 278
Smoker's Home Page, 272–73
Smokers' rights, 146, 154–55, 272–73: see also Nonsmokers' rights
Smokers' Rights Alliance, 7
Smokescreen (Hilts), xi–xii, 250
Smoking bans, 10, 12, 20, 152–59, 279: see also Secondhand smoke
  on airline flights, 138–42, 146, 151, 153, 178
  in restaurants, 11, 37, 153–54, 156, 157, 179
  tobacco company settlement and, 12, 154, 184
  in workplace, 151–52, 153, 156–57, 173–74, 248
Smoking Gun: How the Tobacco Industry Gets Away with Murder (Whelan), 56
Smoking: Making the Risky Decision (Viscusi), 246
Smuggling, 134–37, 259, 265, 266
Snuff, 20, 22–23, 77, 121, 233
Social cost argument, 128–34, 278
Social Security, 131, 133, 214, 278
Solomon, Harold, 203
Sondik, Edward J., 79
South Dakota, 34, 151
Spears, Alexander W., 195
Spiking of cigarettes, 229, 230–31
Sporting events, tobacco company sponsorship of, 94
Stamberg, Susan, 7, 20
Steenland, Kyle, 175
Steinfeld, Jesse L., 144–45
Steinmeyer, F. E., 210
Stigler, George, 247
Stockman, David, 119, 120
Stolwijk, Jan, 170
Stossel, John, 88
Sudden Infant Death Syndrome, 159–60
Suicide, smoking as, 7, 20, 57
Sullivan, Louis, 9, 56, 94, 95
Sunday, Billy, 37, 259
Supreme Court
  on broadcast speech, 90, 112
  Canadian, 112
  on commercial speech, 108–109
  on drug sentencing, 263
  Florida, 211, 212
  Minnesota, 199
  New Jersey, 199
  on prison smoking, 158

on property forfeiture, 264
on right of reply, 113
on searches, 263–64
Tennessee, 30–31, 93, 219
on warning labels, 198–99
Surgeon General's Advisory Committee on Smoking and Health, 1, 41, 192, 235
Surgeon general's reports
  1964, 1, 3, 40–42, 52–53, 64–65, 70, 144, 234–35
  1972, 145
  1986, 140, 151
  1988, 67, 68, 197, 235–36, 240, 242, 249, 255
  1989, 55, 65, 67, 72, 106, 278
  1994, 106, 278
Synar, Mike, 7
Szasz, Thomas, 221

Taddeo, Joseph, 221
Talman, William, 89
Tar, 38, 43, 46, 68, 132, 163, 224: see also Low-yield cigarettes
Target marketing, 95–96
Tax Equity and Fiscal Responsibility Act of 1982 (TEFRA), 119
Taxes: see Tobacco taxes
Teenage Attitudes and Practices Survey (TAPS), 99
Temperance movement, 24–25, 26, 30, 37, 69, 233, 236–37, 259, 268
Tennessee, 30–31, 37, 93, 135, 219
Terry, Luther L., 40–41, 42, 52, 53, 65, 70, 87
Texas, 9, 151, 156, 213, 214, 215
Thank You for Smoking (Buckley), 7
Tisch, Andrew H., 54, 221
Tobacco companies
  events sponsored by, 94–95
  philanthropy of, 94–95
  research sponsored by, xiii–xiv, 48–50, 100, 194–96, 197, 231
  secondhand smoke issue and, xiii, 110, 141–42, 147, 153, 161, 171–72
  settlement agreement by, 12, 74, 93, 115, 123–24, 154, 181–86, 228, 252, 267
  on smoking addictiveness, 181, 188, 214, 220–21, 217, 240, 277
  on smoking hazards, 47–51, 54–55, 181, 187–89, 192, 194–98, 217, 277
  tobacco taxes and, 123, 125
Tobacco Industry Research Committee, 49, 110

Tobacco Institute, 84, 110, 141, 147, 184, 194, 226
Tobacco price support program, 247–48
Tobacco Products Liability Project, 157, 187
Tobacco prohibition, 10, 19, 20–21, 30–31, 34, 37–38, 225–26, 228, 254–55, 265–67, 268
Tobacco stocks, 47, 185–86
Tobacco taxes, xii–xiii, 115, 119–37, 247
    and children, 128, 254
    and cross-border purchases, 134–35
    federal, 119–24
    historical perspective on, 18–19, 21, 121
    regressiveness of, 123, 127
    and smuggling, 134–37
    social cost argument and, 128–34
    state, 115, 124–26, 134–35
Towns, Charles B., 32–33, 143
Trask, George, 25–27, 30, 61, 268
Treatise on Hygiene and Public Health, A (Billings), 62, 63
Trichopoulos, Dimitrios, 148, 149, 174–75
True, 192, 193
Tye, Joe B., 102, 103

United Smokers Association, 154, 155
University of California at San Diego Cancer Prevention and Control Program, 99
Upton, Arthur, 71–72
Uptown, 95
Urban VIII, Pope, 20
U.S. Tobacco, 221
Utah, 37, 125

Valentine v. Chrestensen, 108
Varmus, Harold, 79–80
Vermont, 153
Viceroy, 50
Victoria, Queen, 23–24
Virginia, 124, 135
Virginia Electric and Power Co., 157
Virginia Slims, 36, 95–96, 114–15, 192, 193
Virginia Slims tennis tournament, 94
Virginia State Board of Pharmacy v. Virginia Citizens Consumer Council, 108
Viscusi, W. Kip, 66–67, 132, 246, 278
Volstead Act, 259, 260, 266
Voodoo pharmacology, 222, 225, 237

Wakeham, Helmut, 195–96
Wallack, Lawrence, 117

Warner, Kenneth E., 65–66, 89–90, 91, 102, 106, 120, 126, 127–28, 219
Warning labels, 2, 53–54, 69, 89, 91, 127, 184, 192, 196, 198–99, 209, 251
Wartime, smoking in, 23, 34–35, 44
Washington, 30, 34, 124, 125, 134–35, 153
Washington, D.C., 10, 35, 124, 151
Waxman, Henry, 74–75, 153, 154, 171, 222, 224, 225, 228
W. Duke, Sons & Co., 27
Weinberger, Caspar, 60–61
Weissman, George, 51
Wells, Mary, 172
Wendy's, 157
Werner, Carl Avery, 38
West Virginia, 30, 213
Whelan, Elizabeth, 56, 66, 67, 93, 106, 128, 129, 172
White, Larry C., 56, 107
Whiteside, Thomas, 87, 91
Wickersham Commission, 260
Wiener, Max, 145
Wigand, Jeffrey, 213–14, 231
Williams, Merrell, 208
Wilner, Norwood S., 215, 216
Winston, 2, 3, 50, 216
Wisconsin, 34, 125, 135
Withdrawal symptoms, 238–39, 241–42
Wolf, Sidney, 72
Women and smoking, 18, 24, 35–37, 44, 55, 95, 96, 104, 143, 149
Women's Christian Temperance Union, 29, 37
World Conference on Tobacco, 147
World Conferences on Nonsmokers' Rights, 139
World Health Organization, 234–35, 274
World Wide Web, 272–73
Wortham, Anne, 7
Wright, J. Skelly, 111
W. T. Blackwell & Co., 97
Wyden, Ron, 220–21, 222, 240
Wynder, Ernst L., 44–45, 46, 47, 72, 169, 171

Yeaman, Addison, 188, 215
York, Michael, 55
Young, Patty, 201

Zinberg, Norman, 243
Zwiebel, Jeffrey, 266